A publication of the
Association of American Medical Colleges

New and Expanded Medical Schools, Mid-Century to the 1980s

An Analysis of Changes and Recommendations for Improving the Education of Physicians

J. R. Schofield

New and Expanded Medical Schools, Mid-Century to the 1980s

Jossey-Bass Publishers
San Francisco • Washington • London • 1984

NEW AND EXPANDED MEDICAL SCHOOLS,
MID-CENTURY TO THE 1980s
*An Analysis of Changes and Recommendations
for Improving the Education of Physicians*
   by J. R. Schofield

Copyright © 1984 by: Association of American
                      Medical Colleges
                      One Dupont Circle, Suite 200
                      Washington, D.C. 20036

                      Jossey-Bass Inc., Publishers
                      433 California Street
                      San Francisco, California 94104

                      Jossey-Bass Limited
                      28 Banner Street
                      London EC1Y 8QE

Library of Congress Cataloging in Publication Data

Schofield, J. R. (James R.)
   New and expanded medical schools, mid-century to
the 1980s.

   Includes bibliographies and index.
   1. Medical education—United States—History—
20th century. 2. Medical colleges—United States—
History—20th century. I. Title. [DNLM: 1. Education,
Medical—history—United States. 2. Schools, Medical—
history—United States. W 19 S367n]
R745.S36   1984   610'.7'1173   84-47996
ISBN 0-87589-628-6 (alk. paper)

Manufactured in the United States of America

The paper in this book meets the guidelines for
permanence and durability of the Committee on
Production Guidelines for Book Longevity of the
Council on Library Resources.

JACKET DESIGN BY WILLI BAUM

FIRST EDITION

Code 8426

The Jossey-Bass
Higher Education Series

ᶻᵉᶻᵉᶻᵉᶻᵉᶻᵉᶻᵉᶻᵉᶻᵉᶻᵉᶻᵉᶻᵉᶻᵉᶻᵉᶻᵉᶻᵉᶻᵉᶻᵉᶻᵉᶻᵉ

Association of American Medical Colleges
Series in Academic Medicine
JOHN A. D. COOPER, *Editor*

Foreword

The last two decades have witnessed substantial changes in medical education in the United States, unparalleled since the Flexnerian reforms at the beginning of the century. Abraham Flexner's (1910) *Medical Education in the United States and Canada* encouraged and legitimized a movement toward a more uniform course of undergraduate medical education based on a strong curriculum in the basic biomedical sciences, a position within a university, full-time faculty, and integrated research and clinical facilities. Schools not meeting these high standards soon closed. The changes since 1950 have been directed less toward uniformity than toward creativity and diversity while maintaining the essential scientific basis for medical education. As a result, medical education in the United States and Canada enjoys both a heterogeneity and an excellence unmatched even in other developed nations.

In the middle of this century, pressure grew for expansion in the number of physicians trained, and various incentives ensured a rapid response to society's needs. Since 1960, forty-one new medical schools—nearly a third of those now in existence—have been established, most associated with a university complex, although others show new organizational forms. First-year enrollment has more than doubled, from 8,298 in 1960–61 to 17,186 in 1980–81. Faculty growth quadrupled in the same time, reflecting not only the increased number of medical students but also changes in the faculty's professional activities, such as the increased involvement of the medical school faculty in the education of other health professionals and in the provision of patient care services. Many more hospitals assumed a role in the process of undergraduate medical education as they became sites for clinical clerkships for the growing number of physicians-in-training. These two decades have been particularly challenging for American medical education as the community has grown in size and scope and in complexity while maintaining the highest standards of quality and some degree of uniformity in curricular content.

Today's accreditation process relies on much more than the wisdom, judgment, and observations of just one man. Nevertheless, J. R. Schofield enjoys the distinction of having made more visits to assess the quality of medical schools than anyone since Abraham Flexner. In *New and Expanded Medical Schools, Mid-Century to the 1980s,* Schofield, from this unique vantage point, comments on this historical period and illuminates the pedagogical and organizational lessons learned in this period of exceptional change.

Schofield is able to identify significant components in the administration of a medical school, analyze and assess their impact on the institution as a whole, and indicate particular problems and weaknesses faced by some schools. His "lessons learned" sections should be required reading for anyone with governance or administrative responsibility in health professional education, drawing as they do on Schofield's thirty-five years of experience and his broad perspective on and comprehensive knowledge of undergraduate medical education issues. Throughout his professional career, the author has been an advocate for improving the educational process and has formulated strong opinions on the approaches he favors. Readers may find themselves disagreeing with some of these opinions and evaluations, but they will be grateful for the range of material and analyses presented.

As this century draws to an end, medical schools find themselves again on the verge of major changes as resources constrict and opinion builds that a surplus of physicians is expected. The ultimate significance of this book may be in its ability to help medical educators and policy makers adjust to a new era by avoiding past mistakes. Thus, the Association of American Medical Colleges' Series in Academic Medicine includes this volume as a means of focusing attention on major administrative, structural, and pedagogical issues in medical education.

July 1984   John A. D. Cooper, M.D., Ph.D.
                                           President, Association
                                           of American Medical Colleges

Preface

After careful research, I find that this book contains the first comprehensive description and critical analysis of the activities of American medical schools and their programs for physician education since Deitrick and Berson's (1953) *Medical Schools in the United States at Mid-Century*. Of course, any hiatus of three decades should provide sufficient justification for developing a new audit of medical education; however, the period from mid-twentieth century to the early 1980s encompassed spectacular changes in the activities and programs of the American medical schools. To illustrate, between 1960 and 1980 the enrollment of medical students more than doubled, as did the number of newly credentialed M.D.s enrolled in graduate education in the medical specialties. Medical research grants from the National Institutes of Health to medical schools increased from $11 million in 1952 to $1.19 billion in 1980. This book evaluates these and other changes during three decades.

As I wrote this book, I was mindful that during the last thirty of my thirty-six years of experience as a medical faculty member, academic dean, and manager of medical school accreditation activities I have been asked to describe, explain, and justify the expanding functions of our nation's medical schools to thousands of curious persons who needed answers to a broad spectrum of probing questions. The questions asked of me repeatedly through the years have convinced me that the elaborate process of education of the physician has been poorly understood by many responsible individuals. Included among the questioners have been interested laypersons, practicing physicians, newly appointed medical school deans, and a variety of faculty members; university trustees, chancellors, provosts, and vice-presidents; premedical advisors, applicants to medical schools, and their parents; federal agency officials; U.S. senators and congressmen and their staff members; state legislators and their staff members; state commissioners on higher education and their staff members; governors and their aides; mayors and chamber of commerce officials; foreign visitors; and, last, an increasing number of demanding professionals in all branches of the news media.

Many questioners have asked for reference material in support of my answers, and through the years much literature has been collected and stored in my file boxes, desk drawers, and bookshelves. While this published literature is available to anyone who searches for it, the most complete descriptive data on medical schools and the only critical evaluations of the quality of M.D. educational programs therein are stored in the confidential files of the Liaison Committee on Medical Education (LCME). All such material has been used to extend my own personal experiences as I have written this book.

My duties as an accreditation survey report writer since 1959 and as a secretary of the LCME since 1971 have thrust me into the midst of the enrollment expansion of the eighty-six pre-1960 medical schools and the establishment and early growth of forty new ones. This work has included extended dialogue with numerous deans and members of faculty planning committees about the resources needed for major enrollment increases in the established schools, and I have offered advice and admonishment about national standards of quality to a wide variety of both governmental and university officials before, during, and after the enrollment of the charter class of medical students of the new schools. Having participated in 116 full-scale accreditation inspections of medical schools since 1959, I long ago realized that the LCME had in its possession the only complete and accurate record of the sweeping changes that occurred in medical education between 1960 and 1980, when the size of the entering class of medical students was doubled in an effort to solve the shortage of physicians perceived at mid-century.

So, in 1970–71, I began a special study of the detailed annual reports submitted to the LCME by all the medical schools, giving particular attention to the new ones. These annual reports yield comparable data, which I have followed progressively as the older schools expanded and as the new ones began operation and developed toward maturity. I also studied the reports generated through the process of inspection of all schools by the LCME. Older schools are inspected periodically and especially when enrollment increases are proposed, and each new school is visited annually, beginning two years before enrollment of the charter class and extending through the year the first M.D. degrees are conferred.

Each on-site accreditation inspection by the LCME is conducted by four to six experienced medical educators, whose work is facilitated by presurvey study of an average six to ten pounds of descriptive documentation on the school to be visited. After concluding a comprehensive four-day-long audit of all features of the school, the team members prepare a report that averages 200 pages describing their findings about the quality of the M.D. education program and the resources available to support it. Each report of an accreditation inspection is circulated to the members of the LCME, whose opinions and judgments about the school are buttressed by the comments and evaluations received from the forty-five-person panel of reviewers drawn from the AAMC Executive Council and the AMA Council on Medical Education. Thus, descriptions, factual data, and expert opinions and judgments collected throughout two decades have been available to me as I have conducted the research for this book. It should be emphasized that all data collected by the LCME is kept confidential and that only the formal determination of the status of accreditation of a medical school is made public. In writing this book, I have preserved the rule of confidentially about each separate school but have made liberal use of aggregate data to describe trends, results of experiments, and other events.

In devising the format of the book, I have begun each chapter with a brief historical account of the development of the subject, which is followed by a description of the changes that occurred during the period studied. The descriptive material and its treatment of summary data should be useful to anyone interested in higher education; medical educators will find the elaborate data tables and the citations to the professional literature helpful in performing their own analyses and in making judgments of my conclusions and recommendations, which are located in the "Lessons Learned" segment following each chapter. The serious student who desires to do an elaborate study of the series of subjects may do so by delving into the "Select Bibliography."

The contents of the book have been divided into four parts. In Part One, Chapter One describes the change from a surplus of physicians around 1900 to a shortage by mid-century. Efforts by private and public sectors to solve the shortage as the population increased between 1950 and 1980 are described in detail. Chapter Two describes methods of solving the shortage by expanding the eighty-six pre-1960 schools and by establishing forty new ones.

Part Two treats the administration of a medical school. Chapter Three reviews the changing role of the dean, defines the characteristics of the modern dean, and recommends improved methods for selecting a dean. Chapter Four breaks new ground by defining the nature of the managerial support needed by today's medical dean. Chapter Five is devoted to the administrative tasks that must be performed by the dean who founds a new medical school.

Part Three describes the resources essential for a modern medical school. These include financial resources (Chapter Six), faculty (Chapter Seven), physical facilities for students and faculty (Chapter Eight), the medical library (Chapter Nine), and the teaching hospital (Chapter Ten).

Part Four consists of a comprehensive description, analysis of problems, and recommendations for improving the programs of physician education. Chapter Eleven covers the period prior to

medical school (high school and college); Chapter Twelve concerns
the program of education leading to the M.D. degree; Chapter
Thirteen briefly reviews graduate and continuing medical education
and describes the value to medical education of scholarly activity,
including research, and the contiguity of graduate degree programs
in the basic medical sciences; and Chapter Fourteen offers recommendations for improving the education of future physicians.

The process of educating the physician always has been
considered mysterious and unfathomable to the American people,
whose tax payments have supported many of the recent changes.
Old impressions about the process may need to be replaced with
accurate current descriptions and critical analyses. So, the book has
been written with the intent of satisfying the curiosity of a heterogeneous readership.

The book should be useful to several categories of readers:

- To medical educators who desire to study changes and experiments within the 1950–1980 period, when the education of
  physicians rose near the top of the nation's list of crucial
  priorities. The prose commentary of each chapter should provide
  general perspective to the professional medical educator, while
  the data tables and comprehensive references cited should support serious study of this turbulent period. The recommendations at the end of each section are intended to provoke dialogue
  among faculty members and others about improvements in
  medical education.
- To presidents of universities containing a medical school and
  to other senior officials of universities and related activities of
  higher education, as these heavily burdened persons encounter
  a need to develop an understanding of the complex subject of
  the education of the physician and other members of the health
  care occupations. The premedical advisors of the colleges and
  universities may also find the book useful in defining the
  circumstances of the professional education sought by their
  advisees.
- To public policy makers holding federal, state, and local
  administrative and legislative positions of responsibility as they
  attempt to understand the nature of medical schools, the con-

stellation of resources they require, their financial needs, and their dependence on hospitals and clinics for successful operation.

- To public officials and educators in nations that, in the future, may desire to expand their capabilities for education of physicians or who desire to compare their own system with this experience reported in the United States.

The opinions and judgments expressed in this book, if not cited to other authors, are my own and are not to be attributed to the AAMC, the LCME, or the AMA-CME. While these agencies are aware of my intention to write this book, they are not responsible for its contents.

Washington, D.C.   J. R. Schofield
July 1984

Acknowledgments

~~~~~~

The undertaking of this project was made possible by the Association of American Medical Colleges (AAMC), whose president, John A. D. Cooper, made available many essential resources and encouraged me to devote considerable time to the project during 1981 to 1984. Thomas H. Meikle, Jr., and James G. Hirsch, successive executive officers of the Josiah Macy, Jr., Foundation, arranged for generous grants of funds that facilitated extensive research and preparation of the manuscript. The foundation supplemented the original grant when the scope of the project was expanded beyond its original objectives. Marjorie Wilson and Joseph Keyes, Jr., of the AAMC's Department of Institutional Development, gave much encouragement and support for the project.

I am indebted to Joan Johnson, James Campbell, and especially Robert Van Dyke, who contributed to the project while serving as my administrative assistants from 1976 to 1984. Considerable research for the manuscript was done efficiently by Charles Venin and Dan Davis. Davis also served as my working editor during the final fifteen months of effort to finish the manuscript. He is due considerable credit for his editorial improvement of my frequently interrupted bursts of composition; he also has earned extra credits for tolerating a strong-minded, aging author who frequently argued tenaciously for his very own unique version of the Queen's English. The manuscript was typed through many drafts by June Peterson, whose ability to tame a balky word processor is legendary.

Innumerable persons have made contributions to the content of the book; I have been an active listener and learner from those in my environment for nearly a half century. My companions on 116 accreditation inspections of medical schools, the faculty members and students of these schools, and especially the members of the academic community of Baylor University College of Medicine from 1944 through 1970 all contributed to my insight into the process of medical education.

Special gratitude is herewith expressed to a number of persons who read and criticized early drafts of the book. These experienced and well-known peer reviewers provided me with reactions to my composition and made many suggestions for improvement. All are absolved from any blame or fault to be found in the final, printed version, as I did not accept all their criticisms. The most indefatigable peer reviewers, who read and critiqued the entire manuscript, were Glen Leymaster, Stanley Olson, Carter Pannill, and Donn Smith. In addition, separate chapters or subchapters were improved by suggestions and/or data provided by the following: Chapter One: Edward Petersen, Thomas Turner, George Harrell, John Dietrick, Davis Johnson, Joseph Keyes, and John Sherman; Chapter Three: Marjorie Wilson; Chapter Six: Joseph Rosenthal, John Deufel, Paul Jolly, and Leon Taksel; Chapter Seven: Richard Moy and Ann Peterson; Chapter Nine: David Hoyt and Pauline Innis; Chapter Ten: Susan Carver, J. R. Buchanan, Richard Knapp, Ann Vengrofski, James Bentley, Joseph Isaacs, Peter Butler, and David Worthen. Chapters Eleven and Twelve: Marilyn Heins, George Baker, William Bradford, James Erdmann, Robert Beran, and Philip Wackym. George Gray offered numerous valuable suggestions; his M.D. thesis (Baylor, 1961), "Development of the Curriculum in American Medical Schools," was used frequently as I drafted Part Four of the book. And Kathleen Turner, assistant to the AAMC's president, was very helpful in coordinating arrangements with the publisher.

During late 1983, after my manuscript had been first submitted to the publisher, I reviewed much material collected from colleges, medical schools, academic organizations, and individuals by the AAMC's General Professional Education of the Physician Commission. In these materials, I found considerable support for many judgments and opinions I have written in this book, and I may have been influenced by some expressions as I reviewed conclusions in the manuscript during the editing process. In particular, I found the opinions expressed by L. H. Smith to be impressive.

J. R. Schofield

Contents

xxiii

Contents

Tables and Figures

ਲ਼

Tables

Figures

The Author

J. R. Schofield is director, Division of Accreditation, Department of Institutional Development, Association of American Medical Colleges (AAMC), and a secretary of the Liaison Committee on Medical Education (LCME), the accrediting agency for programs of medical education leading to the M.D. degree in the United States and Canada. He was awarded the B.S. degree for premedical and liberal arts studies at Baylor University in 1945 and the M.D. degree at Baylor University College of Medicine in 1947.

Schofield served as a member of the faculty in anatomy of Baylor University College of Medicine from 1947 through 1970. During 1947 to 1953, he was an active instructor in gross and neuroanatomy. He also served variously as assistant dean, associate dean, dean of academic affairs, and director of graduate studies from 1953 through 1970. In 1956, he was a founder of the informal Southern Regional Association of Academic Deans and subsequently joined in the formation of the AAMC's continuing Group on Student Affairs. During the late 1950s, he chaired an advisory committee for *Medical School Admissions Requirements,* the AAMC's annual publication for premedical students and their advisors. In 1964, he served as chairman of the editorial committee for early issues of *The Advisor,* a newsletter published by the AAMC for the nation's premedical advisors.

In 1959, Schofield was appointed an assistant secretary of the LCME (part time) and began his long service to the process of accrediting M.D. educational programs. During the period from the late 1950s through 1984, he has participated in 116 on-site accreditation inspections of medical schools in the United States and Canada. Since 1971, as the alternating secretary of the LCME, he has worked as one of the three full-time specialists in medical school accreditation in the United States and Canada. His experiences in accreditation include the period of great expansion of programs of medical education that began around 1960 and continued until 1981.

Schofield has devoted considerable time to visiting hundreds of the colleges that produce applicants to medical school. In addition to his visits to medical schools on accreditation surveys, he has served frequently as a consultant and as a speaker at convocation and graduation exercises.

Schofield's active military service included stints in a Navy medical school V-12 unit, 1944–1945; the Army, 1954–1955; and the Public Health Service, 1955–1956. During the latter service, he was national coordinator for Medical Education for National Defense (MEND), a joint program of the AAMC, the Department of Defense, the Public Health Service, and the Office of Federal Civil Defense. This work with the MEND program extended through 1958.

In activities outside his primary profession, Schofield was president of the Texas Academy of Science in 1961; and, during his years of residence in Houston, he was involved in various services to the Chamber of Commerce, the United Fund, the Museum of Natural History, the Sam Houston Area Council of the Boy Scouts of America, and his church.

Throughout his career, Schofield has been interested in the process of learning, especially in young people, and the role of the administrator in facilitating learning and other forms of human performance.

New and Expanded
Medical Schools,
Mid-Century to the 1980s

᠉᠉᠉᠉᠉᠉᠉᠉᠉᠉᠉᠉᠉᠉᠉᠉᠉᠉᠉᠉᠉᠉᠉᠉

*An Analysis of Changes
and Recommendations
for Improving the Education
of Physicians*

Part One

ﾞﾞﾞﾞﾞﾞﾞﾞﾞﾞﾞﾞﾞﾞﾞﾞﾞﾞﾞﾞﾞﾞﾞﾞﾞﾞﾞﾞﾞﾞ

Medical Schools and the Supply of Physicians

ﾞﾞﾞﾞﾞﾞﾞﾞﾞﾞﾞﾞﾞﾞﾞﾞﾞﾞﾞﾞﾞﾞﾞﾞﾞﾞﾞﾞﾞﾞ

From 1960 to 1980, the enrollment of new medical students in the United States more than doubled, and forty new medical schools began their first instruction of students. This unprecedented and rapid expansion contrasted sharply with the development of only sixteen new schools in the fifty years following Abraham Flexner's 1910 report on American and Canadian medical education. During that half century, the production rate of physician graduates failed to keep pace with the rate of population growth. From 1960 to 1980, therefore, an intense effort was made to redress this imbalance and to produce a sufficient number of physicians to provide health care to a population that had expanded from 93 million people in 1910 to 180 million in 1960 and to 226 million by 1980. Part One describes the changes in the nature of American medical schools from 1900 to mid-century and thereafter as they responded to the gradually perceived need to expand the supply of physicians.

Chapter One begins with an account of early American medical education and explains the emergence of a surplus of poorly

1

trained physicians by 1900. Next, there follows an account of efforts to reform medical education between 1900 and mid-century, as a shortage of physicians developed. The balance of the chapter is devoted to a chronological account of numerous efforts to finance the expansion of the production of physicians, an effort which seems likely to result in a potential surplus by the late 1980s.

Chapter Two describes enrollment expansion in the eighty-six pre-1960 schools and devotes much attention to many aspects of the development of the forty new schools launched between 1960 and 1980. The chapter concludes with a number of lessons learned from the development of this cluster of new schools.

From Surplus to Shortage to Surplus, 1900–1980

Early American Medical Education

Throughout the history of the republic, there has been a cycle of famine and feast in the supply of physician graduates. The early colonies lacked both universities and component medical schools and thus depended on the haphazard immigration of physicians who had been trained chiefly in England and Scotland or in the inadequate practitioner/apprenticeship system of the period. Medical schools were established in Philadelphia, New York, and Boston during the final third of the eighteenth century, followed by a few others of university stature early in the nineteenth century. In the beginning, however, these schools had small enrollments of students (Waite, 1937). Affluent young Americans were able to finance the cost of medical study in either the British Isles or Europe, but they were few in number and made only a modest contribution to the chronically inadequate supply of physicians for a nation that was quickly expanding in both population and geographical area.

The trek westward by pioneers from the thirteen original states scattered the population across the continent and produced the first maldistribution of physicians. Then as now, doctors preferred to establish their medical practices in or near the large cities rather than in the frontier hamlets or villages, hard by territory occupied by frequently hostile native Indians. Possibly because there was a paucity of the resources necessary to establish universities after the classical European model (containing colleges of theology, law, arts, and medicine), frontier-minded America pragmatically developed, during the nineteenth century, a unique "factory" for the production of physician graduates: the proprietary medical school. Schools of this type admitted virtually any applicant who could pay the stipulated fees, regardless of prior educational achievement. The faculty typically was composed of a few physicians who owned stock in the enterprise. The curriculum consisted of a series of lectures given over a period of four months and repeated to all students for a second year. No regulation of any kind was imposed on these "schools" (Norwood, 1970). By 1900, these numerous nineteenth-century commercial enterprises had produced an over-supply of poorly trained "physicians," whose abilities were held in general contempt by many people. An editorial in the *Journal of the American Medical Association* reflected this widespread attitude toward the profession:

> That a majority of the profession is incompetent and unworthy is not subject to statistical proof. To the unprejudiced medical observer of the profession of almost any locality, the truth is patent that very many of its members are persons of inferior ability, questionable character, and coarse and common fiber. The little esteem in which the profession is held by laity and government attests to its unworthiness. Patients whose number is legion throw themselves from its arms into the embrace of quackery, and we must admit support is often as effective in the one case as in the other. . . . Unquestionably the cause of the

professional degeneracy lies in the educational requirements made for entrance to the profession; and hence
the question resolves itself into one of medical colleges,
their number, their location and their standards.

Medical colleges exist far in excess of any public
need. Like the country store which doles out its inferior
wares at every cross-roads, a so-called medical college
is found in almost every town of generous size; and
to obtain a medical degree is within the possibility,
intellectual and financial, of any youth, however
lacking in mental and moral fitness. In inverse ratio
to the frequency of medical colleges do we find the
extent of their equipment. In the majority of cases,
they possess few facilities for demonstration; are located in towns where there is not sufficient number
of dependents to furnish requisite clinical material;
and, generally have as instructors men of mediocre
or less ability (Philbrick, 1901, pp. 1700–1702).

Although he tended to concur with this negative judgment, Hender-
son included a note of restrained optimism in his assessment of
the medical profession in the early decades of this century: "I think
that it was about the year 1910 or 1912 when it became possible
to say of the United States that a random patient with a random
disease consulting a doctor chosen at random stood better than a
fifty-fifty chance of benefiting from the encounter" (quoted in Gregg,
1956, p. 57).

The Drive for Higher Standards: The Flexner Survey
and Its Aftermath

In his famous report on medical education, Flexner (1910,
p. 8) concluded that, from 1810 to 1910, 457 medical schools were
established in the United States and Canada. It was his view that
many of these proprietary medical schools were part of a "wave
of commercial exploitation" that swept through medical education
during the final half of the 1800s and produced a surplus of new

physicians. He estimated that in 1910 there were 568 persons for each physician in the United States and in large cities there frequently was one physician for every 400 persons or less. Not all 457 schools identified by Flexner continued to function during the period of his research (1908 to 1910); some had operated only briefly, but 147 in the United States and 8 in Canada still existed, were actually visited by Flexner, and were described in his famous report.

At a testimonial dinner given in New York City by the National Fund for Medical Education in celebration of his ninetieth birthday, Flexner (1956) vividly recalled his preparations before visiting the 155 schools: "I must make an overdue confession. The whole thing was done as a hoax. We knew that the schools would never allow the inspections if the deans learned of our intent to be critical. So we wrote to each dean on the letterhead of the Carnegie Foundation asking simply for an opportunity to visit. Naturally, each dean expected that the officers of the foundation (the most generous of its kind during this period) had selected his school to be the recipient of a major endowment and immediately wrote back expressing a warm invitation."

In a bicentennial retrospective on undergraduate medical education in the United States, Cooper (1976) has traced the efforts to reform medical education made by the Association of American Medical Colleges (AAMC), the American Medical Association's Council on Medical Education (AMA-CME), the Federation of State Medical Boards, and others from the mid-nineteenth century to the present. All these efforts, though impressive, made only a modest impact on the national problem until the publication of Flexner's report in 1910 crystallized public demand for rapid and comprehensive improvements in the quality of medical education.

Improvements in Medical Schools. Jarco (1959), Chapman (1974), Lippard (1974), and others have described the many remarkable changes that occurred after the publication of the Flexner report. The number of schools was reduced from 147 in 1910 to 83 in 1921 and further to 76 in 1929 (see Appendix A) by the consolidation or closing of marginal or inadequate schools. Proprietary schools disappeared, as did a few independent schools; most of the rest became functional, as well as de facto, components of universities.

A full-time faculty system gradually developed, first in the pre-clinical scientific subjects and later in the clinical departments. Uniform academic prerequisites—including studies in biology, chemistry, and physics—for admission to medical school were established. Flexner noted the chaotic and haphazard adherence to premedical academic standards during the period from 1908 to 1910. By the early 1920s, however, two years of college study were required for admission to medical school; by 1938, three or more years of premedical studies had been established as prerequisites. Finally, there were several improvements in the curricula of medical schools: greater emphasis was placed on laboratory studies in the preclinical sciences; university-controlled hospitals and dispensaries were employed to enhance clinical studies; and a graded program of studies of a minimum of eight months per year for four years was adopted in all medical schools.

Accreditation by AAMC and AMA-CME. Flexner's recommended model for the reformation of medical education in America was inaugurated at the Johns Hopkins University School of Medicine in 1894, where a curriculum consisting of four years of graded studies to which were admitted limited numbers of students, all baccalaureate graduates, was established (Chesney, 1943). Emulating the high standards of the world-famous scientific German universities of the late nineteenth century, Johns Hopkins gradually established a requirement that each department be staffed by a "critical mass" of full-time faculty members (Bonner, 1963). The generally poor state of the schools surveyed by Flexner, including many of those controlled by the universities, made this sophisticated model for the education of a physician a very difficult and expensive one to copy. The seventy-six schools that had survived the imposition of the new, higher standards as of 1929 had done so only because they were able to mobilize a substantial pool of the necessary resources. Those that flourished thereafter did so because they were able to acquire a significant, guaranteed annual income/revenue over and above that derived from tuition payments alone. Opie (1970) has written an interesting case study of the impact of Flexner's report on the Washington University School of Medicine.

Although much of the early impetus to reform in the twentieth century is often credited to Flexner, the AAMC and the

AMA-CME sustained the effort to improve the schools during the period from 1900 to 1942. In 1903, the AAMC began the first on-site inspections of medical schools in order to enforce its membership standards. In 1906, the AMA-CME inspected all the schools. In the previous year, it had initiated its listing of Class A (approved) schools and Class B and Class C (unapproved) schools based on the results of licensure board examinations; after 1929, it maintained a single list showing only the approved schools (Johnson, 1947). The AMA-CME played an important role in the reform movement by policing substandard medical schools during the post-Flexner survey period and by developing a published list not only of approved medical schools but also of internships, residencies, and hospitals. As a result of the AMA-CME's efforts, a graduate of an unapproved/unaccredited medical school often had great difficulty (or no success whatsoever) in obtaining an appointment for graduate medical education, a state license to practice medicine, or a hospital staff position in a CME-approved hospital. Under these circumstances, substandard medical schools were forced to close or to acquire the resources and programs required for approval and accreditation. The single national standard for medical education that grew out of the AAMC and AMA-CME's cooperative efforts in accreditation has been adopted by the licensure boards of the states and other jurisdictions as the principal basis for granting licensure throughout this century. Hyde and his colleagues (1954) have written of the power and functions of the AMA at mid-century.

During the mid-1930s, the dean of Syracuse University's School of Medicine, the indefatigable Herman Weiskotten, along with representatives of the AAMC, the AMA-CME, and the Federation of State Medical Boards, inspected every school in a concerted effort to cap the drive to reform American medical education (Weiskotten and others, 1940). In 1942, the AMA and AAMC formed the Liaison Committee on Medical Education (LCME) and thus formally unified the accreditation system and the ongoing process of improving the education of the physician. In the same year, the Association of Canadian Medical Colleges asked the LCME to include its member schools in the accreditation process; as a result, a comprehensive system for scrutinizing and improving programs of medical education throughout North America was established.

1910–1950: Development of the Shortage of Physicians

After the publication of the Flexner report, no additional proprietary schools appeared; indeed, the establishment of new schools slowed considerably—only sixteen appeared between 1910 and 1960 (see Table 1). This modest development of new programs, coupled with the demise of numerous marginal or inadequate schools during the early post-Flexner survey period, resulted in a sharp drop in additions to the ranks of practicing physicians. Table 2 displays the annual number of M.D. degrees awarded and the number of schools involved from 1900 to 1960.

Table 1. Medical Schools Established Between 1910 and 1959.

Date of Establishment	School
1912	Chicago Medical School
1913	Medical College of Wisconsin (Marquette)
1914	Ohio State University College of Medicine
1915	Loyola University of Chicago, Stritch School of Medicine
1925	University of Rochester School of Medicine and Dentistry
1927	University of Chicago, Pritzker School of Medicine
1930	Duke University School of Medicine
1931	Louisiana State University School of Medicine in New Orleans
1943	University of Texas Southwestern Medical School at Dallas
1946	University of Washington School of Medicine
1950	University of Puerto Rico School of Medicine
1951	University of California, Los Angeles, School of Medicine
1952	University of Miami School of Medicine
1954	University of Medicine and Dentistry of New Jersey (Seton Hall)
1955	Albert Einstein College of Medicine of Yeshiva University
1956	University of Florida College of Medicine

Note: Between 1910 and 1960, six older two-year schools of the basic medical sciences expanded their programs and began to grant the M.D. degree: Bowman Gray School of Medicine of Wake Forest University, University of Utah School of Medicine, University of Alabama in Birmingham School of Medicine, University of North Carolina at Chapel Hill School of Medicine, University of Mississippi School of Medicine, and University of Missouri-Columbia School of Medicine.

Source: Association of American Medical Colleges, 1981.

Table 2. Accredited Medical Schools and M.D. Graduates 1900–1960.

Year	Number of Schools	Number of M.D. Graduates	Year	Number of Schools	Number of M.D. Graduates
1900	160	5,214	1931	76	4,735
1901	160	5,444	1932	76	4,936
1902	160	5,009	1933	77	4,895
1903	160	5,698	1934	77	5,035
1904	160	5,747	1935	77	5,101
1905	160	5,600	1936	77	5,183
1906	162	5,364	1937	77	5,377
1907	159	4,980	1938	77	5,194
1908	151	4,741	1939	77	5,089
1909	140	4,515	1940	77	5,097
1910	131	4,440	1941	77	5,275
1911	122	4,273	1942	77	5,163
1912	118	4,483	1943	76	5,223
1913	107	3,981	1944[a]	77	5,134
1914	102	3,594			5,169
1915	96	3,536	1945	77	5,136
1916	95	3,518	1946	77	5,826
1917	96	3,379	1947	77	6,389
1918	90	2,670	1948	77	5,543
1919	85	2,656	1949	78	5,094
1920	85	3,047	1950	79	5,553
1921	83	3,191	1951	79	6,135
1922	81	2,529	1952	79	6,080
1923	80	3,120	1953	79	6,668
1924	79	3,562	1954	80	6,861
1925	80	3,974	1955	81	6,977
1926	79	3,962	1956	82	6,845
1927	80	4,035	1957	85	6,796
1928	80	4,262	1958	85	6,861
1929	76	4,565	1959	85	6,860
1930	76	4,446	1960	85	7,081

[a] In 1944, the medical schools awarded M.D. degrees to two graduating classes due to an accelerated program in operation from 1943 to 1946.

Sources: Journal of the American Medical Association, 1922, *70*, 633; 1940, *115*, 699; 1964, *190*, 613.

In 1910, Flexner estimated that there were 568 persons to each physician (the population to physician ratio was estimated to be 400 to one in the cities); by 1960, there were approximately 725 persons to each physician (Rosenthal, 1980). The reasons for the increase are numerous. This period spanned World War I (1916–1918), the Great Depression of the 1930s, and World War II (1941–1945). The social and economic dislocations these events produced were not conducive to the initiation of expensive new educational programs based on the Flexnerian model. This half-century was one of momentous change. Early in the period, the now-ubiquitous automobile appeared, and the construction of a national system of roads and highways supplementing the already extensive railroad network was begun; as a result, many Americans achieved a remarkable mobility. A large segment of the population left the farm and moved to the city, where jobs could be found. The nation entered a new phase in its century-long march toward industrialization. The new demographic movements and socioeconomic trends of this era paved the way for changes in the medical care system. Hospitals were established in smaller cities, and patients were referred by general practitioners in the hamlets and towns to the burgeoning number of medical and surgical specialists who worked best in a hospital setting. In 1932, Rappleye and his colleagues noted that the number of operating hospitals had expanded from 1,000 in 1900 to 6,600 in 1931.

1950–1980: Support for Expansion of Medical Education

The increasing complexity of American life involved medical education as well. In 1953, Dietrick and Berson published the results of a comprehensive survey of the nation's medical schools at mid-century. In a general analysis of all aspects of the operation of medical schools, the authors called attention to the quiet but massive expansion of various health education programs that had developed in the schools of medicine and showed that, in most instances, finances, facilities, and faculties were overtaxed. They also defined the need for careful accounting of the separate costs of each of the numerous educational programs sponsored by the schools so that potential donors, legislators, and the public could understand the complexity of these unique institutions. This publication undoubtedly was influential in heightening public awareness of the financial circumstances of the older, existing schools, as well as in shaping a nationwide perception that new medical schools must be established to meet the demand for an increased production of physician graduates.

Private Sector Contributions. Private donors and the nation's corporations were drawn into unified financial support of the schools through the organization of the National Fund for Medical Education in 1949. This fund was granted a federal charter in 1954 by Public Law 635 of the 83rd Congress. Organized by university presidents, corporate executives, labor leaders, and officers of the American Medical Association (AMA) and the AAMC, the fund annually attracted contributions from some 3,000 companies, foundations, and individuals during the 1950s and early 1960s until the first element of direct federal support of medical school education of physicians was established in 1965 (National Fund for Medical Education, 1979). In the late 1950s, the AMA organized a system for direct contribution to the medical schools by physicians (Ruhe, 1982). Beginning in 1967, the AMA Education and Research Foundation made direct grants for the operating expenses of special projects to the medical schools from contributions made by physicians and their state and community organizations.

To some extent, the wide public attention focused on the problems of American medical education induced the Ford Foundation to distribute $90 million to the eighty-two existing schools in December 1955. In March 1959, the Ford Foundation set aside $10 million to be used in matching grants administered by the National Fund for Medical Education over a ten-year period. During 1955 and 1956, the Commonwealth Fund made unsolicited grants totaling $13.3 million to nineteen private, nonsectarian, university-affiliated medical schools. Beginning in the 1950s, the Josiah Macy, Jr., W. K. Mellon, and Markle Foundations, along with other donors, increased their support of selected schools and of the national effort to strengthen medical education programs (Lippard, 1974).

In the 1940s, the annual birthrate began to increase dramatically. At this time, while resources for the repair of ailing medical schools were being developed, an awareness of the nation's physician shortage began to spread. In 1948, the shortage and the rising annual birthrate were first publicly recognized by Oscar Ewing, the director of the federal Social Security Agency. In 1949, Dean Smiley, executive director of the AAMC, called attention to the shortage in his article, "Our Need for Doctors." In 1953, Ward Darley, Smiley's successor at the AAMC, warned of the need to strengthen the medical schools' finances before increasing enrollments to alleviate the shortage. And in 1957, the AAMC called for further enrollment increases at existing schools, recommended the expansion of existing facilities, and urged universities in major population centers without medical schools to consider establishing them (Association of American Medical Colleges, 1958).

In keeping with the unique American tradition for solving national problems, private sources led the way in the development of the new medical schools deemed necessary to solve the rapidly developing shortage of physicians. The Commonwealth Fund facilitated the establishment of new schools with its grants to support detailed feasibility studies at the University of Florida in 1952, the University of Kentucky in 1956, the University of Arizona in 1959, Brown University in 1959, the University of Hawaii in 1962, Memorial University of Newfoundland in 1964, State University of New York at Stony Brook in 1968, the University of Nevada in 1968, and Mayo Medical School in 1971. In 1957, a large grant was made to Dartmouth Medical School to support its refounding. In 1960, a grant was made to Michigan State University to finance development of various programs of education and research in medicine and the biological sciences (Willard and others, 1960). The W. K. Kellogg Foundation should be credited with a timely recognition of the physician shortage. Beginning in 1960, this foundation made grants in the amount of $9.655 million to facilitate the actual development of new basic science medical schools at the following universities: New Mexico, Connecticut, Rutgers, Brown, Hawaii, Michigan State, and Nevada. It also provided a grant to assist in an expansion of the basic science program at Dartmouth. During the same period, the Kellogg Foundation made similar grants to facilitate the development of a new school at the University of Sherbrooke, Quebec, and to develop a new curriculum at the University of Newcastle, New South Wales. It also funded a timely study by a task force of the AAMC on the methods of developing new medical schools in 1959 and 1960 (Sparks and others, 1980).

Role of State Governments. In the thirty years following 1950, state governments displayed a new concern for the quality and availability of medical education and health care and made the largest financial contribution toward solving the national problem of the shortage of physicians. The University of California developed a master plan for expanding its facilities for medical education during the early post–World War II period; enrolled medical students in 1951 on its campus in Los Angeles; and, with generous support from the state legislature, planned the development of three additional medical schools, which first accepted students during the 1960s and 1970s. Although it was slow in consolidating its scattered units of public higher education, New York organized the State University of New York (SUNY) system in 1948; and, in 1950, SUNY assumed responsibility for operating financially moribund private medical schools in Brooklyn and Syracuse. In 1962, the private medical school in Buffalo was absorbed by SUNY, followed by the development of a new school on Long Island, at Stony Brook, which accepted its first medical students in 1971. Florida opened its first state-supported medical school in 1956, following the establishment of the privately owned University of Miami in 1952, an institution that later received an annual capitation from the state for each resident medical student enrolled. A second state-owned school was opened in 1971. During the 1960s and 1970s, the states of Texas and Ohio also developed new medical schools as a part of statewide plans to increase the supply of physicians.

In summary, between 1960 and 1980 state governments developed twenty-nine new schools and enacted legislation providing for the annual support of operating expenditures in eight of the eleven new private schools that first enrolled students during that period. At the same time, state support increased significantly for existing state-operated schools and many states devised mechanisms for underwriting part of the cost of educating state residents enrolled in privately operated medical schools.

Struggles to Obtain Federal Support. While the private sector and state governments were actually engaged in the improvement of existing medical schools and the development of new ones, the ponderous federal government began considering possible solutions to the developing shortage of physicians. The first federal initiative came in March 1949, when S. 1453 was introduced in the Senate and several similar bills were brought before the House. S. 1453 proposed a $300 capitation for each school's average prior enrollment and $1,700 for each student enrolled above that average up to 50 percent of each school's budget. New schools were to receive $1,000 for each student enrolled. The bill also included provisions for construction grants for both new and existing schools and scholarships for medical students ("Proceedings of the Washington Session . . .," 1949). (Keep in mind that, in purchasing power, $1,000 in 1959 was the equivalent of $3,450 in 1980.)

S. 1453 was referred to the U.S. Senate Committee on Labor and Public Welfare's Subcommittee on Health and, according to the account in the *Journal of the American Medical Association* ("Proceedings of the Washington Session . . . ," 1949), the benefits of the bill were reduced substantially. The modified bill was approved by the Committee on Labor and Public Welfare and passed the Senate by unanimous voice vote in September 1949 ("Approved Examining Boards in Medical Specialties," 1949). In the House, H.R. 5940, the equivalent of the Senate bill, was reported out favorably by the Rules Committee but did not survive the adjournment of the session. Similar bills were unsuccessful in the next session of Congress. Other attempts to provide basic operating funds for the medical schools were made in Congress in 1951 and again in 1955, but none was successful (Cline, 1952; Wiggins and others, 1959).

In 1956, Congress did pass P.L. 84-911, which appropriated funds for the advanced training of nurses; and, in 1958, the nation's legislators enacted into law P.L. 85-544, which provided funds for the operation of schools of public health. Federal support for the education of physicians, however, was not realized until the mid-1960s.

A review of the legislative history of the 1940s and 1950s does not provide immediate answers to the question of why federal solutions to the national shortage of physicians were delayed. Franklin D. Roosevelt, in his precedent-setting creation of the New Deal of the 1930s, dug a wide channel for the flow of federally controlled tax revenues into programs intended to solve problems plaguing all levels of society. The years after World War II and throughout the 1950s were prosperous ones; the U.S. dollar was almighty in its value, and Marshall Plan funds were rebuilding Europe. As indicated by the initiatives first undertaken in 1949, Congress was interested in contributing to the solution of the problem; but until 1965 no proposal to support the direct cost of medical education was able to clear the political hurdles and become law.

Nonetheless, Congress had long understood the value and espoused the cause of medical research. The National Institutes of Health were established in 1930 by P.L. 71-251; the National Cancer Institute was established in 1937 by P.L. 75-244; and, in 1948, P.L. 80-655 established the National Heart Institute. In 1950, P.L. 81-692 mandated the establishment of other institutes devoted to health concerns (U.S. Department of Health, Education and Welfare, 1976). These new federal institutions developed both intramural and extramural-sponsored research programs, mainly in the medical schools, with generous annual increases in congressional funding during the 1950s and 1960s. The effort to obtain funding for medical research was facilitated by the effective influence of Mary Lasker and others with Senator Lister Hill and Congressman John Fogarty (Strickland, 1972; Drew, 1967). Indeed, federally sponsored biomedical research grants to medical faculty members began to rise to such a high volume in the mid-1950s that, in 1956, Congress enacted P.L. 84-835: the Health Research Facilities Act. This law assisted in the construction of modern laboratories—often in the form of new structural additions to the teaching facilities of the medical schools—to house federally funded research activities. None of these new facilities could be used for the instruction of medical students; federal inspectors audited the use of the space to enforce federal restrictions. Furthermore, in 1946, Congress enacted the famous Hill-Burton Act (P.L. 79-725), which, during the next several decades, facilitated medical care delivery by assisting with the construction of many new (but unfortunately quite small) hospitals and the renovation of old hospitals.

From 1949 to 1965, particularly early in that time span, some members of the medical academic community feared and anticipated an erosion of academic freedom through the federal government's intervention in medical education. This was certainly the case with the leadership of the AMA until the mid-1960s. Following the events through the contemporary pages of the *Journal of the American Medical Association,* I think it is clear that the AMA, until the early 1960s, was influential in blocking passage of any bill providing direct federal funding of medical education, particularly if this provision was coupled with the introduction of any kind of compulsory health insurance. Cooper (1976) has concluded that the leaders of the AMA opposed these federal initiatives because they recalled the harsh financial circumstances of physicians during the 1930s and thus had difficulty recognizing the development of a shortage of physicians in the early 1950s. Rayack (1967), in a lengthy diatribe against the AMA, attributes its opposition to federal initiatives entirely to a desire to restrict the supply of physicians for purely protectionist economic reasons. It is possible that Rayack's litany of allegations against the AMA's actions during the 1930–1955 period formed the philosophical basis of the Federal Trade Commission's attack on the AMA in 1976, many years after the AMA had reversed its stand against federal support of medical education. Clear evidence of a trend toward the AMA's recognition of a developing shortage of physicians, of the necessity for the development of substantial new teaching facilities to encourage enrollment expansion in existing schools, and for the establishment of new schools may be found in the Fifty-Ninth Annual Report on Medical Education by the AMA Council on Medical Education (American Medical Association Council on Medical Education, 1959). The AMA Board of Trustees, however, did not endorse federal support of medical education for several more years.

During the late 1940s and early 1950s, the deans of the AAMC could not reach a unanimous position of approving federal grants to medical education—unanimous views are rarely found in groups of academic people. Yet by 1955, most of the deans could accept the federal government as a source of funding needs, which had to be satisfied before enrollments could be expanded. Officials of the AAMC and the AMA testified before Congress in 1955 and addressed the issue of academic freedom; they were particularly concerned about governmental pressure to increase enrollments at the expense of educational quality, but they were hopeful that the long-established, independent accreditation system would guard against damaging interference from forces external to the university. The role of the LCME became crucial to the maintenance of quality in the M.D. degree programs, both in existing schools as they expanded their enrollments and in new schools as they developed with partial support from the federal government.

After Congress encountered its difficulties in supporting medical education, first in 1949 and later in the early 1950s, a series of studies of the national physician supply were compiled. In 1952, the President's Commission on the Health Needs of the Nation (the Magnuson Commission) concluded that the shortage of physicians could amount to 45,000 by 1960. In the mid-1950s, three governmental commissions were formed to study the problems of medical research and the supply of physicians. Each was given an unmemorable and lengthy title, so the published reports are usually identified by the name of each body's chairman: the Bayne-Jones Report of 1958, the Bane Report of 1959, and the Jones Report of 1960. These reports were instrumental in the shaping of public opinion and contributed greatly to the developing demand for increases in the supply of physicians.

Of the three, the Bane Report had the greatest impact. Its excellent analysis of the problem of physician supply and projections for the future undoubtedly impressed the members of Congress. Fordham (1980) credited it with transmitting a sense of urgency about the shortage of physicians and with providing an analytical data base for the formulation of subsequent federal legislation. The Bane group made several specific recommendations:

- The ratio of 141 physicians (133 M.D.s and 8 D.O.s) per 100,000 people in 1959 should be maintained as the population increases.
- Existing schools should expand enrollments whenever possible.
- New two-year schools should be developed to provide students to fill existing clinical teaching facilities.
- Depending on the level of expansion of existing schools, a minimum of twenty and as many as twenty-four new schools should be built if the 1959 physician/population ratio is to be maintained.

- By 1975, the annual number of M.D. graduates in the United States should rise to 11,000. To accomplish this goal, construction of teaching facilities should begin in the immediate future and be completed in a few years.
- Financial support should be provided for the operation of medical schools.
- There should be careful planning in the location of new schools, with collaboration among federal, regional, state, and private agencies.

The Bane Report offered a blueprint for the expansion of facilities and programs of medical education and defined what had to be done. But the task proposed was so enormous that, by 1960, it was clear that financing from a combination of private-sector and state sources would be inadequate. In 1960 and again in 1962, Congress considered and rejected legislation proposing federal matching grants for the construction of teaching facilities and for loan assistance to medical students. Thomas Turner, dean of the Johns Hopkins Medical School and the AAMC's spokesman in congressional hearings in 1962, emphasized the magnitude of the problem: "The universities must, within the next eight or nine years, create facilities for an additional 4,000 students; or, put another way, we must, in a decade or less, increase by 50 percent facilities that required nearly 200 years of private effort to establish." He stated further that private sources were inadequate to provide the scholarship and loan funds needed by students (U.S. House of Representatives, Committee on Interstate and Foreign Commerce, 1962, pp. 105–115, 339–360).

The first trickle of federal support for the research-dollar-rich and educational-dollar-poor medical schools came through P.L. 88–129, the Heatlh Professions Education Assistance Act, which was passed in 1963. This law allocated one federal dollar to match every local dollar to provide for the construction of additional educational facilities for existing schools; for every local dollar, two federal dollars were provided for the construction of new schools; and federal loan funds were made available to students. A school receiving a construction grant was required to increase the size of its entering class by 5 percent or five students, whichever was greater.

The statute required, as a contingency, that the recognized accrediting agency, the LCME, certify that there was reasonable assurance
that the quality of the educational program would not be diminished
by the enrollment increases. This action established a precedent
that was followed in all subsequent public laws affecting the
education of physicians. The 1963 act authorized $175 million for
construction grants during the fiscal years 1964 through 1965 for
use by all health professional schools (U.S. Department of Health
and Human Services, 1979).

In 1965, Congress crept closer to the provision of substantial
support for medical schools through the passage of P.L. 89-290.
For the first time, all medical schools were entitled to receive "basic
improvement grants," which in 1966 amounted to a "base grant"
of $12,500 plus $250 per full-time student and during 1967-1969
a "base grant" of $25,000 plus $500 per full-time student. Entering-
class enrollment had to be increased by 2.5 percent or 5 students.
Scholarships were created at the maximum of $2,500 per needy
student, loan funds were continued, and $480 million was authorized
for medical school construction for the period 1966-1969.

In 1965, in the midst of the political agitation regarding
federal support of medical education, Congress enacted P.L. 89-
97, which established the Medicare and Medicaid programs. These
two systems of federal (plus state, in the case of Medicaid) support
for the costs of medical services and hospitalization for the aged
and the needy expanded in volume quite rapidly and thus created
an increased demand for the services of physicians, who were already
in relatively short supply. Few persons predicted then that by 1979
the total expenditures for Medicare and Medicaid would grow to
$91.4 billion or 43.1 percent of all personal health care expenditures
(Health Insurance Institute, 1982).

While the federal Medicare and Medicaid programs were
being instituted, the American people, to a great extent spurred
on by the labor unions, began to participate heavily in the various
private medical care and hospitalization plans. By 1980, membership
in these health insurance programs had risen to 183 million
persons—that is, 85 percent of the civilian "noninstitutional"
population (U.S. Department of Health and Human Services, 1980).

In November 1967, the National Advisory Commission on Health Manpower appointed by President Johnson published a series of recommendations, most of which had been offered earlier: new schools of medicine should be formed; existing schools should expand enrollments; less reliance should be placed on foreign medical graduates (who should pass qualifying tests similar to those used to measure the achievements of M.D. graduates in the United States); the M.D. curriculum should be streamlined; and federal aid should be given to students and to expanding medical schools. Although this report broke little new ground, it added to the accumulating momentum of support for expanding the nation's capacity for educating physicians.

The significant breakthrough in federal legislation came in August 1968 with P.L. 90-490, which was passed by Congress with flying colors, perhaps due to its unreserved endorsement by not only the AAMC but also the AMA. (Earlier in 1968, the AAMC and the AMA had issued a joint statement supporting mobilization of the support necessary for the expansion of medical school enrollments to desirable levels.) P.L. 90-490 authorized construction funding of $170 million for fiscal 1970 and $225 million for fiscal 1971 and modified previous provisions by requiring the matching of federal to local funds on a two-to-one basis. "Institutional grants" were established to replace the previous "basic improvement grants"; each school was granted $25,000, and all schools shared in a distribution by formula of the balance of the funds appropriated— in medical schools this amounted to $550 per student. Each school was required to increase its entering enrollment by 2.5 percent or 5 additional students. A special "Physicians Augmentation Program" was developed on the basis of an authority for special projects with the intent of adding 1,000 entering-class spaces. Those schools that contributed to the addition of a national aggregate of 448 entering students received an award that amounted to approximately $20,000 per additional student. Grants to schools in financial distress were created, and loan and scholarship programs were continued. In administering this new law, the U.S. Public Health Service created a system of advisory councils composed of well-qualified medical educators who reviewed applications for construction grants, made site visits, and recommended final action by the U.S. Department of Health, Education and Welfare.

At this stage in the efforts to solve the problem of physician shortages, two events of considerable importance to medical education and health care occurred. The first of these was the publication of the Coggeshall Report in 1965. This report, which was financed by the Commonwealth Fund, reviewed trends in health care and cited their implications for medical education. It also made a series of rather specific recommendations to be followed in the reorganization of the AAMC, including a recommendation for the relocation of its staff offices to Washington, D.C. From 1965 to 1971, the AAMC expanded its constituencies to include—in addition to the original Council of Deans—a Council of Academic Societies, made up of faculty members; a Council of Teaching Hospitals; and an Organization of (Medical) Student Representatives. In 1969, the staff completed its relocation from Evanston, Illinois, to new quarters in the National Center for Higher Education in Washington (Cooper, 1976). Under the new leadership of John A. D. Cooper and with an enlarged professional staff, the AAMC quickly became a major resource for accurate information for both the legislative and administrative branches of the federal government as initiatives concerned with increasing the supply of physicians were considered during the 1970s. One of the early major actions of the enhanced AAMC was its adoption, in September 1970, of a goal to enroll 15,000 entering medical students annually by 1976, the bicentennial of the United States (Association of American Medical Colleges Committee on the Expansion of Medical Education, 1971).

The second event was the 1970 publication of the Carnegie Commission on Higher Education's detailed report on the nation's health and its implications for medical education. Among the many specific recommendations in the report was a call for the expansion of enrollments of entering medical students in existing schools and the establishment of nine new medical schools, thus increasing the annual input from 10,800 in 1970-71 to 15,300 in 1976 and to approximately 16,400 in 1978. Each university health center was urged to expand its services in its geographical area through the development of area health education centers. The commission recommended that the federal government support the necessary expansions in enrollment through loan and scholarship programs for needy students; capitation grants for the instructional costs for each student enrolled, in addition to a "bonus grant" for each student enrolled in an expansion program; fiscal incentives for experiments in curriculum reform; and liberal grants for the construction of university health science centers and area health education centers.

In 1971, P.L. 92-157 was passed by Congress, raising the federal contribution to construction of new buildings and the renovations of old ones to a maximum of 80 percent. This law also provided for the continuation of scholarship and loan funds; inaugurated bonus enrollment expansion awards; and established a system of grants for financial distress, the conversion of two-year programs to full M.D. curricula, newly developing schools, and capitations to each school based on its enrollment. Each school was required to increase entering-class enrollment by 10 percent or ten students and to engage in three of nine specified programs. Table 3 presents a summary of the actual amounts for operating costs received by an illustrative school from 1966 to 1980.

In 1976, Congress enacted P.L. 94-484, which made complex and substantive amendments to preceding health manpower legislation. Capitation was continued, but the amount funded per student was reduced annually (see Table 3). To receive a capitation grant, each school was required to increase entering-class enrollment by 10 percent or ten students and to expand primary care resident training programs from 35 percent of the total first-year residency positions in 1978 to 50 percent in 1980. A very controversial provision required each school to accept for transfer into the third year an "equitably apportioned" number of United States citizens/students from foreign medical schools for a three-year period beginning in 1978-79. Insured loans were developed, and repayment was authorized through medical service in a shortage area under the auspices of the National Health Service Corps. Area health education centers were given legal status and continued funding and each school was required to conduct at least 10 percent of all undergraduate education in two remote sites and to provide a training program for physician assistants or nurse practitioners. One of the sections of this law declared an end to the shortage of physicians in the United States.

In 1977, P.L. 95-83 extended the authority for capitation and required foreign M.D.s seeking graduate medical education in the

Table 3. Illustration of Federal Support of Medical School Operating Expenses, 1966 to 1980.

Fiscal Year	Authorizing Legislation	Authorized — Formula of Capitation Grant (Increase in 1st-year Enrollment)	Authorized — Amount of Authorized Award	Enrollment First Year	Enrollment Total	Capitation Grant Amount Authorized	Capitation Grant Amount Paid	Average Operating Expenses	Percent of Capitation Grant of Average Operating Expenses Authorized	Percent of Capitation Grant of Average Operating Expenses Paid
1966	P.L. 89-290	Greater of 2.5% of previous 1st-year enrollment or 5 students	$12,500 + $250 per student	105	405	$113,750	$ 80,000	$ 4,230,000	2.7	1.9
1967			$25,000 + $500 per student	105	410	230,000	223,000	4,890,000	4.7	4.7
1968				105	415	232,500	232,500	5,520,000	4.2	4.2
1969				105	420	235,000	235,000	6,320,000	3.7	3.7
1970	P.L. 90-490	Greater of 2.5% of previous 1st-year enrollment or 5 students	$25,000 + remaining appropriation prorated on basis of enrollment and graduates	110	425	240,000	240,000	7,200,000	3.3	3.3
1971				110	430	229,000	229,000	8,480,000	2.7	2.7
1972	P.L. 92-157	Greater of 5% of previous 1st-year enrollment or 10 students if previous enrollment greater than 100 (if less than 100, then 10%)	$2,500 per 1st-, 2nd-, 3rd-yr students, $4,000 per graduate	120	445	1,270,000	887,000	9,120,000	14.0	9.7

Year	Legislation	Capitation Grant Amount							
1973			120	460	1,315,000	831,000	10,060,000	13.1	8.3
1974			120	470	1,340,000	856,000	11,030,000	12.1	7.8
1975	P.L. 92-157 Extended through Continuing Appropriation Act		120	480	1,380,000	645,000	13,920,000	9.9	4.6
1976			120	480	1,380,000	416,000	16,100,000	8.6	2.6
1977	P.O. 92-157 Extended by P.L. 94-484		120	480	1,380,000	495,000	19,600,000	7.0	2.5
1978	P.O. 94-484 Extended through Continuing Resolutions until June 5, 1981	Maintain 1st-year enrollment of preceding academic year (or 1976-77, if greater) $2,000 per 120 students	120	480	960,000	665,000	21,800,000	4.4	3.1
1979		$2,050 per 120 students	120	480	984,000	636,000	25,300,000	3.9	2.5
1980		$2,100 per 120 students	120	480	1,008,000	438,000	28,000,000	3.6	1.6
				TOTAL	12,297,250	7,108,500			

Notes: This table illustrates the federal support of medical school operating expenses through capitation grants authorized and appropriated for a typical school with an enrollment in 1965 of 100 students in each class (that is, a total enrollment of 400 students). The illustration is based on the assumption that the typical school has complied with all legislative requirements for receiving the capitation grants (for example, the special project requirements under P.L. 92-157 and the residency and transfer of U.S. citizens in foreign medical schools requirements under P.L. 94-484) and with the mandatory medical student enrollment requirements of each legislative act. The additional awards for bonus grants under P.L. 92-157 and physician augmentation program grants under P.L. 90-490 have not been included in the data and the 5 percent enrollment increase requirements for a school that received a construction grant is *not* portrayed in this table.

Dates indicate years the money was paid to the schools, not the years when the legislation was enacted.

The reader should observe that Congress authorizes funds fairly generously but frequently does not appropriate the full amounts authorized. The columns headed "Capitation Grant Amount" and "Percent of Capitation Grant. . ." show the differences.

Sources: Rosenthal, n.d.; U.S. Department of Health and Human Services, 1979.

United States to pass the Visa Qualifying Examination (VQE), effective January 1978. P.L. 95-215, enacted by Congress in the same year, repealed the requirement that each school accept U.S. citizen transfer students from foreign schools after 1978–79, largely due to the refusal of a number of universities to accept the capitation grant if the requirement to accept those transfer students continued for three years.

The basic provision of P.L. 94-484 for the capitation grants to the schools was continued in effect during 1978–80 by means of a series of continuing congressional resolutions. Efforts were made to enact a new health manpower statute during the 95th and 96th Congresses, but none succeeded.

Table 3 indicates that for the typical illustrative school the portion of total operating expenditures provided by federal grants amounts to only a modest subsidy, which may or may not have covered the additional costs incurred as a result of the successive enrollment expansions required by the several public laws affecting health manpower. Regardless of the aggregate cost to the federal government, the obvious objective of increasing the enrollment of medical students in preexisting schools was achieved. Schools that received a federal matching grant for new construction or major renovation of teaching facilities were required to increase the enrollment of the entering class by an additional 5 percent, a calculation not plotted in Table 3.

Two-year schools of the basic medical sciences that converted to a full M.D. curriculum after the enactment of P.L. 92-157 in 1971 received a one-time grant of $50,000 per student enrolled in the first third-year class; this first third-year class had to be enrolled no later than the school year beginning in fiscal year 1975. P.L. 92-157 also authorized start-up assistance for new schools for a period of one year prior to the admission of the first-year class through the third year in which students were enrolled. The grant for the year preceding that in which the students were first enrolled was limited to $10,000 for each full-time student in the projected charter class; $7,500 was granted for each full-time student enrolled in the first year, $5,000 for each full-time student enrolled in the second year, and $2,500 for each full-time student enrolled in the third year. In addition, the school was also eligible to receive the "capitation" grant; because of the small number of students enrolled in the early classes, this was never a large amount.

Some new schools received direct support for the operation of "special projects" authorized by a variety of the public law cited above. New schools that developed between 1963 and 1976 were able to avail themselves of several authorities for federal matching grants for the construction of new teaching facilities as well as teaching hospitals, with the latter usually supported by a variety of sources, including funds under the Hill-Burton Act.

In 1972, a rather special involvement of federal government in medical education developed through the enactment of P.L. 92-426, which created the Uniformed Services University of the Health Sciences—a "West Point for military doctors," according to its ardent and persistent advocate, Congressman F. Edward Hebert (D-Louisiana), who became the all-powerful chairman of the House Committee on Armed Services in the 92nd Congress ("Military Medical School," 1975). This public law authorized the very useful and popular armed forces scholarships; but its principal component was the authority to establish a medical school in or adjacent to the District of Columbia. This federal initiative was opposed by a long list of professional associations as being "unnecessary," "too expensive," "duplicative of civilian activities," and so on. Due to Hebert's capacity for persuasion, Congress quickly approved P.L. 92-426, but the authorized new school met further opposition before it started. In early 1975, the Defense Manpower Commission unsuccessfully recommended that the new school be terminated ("Military Medical School," 1975). Even after students were enrolled in 1976, the military school encountered difficulties. In early 1977, one of the first actions of the new Carter Administration was to delete from the budget of the U.S. Department of Defense the operating expenses for the school for the next year and to strike the next scheduled appropriation for completing construction of the school's teaching facilities. After extensive deliberation, Congress approved the previously planned appropriations, and the school continued its development (*Congressional Record*, 1975).

The federal government took another initiative in direct participation in medical education when, in 1972, P.L. 92-541, the Veterans Administration Medical School Act, was passed. The three

sections of this law provided some support for allied health education; grants to expand and/or improve existing medical schools
that had "Dean's Committee" relationships with VA hospitals; and
appropriations, over a seven-year period, to facilitate the development of eight new state-operated medical schools. It is clear that
this public law was an initiative of Congress, particularly the House
and Senate Committees on Veterans' Affairs. Ultimately, five new
medical schools and one area health education center of an existing
school were established under P.L. 92-541, all in the jurisdictions
of prominent members of the two committees. One other proposed
new medical school was vetoed by a state governor who believed
that his sparsely populated state would have difficulty in absorbing
the operating costs of a new medical school after the VA retired
from the scene when the statutory seven years of fiscal support
expired. VA hospitals are discussed further in Chapter Ten.

Influx of Foreign Medical Graduates. Besides the efforts to
increase the number of physicians educated in and graduated from
medical schools in the United States, another factor had a significant
impact on the supply of physician manpower until 1980: the heavy
wave of foreign medical graduates (FMGs) immigrating to the
United States during the post-World War II period.

Stevens and Vermeulen (1972) reviewed the FMG situation
during the years prior to 1972. The major influx of FMGs began
after the Fulbright Program of International Educational Exchange
was established by Congress in 1946. The Smith-Mundt Act of 1948
further facilitated the entry of FMGs into the United States through
the provision for exchange visitor (J) visas. The governmental
provisions, intended for much broader purposes, became the legal
basis for the increased flow of FMGs into the much-expanded
programs of post-M.D. specialty (internship and residency) training,
which had been developed to accommodate the bolus of World War
II veterans seeking such training during the period from 1946 to
1950.

Many FMGs who came to the United States on an exchange
visit managed to convert their status to that of permanent immigrant
through marriage with a United States citizen or by admission into
the national quota system. The latter arrangement was modified
by exceedingly permissive legislation in 1965. The new law abolished

Table 4. Comparison of Foreign Physicians Admitted to the United States with U.S. Medical Graduates, 1950 to 1980.

Year	Foreign Medical Graduate (FMG) Immigrants[a]	Physician Exchange Visitors[b]	Total	U.S. Medical Graduates[c]	FMG Interns and Residents as % of Total Interns and Residents[d]
1950	1,878	*	*	5,553	*
1951	1,388	*	*	6,135	10.0
1952	1,210	*	*	6,080	14.0
1953	845	*	*	6,668	18.0
1954	1,040	*	*	6,861	21.0
1955	1,046	*	*	6,977	17.0
1956	1,388	*	*	6,845	19.0
1957	1,990	*	*	6,796	20.0
1958	1,934	*	*	6,861	22.0
1959	1,630	*	*	6,861	23.0
1960	1,574	*	*	7,081	25.0
1961	1,683	*	*	6,994	26.0
1962	1,797	3,970	5,757	7,168	24.0
1963	2,093	4,737	5,730	7,264	24.0
1964	2,249	4,518	6,767	7,336	26.0
1965	2,012	4,160	6,172	7,409	28.0
1966	2,552	4,370	6,922	7,574	29.0
1967	3,326	5,204	8,530	7,743	31.0
1968	3,129	5,701	8,829	7,973	32.0
1969	2,756	4,450	7,216	8059	35.0
1970	3,158	5,008	8,116	8,367	*
1971	5,756	4,784	10,540	8,974	33.0
1972	7,144	3,935	11,079	9,551	*
1973	7,119	4,613	11,732	10,391	*
1974	4,537	4,717	9,254	11,613	*
1975	5,361	2,849	8,210	12,714	*
1976	7,519	2,562	10,081	13,561	23.3
1977	7,037	1,578	8,651	13,607	18.2
1978	4,435	951	5,386	14,393	15.4
1979	3,040	420	3,460	14,966	20.0
1980	*	*	*	15,135	*

Note: An asterisk indicates that data in these categories are not available.

[a] Data for 1950 to 1971 from Stevens and Vermeulen, 1972, p. 95; data for 1972 to 1979 from U.S. Department of Justice, Immigration and Naturalization Service, unpublished data for those years.

[b] Data for 1950 to 1971 from Stevens and Vermeulen, 1972, p. 96; data for 1972 to 1979 from U.S. Department of Justice, Immigration and Naturalization Service, unpublished data for those years.

[c] Data for 1950 to 1960 from *Journal of the American Medical Association*, 1964, *190*, 613; data for 1961 to 1980 from *Journal of the American Medical Association*, 1981b, *246*, 2917.

[d] Data from American Medical Association, *Directory of Residency Training Programs*, 1950 to 1980.

national quotas and gave preference to persons whose occupations were designated by the Department of Labor as being in short supply in the United States. Medicine was so designated. Table 4 shows the history of the movement of FMGs into the United States during the 1950–1980 period. From 1900 to 1950, the annual number of FMGs entering the country averaged below 1,000.

In the early post-World War II period, the AMA and the AAMC through the LCME attempted to develop and maintain a list of foreign schools whose graduates were recommended for consideration on the same basis as graduates of LCME-accredited schools. This list was first published in 1950 but was discontinued in 1955 because of the difficulty of maintaining adequate information about all of the numerous foreign schools. At this time, exchange visitor FMGs began to occupy an annually increasing number of the positions available for post-M.D. training. Concerned about the obviously poor quality of education of some FMGs appointed as house staff, the AAMC and the AMA organized the Educational Commission for Foreign Medical Graduates (ECFMG) in 1956. Its purpose was to evaluate individuals rather than the quality of the schools they attended. The first ECFMG exam was administered in March 1958; each FMG house staff member had to attain a passing grade by December 30, 1960, or residency training would not be allowed to continue. All subsequent FMG candidates for the beginning of hospital training had to pass the ECFMG exam before leaving their native countries (American Medical Association Council on Medical Education and Hospitals, 1960). Stevens and Vermeulen described the development of testing of the qualifications of FMGs (1972) and Stimmel and Smith (1978) reported relatively poor performance by FMGs on licensing exams. Weiss and others (1974a, 1974b) believe that during the 1970s many thousands of FMGs were rendering substantial medical care under poor or no supervision in marginal training programs, state hospitals, and elsewhere, and without any kind of license.

The causes for the enormous migration of FMGs into the United States after World War II are subject to debate. Without doubt, the affluent life-style that American physicians began to enjoy during the 1950s has been a powerful attraction. Numerous hospitals, unaffiliated with medical schools and unsuccessful in recruiting American M.D. graduates, have found that FMGs are an inexpensive source of physician services, particularly in the deteriorated core of the older cities, where house staff physicians have long been in short supply. Such hospitals have been quite adroit in recruiting FMGs and protecting their status once they arrive. But there can be no denying the obvious: The tardy development of solutions to the post-World War II national physician shortage created an irresistible vacuum that drew in many thousands of FMGs.

However, as Table 4 indicates, the enactment of P.L. 94-484 in October 1976 began to check the influx of FMGs. Since the law declared an end to the physician shortage, no more preference could be given to FMGs for exchange visitor visas or immigration (Stevens and Vermeulen, 1972, pp. 25–47). A tough new "entrance" examination, the Visa Qualifying Examination (VQE), comparable to Parts I and II of the National Board of Medical Examiners (NBME) examination, replaced the ECFMG test for foreign FMGs (but not for U.S. citizen FMGs), producing an immediate improvement in the educational quality of the reduced number of FMGs selected for residency training. At the beginning of 1981, adjustments to the new rules by foreign countries were still being made; the State Department had received protests from at least one foreign government, none of whose M.D. graduates could pass the VQE. And, in 1982, the ECFMG modified its test so that, effective in 1984, it will be comparable in difficulty to Parts I and II of the NBME examination. This new test—the Foreign Medical Graduate Examination in the Medical Sciences (FMGEMS)—will replace the older ECFMG and the VQE measurements and is to be given to all foreign medical graduates.

The Physician Supply After Two Decades of Effort

Table 5 shows the results of the twenty-year attack on the post-World War II shortage of physicians by the nation's universities, teaching hospitals, private donors, foundations, state governments, and the federal government. Between 1960 and 1980, the number of accredited schools increased from 86 to 126; the size of the entering class of medical students grew from 8,298 to 17,204, while M.D. graduates expanded from 6,994 to 15,667, with additional

Table 5. Growth in Medical Schools, Entering-Class Sizes, and M.D.
Graduates, Academic Years 1960–61 to 1981–82, with Projections for
Academic Years 1983–1984 to 1986–87.

Year	Number of Schools	Entering-Class Size	Number of M.D. Graduates
1960–61	86	8,298	6,994
1961–62	87	8,483	7,168
1962–63	87	8,642	7,264
1963–64	87	8,772	7,336
1964–65	88	8,856	7,409
1965–66	88	8,759	7,574
1966–67	89	8,964	7,743
1967–68	94	9,479	7,973
1968–69	99	9,863	8,059
1969–70	101	10,401	8,367
1970–71	103	11,348	8,974
1971–72	108	12,361	9,551
1972–73	112	13,726	10,391
1973–74	114	14,185	11,613
1974–75	114	14,963	12,714
1975–76	114	15,351	13,561
1976–77	116	15,667	13,607
1977–78	122	16,134	14,393
1978–79	125	16,620	14,966
1979–80	126	17,014	15,135
1980–81	126	17,320	15,985
1981–82	126	17,234	15,728
1982–83		17,150	16,129
1983–84		16,723	16,753
1984–85		16,742	16,922
1985–86		16,734	16,914
1986–87		16,778	16,908

Sources: Data for 1960–61 to 1980–81 from Journal of the American
Medical Association, 1981b, 246, 2917. Data for 1981–82 and 1982–83 to
1986–87 projections from Journal of the American Medical Association,
1982, 248, 3249.

expansion of annual graduates projected as the newest schools
achieve their planned enrollments.

Figure 1 displays the projected impact of the increased
production of M.D. graduates. In 1960, there was one M.D. to 754
people; in 1980, the ratio shifted to 515 per M.D., and the known

Figure 1. Number of People per Physician in the United States, 1950–2000.

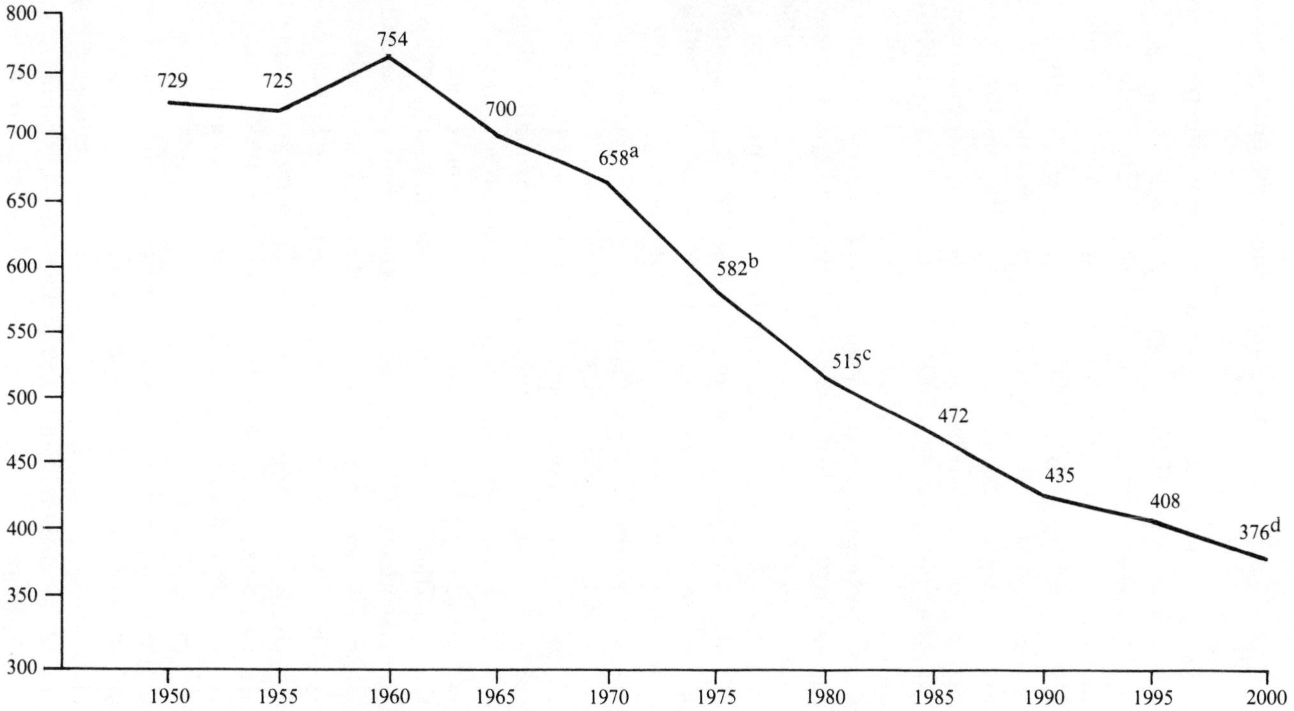

Sources: a. 1950-1970 data from U.S. Department of Health, Education, and Welfare, December 1974, p. 31.

b. 1975 data from American Medical Association, 1977, p. 108.

c. 1980 data from *American Medical Association Newsletter*, July 26, 1982, p. 4.

d. 1985-2000 estimates from Bureau of Health Manpower, 1977.

number of students in the pipeline headed to the practice of medicine by 1990 could bring the ratio to 435 persons per M.D.

Will 435 persons per physician in 1990 be too few, just right, or too many? As early as 1959, Ginsberg, in a series of writings and public utterances published in 1969, warned of the difficulty of predicting the demand for physicians' services and suggested the possibility of a surplus. Castleton (1971) and M. Wilson (1972) have questioned the need for additional new schools. In 1976, the Carnegie Commission on Policy reversed the position it had taken in 1970 and warned of a potential surplus. In the same year, P.L. 94-484 declared that "there is no longer an insufficient number of physicians and surgeons in the United States." In 1978, Joseph Califano, Secretary of Health, Education and Welfare, expressed his view that the United States faced a severe oversupply of doctors in the coming decade (Califano, 1979). In 1980, the Graduate Medical Education National Advisory Committee recommended that "all medical schools should reduce entering-class size in the aggregate by a minimum of 10 percent by 1984 relative to the 1978-79 enrollment, or 17 percent relative to the 1980-81 entering class. The number of FMGs entering the United States, estimated to be 4,100 by 1983, should be severely restricted. If this cannot be accomplished, the alternative is to decrease further the number of entrants to United States medical schools or to close the weakest of them" (p. 52).

Using a slightly different approach, Reinhardt (1977) advanced the view that the demand for physician services is virtually limitless and may increase in proportion to the supply of physicians. Ginsberg (1969, 1980) continued to repeat the warning he first gave in 1959: Each physician adds to the cost of the medical care system of the nation—$200,000 in 1959 and $350,000 in 1980; thus, the greater the number of physicians, the greater the aggregate cost of health care.

In 1980, the results of a study financed by the Rand Corporation, "The Changing Geographic Distribution of Board Certified Physicians," were published (Schwartz and others, 1980). According to the authors, from 1960 to 1977 smaller communities in the United States were the beneficiaries of an influx of medical specialists; however, the absolute increase in specialists per 100,000 persons was greater in metropolitan areas. Thus, it appears that the urban centers of the United States have felt the primary impact of the physician surplus that had developed by the end of the 1970s. The *Wall Street Journal* reported that San Francisco has one doctor for every 216 persons; the practice of house calls on patients has been revived; appointments with physicians are made quickly; and a number of salaried positions for physicians have long lists of applicants ("Will Surplus of M.D.s Be Good for Patients? Look at San Francisco,"1980). In the early 1980s, articles in the *Washington Post* and *American Medical News* forecast a continuation of the surplus in those urban areas that are most attractive to physicians and the persistence of shortages in less attractive urban and rural areas ("In Portland, the Doctor Is In, and In, and In," 1981; "California Considering Action to Deal with a Physician Surplus," 1981).

Lessons Learned

After this review of the cycle of shortage and surplus in physicians, it is appropriate to draw some conclusions from the experience.

1. *Physician Supply in the 1980s and Predictions for 2010 A.D.* To my knowledge, no acceptable measure of the actual demand for physician graduates has yet been advanced. With the aid of infallible hindsight, it is easy now to conclude that, from 1910 to World War II, the country fell behind in the production of physicians as the population continued to grow—and grew very rapidly from 1940 to 1960. The imbalance was compounded as Medicare and Medicaid programs created more demand for physician services, as did the increasingly heavy subscription to private health care/ hospitalization insurance. The extolling of miracle cures and discoveries in the media also raised the American people's expectations from medical science—expectations that were enhanced by the performances of the celebrated members of what has been called "Mary Lasker's Health Syndicate" (Drew, 1967), in numerous congressional hearings.

When the physician shortage was recognized during the 1950s, many groups—but not the federal government—moved to solve the problem. Congress refused to approve direct aid for medical education until the practicing branch of the House of Medicine was able to join hands with the academic branch. This took almost fifteen years too long. When the financial aid to establish a new school was finally provided, seven to ten years were needed from the granting of a legal charter to the graduation of the first M.D.s in small numbers. The delay, plus the changes in demand for medical care detailed above, created the vacuum that drew in the horde of FMGs, some well trained, others grossly inadequate by post-mid-century U.S. standards.

Now, in the early 1980s, many of us believe that the students currently in the physician education/training "pipeline" are so numerous that we soon shall see a functional surplus in the United States. The problem is that all Americans, clustered around several thousand foothills, have been conditioned for forty years to suffer a shortage of physicians and they are reluctant to hear, much less believe, pronouncements about impending surpluses—especially if such sounds emanate from the self-styled Olympians who reside a mile or so east of the Potomac River. So the overproduction may continue for some time.

If the near future is a rerun of the past, we should expect some reduction of medical student enrollment, increasing constraints on the immigration of FMGs, and ultimately some (but not full) correction of the maldistribution of practicing physicians—likely by the last half of the 1980s. A few new or old schools may close due to the general financial constraints expected during the 1980s, including the demise of federal capitation and/or reduction of state appropriations to both public and private schools. Around 2010 A.D., in time for the centennial of Flexner's report, the population increase could run ahead of the physician supply; a whole new build-up could begin again, with a need for upgrading aging facilities and external (federal) support for expanded enrollments.

2. *Federal Support Versus Federal Control.* In the 1950s, some expressed concern that the federal government, if it began to provide financial support for the various activities of the nation's medical schools, would also seek to exercise control over their administrations and faculties. Federal support of the medical schools has developed, and their circumstances, over a thirty-year period, have

been greatly modified as a result. In 1967, Hinsey wrote of the schools' problems in dealing with multiple agencies of government in such matters as arranging for the renovation of an established institution or the building of a new one; he particularly deplored the damage done to institutional integrity by the extramural influences over project research grants to faculty members. Also, he described the difficulties encountered by medical school administrators laboring under governmental accounting requirements. In 1980, Petersdorf reviewed U.S. Department of Health, Education and Welfare Secretary Califano's 1978 address to the AAMC (Califano, 1979) and, among other topics, criticized Califano's call for changes in the medical curriculum to make students more responsive to the demographic, social, and economic factors that affect health care. Petersdorf also made the point that the government can suggest curricular reformation but should not mandate it—to make any subject a prerequisite for financial support of medical education is intellectual blackmail and violates one of the essential freedoms of the university to determine the course of study for its students.

Unfortunately, P.L. 94–484, in 1976, contained provisions that indirectly induced curricular change and dictated instruction of a minimum of 10 percent of clinical subject material in a nonmedical center setting. One need not be paranoid to be wary of a potential trend in future public laws that could result in a substantial erosion of the tradition of academic freedoms in medical education.

Governmental accounting requirements, the subject of Hinsey's complaints in 1967, also appear to have reached a dangerous level that justifies grave concern; witness Circular A-21 of the 1979 Office of Management and Budget, which has had a disastrous impact on the universities. An article in *Science* estimated that at Stanford University alone, where A-21 will require a time-and-motion reporting of the activities of faculty members holding research grants, required reports will rise from 3,000 to 80,000 and administrative costs will be increased by $250,000 to $300,000 a year (Walsh, 1980).

In a personal communication in 1981, John Sherman, AAMC vice-president and former deputy director of the National Institutes

of Health (NIH), expressed the following view of the evolution
of federal government/medical school relationships:

> Of even greater significance than the sizable
> efforts and the associated costs, both tangible and
> intangible, of the accounting requirements is the
> nature of contemporary attitudes and behavioral
> patterns among institutional officials and faculty
> members concerning the terms and conditions of
> federal grants to medical schools for health-related
> activities. I suggest that because of the unusual char-
> acteristics of the relationship between those institu-
> tions and government agencies, particularly the
> National Institutes of Health, during the formative
> days of that agency's research grant program, there
> may have been established, inadvertently but strongly,
> some misconceptions about the eventual nature of
> arrangements generally between the federal and non-
> federal sectors. As one who not only observed but took
> part in what had to be one of the most exciting eras
> in our nation's history involving public aspirations
> for improvements in health as a major policy objective,
> I believe that hindsight forces a conclusion quite
> contrary to what some of us envisioned as that era
> began shortly after World War II. I refer to the fact
> that numerous individuals involved in the establish-
> ment and development of the research grant programs
> managed by the NIH presumed that it would be
> possible to disprove what we regarded as an unfair
> and inappropriate cliche, namely, "federal funds me-
> ant undue federal influence." The heady atmosphere
> of those days was highlighted by an unusually effective
> and close working relationship in the development
> of policies and programs between leaders in the grantee
> institutions and the biomedical research community
> as well as their counterparts in government. This was
> a circumstance which in retrospect was definitely on

the positive side as far as the public good was concerned. The attitude of the NIH grant funds created
a belief that perhaps that cliche, indeed, did not
necessarily apply to all activities touched by federal
dollars.

Thus, there was raised almost a generation of
institution administrators and faculty as well as federal
program officials who were largely convinced that it
was possible to arrange a set of conditions by which
the public purpose was well served with a minimum
of restrictions on the use of the funds and the individuals responsible for their expenditures. Although
the purpose and conditions involved in federal support
of the education of health professionals were necessarily significantly different from those obtained for
research support, those differences were overlooked by
many because of the experience derived from the
research program. Too late have we realized that what
we considered to be a myth was not and that probably
there can be no exceptions to the consequences of
federal funding as we now recognize them. While one
may lament the extremes to which undue federal
influence has developed along with financial support
of both education and research, that in no way alle-
viates the pain of the rude discovery that our early
beliefs were sadly in error.

The reasons for the increase of federal influence on the schools
of medicine from 1950 to 1980 shall be debated for some time to
come. Among the reasons cited most frequently are the burgeoning
size of the federal bureaucracy and the concomitant spread of the
bureaucratic mentality: as the number of employees in the numerous
agencies of the executive branch increases, so does the tendency
of many of them to succumb to a prevalent chronic malady "of
unknown origin," limited to the environs of the District of Columbia
and generally characterized by strong personal feelings of intellectual
superiority, which are unjustified by the facts. During the 1970s,
the increase in executive branch personnel was nearly matched by

a significant swelling in the size of the various staffs serving the members of Congress and their committees. Congressman James M. Collins (R-Texas) reviewed this matter early in the 97th Congress (Kilpatrick, 1981), citing 817 total committee staff members in 1972 and 1,030 in 1979, with their cost increasing from $14 million to $96 million in the same period. One could infer that the malady, long endemic among the agencies, has spread into the congressional staffs; as a result, public laws in the mid-1970s began to include those numerous specific detailed and mandatory prescriptions and prohibitions long prevalent in the regulations written by the agency staff members when given a new public law. As an illustration of the impact of this federal disease among congressional staffs, I give you P.L. 94-484.

So, in the future, be wary of governmental employees who come bearing grants—with grants come onerous requirements, sooner or later. Further, funds that are authorized by Congress frequently are not appropriated in the full amount authorized.

2

Solving the Physician Shortage, 1960–1980

The shortage of physicians that had developed in the United States by the late 1950s could be solved only by increasing the annual enrollment of entering students. There were two paths to the accomplishment of this objective: one was to expand enrollments in the eighty-six older schools; the other was to build new medical schools. Neither path was easy to travel, but each eventually led to a substantial growth in the ranks of American physicians. In 1960, the eighty-six older schools enrolled 8,298 entering medical students. By 1980, the same schools (plus the University of California at Irvine, which converted from a school of osteopathy in 1974) had increased their enrollments of entering medical students to 13,753—an increase of 5,455. In the same year, the forty new medical schools that had been established since 1960 enrolled 3,443 new students, a number that could grow to 3,600 by 1985 if these schools achieve their established enrollment goals.

Of course, statistics alone do not convey the complexity of the means by which these increases were achieved. The first section of this chapter examines various facets of the enrollment increases that occurred in the eighty-six schools established before 1960: the

41

factors that limited their expansion, the role of federal programs as incentives to expanding enrollments, and the impact of the increases on these schools. The core of the chapter consists of a detailed discussion of the forty new schools founded between 1960 and 1980. Although the 1980 entering-class enrollment in the new schools was less than that in the old schools, the forty new medical schools did make a contribution to solving the national problems of a physician shortage. Their significance, however, extends far beyond their role in producing more physicians for the United States: each provided a unique opportunity for studying the critical elements of the early phases in a medical school's development.

The subsequent discussion of the forty new schools focuses on two of these elements: (1) the general and specific reasons advanced by those groups and individuals who advocated their development and (2) the types of sponsorship that characterize them. In the section headed "Lessons Learned," I have drawn on my personal observations of and experience with the forty new schools in sketching the ideal conditions and the realities of developing new programs in medical education and in offering guidance to those who may, in the future, be faced with the option or necessity of founding new medical schools. I conclude with a note of extreme caution to those who, in response to a developing shortage of physicians or to other problems involving medical education, may be tempted to found new medical schools as a panacea to these ills. The establishment of a new medical school is an enormous task that consumes nearly unfathomable amounts of money, time, and human energy; and its development will demand reliable supplies of these resources throughout its life. In terms of efficiency and guaranteed results, the expansion of existing facilities and programs of medical education may be the preferred alternative for future policy makers and planners concerned with the field of medical education.

The Eighty-Six Older Schools

Factors Limiting Expansion of Enrollments. In the eighty-six medical schools established before 1960, entering-class enrollments were expanded gradually and in direct relationship to state initiatives and the various federal public laws enacted during the 1970s, which required successive percentile increases in the entering-class size as a condition for the receipt of federal capitation grants (see Table 3). Four factors often limited expansions of the entering-class enrollments in these schools: (1) the existing seat space in lecture rooms and student laboratory work areas, (2) the availability of a sufficient number of patients in teaching hospitals owned by or affiliated with the university, (3) the size and professional characteristics of the medical school faculty, and (4) the additional operating funds required to support the larger entering-class enrollments.

Most of the eighty-six schools were able to achieve small enrollment increases by making minor rearrangements in the available space or by adding lecture room seats and laboratory work areas. More substantial enrollment increases—those above 10 percent—usually required a large-scale modification of existing buildings or the construction of new ones. Between 1963 and 1968, the federal government underwrote the construction of new teaching facilities on a one-to-one dollar-matching basis; after 1968 and until the expiration of the program in the mid-1970s, the federal share was doubled. As a result, many schools were able to finance the construction of new teaching facilities that replaced inadequate and antiquated buildings and made possible large increases in the enrollment of entering students.

Federal Incentives for Enrollment Increases. In addition to capitation grants, special financial incentives for the expansion of medical student enrollments were written into P.L. 90-490 and P.L. 92-157, which Congress enacted into law in 1968 and 1971, respectively. The first incentive, the Physicians Augmentation Program, paid an average of $20,000 to each medical school for each student newly enrolled in excess of the number required for receipt of the capitation grant. The second incentive authorized a payment of "$1,000 for each enrollment bonus student; $4,000 for each graduate completing studies in more than three years; and $6,000 for each student completing studies in more than three years or less." These clever devices, arranged by crafty federal employees in the legislative and executive branches of the government, succeeded in catching the attention of medical school deans and their departmental chairmen. The federal statutes, however, did evince a concern for the maintenance of high academic standards: they required the LCME to certify that any proposed expansion of an entering class would not jeopardize the quality of the medical school's M.D. degree curriculum.

While these incentive programs were in operation, the LCME considered proposals for the expansion of enrollments, approved many, modified the size of the expansion proposed by some, and rejected those submitted by a small but significant number of others. Most of the proposals were designed with the objective of maintaining good academic standards; a few were submitted by medical school officials who seemed willing to risk the sacrifice of academic quality by offering to double their enrollments within a few months in order to obtain the federal funds—just as the Old Testament figure Essau was willing to sell his birthright for a mess of pottage.

Impact of Enrollment Increases. The size of the increase in entering-class enrollments varied from school to school; ultimately, each school had to expand the entering class by 20 percent over its 1960 baseline in order to qualify for the several authorized federal capitation grants. Table 6 displays the expansion in percentiles of entering-class enrollments from 1960 to 1980 in the eighty-six older schools; Tables 7 and 8 chart the growth of the entering classes in these schools from 1960 to 1970 to 1980. (See Appendix B for a school-by-school listing of the percentage increase in entering-class enrollment of the eighty-six pre-1960 schools in 1960 and 1980.)

In order to accommodate the expansion of the medical schools' entering-class enrollments, additional physical facilities were needed; consequently existing buildings were renovated or new and larger ones were constructed. These enrollment increases not only led to modifications of a medical school's physical plant but also caused changes in its educational program. During the 1970s, fewer student laboratory exercises in the basic sciences were offered. In some schools, students had few or no laboratory studies in biochemistry and physiology; anatomy and pathology continued to include gross and microscopic laboratory studies. The increased numbers of students assigned as clinical clerks in the teaching hospitals, together with an expanded corps of hospital residents and clinical fellows, congested these institutions and thus diluted

Table 6. Expansions of the Entering-Class Enrollments in the Eighty-Six Medical Schools Established Before 1960, 1960–1980.

Percentage Increase in Enrollments	Number of Schools	Percentage of Schools
1 to 25	5	5.8
26 to 50	25	29.1
51 to 75	17	19.8
76 to 100	21	24.4
101 to 125	10	11.6
126 to 150	5	3.5
151 to 200	3	5.8
TOTAL	86	100.0

Sources: Entering-class enrollment data for 1960 from *Journal of the American Medical Association*, 1961b, *178*, 645–646. Entering-class enrollment data for 1980 from *Journal of the American Medical Association*, 1981e, *246*, 2965–2967.

Table 7. Average Number of Students in Entering Classes of the Eighty-Six Medical Schools Established Before 1960, in 1960, 1970, and 1980.

Year	Total Number of Students	Average Number of Students in Entering Classes
1960	8,298	96
1970	10,539	122
1980	13,753	159

Sources: Journal of the American Medical Association, 1961c, *178*, 647; 1971, *218*, 1206–1207; 1981e, *246*, 2965–2967.

Table 8. Range of Entering-Class Sizes of the Eighty-Six Medical Schools Established Before 1960, in 1960, 1970, and 1980.

Year	Low	High
1960	24	207
1970	66	250
1980	66	357

Sources: Journal of the American Medical Association, 1961b, *178*, 645–646; 1971, *218*, 1206–1207; 1981e, *246*, 2965–2967.

each student's "hands on" experience with patients. To cope with the crowded conditions and the need to provide students with a solid clinical education, most schools were forced to extend their teaching activities into more and more affiliated, community, and veterans hospitals. These extensions of teaching activity usually occurred in the city where the medical school was located; in some instances, however, clinical branch campuses were developed— sometimes at a considerable distance from the site of the medical school and the faculty based there. In most cases, the dispersion of clinical teaching activities required additions to the medical faculty. Furthermore, it has often produced concern about the equivalency of the clinical learning experience from site to site. Finally, the emergence of the fully elective fourth year in the standard M.D. degree curriculum was the result, in part, of the increased load on the medical school faculty that resulted from the expansion of entering enrollments.

The Forty New Schools

Reasons for Development. The men and women who advocated the establishment of the forty new schools in the period from 1960 to 1980 stated a number of different reasons and objectives in their proposals. In every case, two conditions were cited as reasons legitimizing the establishment of a new school: (1) the number of physicians providing health care for the relevant area was inadequate, and (2) a large number of applicants with acceptable qualifications for admission to the study of medicine created pressure for new programs in medical education.

Some private and many state-supported schools were founded for the purpose of producing family physicians to serve the residents of small towns and rural districts. Another factor in the establishment and development of these schools was the availability of substantial federal funding for school and hospital construction, start-up and operating grants, student loans and scholarships, and research grants—all supplemented by local funding.

Other new schools were built to satisfy a particular need or for a specific purpose. The Uniformed Services University of the Health Sciences School of Medicine was founded to provide future physicians with careers as military medical officers. More-house College School of Medicine was established to increase the ranks of black physicians. Religious and evangelical objectives were primary in the construction of a medical school at Oral Roberts University. P.L. 92-541 provided for the continued operation of older Veterans Administration hospitals in conjunction with the new medical schools founded at the University of South Carolina, East Tennessee State University, Wright State University, Texas A&M University, and Marshall University. Existent programs in graduate medical education were undergirded by the development of undergraduate M.D. curricula at Mayo Medical School, Mount Sinai School of Medicine, and Rush Medical College. The medical school and center founded at Pennsylvania State University was founded because a major donor, the Hershey Foundation, wanted to make a substantial commitment of funds to the development of a facility for medical education.

Characteristics of the New Schools. The forty new schools established between 1960 and 1980 are listed in Table 9. The date of enrollment of the charter class of medical students has been adopted as the critical event in the school's early development, and this date is used throughout the book as the milestone in comparison with which other date/time references are made. Use of the date of the granting of a charter by a state government to operate a medical school was considered but rejected because not all such actions in the past have resulted in the commencement of instruction.

Three of the new schools are privately owned and operated; six are privately owned but receive some form of state support. Twenty-five—that is, the majority—are state institutions; five other schools are state institutions that receive (or received) some support from the Veterans Administration. The one remaining new school is a federal institution founded for the express purpose of educating physicians for the military. In 1980, two privately owned schools mounted unsuccessful campaigns to obtain operating funds from their state governments. One privately owned school is sponsored by a religious organization and funded by contributions from its members.

As of 1980, two new schools offered only the basic science components of the standard, four-year M.D. curriculum. Students

Table 9. The Forty New Medical Schools Established Between 1960 and 1980.

School	Type of Ownership	Charter Class Enrolled	First M.D. Degrees Conferred	Entering Class Size, 1980	M.D. Degrees Conferred, 1980
University of Kentucky College of Medicine	S	9/1960	6/1964	108	116
Brown University Program in Medicine	P/S	9/1963	6/1975	60	61
University of New Mexico School of Medicine	S	9/1964	6/1968	63	70
Michigan State University College of Human Medicine	S	9/1966	6/1972	105	107
University of Medicine and Dentistry of New Jersey/Rutgers Medical School	S	9/1966	6/1975	108	91
University of Texas Medical School at San Antonio	S	9/1966	6/1970	202	135
University of Hawaii John A. Burns School of Medicine	S	9/1967	9/1975	69	72
University of Arizona College of Medicine	S	9/1967	6/1971	88	60
Pennsylvania State University College of Medicine	S	9/1967	6/1971	99	96
University of California, Davis, School of Medicine	S	9/1968	6/1972	100	104
University of California, San Diego, School of Medicine	S	9/1968	6/1972	128	109
Mount Sinai School of Medicine of the City University of New York	P/S	9/1968	7/1970	100	119
University of Connecticut School of Medicine	S	9/1968	6/1972	82	84
Medical College of Ohio at Toledo	S	9/1969	6/1972	130	111
Louisiana State University School of Medicine at Shreveport	S	9/1969	5/1973	100	96
University of Massachusetts Medical School	S	9/1970	6/1974	100	96
University of Texas Medical School at Houston	S	9/1970	12/1973	200	107
State University of New York at Stony Brook Health Sciences Center School of Medicine	S	9/1971	6/1974	76	54
University of Nevada, Reno, School of Medicine	S	9/1971	6/1980	48	36
University of South Florida College of Medicine	S	9/1971	12/1974	96	96
University of Missouri-Kansas City School of Medicine	S	9/1971	6/1973	100	72
Rush Medical College of Rush University	P/S	9/1971	6/1973	120	122

School	Ownership				
Mayo Medical School	P/S	9/1972	6/1975	40	44
Texas Tech University School of Medicine	S	9/1972	4/1974	80	42
University of Minnesota-Duluth School of Medicine	S	9/1972	—	48	—
University of South Alabama College of Medicine	S	1/1973	6/1976	64	56
Southern Illinois University School of Medicine	S	6/1973	6/1975	72	74
Eastern Virginia Medical School	P/S	11/1973	9/1976	96	65
Wright State University School of Medicine	S/VA	9/1976	6/1980	100	31
Uniformed Services University of the Health Sciences School of Medicine	F	10/1976	6/1980	130	28
University of South Carolina School of Medicine	S/VA	9/1977	6/1981	48	22
Texas A&M University College of Medicine	S/VA	9/1977	6/1981	32	32
East Carolina University School of Medicine	S	9/1977	6/1981	52	28
Northeastern Ohio Universities College of Medicine	S	9/1977	6/1981	93	42
Marshall University School of Medicine	S/VA	1/1978	6/1981	36	18
Ponce School of Medicine	P	1/1978	6/1981	40	—
School of Medicine at Morehouse College	P/S	9/1979	—	32	—
East Tennessee State University Quillen-Dishner College of Medicine	S/VA	9/1979	—	72	—
Oral Roberts University School of Medicine	P	11/1978	—	36	—
Universidad del Caribe School of Medicine	P	1/1979	—	80	—
Total				3,443	2,496

Key to Symbols: P: Privately Owned   P/S: Private with State Support
S: State Owned   S/VA: State Owned with Veterans Administration Support
F: Federally Owned

Notes: During the 1970s, several new schools established in the 1960s as two-year schools converted to the full, four-year M.D. degree program: the Michigan State University College of Human Medicine in 1970, the University of Medicine and Dentistry of New Jersey/Rutgers Medical School in 1972, the Brown University Program in Medicine and the University of Hawaii John A. Burns School of Medicine in 1973, and the University of Nevada, Reno, School of Medicine in 1978. At the University of Minnesota-Duluth School of Medicine, students transfer to other schools for their third and fourth years.

Sources: Data on type of ownership from Rosenthal, 1980, pp. 885–887. Other data from Liaison Committee on Medical Education, Confidential records.

completing the two-year program at the University of Minnesota—
Duluth were guaranteed the opportunity to transfer to the School
of Medicine at the University of Minnesota-Minneapolis. Morehouse
College School of Medicine was organized with the intent to offer
the full program leading to the M.D. degree, but it deferred
development of the clinical years of the full curriculum until after
1982.

    In 1973, the LCME adopted a policy against accrediting
independent two-year schools of the basic medical sciences. This
action was taken in consideration of the difficulties encountered
by students of the two-year schools in arranging transfer to institutions granting the M.D. degree; the LCME policy is also founded
on a concern about the ability of the medically isolated basic science
school to offer effectively the full spectrum of subject material in
the first two years of the full M.D. degree curriculum. In support
of the LCME policy, it should be noted that all two-year basic
science schools in operation prior to 1960, as well as those new
schools that began as two-year schools, have voluntarily expanded
their programs to the full M.D. degree curriculum (except for the
University of Minnesota—Duluth School of Medicine and Morehouse College School of Medicine). For similar reasons, the LCME
does not accredit any independent two-year schools offering only
clinical instruction.

    The enrollment/graduation data displayed in Table 9 include
the size of the new schools' entering classes; in some schools, this
number is smaller than the number of graduates because these
schools accept transfer students into the second or third year of

Table 10. Contributions of the Forty New Medical Schools to the Supply
of Physician Graduates in 1980

	1959–1960	1979–1980		
	Total All Schools	Eighty-Six Older Schools	Forty New Schools	Total All Schools
First-Year Enrollment	8,173	13,571	3,443	17,014
M.D. Graduates	7,081	12,523	2,612	15,135

Sources: Journal of the American Medical Association, 1981b, 246,
2917; 1981e, 246, 2965–2967.

the program. Furthermore, as of 1980 the youngest schools were still engaged in incremental growth of their enrollments toward planned levels under the annual review of the LCME. Table 10 charts the estimated contributions of the forty new schools to the supply of physician graduates. Figure 2 is a map of the locations of the forty new schools. States that developed their first medical school during the period from 1960 to 1980 are Nevada, Arizona, New Mexico, Hawaii, and Rhode Island.

During the 1970s, proposals for new schools that received moderate to major planning efforts but did not reach fruition were developed in Maine, Delaware, Wyoming, and the Navajo Indian nation. As of 1980, Alaska, Montana, and Idaho lacked medical schools; however, each participated in a consortium based in Seattle at the University of Washington (this consortium, the Washington/ Alaska/Montana/Idaho [WAMI] program is described in Chapter Twelve). The states of Maine, Delaware, and Wyoming have made contractual arrangements with various medical schools for the enrollment of specified numbers of their resident premedical students. In summary, by 1980 every one of the fifty states was involved, either directly or indirectly, in some form of medical education.

Existing universities have provided official sponsorship for thirty of the forty new schools. Three new schools have had or do now have a relationship with one or more universities. The Northeastern Ohio Universities School of Medicine is governed by an independent board of trustees, although by charter it is closely related to three nearby universities: Kent State, the University of Akron, and Youngstown State University. Mount Sinai School of Medicine was originally chartered as an independent institution, but in 1967 it became a component of the City University of New York. Rutgers Medical School originated as a component of Rutgers University but later was incorporated into the University of Medicine and Dentistry of New Jersey. Seven new schools operate as independent institutions; as of 1980, each offered only the single program leading to the M.D. degree but was engaged in the development of other programs so as to constitute a university of the health sciences.

Twenty-four of the thirty university-sponsored schools have their principal location on or adjacent to the campus of the

Figure 2. Locations of the Forty New Medical

Key:
1. Univ. of Ky. College of Medicine
2. Brown Univ. Program in Medicine
3. Univ. of N. Mex. School of Medicine
4. Mich. State Univ. College of Human Medicine
5. Univ. of Medicine and Dentistry of N.J./Rutgers Medical School
6. Univ. of Texas Medical School at San Antonio
7. Univ. of Hawaii John A. Burns School of Medicine
8. Univ. of Ariz. College of Medicine
9. Penn. State Univ. College of Medicine
10. Univ. of Calif., Davis, School of Medicine

11. Univ. of Calif., San Diego, School of Medicine
12. Mount Sinai School of Medicine of the City Univ. of N.Y.
13. Univ. of Conn. School of Medicine
14. Medical College of Ohio at Toledo
15. LSU School of Medicine at Shreveport
16. Univ. of Mass. Medical School
17. Univ. of Texas Medical School at Houston
18. SUNY at Stony Brook Health Sciences Center School of Medicine
19. Univ. of Nev., Reno, School of Medicine
20. Univ. of South Florida College of Medicine

Note: The medical schools are numbered in the order in which they were established.

Schools Established Between 1960 and 1980.

21. Univ. of Missouri—Kansas City School of Medicine
22. Rush Medical College of Rush Univ.
23. Mayo Medical School
24. Texas Tech. Univ. School of Medicine
25. Univ. of Minn.—Duluth School of Medicine
26. Univ. of South Ala. College of Medicine
27. S. Ill. Univ. School of Medicine
28. E. Va. Medical School
29. Wright State Univ. School of Medicine
30. Uniformed Services Univ. of the Health Sciences School of Medicine
31. Univ. of S.C. School of Medicine
32. Texas A&M Univ. College of Medicine
33. E. Carolina Univ. School of Medicine
34. Northeastern Ohio Univ. College of Medicine
35. Marshall Univ. School of Medicine
36. Ponce School of Medicine
37. School of Medicine at Morehouse College
38. E. Tenn. State Univ. Quillen-Dishner College of Medicine
39. Oral Roberts Univ. School of Medicine
40. Univ. del Caribe School of Medicine

sponsoring university. Two new schools, Southern Illinois University School of Medicine and Texas A&M University, provide instruction in the basic science subjects on the parent campus, but clinical instruction is arranged in other cities. Clinical instruction is arranged in various ways that are described in Chapter Ten. In general, most new schools use their own university hospital and/ or one or more affiliated hospitals scattered within or near the same city where basic science instruction is held.

A Note on New Foreign Medical Schools

In addition to the forty new medical schools in the United States considered here, some mention should be made of the new schools in the developing Caribbean Island nations and Mexico. These schools were founded to enroll large numbers of United States citizen premedical students who fail to gain admission to the study of medicine in the United States. Lawrence (1978, 1980) has described the apparently dismal circumstances of several schools that were established during the 1970s in the Caribbean; Relman (1978) has reviewed the problems these schools pose as has the *Wall Street Journal* (Bronson, 1979).

In a 1980 report to Congress, the U.S. General Accounting Office (GAO) reviewed the problem and estimated that between 10,000 and 11,000 United States citizens were enrolled in foreign medical schools, with the largest number in approximately ten schools in Mexico and the Caribbean Island nations. In the same year, the GAO inspected six foreign medical schools that enrolled a majority of United States citizens: none was found to offer a program of medical education leading to the M.D. degree that was comparable in quality to schools accredited by the LCME in the United States and Canada. If the findings of the GAO were accurate, the United States citizens enrolled in these schools are likely to encounter difficulty after graduation in gaining admission to programs of graduate medical education in the United States and in achieving licensure to practice medicine in the states. Evidently, some foreign governments have been opposed to the establishment of these dubious ventures in medical education within their jurisdictions: Charles (1979) has described the government's rebuff of proposals by eight different entrepreneurs to establish a "medical school" in the Bahamas.

Lessons Learned

Since an exhaustive account of the development of each new school would be impossible to render within the confines of this book, I have selected certain experiences and events that, in my opinion, provide valuable lessons for medical educators and those who may in the future feel a need for additional programs in medical education.

1. *Early Initiatives in Developing the New Schools.* The histories of the forty new schools, which the staff of the LCME has collected, describe a number of early initiatives that inaugurated the developmental process. The most frequently recorded impetus was that provided by a single physician who was able to convince his colleagues in a local medical society or state medical association to appoint a committee to explore the possibility of developing a new school. In two instances, physicians sought and won seats in state legislatures with the express purpose of using those forums to promote the establishment of new medical schools. In other cases, local newspaper editors, chambers of commerce, and businessmen provided the initial momentum. In California, New York, Texas, Illinois, and Ohio, the state agency for higher education undertook statewide studies of the physician supply (Porterfield, 1965); after a state or regional shortage was determined, new medical schools were explored as possible solutions to the problem.

In several instances, universities and their faculties became involved in regional or statewide efforts to found a new medical school, a situation that sometimes led to difficulties in the developmental process. For example, when a new school was under consideration by the Arizona state legislature, intense rivalries for the franchise developed between the University of Arizona and Arizona State University and between their respective locales, the cities of Tucson and Phoenix. Eventually, Tucson and the University of Arizona won (Volker, 1962a, 1962b). Sometimes, intrauniversity strife has attended the establishment of a new medical school. At Brown University, several faculties in the College of Arts and

Sciences opposed the institution of a program in the basic medical sciences; several years later, the opposition flared up again when a decision was made to expand the controversial program to the full M.D. degree curriculum. Yet, in other institutions, faculty members in the biological and physical sciences actually led the early discussions about adding medical education to existing university programs.

In the majority of the forty new schools, once public agitation for a new school gained ground, the president of one (and sometimes more than one) university in the area had to study the magnitude of the task before providing an institutional response (if no university became involved, then some other person or group had to undertake this study). Some university presidents involved with the establishment of the new schools expressed, either publicly or privately, some reluctance to take responsibility for starting a new medical school. They undoubtedly knew of the aphorism of some unknown academic sage: no university president can expect to achieve equanimity if his university operates either an intercollegiate football program or a medical school.

2. *Guidance for Planners for New Medical Schools.* Since the late 1950s, the AAMC has provided helpful written guidance on the development of new medical schools. An outline of the initial steps in the developmental process was included in the Bane Report of 1959; and in 1960 an AAMC task force chaired by William Willard and supported by a grant from the W. K. Kellogg Foundation prepared a report that was published in the *Journal of Medical Education* and became a major informational resource for anyone interested in the establishment of new programs in medical education. This report and the Bane Report of 1959 have been the chief sources of the advice and information provided by the staff of professional medical educators assigned to LCME functions at both the AAMC and the AMA-CME.

The planners of a new medical school in the United States or Canada would be well advised to seek guidance from the LCME staff *from the outset of their deliberations* (in other countries, the appropriate government minister may be the focal point of departure for serious planning efforts). During the twenty-year period in which the forty new schools were founded, LCME staff members acquired extensive, direct experience in providing guidance to university presidents, early study groups, and the founding deans of most of the new schools. LCME staff members have arranged numerous ad hoc consultations and on-site visits in connection with proposed schools. They have also recommended experienced medical educators who might be retained to conduct reliable studies of the feasibility of a proposed school. Reference materials, current data about trends in all phases of medical education, and current information about government and private sources of funding were obtained at no charge from the LCME staff. In selected circumstances, LCME staff members have agreed to make a brief site visit to confer with the president of the sponsoring university and the early study group.

If a formal commitment is made to develop the proposed school through the granting of a state charter, action by a state legislature, or the assignment of a large endowment (an unlikely possibility in the 1980s), a formal feasibility study should be conducted. Feasibility studies were used in some of the forty new schools to good advantage; in others, the consultation was of poor quality and misleading in some respects. (A number of these studies, as well as definitive plans for the early development of new schools, have been collected by the LCME staff; although some are confidential and few have been published in the retrievable literature, most have been printed for local or limited distribution.) Again, the LCME staff is the best-informed source for leads on reputable individuals or groups who may be available for a feasibility study prior to the appointment of the founding dean. Caution should be used in employing a commercial consulting firm to conduct the study. Advice and professional evaluations are rarely any better than the experience and credentials of the principal project director, who should work full time and on site for three to six months. Before they employ a commercial firm, the planners should try to determine who will be assigned to the project and should inquire into the qualifications and productivity record of those persons in the management of programs of medical education.

The cost of a feasibility study will be quite large if it is assigned to a commercial firm; a reputable medical educator with the assistance of local individuals may cost less. If possible, the state legislature should be petitioned to appropriate funds for the study—certainly, if the proposed school is to be funded by the state. In the period from 1950 to 1980, private foundations were very helpful in supporting studies of the feasibility of new schools, but there is now some doubt about the availability of such resources in the future.

3. *Determining the Need for a New School.* The principal objective of a feasibility study is to determine the need for a proposed school of medicine. One of the first tasks in this respect is to analyze the geographic community, its medical profession, and its institutions of higher education. The following items constitute a general, though incomplete, agenda for such an analysis.

- *Population.* Demographic trends of the past thirty years should be studied, and those for the next thirty years (at minimum) should be projected. The various age groups of the population should be analyzed by deciles, and those in the future should be projected. According to Smythe (1972), there was one medical school for every 2.02 million persons in the United States in 1960. In 1980, there was one school for every 1.79 million persons (1980 U.S. Census data).
- *Income Levels.* Data on the average income of the population should be collected and compared with that of other states and cities.
- *Medical Profession.* The number of physicians currently in active practice should be computed and analyzed, along with their ages and their distribution by type of specialty or practice. Data on the number of physicians licensed by the state during each of the past twenty years should be collected. The ratio of practicing physicians to state and community populations should be analyzed and compared with that of other states, cities, and the United States as a whole. Information concerning organized group clinics and health maintenance organizations should be collected, along with the numbers of physicians active in each of these.
- *Higher Education.* The analysis should include a list of all four-year universities and colleges in the relevant area; enrollments

at the baccalaureate, master's degree, and doctoral degree levels should be computed for each institution. Graduate and professional degrees awarded by each institution should be computed; in this respect, it is very important to obtain data on any existing educational programs in dentistry, nursing, pharmacy, and other allied health fields.

- *Area Hospitals.* Each area hospital with more than 200 beds should be listed, along with its location (in relation to the proposed school), the nature of its ownership, the number of beds, its daily occupancy rate during the past five years, and the special services it provides. This information will be necessary for the formulation of the school's undergraduate clinical program. In addition, area hospitals should be analyzed as potential resources for graduate medical education. Any accredited residency training programs should be listed, along with the number of approved and filled positions in each program during the past five years.

- *Supply of Potential Medical Students.* Data on area and state residents entering medical school during the last fifteen years should be collected, including their numbers, their colleges of origin, and the medical schools in which they enrolled. A ranking of medical school entrants per 100,000 population by state should be developed.

- *Activities of Existing Area Medical Schools.* The geographical relationship between each existing medical school in the area and the proposed school should be shown. The educational activities and programs of each existing school should be listed and studied. Finally, as an alternative to the development of a new school, the feasibility of extending existent programs into the locale of the proposed school should be assessed.

    4. *Unique Resources Required by a Medical School.* A society cannot function properly if poor health or chronic disease is a pervasive phenomenon among its members; one need only recall how the plagues of the Middle Ages crippled and nearly destroyed entire populations to recognize the simple, though often neglected, truth of this basic observation. Since the time when the Black Death

laid waste much of fourteenth-century Europe, medical science has advanced to the point that many illnesses that once paralyzed a whole society no longer pose such a threat; and with this hard-won health and physical security have come prosperity and the end to many forms of human suffering.

It is no mere coincidence that the real momentum in the millennial advance of medical science was gathered during the last hundred years, the period in which the modern medical school has come into being. Among all the different social, political, economic, and educational institutions of a society, the modern medical school occupies a prominent, if not unique, position. In it resides the primary responsibility for the education of those individuals whose life work is the treatment and prevention of disease and the promotion of physical and mental well-being. One of the fundamental reasons for the singularity of the medical school as a societal institution is the unparalleled constellation of resources it requires in order to fulfill its role.

Chapters Six through Ten present extensive discussions of the fiscal resources, the physical facilities, the faculty and personnel, and the kinds of students required for the optimal development of a medical school. Here we underline the importance of two major resources: the *teaching hospital* and the *sponsoring university*.

A university can organize a law school without operating an actual court of law, develop an engineering school without contracting to build bridges (Booker, 1963), or open a business school without founding a corporation. When a university establishes a *medical school*, however, it will find that it has entered the actual practice of medicine to a major degree, either in its own hospital or in one or more hospitals with which it is closely affiliated. Academicians accustomed to the comparatively uterine-like environment of the university always grow anxious at the prospect of sharing their ivory tower with a faculty of medicine, some of whose members actually engage in clinical practice. Debates about pure versus applied science rattle eardrums in the faculty luncheon club. Despite expressions of qualms and numerous alarums, the plain, undeniable fact is that medicine is based on a continually expanding body of scientific knowledge that must be tested and applied in the prevention and therapy of disease and the repair of trauma in order to be of any use. This body of scientific knowledge is introduced to medical students in large increments, beginning early in the four-year M.D. degree curriculum, while multiple demonstrations of expert medical care of patients by faculty (with the assistance of advanced, post-M.D. students) make up the educational program in its final half. In the United States and Canadian systems, much of the education of the undergraduate and graduate medical students must be centered, therefore, in the only facility in which expert and complex medical care can be provided—that expensive institution known as a hospital. Ambulatory clinics and the private offices of physicians can and also should serve as classrooms for medical students, but the hospital that has been designed and is administered for teaching purposes is an essential resource for the development of a new medical school. Chapter Ten includes a detailed discussion of the teaching hospital—based, in part, on observations of those thirteen new schools that built their own teaching hospitals in the period from 1960 to 1980 (the remaining twenty-seven developed affiliations with one to nine existing hospitals).

If the university elects to build and operate its own teaching hospital, the medical faculty will staff it and formulate and enforce its policies for education and medical/surgical practice. If the new school expects to affiliate with an existing hospital, the trustees, administrators, and physician staff of that hospital must be drawn into the matrix of discussion regarding the feasibility of the proposed school before a commitment to commence instruction is made. The medical faculty's introduction into the environment of a well-established but newly affiliated hospital may be compared with the arrival of a new bride in her mother-in-law's house—interpersonal friction is often likely to develop.

Another of the medical school's important resources is the *sponsoring university,* but one may rightly ask: Is a medical school a proper part of the university? Does the incorporation of a medical school within the curricular family of a well-established university provide mutual benefits to both? There is ample historical evidence for affirmative answers to both questions. As early as 1156 A.D., the University of Bologna complemented its faculties of law, theology, and arts with one in medicine (Singer and Underwood,

1962); later, in the thirteenth and fourteenth centuries, the great universities founded in Paris, Oxford, Montpellier, Cambridge, and Padua did the same (Garrison, 1966). This long-standing tradition has continued to the present in Europe.

The review of the history of medical education in the United States in Chapter One showed that the nation took a detour from this tradition of including medicine within a university setting with the rising tide of the independent, proprietary schools in the nineteenth century. After the publication of Flexner's report in 1910, the status of these schools declined and, from 1910 to 1975, no new independent medical schools were established in the United States. Most medical schools in the United States are integral components of well-established universities that offer advanced education in the humanities, the physical and social sciences, and the professions, such as business, law, and architecture. Of the forty new schools established between 1960 and 1980, thirty-three are owned by or related to established universities; seven are independent institutions, but two of these are controlled by state boards of higher education. Appendix C further illustrates the precedence of university-related medical schools based on the Carnegie Council's (1976b) classification of institutions of higher education in the United States.

The virtues of an established university as the most desirable home for a medical school have been extolled by many. In his presidential address to the AAMC in 1955, Lippard presented a classic justification for the unqualified inclusion of medical education within the university family. For many years the LCME has included the following statement in its accreditation standards: "A medical school should be incorporated as a nonprofit institution. Whenever possible, it should be part of a university, since a university can so well provide the milieu and support required by a medical school" (Liaison Committee on Medical Education, 1973a, p. 3). Saxon (1976) strongly favored university sponsorship of a medical school, as well as its location on the campus of the sponsor; in particular, he cited the opportunities for intellectual exchange with nonmedical scholars and chided the medical faculty for its frequent failure to take full advantage of such opportunities.

Medicine is a profession that serves society and thus must reflect society's values and needs. The process of educating students to serve in that profession must similarly take account of the values and needs of society. In the nineteenth century, medical education in the United States was strongly influenced by the independent proprietary schools. They proved unable to respond to the task of providing their students with a sound, scientific education. The university rescued medical education from this circumstance and set the stage for the transformation of medicine into a truly scientific profession.

A century later, the concern is no longer that medical education is not scientific but that it seems to have become engulfed by science and technology. Again, it is to the university that society must look for a remedy. To be sure, the inclusion of medical education within the university structure has only intensified one of the university's foremost problems—how to correct the pernicious imbalance between the sciences and humanities brought about, in part, by the dramatic growth of science. Yet, the likelihood of finding a solution within this unique social institution is far greater than without.

Now, in the final half of the twentieth century, medicine has become a social force of unfathomable scope and depth. If it is to avoid academic insularism, teratological growth, and the hazards posed by external forces (such as those that often emerge from an expedient, short-sighted government), it needs the checks and balances that only a well-established university with the full range of academic disciplines can provide. Those who advocate the establishment of a new school outside the university or the moving of established schools farther from the disciplines of the university would deny medical education the strength of that institution from which it can draw the greatest benefit.

5. *Individuals and Institutions Concerned in the Operation of a Medical School.* The unusual nature and scope of the resources that are necessary for the establishment and ongoing development of a new medical school require its planners and administrators to engage in continuous interface with a wide variety of individuals and institutions, both public and private. If the new school is a component of a state university or depends to any degree on state

funds for its support, its planners and administrators will be engaged
in dialogue with various levels of the state government from the
earliest planning phases. The governor, the members of the state
legislature, the state commissioner for higher education, and the
state board of higher education—all will be integral to the founding
and development of a new medical school with state support. The
mayor(s) and other municipal officials of the city (or cities) wherein
the new school is located will become key individuals in its
development, as will the local chamber of commerce and other civic
organizations, business and labor leaders, members of the clergy,
and consumer groups. Medical societies at both the state and local
levels will be instrumental in garnering support for the new school
among practicing physicians. The staff, administrators, and trustees
of every hospital that figures as a potential affiliate of the new
school will be important in developing clinical programs and
facilities. Potential donors, whether individuals or private foundations, will be integral to the establishment of reliable financial
support for the new venture. Finally, if the new school is to be
a component of an existing university, individuals and groups at
every level of its hierarchy will be drawn into the matrix of
institutional support for its establishment and future support. More
likely than not, the regents or trustees of the existing university
will be key individuals in the committee appointed to develop the
new medical school. It goes without saying that the president and
other administrators of the university will play central roles in the
life of the school, along with the deans and faculties of any other
existing health education programs. And the various faculties of
the university—including those of the graduate and professional
schools and of the natural, physical, and social sciences and the
liberal arts—will be necessary in the formation of a supportive
intellectual ambience for the new school.

6. *Some Final Words of Caution on Developing New Medical
Schools.* It is the policy of the LCME, supported by the AMA and
the AAMC, to evaluate standards for the purpose of accrediting
any school that may make application. Neither organization has
any policy that limits the number of medical schools in the United
States or Canada. Nevertheless, individuals and organizations un-

dertaking the establishment of new medical schools in the future should consider carefully their answers to the following questions:

- Is there a chronic, functional shortage of physicians (nationally, regionally, or locally) that cannot be alleviated by the projected production of physician graduates within a ten-year period in the future?
- Is there an abundant supply of well-qualified applicants for medical school in the region where the new school is proposed?
- Is there a demonstrated need for the development of new programs in graduate medical education (that is, residencies) that could be facilitated by a new medical school or the significant upgrading of existing but foundering graduate medical education programs?
- Is there an area of growing population not currently served by or incapable of being served by an existing school through the development of a clinical branch campus or by other means of extension from a focus of proven strength in the full spectrum of programs for physician education?

In 1980, the forty new schools enrolled 3,433 entering medical students. Between 1960 and 1980, the eighty-six older medical schools in the United States expanded their entering-class enrollments by an aggregate of 5,455. In terms of costs and benefits, expanding the enrollments in existing schools was a more efficient and effective means of solving the physician shortage than establishing new medical schools. If, in the future, the nation experiences another shortage of physicians and an unequivocal justification for the expansion of opportunities for the study of medicine develops, a careful examination should be made of the utility of expanding enrollments in existing institutions versus that of establishing new medical schools.

Furthermore, the types of ownership and sponsorship of the forty new schools indicate that the private sector may not be able to develop and sustain properly a new medical school in the future. The absence of permanent fiscal support from a state or the federal government may ensure that a new medical school has only a brief existence. Chapter Six demonstrates that operating a medical school on the basis of tuition-derived income alone is impossible.

Finally, the stronger the programs of the sponsoring university, the easier the gestation and neonatal growth periods of its new medical school. In my opinion, independent medical schools developed *de novo* are quite vulnerable to a variety of external threats and may not survive.

Part Two

ϗϗϗϗϗϗϗϗϗϗϗϗϗϗϗϗϗϗϗϗϗϗϗϗϗϗϗ

Medical School Administration

ϗϗϗϗϗϗϗϗϗϗϗϗϗϗϗϗϗϗϗϗϗϗϗϗϗϗϗ

The role and functions of the chief executive officer (the dean) and the size and functions of his supporting staff (the deanery) changed substantially from mid-century to the early 1980s. Chapter Three reviews the changing nature of the deanship in the older, well-established schools, beginning at mid-century, and describes variations in the powers of deans and the numerous relationships of the dean. Critical attention is given to the frequently observed problems in the search for and selection of a new dean. The "Lessons Learned" section sets forth general principles and specific practices recommended for improving the procedures followed in selecting a new dean.

Chapter Four describes the universal expansion of the dean's administrative staff since mid-century and lists and defines the types of academic and managerial officers most schools now include in the deanery. The "Lessons Learned" section contains recommendations concerning the status of various members of the administrative staff and emphasizes the need for a chief academic officer, who preferably should work full-time in directing the academic programs of the school.

Chapter Five is based on the considerable literature published by the developers of the forty new schools established between 1960 and 1980. Administrative and academic problems encountered by the founding deans are discussed in the "Lessons Learned" section. Judgments made on these schools during the 1970s by the accrediting body, the LCME, are employed in the construction of a series of recommendations for development of new schools in the future.

3

The Dean: Functions, Characteristics, and Problems of Selection

The title *Dean* has ancient origins among the Greeks and Romans. Jerome, A.D. 400, in his translation of the Bible, the Vulgate, used the Latin word *Decanus* as the title of the person who had administrative responsibility over ten monks in a monastery. As the early universities emerged, often from the monasteries, the title was applied to principal administrators of academic programs; meanwhile, the title continued in use in ecclesiastic settings.

The physician who earned the medical degree before 1950 will likely remember the dean of his medical school as a dignified senior citizen who presided over convocations, graduation exercises, and other ceremonial functions but was otherwise unseen. Prior to World War II, some deans limited appointments to one or two afternoons per week—often for only two or three hours. During this period, most medical school deans had relatively little to administer. The faculty was small, as was the student body. Biomedical research activity was either nonexistent or quite modest in scope, as measured by the magnitude of external fiscal support.

More often than not, the dean continued in active clinical practice or devoted the bulk of his* time to teaching or some other type of scholarly activity.

Changing Role of the Dean

During World War II, the role of the dean began to change; the metamorphosis this office underwent accelerated during the 1950s; and, by the end of the 1960s, a new species of chief executive officer could be found in every medical school in the United States. Obviously, the deanship *had* to change as the role and mission of the medical school expanded in response to the forces impinging on it from within and without.

First, World War II had forced the schools to adopt accelerated programs for medical education. Upon demobilization, the veterans who had been unable to go to medical school applied for admission in great numbers. In addition, many physicians who had seen service as general medical officers desired to continue their medical education, thus making unprecedented demands for training in medical specialities. A vast expansion of positions for residency training occurred within a remarkably short time. In 1940, 12,328 interns and residents were enrolled in specialty training; in 1950, the number had grown to 21,525; in 1960, to 37,562; in 1970, to 51,015; and, in 1980, to 61,819 (*Journal of the American Medical Association*, 1975, *231*, 49; 1981d, *246*, 2940). Prior to World War II, internships developed all over the country, although it was not until 1923 that the number of internships available was sufficient to enroll all annual M.D. graduates. Advanced residency training in the clinical specialities was heavily concentrated in a few older medical schools in the hospitals owned by them or in affiliated hospitals that were often large municipal charity facilities. The escalating demand for residency training in the post-World War II period led to the rapid

*The traditional use of the pronoun *he* has not yet been superceded by a convenient, generally accepted pronoun that means *he* or *she*. Therefore, the author will continue to use *he* or *his* while acknowledging the inherent inequity of the traditional preference for the masculine pronoun.

development of formal programs to train clinical specialists on the many medical foothills throughout North America—a trend that broke the earlier elitist monopoly found on medicine's Mt. Olympus (claimed to be located variously in Boston, New York, Philadelphia, Baltimore, and elsewhere).

Second, the proliferation of specialty training programs accelerated a previously sluggish trend toward the establishment of full-time medical faculty positions in the clinical fields—positions that once were occupied by volunteer or part-time faculty members who were primarily engaged in the private practice of medicine. Table 11 illustrates this growth in full-time positions in medical school faculties.

Third, the significant advances in the biomedical sciences that were initiated during the 1920s and 1930s and continued during and after World War II greatly improved the therapeutic skills of physicians (Roberts, 1981). For example, the arrival of the sulfonamides in the 1930s, followed by the development of a specific chemical-therapeutic drug for tuberculosis and the families of antibiotic, anti-infection drugs, dramatically reduced mortality rates and, together with improved anesthesiology, made possible the surgical correction of formerly untreatable medical problems. The improved poliomyelitis vaccine prevented virtually all forms of that disease. In response to these highly publicized advances in medical science, the public began to demand an intensification and expansion of the scope of medical research. Congress, always sensitive to the voice of the public, met this demand by providing for the rapid growth of the National Institutes of Health (NIH). The NIH

Table 11. Growth in Full-Time Medical School Faculty, 1950–1980.

	1950	1960	1970	1980
Basic Science Faculty	2,520	4,003	8,283	12,840
Clinical Faculty	2,900	7,108	19,256	37,696
Totals	5,420	11,111	27,539	50,536

Sources: Journal of the American Medical Association, 1951, 134, 695; 1961a, 178, 632; 1972, 222, 974; 1981a, 246, 2914.

program of extramural research grants to medical academicians supported the expansion of medical faculties and provided nearly full funding for the research undertaken by these medical scholars and teachers (see Table 12).

Fourth, increased medical specialization, with its dependence on complex technology, virtually forced physicians to shift much of the delivery of medical care to the hospitals, the number of which expanded with the assistance of appropriations from the Hill-Burton Act of 1946. Furthermore, the states and, later, the federal government invested heavily in the construction of elaborate new patient-referral/academic teaching hospitals for new and existing medical schools. Larger numbers of full-time clinical faculty members began direct clinical practice, beginning with referrals from private physicians and, in some schools, extending later into group prepaid clinical care and other forms of comprehensive medical coverage.

Finally, medical school enrollments multiplied during the post-World War II period, not only in the traditional M.D. degree program but also in the rapidly proliferating series of new educational ventures in other health occupations. At least in the beginning, these new programs meant added responsibilities for the faculties of medicine and rendered their administration more complex.

By the 1980s, the mid-century description of a medical school as the site where medical students are taught had become obsolete. Thus, from 1950 to 1980, the dean of a typical medical school

Table 12. National Institutes of Health Research Grants
to the Medical Schools, Selected Years.

1952	$ 11,700,000
1954	16,700,000
1960	92,600,000
1964	224,000,000
1970	320,323,000
1975	620,651,000
1980	1,192,163,000

Sources: National Institutes of Health, 1952, 1954, 1960, 1964, 1970, 1975, and 1980.

gradually acquired administrative responsibilities and duties comparable to those of the chief executive officer of a major corporation; however, the broad authority vested in the corporate executive has been denied the dean of medicine. In his chairman's address to the AAMC in 1969, Glaser observed that the deanship had become a less attractive position, with a rapid turnover in office as a result. The lack of appeal, to a large extent, may be attributed to the small percentage of the budget over which the dean has active control. The faculty's biomedical research scientists have been able to exercise great independence from their institutions on the basis of the research grants they receive from the NIH. The clinicians of the medical school faculty (abjuring genteel academic poverty) receive substantial incomes from clinical practice. According to Cluff (1982), income derived from this source increased 4,000 percent from 1960 to 1977; and in 1981 the AAMC reported that, as of 1979, the clinical earnings of the faculty amounted to 37 percent of the aggregate revenues of the nation's medical schools.

In short, the dean whose responsibilities formerly consumed only part of his time has been gradually superseded by one whose duties now require a full-time commitment. This expansion of the role of the dean has required, in turn, the development of a diverse academic support staff consisting of a full-time senior associate dean and a cadre of full- and part-time assistant deans for specialized and technical functions. The fiscal aspects of the burgeoning programs of the medical school have become more and more complex, requiring professional management by a qualified financial officer, who, in turn, must have a support staff. Some idea of the complexity of medical school administration can be garnered from the fact that, in the 1979–80 academic year, 44 of the 126 accredited medical schools reported expenditures in excess of $50 million, exclusive of the separately budgeted cost of operating a university teaching hospital, which by itself can run as much as $200 million annually.

Administrative Relationships of the Dean

From school to school, the functions and powers of the dean vary significantly. In the older ones, there is often a federation of

departmental baronies, each jealously and aggressively defended by
the powerful baron of that particular discipline. Under these
circumstances, the dean has limited powers; like the monarch of
the United Kingdom, the dean reigns but does not rule. By 1980,
77 percent of the 126 schools had appointed a vice-president for
health affairs (or similar officer) to whom the dean of medicine
is required to report, along with the deans of the other health
education schools, such as dentistry, pharmacy, nursing, and allied
health. In an administrative arrangement such as this, the dean
of medicine can find himself squeezed between the authority
exercised by his superior, the vice-president, and the aggressively
protective behavior of those whom he in turn administers, the
departmental barons. More likely than not, the dean will find his
residual powers greatly diminished as a result. To make matters
even more difficult, the administrator of the typical university-
owned or affiliated hospital is often required to report directly to
the vice-president for health affairs. This situation can offer a distinct
advantage to those clinical departmental chairmen who are the
primary consumers of the space and budgetary funds belonging
to the hospital: those who choose to do so can bypass the dean's
administrative controls and deal directly with the hospital administrator. A dean who enters this type of arena expecting to function
as a football quarterback may quickly discover not only that the
principal players often fail to respond when he calls the signals
for a play but that he never quite manages to get his hands on
the ball.

      Of the ninety-seven schools with a vice-president for health
affairs, thirty-two have bestowed that title on the dean of medicine.
This arrangement may solve a number of the problems sketched
above, but it also creates a potential for anxiety and rivalry among
the deans of the other health education schools, who may not trust
the medical dean to deal equitably with them when wearing his
vice-presidential hat. There have been several recent experiments
in appointing to the vice-presidency for health affairs people of
entirely nonmedical backgrounds, such as business or administration of higher education. On these, the final verdict has not yet
arrived; however, early reports are quite discouraging for the
concept.

Characteristics of the Modern Dean

In her definitive study of the deanship during the period from 1960 to 1980, Marjorie Wilson analyzed the characteristics of 322 deans. She found that the average age of the deans of this period was forty-seven to forty-eight years when they were appointed to their posts and that their tenures in office ranged from four to twelve years, not the much briefer "half-life" reported by Glaser in 1969. Thirteen percent of these deans had previously served as deans of other medical schools, 36 percent had been assistant or associate deans, and 33.5 percent had been departmental chairmen. Two thirds of the deans were appointed from within the institution. A few deans came to office after a period of service in the government or a national association. Forty-three percent had received previous professional training in internal medicine, 10 percent in pathology, and 4 to 8 percent in pediatrics, surgery (in its various forms), psychiatry and neurology, anatomy, and preventive medicine. Ninety-four percent had earned the M.D. degree; 6 percent held the Ph.D. or other doctoral degree; thirteen of the 322 held both the M.D. and Ph.D. degrees. A significant number of the deans had served as chief resident while involved in graduate medical education (Wilson and McLaughlin, 1984).

Wilson's study supports the general conclusion that these deans were selected on the basis of strong prior achievements in a selected professional medical specialty and prior experience in some form of educational administration, usually in a medical school, with the exceptions being those who came to the school from national service of some kind. The majority of the deans assumed office with neither formal education nor significant training in the modern principles of management. Yet they were responsible for the management of major institutions with large budgets, a large staff of highly credentialed faculty, superior students, and numerous technical staff members, all engaged in complex programs of education, biomedical research, and the care and treatment of patients.

In 1972, in a major effort to prepare deans for their expanding responsibilities, the AAMC developed the Management Advancement Program to provide medical school deans (and, later, departmental chairmen and others) with instruction in the principles of management by professors from various schools of business. This program has been quite successful in achieving its objectives; the best results became evident after the business school professors themselves began to recognize the difference between managing corporate entities organized entirely for profit and managing medical schools and academic health centers. The latter do not have the benefit of profit-and-loss statements to evaluate their success; they are nonprofit institutions with organizational structures that range from efficient and understandable to inefficient and inscrutable.

Functions of the Dean

Obviously, no single pattern of "deanly" activity is found in the 126 United States and 16 Canadian schools. In some schools, the dean is limited to the role of secretary to the faculty; in one school, the departmental chairmen annually appoint the dean for a one-year term. At the other end of the scale, some deans are vested with substantial executive powers, which may include supervision of medical education as well as many aspects of medical care throughout the state. Moreover, there is often a wide distance between the faculty's perceptions of the dean's functions, the dean's own expectations and ideas of his responsibilities, and what the dean can realistically accomplish with the authority at his disposal. Rogers (1975) has written of the problems encountered by a dean who does not possess the authority necessary for the discharge of his duties, of the trivial nature of much of the dean's activities, and of the dean's need to develop a supportive ambience for the faculty and employees of the institution he administers. According to Zaleznik (1979) and Wilson (1980), some deans function as "managers" and others as "institutional leaders." The archetypal manager/dean devotes himself to the details of administering the numerous activities of the schools and responds to the expressed needs of the faculty, students, and personnel. The leader/dean, by contrast, may be quite bored with the quotidian routine of "keeping store" efficiently, is less involved with the people of the institution, and prefers to devote much of his working day to solitary contemplation and the creation of broad, new battle plans that he, as the admiral of the fleet, then intends to launch.

Few of the numerous deans I have observed for many years have been successful in developing a pure role as an institutional leader. Through the years, a majority of them have reported that most of their long working days are consumed with continuous, serial visits from faculty members, administrative personnel, students, and extraneous visitors. A visitor who does not present a problem to be solved is rare. Some insecure faculty members and/ or chairpersons seem to need a frequent visit with the chief executive officer just for therapeutic reassurance. Even when the dean is at home during the late evening, a faculty member may telephone to review yet another unsolved problem, often with the apology, "I did not want to bother you at the office since you seemed so busy there." Under such circumstances, little time is left for contemplation and analysis of the major problems of the institution; even less time remains for the creation of innovative solutions which, if implemented, would enhance the effectiveness of the institution.

While much variation exists among the 127 accredited schools during the early 1980s, the following major activities are commonly expected of a dean who is the chief executive officer. If the dean is subordinate to a vice-president for medical affairs, the list may be reduced significantly.

- Allocation of institutionally owned funds in the budget.
- Assignment of office and laboratory space to programs, departments, and individuals.
- Control of the process of appointment of new departmental chairpersons.
- Supervision of administrative committees of the faculty.
- Appointment and supervision of the individuals on the dean's staff.
- Maintenance of accurate knowledge of relevant trends and changes in local, state, and national public policies that affect the institution.
- Creation of new plans for improvements in the institution and persuasion of the general publics involved to support them.

- Enhancement of the short- and long-term resources of the institution.
- Management of, or arbitration of problems connected with, earnings derived from the faculty's clinical practice plan. This activity is likely to increase in significance as schools are forced to depend more and more heavily on faculty earnings for their operational expenditures.
- Facilitation of the performance of students, faculty members, and other employees of the institution.
- Management of unanticipated problems that produce crises and threaten disruption of the usual activities of the academic community.

Obviously, the tasks just outlined aggregate to a demanding, full-time occupation for the dean. Most deans, when newly appointed to the office, expect to become engaged in the institution's variant of these tasks, but many find that the time-consuming personal demands made upon them by the faculty prejudice optimal performance. It appears that many faculty members expect their dean to be all things to all people, as may have been possible earlier in the century when a medical school generally was very modest in size. Or, the dean may be at fault by insisting that he receive personal reports from an excessive number of people and/or he may fail to delegate supervision of numerous ongoing activities to competent associates or assistants on his staff.

The dean faces an inexorable dilemma: if he is too aloof from the members of the academic community, he may lose contact with the changing events within the institution and thus risk the loss of his ability to exercise effective leadership. If the dean devotes his time excessively to providing personal services to all who demand his time, he may be a popular fellow but not particularly effective in dealing with major problems. Some effective deans follow a deliberate policy of calling on faculty members in their laboratories and visiting areas where instruction to students is in progress. Such a policy gets the dean out of his office and gives him an opportunity to become personally acquainted with the people he is expected to supervise. A noticeable number of deans, through the years, have been able to balance these conflicting demands satisfactorily. A

smaller number have even found time to continue personal professional activities not connected with administration; these highly
effective deans usually have benefited from the support provided
by a staff of competent associates. Chapter Four will review patterns
of organization of the dean's staff.

Problems in Selection of Deans

Earlier in the century, the selection of a dean was a function
dominated by the autocratic university president common to that
era. the president may have sought some advice from the pertinent
faculty; but, more likely, he depended heavily on his peers, the
presidents of other universities, for recommendations of candidates,
or else he appointed a faculty member already in residence to the
vacant position. A candidate for a vacant deanship related primarily
to the president, his prospective employer, during an exploratory
visit. While this system had its problems, it was efficient if the
president was experienced, well connected, and well informed about
the needs of the institution. By contrast, in the early 1960s and
1970s, autocracy largely gave way to egalitarianism in university
management; this change in institutional behavior often caused
many problems for prospective candidates and for the school in
need of a dean.

Despite a number of critical papers on the subject published
in recent years (see the select bibliography for this chapter), many
selection committees for the deanship continue to amaze and amuse
onlookers, frustrate the medical academic community, consume
inordinate amounts of time, and expend unnecessarily large
amounts of money. As an example of the costs of searches for
executives, in 1976 the University of Colorado spent $16,000 to find
a chancellor for its medical center and $33,000 to find a president
(Jacobson, 1976). Search committees often reach an unwieldy size
due to demands that each indentifiably separate constituency of
the school be represented in the search. Since two representatives
are often appointed from each constituency, this is widely called
a Noah's Ark type of committee.

From my studies of the published criteria used by numerous
dean search committees, I am forced to conclude that many expect

the candidate to match the eloquence of Winston Churchill, the craftiness of Machiavelli, the infinite wisdom of Confucius, the audacity of Crazy Horse, the fiscal acumen of J. P. Morgan, and the durability of Minnie Pearl—not to mention the stipulation that he should possess the entire body of biomedical and clinical knowledge accumulated since 3150 B.C., when Imhotep was actively providing his pharaoh with medical care.

A large, representative search committee often contains a number of persons who have had no prior experience in such matters. It is not too surprising, therefore, to observe that the committee's first preferred list of candidates may consist of the five most recent Nobel Prize winners and a group of the most prominent medical educators known to the English-speaking world. If requests for interviews are made with these ideal but probably unattainable prospects, the committee very likely will receive a series of rejections; however, several months may be lost in this process. (Some recent selection processes have consumed eighteen to twenty-four months before actual nominations were made—a substantial portion of the average tenure of a dean).

The second stage of the selection process is usually guided by a more realistic attitude: reams of correspondence have been collected from far and wide, and the working list of nominees has reached several hundred names. At this point, the committee decides to hold interviews. After numerous ballots by the committee, a preferential order for extending invitations is established. Time is usually consumed in obtaining the agreement of the first prospect on the preferred (short) list to visit for interviews.

The members of the committee then harangue each other about the format of the candidate's visit. The result is always the same: The prospect is summoned for a two-and-a-half day visit crammed with interviews with eager questioners who change identity every half hour, beginning at dawn and extending until nearly midnight. All the represented constituencies on the committee demand time to interview the candidate—no one may be left out. The highly desirable candidate becomes fatigued and bored and often loses interest in the position.

After a series of interviews with the candidates on the short list, the committee members debate at length and finally decide, often without consensus, to recommend that the job be offered to someone—perhaps the valiant soul who maintained his equanimity throughout the marathon of interviews extending through a fourteen-hour day. Usually, a significant amount of time has elapsed between the interview and a definitive action by the committee.

The committee then reports its recommendation to the vice-president, provost, or president (or all of them); the president must then obtain authority from the trustees of the university to make the appointment. All the while, more time passes. In the meantime, there is high probability that the desirable candidate who entered this competition with a tentative decision to relocate from his present place of employment has been cultivated by other institutions and may have developed a strong preference to go elsewhere.

If he is still available, however, the next event is a return visit by the dean-designate, usually with spouse, heirs, and assigns in tow. This visit is usually arranged for the benefit of the candidate. Sometimes the candidate accepts the job during the return visit but, upon his return home, calls to withdraw his acceptance. With so much time, money, and effort invested, the search committee may renew its offer; the nominee may accept again, only to reconsider and reject the offer again. The record known to me for such cyclic indecision is held by a nominee who accepted the offer of a deanship three times and rejected the same offer three times, consuming five months of the committee's valuable time.

If the search committee fails to snare its first choices, it will return to its list of nominees, delete those who have accepted positions elsewhere, and renew its overtures to the remaining prospective candidates. Two or three "near misses" with desirable candidates may finally induce the members of the committee to streamline their procedures, empower a smaller, "executive" sub-committee to act quickly, and, in general, become more realistic about the type of person their medical school can reasonably be expected to attract.

Hoping to reduce the personal anguish and waste of time often involved in searches for deans, I have included in the following section a number of suggestions for improving the selection process.

Lessons Learned

1. *Need for a Separate Vice-President for Health Affairs.*
While circumstances vary among the universities, there may not
be adequate justification for having both a vice-president and a
medical dean in all the schools. Diminished resources in the 1980s
may justify a careful reexamination of the need for a separate vice-
president in some but not all universities. Frequently, the LCME
site visitors have reported ambiguity in the definitions of functions
of the vice-president and the medical dean and have made the
judgment that "effective relationships between the two officers were
dependent upon the good will of the incumbents of the offices."
During the past decade, the LCME visitors have encountered a
number of problems caused by poor relationships between a vice-
president and a medical dean. Often, for example, a newly appointed
vice-president begins his service with a poor definition of his
position. While an original function of the vice-president is to
coordinate the activities of the deans of the several health profession
schools, some vice-presidents also assume the supervision of the
university hospital, thereby diminishing the role of the medical
dean. The successful combination of the two titles in one person,
observed in a number of universities, indicates that this system merits
careful consideration.

2. *Functions of the Dean.* The role of the dean needs careful
analysis periodically. Such analysis could occur when the position
is vacated and a new dean is being sought; when the performance
of the dean is evaluated at intervals of five years, as is the custom
in some universities; or when the medical school conducts its
institutional self-study on a ten-year cycle under guidance by the
LCME. If the medical school undergoes major changes, such as
those that occurred in most of them between 1960 and 1980, the
activities of the dean must undergo modification accordingly. The
academic community should be encouraged to develop insight into
the primary role of its dean—who no longer is the "decanus" for
ten monks.

3. *Adequate Staff for the Dean.* If the dean is to discharge
his principal duties effectively, he should be provided the resources
necessary for appointment of a cadre of associates and assistants

to whom he can delegate supervision of most of the regularly operating programs of the school.

4. *Selection and Recruitment of the Dean.* The volume of complaints and criticisms I have heard about the selection process from candidates, the residual bitterness found among faculty members after a prolonged search, and the disruptions of the programs of a school due to an extended vacancy during a long search have convinced me that the process needs constructive criticism. Working from an awareness of these many pitfalls, I offer the following detailed suggestions in the hope that they may stimulate some search committees to modify their procedures for selecting and recruiting deans.

a. Charge to the Search Committee. The president of the university must ultimately make a recommendation to the board of trustees, which will officially appoint the new medical school dean. Thus, the president should appoint and charge the search committee. The committee should be given the general charge of submitting one to three nominees to the president, one of whom would then be selected by the president and offered the position first. At the initial meeting of the committee, the president or his representative should define the committee's functions, explain its responsibilities, and emphasize the scope, importance, and urgency of the task. Minutes of all committee actions should be kept, and all correspondence should be preserved.

The committee should provide the president with a progress report every three or four weeks, and nominations, if at all possible, should be delivered to the president within four to five months after the committee has begun its work. If this deadline is not met, the president should consider either dismissing the entire committee and appointing a new one or replacing about half of its members with new blood. The president should ensure that the committee members understand the time constraints on their deliberations *from the outset.* A medical school without a permanent chief executive officer is in a state of crisis, and strenuous remedial measures are justified to meet that crisis. The president might consider presenting each member of the committee with a copy of C. P. Snow's *The Masters,* which illustrates in fictional form a dispute among faculty members over the selection of a new chief executive officer.

b. Composition of the Committee. Because many of the problems in the milieu of a medical school stem from the interface between medical education and patient care—as research has become somewhat less dominant recently—the majority of the committee members should be drawn from the ranks of the clinical departments. Basic medical scientists with a broad view of the institution's public role should form the next largest group. Nonmedical faculty members, such as those from the business school, the humanities, and the law school, might be included; however, these committee members should be charged by the president to modify committee issues rather than initiate them. An active alumnus with some significant post-M.D. study and experience outside the local medical center might be a very helpful member in the committee's proceedings.

The student body of the medical school should also be involved in the selection process. This includes undergraduate medical students, graduate students, interns, residents, and fellows, all of whom may seek some voice in the committee's proceedings. Yet the inclusion of students as voting members on the search committee often complicates matters. One way of bypassing such complications is to form a student advisory committee with representatives drawn from each of the various levels of the student body. This advisory committee could meet with visiting candidates, write evaluations on each, and then make its preferences known to the search committee. Or, soon after it has been officially constitutioned, the search committee could call one unstructured meeting to hear the views of the medical student body with regard to the selection of the new dean.

Search committees should also display a good mix of ages among their members. Local contenders for the deanship should be excluded from membership on the committee; and, if a committee member develops an interest in the post, he should resign.

All things considered, a search committee composed of six to ten members is the most efficient. A committee with fifteen or more members will likely consume more time, not to mention money, and one with twenty to forty members will spook any experienced prospect for the deanship.

It goes without saying that the chairman of the search committee is the key figure in its deliberations and in the successful completion of its work. An articulate, effective diplomat who can preside well over the committee, mediate among its various constituencies, and attend to the numerous details of its work should be appointed to this position. He should be relieved of other time-consuming duties during his tenure so that he can devote his time to the awesome task of maintaining communication with all the parties involved, including the local academic and medical professional community. He should also be provided with an adequate support staff to assist him in the discharge of his duties. Furthermore, it is wise to appoint two vice-chairmen who, with the chairman, would constitute a steering nucleus for the full committee, especially if it is large in size.

Of course, the search will require the expenditure of money, and an adequate expense account should be established for this purpose. For instance, the expenses of candidates invited to interview with the committee should be paid either in advance of the visit or by reimbursement within forty-eight hours afterward. Frequently, a visiting candidate has had to wait many months for the reimbursement of his travel expenses.

c. Criteria for Selection. At the outset of its work, the search committee should establish general criteria for the selection of the dean; in other words, the committee should decide in general terms the kind of person it wants to fill the position. The president (or university official) who appoints and charges the search committee should instruct it to seek prospects whose talents and experience match the general needs of the institution; to be sure, the committee members may need to discuss and debate the accuracy of this component of their charge, but some consensus on objectives must be achieved before a satisfactory and well-aimed search can begin. For example, an institution with shrinking revenues and a crying need to reduce expenditures will require an executive quite different from one who is expected to plan and implement a major expansion of the basic science teaching facility or a massive new effort in biomedical research. If the search for a dean is to take place before the expected retirement of a significant number of departmental chairmen, then the new dean will need the special skills of an academic recruiter. If the medical school has completed an LCME-required institutional self-study not long before the search became necessary, the major problems and needs of the institution may have been defined and projected; this would enable the committee to proceed on a more concrete basis in the search.

d. How to Start. The selection process begins with the appointment of the committee and the president's charge. Next, a list of candidates for the deanship should be developed. At this point, faculty members and students should be consulted. The senior professional staff of the AAMC and AMA-CME can be very helpful here by providing suggestions for candidates as well as the names of former chairmen of selection committees in other schools who have recently gone through the same ordeal. In view of the federal government's insistence on affirmative action in all university personnel activity, the university's dean of faculties or the designated affirmative action officer should be consulted. One or more dignified advertisements announcing the search and inviting nominations or applications should be published in medical journals and other periodicals; the *Journal of Medical Education,* published by the AAMC, has often been used for this purpose. These efforts to widen publicity will help satisfy demands for a public search in contrast to a covert, closed one. Finally, the deans of other medical schools and university vice-presidents for medical science should be contacted for suggestions and advice.

e. Finding and Contacting Candidates. Even though a search beyond the school itself may be indicated, the committee members should understand that this endeavor is expensive and very time consuming. Of the 322 deans appointed between 1960 and 1980, two thirds came *from within* the institutions they were chosen to lead, many having served as associate deans or department chairmen (Wilson and McLaughlin, 1984). Frequently, a search committee expends large amounts of energy, money, and time in an external search only to be rejected by a series of prospects; then, as if by default, it turns to a local candidate. It is only fair, as well as practical, to give consideration to local prospects early in the search.

In contacting a prospective candidate for the deanship, the courteous approach is to telephone or write, asking if he has any interest in the post and requesting a curriculum vita and a short list of references. It is embarrassing to a candidate—and may result in a quick rebuff from him—if he learns through the grapevine that he has been or is being investigated for the position before he has agreed to be considered.

f. Checking Credentials. In checking the credentials of a prospect who has agreed to be considered for the post, the usual practice is to ask him for the names of several persons to be used as references. With exceedingly rare exceptions, letters returned from these named individuals contain only praise and congratulations. After all, who in his right mind would list a severe critic as a reference? The search committee may also request the names of former supervisors of the candidate. Such persons may offer fairly objective judgments about the candidate's various abilities, but this is not a guaranteed result. The former mentor may want his protege to be appointed so much that unfavorable criticisms may be conveniently forgotten when the letter is written. Occasionally, the mentor wants, in the worst way, to be rid of a bothersome associate and will praise him excessively in a letter of recommendation. Finally, in today's litigious age, many people are reluctant to record major criticisms of a candidate in a letter. There is a clear need, then, for more precise validation of the professional reliability of a candidate for a deanship, departmental chair, or other sensitive position.

In order to receive definitive answers about a candidate, the committee should ask definitive questions. Questions regarding the candidate's use of illegal drugs or alcohol are not out of order. (Billings and others [1981] have reported on the problem of alcoholism among administrators and faculty members at one old and well-established school). Nor should the committee hesitate to inquire about the candidate's honesty in reporting the results of research and other data. Although a candidate's care and efficiency in the management of his personal finances is a sensitive subject and should be treated with sensitivity, the committee should keep in mind that a dean who is negligent in the fulfillment of his personal financial obligations may also be negligent in the management of the medical school's complex financial resources. Finally, attempts should be made to rate the candidate's reputation with medical students, including graduate students, residents, and interns. This is a legitimate task for the students. The AAMC's Organization of Student Representatives comprises a network with branches throughout the nation's medical schools. The students involved can easily obtain an informative report on the candidate's behavior toward those who follow him in the pecking order of an institution. In this respect, the committee members would do well to recall that every human being tries to look his best when a superior is watching but that true character emerges in and through the continuing relationships one has with one's subordinates.

g. Formalities of the Appointment. Once the institution makes a formal offer, the recipient should be requested to respond as soon as possible, at least within four weeks. If the nominee has visited the institution once or twice (with spouse and family during one of those visits), he should be able to reach a decision about the job in short order. Procrastination in making the decision to reject or accept the offer is, at this stage, a negative prognostic sign—if this is the case, the committee should become seriously concerned about the possibility of losing the candidate. If the candidate simply cannot make a decision, there is often a good reason for the delay: either he is holding out for an appointment elsewhere, or his spouse is reluctant to relocate. The committee should then make delicate efforts to learn the exact reason(s) for the hesitation.

The letter of appointment should include language establishing the date the job will be assumed on a full-time basis. This date often must be set five to six months from the date of acceptance for a person who must relocate; a delay of a full year should be discouraged by the committee and the president. Arrangements should be made for the dean-elect to travel frequently to the medical school to plan the work to be done, meet with key personnel, and arrange other details, many of which may be personal in nature. The new dean should arrive on the job with his appointment calendar free of heavy obligations so that he can honestly and energetically serve his new institution. In one known instance, a dean moved to town so heavily booked up with future speaking engagements that no local chairman could get an appointment with him for at least three months! The members of the search committee and the university administration would do well to remember that an inside candidate can assume the duties of the deanship very soon after his appointment.

h. Rank, Salary, and Fringe Benefits. Inevitably, the writing of the formal letter of appointment of the dean will be preceded by negotiations concerning the terms of the appointment; however, so much misunderstanding has occurred over these matters that a review of them is needed.

The letter of appointment is the contract of employment between the university and the dean, its employee. All details involved in the prior negotiations should be written into the letter. Verbal assurances may have little or no standing after a few years go by or after there is a change of chief executive of the university. The effective date of employment and commencement of salary should be specified. If the salary is not to commence until the dean arrives on site, the letter should make this clear. If the dean is to travel to the site once or numerous times before moving to town, provision should be made for the cost of such trips. Also, the dean should make appropriate arrangements with his prior university employer for brief absences to visit his new place of employment.

Most universities have hoary rules concerning the appointment of any person to the rank of full professor; granting of tenure also is rigidly regulated. However, the person offered a deanship should be granted a full professorship, with tenure *as a professor* in the appropriate field of competence. The appointment as dean never carries with it permanent tenure *as dean*. The most common practice is for the chief executive of the university to recommend to the regents or trustees that a dean be appointed for one year; or, the dean may continue to serve *as dean* at the pleasure of the chief executive of the university. Occasionally, a dean is appointed for a term of three to five years; increasingly, all deans are asked to undergo a periodic formal evaluation of performance as a condition for continuation in office.

A new medical school needs stability in its management during the early years of development; if the founding dean has been selected carefully, he should be supported in office through the three-year period of early growth before students are first enrolled and then through the movement of the charter class to the date their M.D. degrees are to be conferred. After seven or eight years, a formal evaluation of performance may be indicated, with its results bearing on the decision to continue the founding dean in office.

Eighteen of the forty founding deans remained in office at least seven years; one died after two years of service.

The AAMC annually studies the salaries of the medical school deans and their fringe benefits. Such data can be obtained by the university's chief executive officer for use in formulating the salary offer. No doubt, the candidate will have access to the same data. Fringe benefits vary considerably but, in the aggregate, often exceed 20 percent of salary. A Teachers Insurance and Annuity Association/ College Requirement Equities Fund (TIAA-CREF) retirement plan or some other system that vests the full contribution to the individual is essential. Other benefits usually found are Social Security, group term life insurance, disablity insurance, travel/accident insurance, medical care, and hospitalization insurance. Options for coverage of dependents are always included. A few universities can arrange deferred compensation. The provision of a university automobile for use on school-related activity is common or an allowance may be paid for use of the dean's vehicle on school activity. Most deans have an expense allowance to cover specified administrative and official entertainment expenses, usually on a reimbursable basis.

The letter of appointment must define the university's policy on the payment of moving expenses for the dean's household goods, office, and professional equipment. An agreement should be reached on the disposition of extra professional earnings by the dean. These include royalties from writings published while in office, honoraria from speaking engagements, fees from consultation activity, earnings from clinical practice, and similar activities. If the university has established rules for handling such earnings, the prospective dean should be told of them during the period of negotiation. If no such rules are in place, the letter of appointment should include all points of agreement.

5. *Selection of a Founding Dean.* Selecting a dean whose responsibility is to establish a new medical school is quite a different procedure from selecting a dean for an established institution. The old school usually has a fully functioning and well-balanced faculty in place, one member of which, more likely than not, is serving as acting dean. There are many more variables and unknowns in selecting someone to serve as the founding dean of a new medical school.

In both situations, the university president must initiate and organize the search and appoint the members of the search committee; but, in constituting the search committee for a founding dean, he must do so without the benefit of contributions and advice from seasoned medical faculty members. A president who has had no experience in supervising the administration of a medical school may know very little about the intricacies of this task. If this is the case, he should seek expert counsel. If the university president has become acquainted with the professional staff of the LCME during the early stages of planning and developing the new medical school, he can turn to it for the advice and counsel he needs. The staff of the LCME and the AAMC, upon request, can also provide the university president with suggestions for ad hoc consultants who are professional medical educators to serve on or assist the search committee in its work.

In order to complete the process of selecting the founding dean, the search committee must contain members who are active medical educators; or it should seek from well-informed medical educators an analysis of the professional qualifications of the candidates in whom the committee has a serious interest. (Remember, a well-trained turtle will know where to bite another turtle.) Failures of founding deans have often been related to an inadequate professional screening process at the time of their selection. Members of the medical community, such as well-regarded practicing physicians, may not have the training or expertise to judge the professional qualifications of candidates for a founding deanship, but they should be involved in the process in some manner.

What should the criteria be for a founding dean? The individual chosen for this position will occupy a much more public role than a dean who is chosen to succeed another in an established institution. And, since the founder of a new school must recruit the charter faculty and participate in the admission process of the first classes of students, his character, administrative technique, and ethical standards will stamp the school, directly and indirectly, for many years to come. Judgments of personal characteristics can be provided by anyone who is wise; no special status need be assigned to the professional medical educator.

The position of founding dean is no place for an amateur to learn by trial and error. The planning for the opening and operation of a new medical school is invariable undertaken within strict time constraints and with a limited number of resources and people to assist with the job. "Know-how," then, is essential. It follows that the founding dean needs a solid background of experience in the management of a well-developed medical school. Effective prior experience as the dean of such an institution or as a deputy dean with a broad spectrum of duties would be a preferred attribute of the potentially successful candidate. Experience as an associate dean or assistant dean for a specialized function would be useful, but only to the extent that that position also entailed exposure to and involvement with general management. A candidate with experience in the chair of a department *might* be adequate as a founding dean, but only if he is capable of making the difficult transition from intense partisanship on behalf of a single discipline to the impartial role of a general manager of and mediator among many disciplines. It should be noted at this point that a founding dean should *never* simultaneously occupy a departmental chair. This proscription has arisen from a number of unhappy experiences in the recent development of new schools.

In the forty new schools, seventy-six people served as deans from 1960 to 1980. Their average age was forty-nine at appointment; the range was thirty-eight to sixty-one. All were male. Six percent previously had been deans elsewhere, 46 percent had been either associate or assistant deans elsewhere, and 40 percent had previously served as departmental chairmen. As to academic qualifications, 37 percent were internists, 12 percent were pediatricians, 11 percent were pathologists, and 9 percent were surgeons. The remaining 31 percent were scattered throughout eleven different specialties (Wilson and McLaughlin, 1984).

The locale of a founding dean's prior experience is also a significant factor for the committee to consider. Most of the nation's established medical schools are managed well and efficiently, but a few seem to have established a tradition for mediocrity in their academic and administrative functions. Poor prior experience always has a negative value. Playing a significant role in the recent development of another medical school might be an asset; but the quality of that experience and the record of development of that school must be examined carefully. Again, a poor model is unworthy of transplantation.

"If you are appointed dean, whom can you recruit for your planning staff and for a critical mass of departmental chairs, and how quickly?" No candidate for the position of founding dean should be given an official, final appointment until he can give a substantive answer to this query. The innovative, self-starting founding dean will be able, early in the process, to identify a number of persons who have the requisite experience and abilities to perform the tasks associated with the early stages of the school's development. The quality of these individuals will establish the magnitude of academic and professional excellence of the school for its first twenty-five years or longer; the quality of these key people may also be subjected to the judgment of external professional medical educators.

The founding dean's school of origin becomes an even more significant factor for this reason: if it is a well-established and efficiently operating school, it will have a supply of able faculty members, some of whom might be recruited under the banner of one of their effective administrators as he migrates to engage in academic pioneering. The whole process of recruiting faculty and staff will be facilitated if the founding dean has previously earned a national reputation or some other form of wide recognition outside the school of origin. This could be attained, in addition to the area of his specialization, through service on nationally organized committees and task forces of the AAMC or a similar entity, by serving on LCME accreditation survey teams, or through academic consultation.

Chapter Two includes a list of the various institutions and individuals with whom the medical school must relate and maintain enduring ties. The founding dean must possess impressive skills in making verbal and written presentations to all the groups and individuals on this extensive list. A broad knowledge of what to do and how to do it is not enough when the development of a new medical school is at issue; the founding dean is expected and required to describe and justify the developmental activities for the school in a convincing manner and with sensitivity to the political implications of his words and deeds.

Beyond the more objective criteria related to a candidate's professional experience, there are more personal criteria, such as health and stamina. The work load with which a founding dean is saddled is staggering in scope; it usually becomes larger than was anticipated at the outset. The successful founding dean should be a self-starter with a large reservoir of energy that can be easily replenished. An intellectually and physically stressful workday extending from twelve to fourteen hours, six and sometimes seven days a week, is routine. A candidate who is prone to peptic ulcers, ulcerative colitis, migraine, labile hypertension, or other stress-related diseases may risk developing full-blown manifestations of the problem in a founding deanship. A candidate who is known to turn to alcohol or drugs for release from the strain of a job will likely develop a disabling dependence on these crutches in the daily heat of the founding deanship.

The ideal candidate should also be emotionally stable, humane and sensitive, adaptable, and realistically but infectiously optimistic. The awesome task of charting and directing the development of a large, new, and locally unfamiliar institution—which by its very nature is controversial—is not always easy and orderly. The founding dean must possess sufficient equanimity to adapt to any unexpected glitch with a realistic optimism that inspires confidence in the individuals he leads. He should be sensitive to the human needs of the faculty, staff, and students, especially during the formative years of the young school, if the institution is to become anything other than an impersonal bureaucracy administered by dull, robot-like people.

Well-entrenched habits of effective personal organization and the ability to make good decisions expeditiously are also assets to a founding dean. An individual who is unable to manage himself well and to operate effectively, who procrastinates and postpones the nettlesome and unpleasant, is not likely to get his assigned job done, regardless of his natural intelligence or impressive technical and professional credentials.

The founding dean's spouse and children must be prepared to share with him the demands his position entails—often to a very uncomfortable degree. The family's life-style should be reviewed in a mature manner prior to the candidate's acceptance of a job offer. The family should be prepared to accept the consequences of the job, some of which are necessarily unforeseen, and should assure the committee and the university president of their ability and willingness to cope with the situation as it evolves. Unwillingness on the part of a spouse to join the leading prospect as the job is assumed on site may soon doom the new dean's ability to handle the job; this matter should be tested specifically before a final offer of employment is made.

6. *Personal Satisfaction in a Deanship.* The medical school dean does not perform activities for which he has had extended professional training and general experience. The bulk of his day-to-day functions are directed toward the specific activities of his faculty and students. To the point: the dean is there to facilitate the work of the faculty, students, and support staff of the medical school. If he devotes himself to this broad task effectively, he must relinquish the personal satisfactions and new rewards to his ego that might accrue to him were he to devote himself to making scientific discoveries or achieving a high clinical expertise. Through the years, many deans who voluntarily left the office after a short tenure have told me that one reason for dissatisfaction was their discomfort in adapting to the role as a general facilitator for the academic community at the expense of personal intellectual and professional pursuits. It appears that insight into and acceptance of this characteristic of the deanship are essential for success in this office.

The average deanship carries with it a relatively modest amount of power. With the demise of the divine right of kings to absolute power, the only contemporary location of an office that carries with it substantial, unchecked power is a brutal military dictatorship. During the past thirty years, the university's hierarchy, the departmental chairpersons, the faculty, and the students have eroded much automatic power from the deanship. What is left for the dean is an opportunity to convince his numerous publics that he provides valuable leadership to the institution—or is useful to a constituent public or a number of individuals therein. A dean who is effective in the performance of the numerous tasks that gravitate to the deanery and of those initiatives he deems essential to the efficient functioning of the institution will acquire power from all the special interest groups that previously usurped it. Rich personal satisfactions can be enjoyed by the dean who is successful in achieving the full effectiveness of his office.

In conclusion, and with a humorous approach, a deanship may be likened to the job of impresario of a corps de ballet. The classical illustration is to be found in Jules Perrot's "Pas de Quartre," first performed in the mid-1840s, wherein four rival leading prima ballerinas are choreographed to dance on stage simultaneously. The dean may have a dozen or more prima ballerinas (departmental chairmen) on his stage at all times, and odds are that at least one of the twelve will claim to be a prima ballerina assoluta—the ultimate of the species.

The medical deanship is a unique occupation: those without insight do not last very long. Those who make the job work can lead their colleges to greatness in one or more areas, but personal recognition may not be available outside Heaven!

🙰🙰🙰🙰🙰🙰🙰🙰🙰🙰🙰🙰🙰🙰🙰🙰🙰🙰🙰🙰🙰 4

The Deanery: Managerial Support for the Dean

🙰🙰🙰🙰🙰🙰🙰🙰🙰🙰🙰🙰🙰🙰🙰🙰🙰🙰🙰🙰🙰🙰

As the educational, research, and service programs of the medical school have expanded, the dean's staff—the deanery—has been forced to grow commensurately. Prior to World War II, in many of the schools, the office of the dean was managed with tight reins by a mature, competent, and well-organized secretary who acted as court chamberlain to the faculty, den mother to the students, and plantation overseer for the purchasing, personnel, and maintenance activities of the school. Some of the latter functions may have been managed by the administration of the university rather than that of the medical school. During the 1950s, some expansion of the deanery began to occur as the activities of the schools began to increase. Table 13 shows that, by 1960, most of the eighty-six schools established before that date had created one associate deanship and one assistant deanship. By 1980, the same schools had a total of 668 associate and assistant deans—an average of almost seven per school. The other officials in the deanery more than doubled during the same twenty-year period. (See Table 13.)

Table 13. Expansion of the Deanery in the Eighty-Six Medical Schools Established Before 1960, 1960–1980.

	1960–61	1980–81
Associate Deans	76	433
Assistant Deans	80	235
Other Officials	167	364
Total	323	1,032

Sources: Association of American Medical Colleges, 1960, 1980b.

Functions Requiring Management

The wide diversity of the medical schools is reflected in the various arrangements for the deanery. Since about 1960, most schools have included new persons in the deanery in an evolutionary manner in response to emerging need: there is little apparent evidence of organized planning, and there is no consistent pattern of full-time versus part-time assignment of those involved. However, despite the variations found in assignment of people to duty in the deanery, numerous managerial duties must be accepted and discharged in all schools with comparable programs, albeit in varying quantities. Following is a list of functions and programs that require management; most are likely to be found in a typical school with mature development.

I.   Nonacademic functions
    A.   Business affairs
        1.   Budget and payroll
        2.   Personnel
        3.   Purchasing
        4.   Building and grounds; (maintenance and parking facilities)
        5.   Food services; vending machines
        6.   Book store
        7.   Print shop; duplicating facilities
        8.   Mail service

        B.   Planning

        C.   Development (gifts and endowment)

        D.   Public information

        E.   Alumni activities

        F.   Legal affairs

        G.   Governmental relations

II.   Academic functions

        A.   Educational programs

             1.   M.D. degree program (for medical students)

             2.   Graduate medical education (for hospital residents and fellows)

             3.   Continuing education (for practicing physicians)

             4.   Graduate education in the sciences basic to medicine (for graduate students and fellows)

             5.   Other health education programs organized within the medical school

        B.   Scholarly activities of the faculty

             1.   Biomedical research

             2.   Seminars

             3.   Visiting lectureships

        C.   Supporting services for academic programs and activities

             1.   Admissions activities (including minority student recruitment)

             2.   Registrar

             3.   Student affairs (financial aid, health service, housing)

             4.   Multiple-discipline laboratories

             5.   Library (learning resource center)

             6.   Faculty records

             7.   Grants and contracts management

             8.   Vivarium (laboratory animals)

             9.   Computer services

III.   Medical care and clinical educational activities

        A.   University hospitals (in 73 schools)

        B.   Veterans' hospitals (in 94 schools)

        C.   Affiliated hospitals (all schools)

D.   Special medical care centers and institutes (many schools)

E.   Patient referral activities; faculty practice plan (nearly all schools)

F.   Health maintenance organization (a few schools; others starting in the 1980s)

It is obvious that the dean/chief executive officer (CEO), who is an educated but ordinary mortal, cannot personally manage the array of programs and activities outlined. Therefore, most deans delegate some degree of authority for management, under various kinds of supervision, to members of their staff.

The nonacademic functions have been delegated most easily by the dean, who generally comes to his office with credentials in medicine, not in business management. Business affairs, in a well-developed institution, can be quite large as measured in volume of annual cash flow. Meeting the demands of fiscal accountability requires numerous trained personnel in a school that receives $20 to $50 million per year from a state government and $10 to $40 million grants and contracts from numerous agencies. Indeed, external auditors may be on the premises continuously. It is not surprising, therefore, to find that the nonacademic managers usually report directly to the dean. Because of the size of fiscal operations of many medical schools, fiscal management often is located in the medical school as a responsibility of its CEO, either semi-independent or as a branch of the university's fiscal offices. Development, public information and alumni activities somewhat related, may be directed by one person with the support of specialized subordinates.

Academic functions and their essential supporting services are more difficult for a dean to delegate than are the nonacademic functions. However, the list of functions is still far too long for him to manage personally, even though his training and experience may equip him to do so. Thus, deans appoint numerous associate deans, assistant deans, program and service directors, assistants to the dean, administrative assistants, and aides to be primary managers for assigned duties; these range from narrow, part-time assignments to very broad delegations of authority.

In the early 1980s, about one fourth of the schools have designed a principal officer as deputy dean, vice-dean, executive associate dean, or senior associate dean. Responsibilities for this officer vary; many incumbents are involved in general management of the school and bear the dean's authority in his absence. Duke University, in 1970, altered the administration of its medical school by appointing a vice-president as CEO and a director (dean) of medical and allied health education. Subsequently, a few other schools have appointed a chief academic officer (CAO), usually called dean of academic affairs. This CAO has become the principal academic program leader of the school, under the supervision of the CEO, who is sometimes titled vice-president and otherwise titled dean. Most schools, however, have splintered the academic programs by assigning portions and pieces of management to faculty members who divide their time between administrative duties and primary professional activities.

Management of those institutions (or coordination of activities within them) which house medical and clinical educational activities is almost always delegated to qualified persons who may be appointed associate deans. These institutions have grown very large since mid-century, and their complexity generally requires expert, full-time management. Few deans have attempted to manage a hospital while simultaneously serving as CEO of a medical school.

Administrative Committees of the Faculty

Some of the standing committees of the faculty required by the by-laws of the school are concerned with administrative activities. While these committees are not part of the deanery of the school, they frequently are either chaired or staffed by officers of the administration. The most significant standing committee is the dean's advisory committee. Its membership typically consists of the chairpersons of all major departments, with rotation of members from smaller departments, and directors of institutes or centers. Ordinarily, the dean is chairperson and associate deans and selected assistant deans may be ex officio members. This committee reviews current managerial problems of the medical school and advises the dean in the formulation of solutions. The committee is commonly advisory in nature; but, in a few schools, it may have executive powers that exceed the authority granted to the dean.

Following is a list of standing committees, subject to some variation, that engage in certain managerial/administrative activities under policies developed by the faculty's academic policy-making body, sometimes called the senate (of the medical school) or the faculty council:

> Admissions (of medical students)
> Curriculum for the M.D. degree
> Promotions and graduation of medical students
> Student honors and awards
> Graduate education in the sciences basic to medicine
> Graduate medical education
> Clinical teaching resources
> Library
> Biomedical resources (vivarium, computers, radioactive substances, and others)
> Human investigation
> Veterans' Administration Hospital Dean's Committee

While these committees consist of faculty members, each function that has a significant operational component usually is directed by some person involved in the deanery. To illustrate, a medical school may have space for 150 beginning medical students annually and may receive 1,000 to 5,000 applications for these positions. The faculty's committee on admissions, representing the faculty at large, sets the policies for selection of the medical students, but a full-time director/assistant dean usually is placed in charge of the massive operations of the committee's selection process. Other committees may have smaller operational components than the admissions committee, but most depend on a specialized manager who reports to the committee as well as to a designated dean.

Chairpersons of Academic Departments

The final component of administration of a medical school consists of the department chairpersons. The number of departments in the schools ranges from one to several dozen. Each department is authorized by university statutes or by-laws; once established, it has been rare for a department to be dissolved, despite modifications in the body of knowledge that must be taught due to sweeping changes in biomedical technology. Some departments have specific endowments or have access to very large income from external granting agencies or from direct earnings from the clinical practice of its members. The chair of a large, affluent department is a potent force in the administration of a medical school; some such chairs have operated their departments in a large measure of independence from the CEO, the CAO, or other members of the deanery.

Formerly, a person appointed to a chair might have held that position of power for several decades. Within the past decade, however, many schools have appointed chairpersons for a term of five to seven years. Toward the end of such a term, the dean organizes a review of the performance of the incumbent; the results may determine whether the chairperson is appointed to a second term.

Lessons Learned

1. *The Dean and the Deanery.* Someone appointed to the deanship of an established school from the outside will encounter his first substantial challenge in the need to determine exactly what each person in the deanery actually does and how well he does it. A few deans have failed to be effective executives because of their inability to gain control over the mediocre but well-entrenched bureaucracy they inherited or because they failed to obtain the fiscal resources necessary for the development of an expanded, efficient one. In an attempt to exercise control, an inexperienced, compulsive new dean may reorganize the school so that all of the middle- and lower-level managers, as well as the departmental chairmen, report directly to him; in a short time, such a move will create a bottleneck rendering timely administrative decision making impossible. In any contemplated reorganization of medical school administration, the dean should be concerned with maintaining continuity in the management of essential, ongoing programs which may be required to meet a fixed time schedule of operation.

The dean/CEO should schedule routine meetings (on a weekly, biweekly, or monthly basis), lasting at least one but no more than two hours, with all or selected members of his administrative staff for the purpose of providing effective group communication. Every member of the staff should be on the distribution list for memoranda from the dean and for selected items of information of a general interest. Other means of communication among the members of the group should be devised.

Whether the school is modest or sprawling in size and complexity, the dean must limit the number of middle- and lower-level managers who report to him directly on a routine basis. Every aspect of the administration can be reviewed at the time the annual budget is considered, or brief annual reports can provide an overview of who does what and why. An effective dean will delegate responsibility and authority to carefully selected subdeans or directors and managers of ongoing programs, services, and activities. Of course, prompt attention must be given to a festering problem that a middle manager has failed to solve; sometimes the best solution may be the replacement of the middle manager. Proper delegation to able staff members will allow the dean to have more time to leave his office and circulate around his school for the purpose of engaging in useful dialogue with faculty members, students, and employees.

2. *Chief Academic Officer.* Those few schools that have vested authority for direction of all educational programs and related academic functions in one full-time individual have achieved admirable progress in the evolution of medical school administration. It should be remembered that a full-time faculty is a rather recent development in this country and that the presence of a full-time dean in nearly all schools has a history extending only thirty to forty years. So I make a plea for designation of a well-qualified faculty member who has a broad interest in medical education as the CAO on a full-time basis. Direction of the educational programs of a school is a different function from that of the CEO, who must acquire resources for the school and facilitate the performance of its people.

3. *Status of Members of the Deanery.* The recruitment of members of the faculty to serve as associate or assistant deans is a responsibility of high priority for the dean. If possible, the CAO

should serve full time because this office is so crucial to the development and maintenance of the quality of the educational program. If the CAO occupies his office on a full-time or nearly full-time basis and if he gives evidence of stability and quality in the performance of his duties, his contributions should be recognized by the designation of an appropriate academic rank, such as professor of medical administration in an independent division or department chaired by either the CEO or himself, preferably the latter. If such a division or department of medical administration is formed, appropriate academic rank can be assigned, if justified, to other members of the deanery. Vanderbilt University has employed such an arrangement since 1969.

The other associate and assistant deans are usually appointed on a part-time basis and are therefore able to continue professional activity in their respective disciplines. The CEO and CAO should be alert to a developing interest in administration on the part of promising younger members of the faculty and should arrange for such persons to be assigned for a term of service to committees of the faculty or as members of the deanery. The ideal objective is to provide the outstanding younger faculty members—who may eventually seek a departmental chair or deanship—with definitive administrative experience. The attainment of this objective would increase the pool of well-qualified and able candidates for executive positions in medical school and departmental administration.

4. *Succession of Authority in the Deanery.* The CEO, advised by his administrative advisory committee, should establish a clear line of delegation of administrative authority to be followed during his absence or subsequent to his departure from office. Institutions can lose efficiency of operation rapidly if multiple subdeans and departmental chairpersons are allowed to jockey for authority in the vacuum of power left by an absent, ailing, or resigned CEO. Of course, the university president must appoint an acting dean; but until he does so, the school has to be kept running—some portions of it day and night.

Founding
a New Medical School

The extensive experience gained in the founding of forty new medical schools between 1960 and 1980 has demonstrated the great differences between the administration of old, established schools and new ones during their early years before and soon after the first students are enrolled. The newly appointed founding dean is quite alone when he arrives to undertake his task. During his early crucial months, he does not have access to a well-staffed faculty or a deanery of resourceful professionals upon whom he can depend for technical advice or working support. Furthermore, the founding dean has to solve many of the problems that beset the deans of older schools; and, in addition, he must cope with problems of significant magnitude that are unique to the development of a new institution.

The Founding Dean's Major Tasks

The general objectives for development of a new school have been established by the LCME, the national accrediting body; therefore, the founding dean is able to begin his labors with a clear understanding of his responsibilities. Following is the list of major tasks to be performed; experience has proven the need to attend to all tasks more or less simultaneously.

- Secure the resources necessary for the implementation of a program of medical education leading to the M.D. degree—a program that meets, at the very least, the minimal national standard for accreditation, as well as any special local objectives for the medical school.
- Establish or improve programs in graduate medical education in hospitals owned by or affiliated with the new medical school.
- Establish appropriate advanced degree programs or other programs in the basic medical sciences.
- Develop a program of continuing medical education for the benefit of the practicing physicians in the city and surrounding area.
- Develop the resources necessary for, and foster the innovative spirit prerequisite to, contributions to the body of medical, scientific knowledge through research and scholarly activity.

Information About the Founding of New Schools: 1960–1980

The two principal sources of information about administrative activities of a founding dean are the confidential records of the LCME and the formal publications of the founders of new schools. The LCME has collected substantial descriptive data and recorded serial evaluations of the fifteen schools established in the 1960s and the twenty-five schools launched during the 1970s. The pattern of surveillance by the LCME has been essentially unchanged for the period studied.

1. The professional medical eduactors who staff the LCME were visited by university officers who described their tentative proposal for a new school and sought criticism of it.
2. Eighteen to thirty months before enrollment of the first class, the LCME staff conducted a consultation visit on site.
3. At least twelve months before the first matriculation date, the LCME inspected the resources available to the proposed new

school and determined whether provisional accreditation could
be granted.

4. Beginning with the year of enrollment of the charter class, and
   each successive year until the graduation of the charter class,
   an annual inspection was held.

5. Reinspections were held at intervals of two to four years until
   the school achieved mature growth and a stable state. LCME
   staff members or survey team members wrote a definitive report
   for consideration by the official accrediting body on each event
   outlined. All of these reports (many of which consist of 200 pages)
   and the critical comments accumulated from LCME members
   and their forty to fifty reviewers have been analyzed in preparation
   for writing the "Lessons Learned" segment of this chapter.

The second source of material is the accumulation of writings
by the founding deans, their successors, or an early faculty member
participant in the development of a new school. The deans of the
forty schools studied and their medical librarians were asked to
send a bibliography or actual reprints on early development of their
schools. The select bibliography for Part Two of this book contains
a comprehensive listing of everything known to be in the retrievable
literature on the early development of these schools. A number of
these papers were commissioned by the Josiah Macy, Jr., Foundation
and the W. K. Kellogg Foundation and published in book form;
others were collected and published in medical/academic journals,
such as the *Journal of the Mount Sinai Hospital.*

Instead of summarizing all the materials on the new schools,
I have prepared a review of the numerous events and problems
that inevitably occur soon after the founding dean is appointed.
Each event presents a special administrative problem or entails a
particular responsibility for the founding dean; one or more recommendations for solving or dealing with each is offered. The accounts
of the personal experiences of the founding deans form the "yin"
and the confidential, contemporary record of judgment of each
school by the LCME constitutes the "yang" of a synthesis of
recommendations for use in the future. Under the strong influence
of hindsight, I have further evaluated these two sources of information and the often conflicting opinions they contain in expressing

my own recommendations concerning the establishment of a new medical school. All recommendations are general in character and should be modified to meet special circumstances in an individual school.

Lessons Learned

1. *Pressure for an Early Start of Instruction.* Immediately after receiving his appointment, a founding dean becomes the focus of attention within the university, the local medical profession, and especially the media. In most cases, these groups and the public in general have witnessed the passage of several, sometimes many, years from the time the school was first proposed to the time the authority to establish it was finally obtained. The founding dean should therefore expect to be badgered at once to announce the anticipated date of enrollment of the charter class of medical students. The founding deans of the new medical schools established between 1960 and 1980 discovered that there is a widespread, genuine absence of insight into the amount of time involved in accumulating the vital resources that are needed before students can be provided with learning opportunities and programs that meet—again, at the very least—minimal national standards of medical education. For example, it has been common for a founding dean who begins his work early in the calendar year to encounter a widely held expectation that students will be enrolled in the autumn of that same year. This unrealistic but common expectation has often forced the founding dean to call on external experts to soften the local demand for an instant start of instruction. The situation can become even more difficult if the dean foolishly allows himself to get caught up in the local agitation for a quick start and makes a public announcement of a starting date, which later he is forced to extend not once but several times. To illustrate, the regents of the proposed new Uniformed Services University of the Health Sciences were appointed in May 1973. After their first meeting during that same month, a spokesman for the regents indicated their intent to enroll 300 entering medical students in the autumn of the same year. Actually, a charter class of 32 beginning students was enrolled in October 1976.

The time required by the founding dean to start instruction of medical students is inversely related to the availability of critical major resources, such as full financing, an established teaching hospital, appropriate physical facilities and equipment, and, most important, a carefully selected cadre of faculty members. These individuals should be on site during the time needed to develop the myriad details of the medical curriculum and to assemble the requisite teaching materials. The interval between the arrival of the founding dean (full time and on site) and the start of instruction of the charter class of medical students averaged thirty-six months for the cohort of forty new medical schools established between 1960 and 1980.

Thus, those who are impatient and agitate for a quick start of instruction need to be advised and convinced that students, once enrolled in a typical four-year program of instruction leading to the M.D. degree, must be assured of the availability of the full constellation of resources required to support that program—*before* they begin their studies. In light of this, early public statements by the dean should include descriptions of these resources and of the necessity of the simultaneous development of programs for the M.D. degree, graduate medical education, continuing medical education, and basic science graduate degrees; he should also emphasize the time required for the recruitment of a critical mass of faculty members who are indispensable for the development of all educational programs and the scholarly activity which undergirds all types of learning.

The need for an adequate growth period in a new school before the commencement of instruction has been evident for many decades. This is illustrated by the timetable (Table 14) for the development of three medical schools that have attained high academic quality: the medical schools of Johns Hopkins University, Rochester University, and Duke University.

2. *Developing the Administrative Headquarters.* In most circumstances, the dean began his work in temporary quarters located on the campus of the sponsoring university or in offices leased near the campus. Several of the new medical schools were able to use campus facilities that were no longer needed because of changing programs. At Michigan State University and Texas

Table 14. Interval Between Appointment of Founding Dean and Onset of Instruction in Three Exemplary Medical Schools.

School	Date of Founding Dean's Appointment	Date of Onset of Instruction	Interval	Date of Opening of Teaching Hospital
Johns Hopkins University School of Medicine	April 7, 1884	October 1893	114 months	May 7, 1889
University of Rochester School of Medicine and Dentistry	July 1, 1921	September 17, 1925	52 months	January 4, 1926
Duke University School of Medicine	January 21, 1927	October 2, 1930	44 months	July 21, 1930

Sources: For Johns Hopkins: Chesney, 1943; for Rochester: Romano, 1975; for Duke: Gifford, 1972.

Tech University, surplus dormitory facilities were used, and with good efficiency, because such buildings often contained substantial space for the expanding faculty and support staff of the rapidly developing school. Eastern Virginia Medical School used a former nursing school building, and the University of California-Davis and others used "Butler" type temporary structures for temporary headquarters; otherwise, business office space was leased for this purpose.

3. *Original Support Staff.* A frequent mistake made by some of the founding deans was to hold early expenditures at a low level, perhaps because of budgetary constraints, by postponing the development of an adequate support staff. The resulting situation often led to the recommendation by LCME staff consultants during early on-site inspections that the founding dean be given additional support so that he could be relieved of mundane, routine duties.

Soon after he accepts appointment and before he assumes his duties on a full-time basis, the founding dean should visit the new medical school, make arrangements for the first administrative headquarters, and hire an experienced and resourceful executive secretary. This person should be scheduled to begin employment several months before the founding dean moves to town: at the very least, the executive secretary should begin work at the start of the period of transition during which the dean will be making frequent trips from his former locale of employment to the new setting. The sooner an efficient office of the dean is established, the sooner the dean can concentrate on the solution of the numerous developmental problems facing the new school.

Soon after they arrived to assume their new positions, some founding deans employed an administrative assistant or assistant to the dean to perform many managerial chores. Some of the significant yet time-consuming services such a person can perform are: meeting visiting candidates for faculty positions at the airport and returning them there, taking such visitors on local tours, aiding visitors in their searches for housing, driving the dean on an out-of-town speaking tour (thereby allowing the dean to compose his speech in the car), and handling a significant amount of the informational flow via the telephone.

An experienced fiscal planner should be found and employed by the founding dean at an early date. Prior to hiring the fiscal planner, the dean should determine whether this person can be expected to become the chief business and fiscal officer of the school once operations achieve some magnitude. The person occupying this position would be expected to work with the university comptroller and the personnel and purchasing officers until the medical school is independently managed. It should be noted here that none of the new schools was able to respond rapidly to the legitimate needs of a new and growing faculty of medicine through the use of preexisting university fiscal, purchasing, and personnel services. Ultimately, each new medical school found that its explosive growth could be sustained in an adequate manner only when the persons responsible for major administrative functions were fully integrated, physically and bureaucratically, with the dean's staff and thus became available for daily contact with the dean and the faculty. Priority also should be given to the early employment of the director of the library and learning resources, so that the acquisition of materials can begin promptly.

4. *Original Professional Planning Group.* Of all the executive actions to be taken by the founding dean, none shall have a greater and more lasting impact on the future of the institution than the selection of the original members of the faculty. They should possess the superior credentials that would enable them to maintain a high degree of academic and scholarly performance as they and the dean continue to recruit other original members of the developing medical academic community.

These key faculty members should arrive very early on the scene, either with the founding dean or immediately after he arrives, in order to participate in the extensive, definitive planning to be accomplished during the first third to a half of the average thirty-six-month interval between the appointment of the dean and the commencement of student instruction. One founding dean, John Tupper, of the new medical school at the University of California at Davis, was able to bring with him (or soon thereafter) seven faculty members. Later dubbed "Snow White and the Seven Dwarfs" by the medical students, Tupper and his seven associates—representing the major fields of the basic and clinical sciences—were effective in devising at an early date a plan for the development of the new school; their efficiency and foresight enabled them to begin instruction thirty months after Tupper arrived on site.

Undoubtedly, all forty founding deans wanted to recruit faculty members of a superior quality as soon as possible. It is likely that each had some preferences as to which discipline(s) would be initially represented. To be sure, there are random factors involved in recruitment and in the order of arrival of newly appointed faculty members. But, judging from the record of experience, I think the ideal objective is for the dean to recruit initially two sturdy basic scientists and two clinicians to serve as a minimal planning group for the development of the physical resources and the preliminary design of the curriculum. Preferably, the two basic scientists should be (1) a pathologist or a pharmacologist with an M.D. degree and (2) a biomedical scientist in anatomy, physiology, biochemistry, or microbiology. On the clinical side, I think, it is very important to recruit the chairman of internal medicine as a matter of first priority; this action could be followed by the appointment of a psychiatrist or a pediatrician. If the new medical school has established as one of its objectives the education of nonurban practitioners, then a professor of family medicine could be recruited. In any case, experience has shown that the appointment of a chairman of surgery should be deferred until the school is well launched and its officials have had adequate time to develop a harmonious relationship with the local practicing physicians.

If the members of the faculty can be recruited in more or less the order outlined above, then the founding dean should appoint one of the basic scientists to be responsible for details of the planning of the basic science teaching facility, which will also contain offices and research laboratories for faculty members from all disciplines and for administrative officers and support space. This was done at the University of Arizona and other schools. Indeed, one of the criteria to be employed in the selection of the original basic scientist might be prior experience in the performance of this kind of activity or some aptitude for such.

On the clinical side, the chairman of internal medicine would be a likely candidate for the rather complex task of dealing with the affiliated hospital(s) to be used by the school in its teaching programs for both medical students and hospital residents; or, if the medical school intends to construct and establish its own teaching hospital, the chairman of internal medicine would logically assume responsibility for the very involved and intricate task of its planning.

The dean also should consider appointing the original basic scientist (mentioned above) and the clinician (the chairman of internal medicine) to posts as acting associate deans for their respective functions. In the past, when a dean has served as the chairman of one of the departments in the medical school, the results have often been negative. But it is common for a departmental chairman to serve as an acting associate dean for basic science and a clinical chairman to serve as acting associate dean for clinical affairs, at least during the first several years devoted to the planning of physical resources, hospital affiliations, and the development of community relations. The myriad tasks involved in the launching of a new medical school are immense in scope; if the dean holds authority and ultimate responsibility for all of them himself, then each may require an extended period of time for its completion.

The planning staff should be increased as additional members of the faculty are recruited. As soon as the right person can be identified, an associate dean for academic affairs should be designated to manage the development of the curriculum. At least two years before the charter class is enrolled, an additional member of the faculty should be appointed assistant dean for student affairs and admissions. At the same time, another individual should be recruited for the academic support staff as registrar. As the circumstances of the rapidly developing school continue to evolve and change, modifications in these academic support staff assignments will be required. As additional faculty members are recruited, some or all can be given either temporary or long-term assignments in the deanery or as members of ad hoc task forces or standing committees of the faculty.

This continually growing group of people will require suitable office space, both in the initial growth phase of the institution and after the eventual occupancy of the newly constructed medical school building. Planners tend to assign too little space to the administrative functions of a new medical school; years after they have completed the ordeal of launching the new medical school, many of the founding deans have reported that this error was made in the early planning phases of their schools. In my experience, members of the faculty often have not understood why large areas have to be devoted to the administration; however, these same faculty members are the ones who demand extensive and elaborate administrative services and become quite irate if these services are not delivered promptly and efficiently.

5. *Early Fiscal Planning.* In the course of assembling the faculty planning group, the dean and his newly appointed fiscal officer may discover, without warning, that the chief fiscal officer of the university or the budget committee of the state legislature requires a proposed budget for the medical school, not only for the next fiscal year but for the next five. The preparation of a budget for five years in the future is a difficult task even in an established, stable institution; projecting a budget for a new institution with any suitable accuracy for a period of five years is an event uncommon in the experience of an academically trained medical professional who has recently become a founding dean.

Chapter Six includes information that will be useful for budget preparation. Preceding the preparation of a budget, however, it is imperative that the founding dean and his staff formulate an orderly plan for the accumulation of the resources necessary for the implementation of the several programs of education and scholarly activity which constitute a medical school. Obviously, the nature and magnitude of the necessary resources depend upon the style and complexity of the plan for each program to be instituted. The dean has two very different options in formulating the M.D. educational program: (1) He may elect to replicate a combination of elements of highly successful programs long in operation elsewhere; this can be done quickly and efficiently and at a predictably moderate cost by a competent faculty due to the fact that an established program is usually well understood. (2) The dean may choose to design an innovative program composed of new and untried elements. In my opinion, the second option requires a substantially larger number of faculty members who are not only professionally competent but also highly creative and deeply interested in medical education and the welfare of students. Perfection of a new, innovative plan is likely to require more time than the construction of a replica. Students who are enrolled in an untested scheme are vulnerable to the possible failure of an innovative program; also, the need for frequent mid-course adjustments may be unsettling for both students and faculty. And it is usually more costly to innovate. In summary, experimentation and innovation are highly desirable, but they should never be attempted unless the institution possesses the very rich and abundant resources required for successful implementation. Additionally, there must be valid assurance that the students will not suffer if the novel plan fails because of faulty design, poor execution, or inadequate resources.

6. *Planning Permanent Facilities.* Once it has been established, a medical school can be expected to continue in operation indefinitely; thus, the determination of its location is an extremely important matter. Unfortunately the selection of a site is often made on political grounds rather than on the basis of logical, functional considerations. The dean, the university president, and the trustees should attempt to locate the new school where it can function most effectively; they may find external consultation arranged by neutral national associations to be quite valuable if each of several rival factions aggressively contends for selection of a favorite site. Chapter Eight is devoted to the physical resources of a medical school and provides greater detail about the selection of a site and its implications for the educational programs of the medical school. The founding dean should be aware, however, that the process of selecting a site is likely to involve him and his school in public debate and may subject him to commercial manipulation, which he must avoid at all costs.

If an entirely new building is to be constructed, or even if an existing structure is to be modified extensively for use as a medical school facility, the founding dean and his planning group must seize the initiative in (1) selecting an architect, (2) developing a comprehensive list of the functions to be housed in the building, both in the early years of operation and during its first quarter century, and (3) refining the conceptual design of the proposed building or renovation. Chapter Eight also provides a detailed discussion of "good" and "bad" medical school design features. Early in the planning process, the founding dean and key members of the planning group should collect information about the most modern facilities that have been constructed elsewhere; in particular, faculty members who work in these facilities should be solicited for their evaluations of novel design features. After the architect is selected, the dean and key planners should escort him on a brief educational tour of several well-designed medical school buildings.

The planners should keep in mind that a medical school must house a variety of specialized facilities. These include:

- Facilities for the instruction of students of a predetermined quantity in all of the different educational programs to be operated by the school, including classrooms of various sizes for use during lectures to an entire class, small-group teaching rooms, and student laboratories.
- Offices and meeting rooms for the administrators constituting the deanery.
- Offices and research laboratories for the projected number of faculty members, graduate students, and fellows; facilities for the library and learning resources and student study.
- Special facilities required for the support of research activity, such as animal care resources, computer laboratories, radioactive material storage and disposal, and others.
- Food service areas, lounges with student lockers, recreation facilities, and other space for amenities for students and personnel.
- An assembly room with a capacity of 500 to 600 people.
- Facilities for the ambulatory clinical care of an expanding number of patients.
- Maintenance shops, receiving docks, and vendor delivery areas.

In addition, site planning must also make provision for automobile parking and access by public transportation, such as buses, taxis, and so on. In planning the new facility, the architect should be required to provide for the eventual expansion of all of its functions.

7. *Planning Clinical Teaching Activities and Facilities.* Within two years after they have begun their studies, the members of the charter class of medical students will become full-time clinical

clerks in the general hospital(s) planned for use in the M.D. program and in the several programs of graduate medical education. Therefore, the clinical teaching hospital(s) to be used as the site of medical student instruction must be available on this schedule. If a university hospital is to be constructed, the dean and his deputy for clinical programs must begin work on the plans for this massive project as soon as possible after the appointment of the dean.

If, in the early planning for the new medical school, the use of existing hospitals for its clinical teaching facilities has been anticipated, then negotiations regarding the details of an affiliation contract between, on the one hand, the dean and his clinical deputy and, on the other, the administrator, the chief of the medical staff, and the chairman of the board of trustees of the hospital, must be launched at an early date. During the early planning and development of the feasibility studies for the new school, vague, general assumptions have frequently been made about the proposed relationship between a school and one or more preexisting community hospitals; these assumptions must be converted into mutually acceptable managerial relationships between the medical school and the hospitals as soon as possible.

Not only must an educational program be organized for medical students in the primary clinical clerking fields of internal medicine, pediatrics, psychiatry, obstetrics/gynecology, and surgery, in addition to elective studies in a great variety of subspecialties; the school also must organize programs of graduate medical education in these five major fields of clinical clerking so that residents and students can study patient care as a coordinated team under the supervision of faculty, as is the prevailing custom throughout North American medical colleges.

8. *Interim Facilities for Research and Planning for Graduate Degree Programs in the Biomedical Sciences.* Faculty members who possess the scientific credentials most desired in the founding of a new medical school are unlikely to respond favorably to recruiting overtures if acceptance of a position is sure to result in an interruption of several years in their ongoing research activity, which is usually supported by a granting agency external to the host university. Thus, the founding dean must be provided with the means to develop a growing list of research facilities, including

animal care resources, to meet this need. Space must be provided in a location that will hold constant until the researcher can move his laboratory into the permanent facility. The researcher's granting agency may or may not approve the relocation of the grant as well as large items of scientific equipment to the new school; another difficulty may arise if the university where the researcher was formerly employed owns equity in major equipment used by the researcher. Certain equipment cannot be transported and may have to be replaced. These specific matters must be given a high priority by the founding dean or by his deputy for clinical and scientific matters. If solutions to these problems of the prospective faculty member cannot be delivered promptly, there is considerable risk that the new school will end up with faculty members substantially lacking in the capacity to engage in formal research activity. This was the unfortunate situation in several of the modestly endowed new medical schools established between 1960 and 1980.

The intellectual climate needed to implant and foster scholarly activity in a new medical school is fragile in the beginning and requires a substantial commitment from the founding dean, the sponsoring university, and the financial backers of the new venture. If the medical school is to be developed by a well-established university that has already reached maturity in the provision of graduate studies in the social and natural sciences and of professional studies in law, business, and so on, then the needs of the new medical school faculty will not be considered either novel or unusual. Newly appointed biomedical scientists can likely find established researchers and scholars in other departments of the university; this would, of course, enhance the potential for collaboration in a variety of scientific studies, including graduate studies in the sciences basic to medicine. A university which is less developed and lacks the full range of disciplines may have little to offer the new medical school; the founding dean may then be left to his own initiative.

Regardless of the wider academic setting of the new medical school, the founding dean should begin immediately to provide the means for the development of scholarly activity. The newly appointed director of the library and learning resources should establish a constantly growing flow of current medical literature to the new faculty as it expands. Although they may be preoccupied with resource planning, the newly appointed faculty members should also consider the development of a series of scholarly presentations to the university and medical community; this series could be enhanced by formal papers presented by candidates for faculty positions who have been invited to visit the new school during recruitment activities.

The development of full-scale doctoral degree programs by the new medical faculty may require a number of years, but there is ordinarily no barrier to appointing postdoctoral fellows who might accompany their mentors from their universities of prior employment.

If the practicing physicians of the surrounding medical community do not have access to an organized program of continuing education pertinent to the private practice of medicine, the founding dean and his new faculty members should make an early effort to establish an annual program with the objectives of refreshing the knowledge of these practitioners and assisting them in the mastery of recent developments in clinical therapy. Obviously, the newly appointed clinicians on the faculty could participate in such a program, along with selected guest speakers and instructors from other teaching centers. Inasmuch as the private practitioners of the surrounding medical community are understandably concerned about the possible impact of the new school on their own professional activities, the founding dean would be well advised to demonstrate to the practitioners the positive value of the school as soon as possible.

9. *Fund Raising for Support of the New School.* Every new medical school requires enormous resources. During the period from 1960 to 1980, it was rare for a sponsoring university to provide from its endowment or other fixed income the full cost of the constellation of resources needed to establish and develop a new medical school to maturity. Federal and state governments—particularly the latter—often provided the bulk of the needed funding; the private sector, including individuals and corporations, provided the rest. The founding dean who was an effective fund raiser usually came to office with the necessary skills of persuasion or was able to acquire them early in his tenure.

Private institutions are usually well adapted to fund raising; those that are state supported may be slow to develop and sustain organized fund-raising activity. Regardless of its sponsorship, the new school's financial status is such that its leaders should get organized as soon as possible to seek endowments for professorships, the library, and other special projects; in addition, funds for student financial aid, research facilities, special equipment, recreational facilities, and other amenities for students and employees are needed. Particular care should be taken to ensure prompt and appropriate acknowledgment of a gift, as well as a system of recording such in the permanent archives of the institution.

Part Three

꠸꠸꠸꠸꠸꠸꠸꠸꠸꠸꠸꠸꠸꠸꠸꠸꠸꠸꠸꠸꠸꠸꠸꠸

Essential Resources for a Medical School

꠸꠸꠸꠸꠸꠸꠸꠸꠸꠸꠸꠸꠸꠸꠸꠸꠸꠸꠸꠸꠸꠸꠸꠸꠸

The successful initiation, development, and long-term operation of a program of medical education leading to the M.D. degree can no longer be undertaken unless the officials responsible for the program can marshall the full constellation of certain essential resources and guarantee their supply for many years in the future. In fact, the quality of a medical school's M.D. program and other activities is directly related to and dependent on the quantity and quality of these necessary resources: the faculty, finances, physical facilities, library, and teaching hospitals of the medical school. When the LCME has detected deficiencies in the quality of an M.D. educational program, inadequacies in one or more of these resources have been judged to be the cause of the deficiencies.

Between 1960 and 1980, forty new medical schools were established in the United States and four were founded in Canada; each new school has been surveyed annually during its first five to six years of operation and at short intervals thereafter. These surveys of the new schools have provided the members of the LCME and its professional staff with the opportunity to observe and evaluate critically certain experiments in the use of unusual resources to develop educational programs leading to the M.D. degree. In what follows, some of the successes and a number of the failures among these experiments will be discussed.

For example, during the period from 1960 to 1980, several proposals were advanced to establish an M.D. educational program in what was generally called "a medical school without walls." These proposals varied from school to school, but most appeared to be characterized by an intent to enroll sizable numbers of students at a rapid pace without any physical facilities and without employing any basic scientists. Instead of depending on a cadre of full-time teachers to direct the students' education, the schools expected practicing physicians to serve as preceptors who would impart both the scientific base of medical knowledge and the skills needed to apply it to patients. In most of these varied proposals, the use of the organized teaching hospital was to be avoided; clinical medicine was to be taught in the office of practicing physicians, as was the practice in the preceptor system of colonial America. Such proposals to institute a new program of medical education without major resources were not found acceptable by the accrediting authority and ultimately were abandoned. Also, these proposals were never able to gain approval or financial support from either state or federal governments.

The medical schools of North America are so diverse that it is difficult to provide a precise, "mathematical" definition of essential resources. A single successful model does not exist. What follows, however, is a review of the resources available to and required by the schools of medicine in the United States and Canada during the late 1900s. Chapter Six discusses financial resources; Chapter Seven describes faculty; Chapter Eight reports development of new physical facilities during the past twenty years; Chapter Nine evaluates the changes in medical libraries; and Chapter Ten deals with the hospital as the principal site for teaching clinical medicine.

Financial Resources

ఌఌఌఌఌఌఌఌఌఌఌఌఌఌఌఌఌఌఌఌఌఌఌఌ

The most vital resource required for both the original establishment and the long-term development and operation of a medical school is a stable, secure source of income. The next most essential resource is funding for the construction or renovation of physical facilities and for the purchase of furnishings and equipment. The subject of physical facilities is treated in Chapter Eight. In this chapter, the discussion is of the funding for the various programs of the medical school.

Table 15 displays data concerning the changing sources of income and the types of expenditures of the medical schools at ten-year intervals beginning in 1940 and extending through 1980. The data for 1940 and 1950 are derived from Dietrick and Berson's *Medical Schools in the United States at Mid-Century* (1953); the data for 1961, 1970, and 1980 are drawn from the LCME annual questionnaires completed by all schools and from the analyses of these data by the AAMC's Division of Operational Studies. Interested readers can also consult the annual reports on finances for medical education contained in the *Journal of the American Medical Association*.

Sources of Annual Income

Tuition. Early in the history of the United States, the income of the typical medical school was derived entirely from the tuition

Table 15. Trends in Income and Expenditures of Public and Private Medical Schools, Fiscal Years 1940, 1950, 1961, 1970, and 1980.

	1940		1950		1961		1970		1980	
	Public	*Private*	*Public*	*Private*	*Public*	*Private*	*Public*	*Private*	*Public*	*Private*
Number of Schools Reporting	22	37	22	37	44	43	48	45	73	46
Total Income	10.0 100%	15.8 100%	36.5 100%	50.3 100%	194.1 100%	242.0 100%	685.8 100%	829.1 100%	3,178.0 100%	2,523.0 100%
Tuition and Fees	20.0%	35.2%	10.3%	20.0%	4.8%	7.8%	2.4%	4.8%	89.0 2.8%	219.0 8.7%
Endowment	19.4%	41.1%	6.8%	27.0%	0.3%	6.7%	0.2%	3.7%	2.0 0.1%	52.0 2.1%
University Funds	—	—	—	—	1.1%	1.5%	2.3%	3.2%	84.0 2.6%	27.0 1.1%
Gifts	11.4%	26.0%	12.6%	22.5%	0.5%	3.6%	0.9%	1.8%	31.0 1.0%	49.0 1.9%
Sale of Services	—	—	—	—	1.3%	2.2%	0.5%	2.0%	36.0 1.1%	23.0 0.9%
State and Local Governments	49.2%	2.6%	53.4%	7.5%	31.0%	3.5%	29.0%	3.3%	1,105.0 34.8%	86.0 3.4%
Sponsored Programs	—	—	16.9%	23.0%	14.5%	56.0%	51.8%	63.2%	949.0 29.9%	1,071.0 42.4%
Recovery of Indirect Costs/ Grants and Contracts	—	—	—	—	3.7%	4.7%	5.1%	7.4%	104 3.2%	215 8.5%
Faculty Practice	—	—	—	—	3.2%	2.7%	7.5%	4.6%	436.0 13.7%	444.0 17.6%

Hospitals and Clinics	—	—	—	—	—	—	—	—	231.0 7.3%	244.0 9.7%
Miscellaneous Sources	—	—	—	—	9.6%	11.2%	0.2%	6.1%	111.0 3.5%	93.0 3.7%
Total Expenditures	10.0 100%	15.8 100%	36.5 100%	50.3 100%	194.1 100%	242.0 100%	685.8 100%	829.1 100%	3,178.0 100%	2,523.0 100%
General Operating	91.1%	87.0%	75.4%	62.2%	55.5%	44.0%	48.0%	36.8%	2,034.0 64.4%	1,172.0 46.5%
Sponsored, Restricted Programs	8.9%	13.0%	24.6%	37.8%	44.5%	56.0%	51.9%	63.3%	1,103.0 34.6%	1,283.0 50.8%
Research	—	—	—	—	32.8%	42.9%	28.0%	35.9%	577.0 18.1%	653.0 25.9%
Federal	—	—	—	—	24.3%	29.7%	22.9%	27.1%	467.0 14.7%	541.0 21.4%
Nonfederal	—	—	—	—	8.5%	13.2%	5.1%	8.8%	110.0 3.4%	112.0 4.5%
Teaching/Training	—	—	—	—	11.3%	11.1%	13.6%	12.6%	209.0 6.6%	177.0 7.0%
Public Service	—	—	—	—	0.5%	1.9%	10.3%	14.8%	163.0 5.1%	240.0 9.5%
Administrative (Restricted)	—	—	—	—	—	—	—	—	153.0 4.8%	212.0 8.4%
Transfers (Restricted)	—	—	—	—	—	—	—	—	111.0 1.2%	68.0 2.7%

Note: All monetary amounts are in millions of dollars for each year cited.

Sources: Dietrick and Berson, 1953; *Journal of the American Medical Association*, Division of Operational Studies data for 1961, 1970, and 1980.

and fees collected from its students. Although the University of Virginia School of Medicine paid a salary to its first full-time professor in 1825 and the University of Michigan Medical School opened its doors in 1849 with a salaried faculty, most medical schools during the 1800s financed themselves with tuition and fees. Many medical schools of this period were owned by physicians; thus, the fees collected from the students were also a source of profit. According to Norwood (1944), in the early 1800s a student first paid a matriculation fee of three to five dollars. The student then was required to pay a lecture fee to each instructor whose course he was required to take; the instructor then issued the student a "ticket" providing access to the course. Instructors who did not formally print and issue tickets to their courses often used the backs of playing cards as receipts! Separate tickets were sold for dissection exercises and for scheduled attendance at hospitals and clinics. With a set of such tickets, the student could sign the school register in the dean's office and then attend classes and receive credit for his attendance. The total cost of study for two years ranged between $350 and $650 in the mid-1800s. In 1910, according to Flexner, the four-year course of medical studies in Baltimore, Philadelphia, or Chicago cost the student about $1,420. Of the 147 schools visited by Flexner during the 1908-09 academic year, 120 depended entirely on tuition and fees to finance their operating costs; the remaining 24 were schools related to universities and received income from private endowments or appropriations from state legislatures.

By 1940, average income from tuition had declined to 20 percent of total revenues in public schools and 35.2 percent in private schools. By 1950, tuition amounted to 10.3 percent of the total in public schools and 20 percent in private schools. In 1961, the comparable figures were 4.8 percent in public schools and 7.8 percent in private schools. In 1970, tuition reached a low level by amounting to 2.4 percent in public schools and 4.8 percent in private schools. In 1980, tuition as a percentage of total revenues rose slightly to 2.8 percent in public schools and 8.7 percent in private schools. (See Table 15.) It is clear, then, that from 1940 to 1980 tuition dwindled to the status of a relatively modest fiscal resource for the operation of a medical school. The two medical schools that charged the highest annual tuition and fees during the 1981-82 academic year—tuition that averaged $15,675—received 28 percent each of their total incomes from tuition (LCME data). These two private schools and a few others are exceptions to the general trend; they appear to be testing their ability to attract and enroll a class of qualified students during a period when economic constraints have become a national phenomenon and various forms of financial support for medical students are declining sharply.

During the 1970s, a number of commercial medical schools were developed in various Central American countries by profit-seeking entrepreneurs. These schools have very low admission standards (or none at all); thus, large numbers of North American and Canadian students have been enrolled in these schools, which offer an incomplete and inadequate assemblage of the resources necessary for the operation of a medical school of high quality. There can be no doubt that a medical school that disregards prevailing standards of educational quality can operate on the basis of income derived from tuition alone—and make a profit if enough students are enrolled. In the United States and Canada, where the process of accreditation provides public assurance of high quality in accredited schools, experience has demonstrated that the necessary resources cannot be assembled and maintained if a school depends on tuition alone for its income.

Note should be taken here that in some state schools all funds collected from tuition payments revert to the treasuries of the states; of course, in these instances the medical schools also, in turn, receive appropriations from the states. In a few private medical schools, the collected tuition is absorbed by the university, which, in turn, may provide certain services to the medical school.

Endowment, Gifts, and Grants. Income from endowments amounted to 41.1 percent of the total income for private schools in 1940. By 1950, it had declined to 27 percent; by 1961, to 6.7 percent; by 1970, to 3.7 percent; and, by 1980, to 2.1 percent. In publicly supported schools, endowment income amounted to 6.8 percent of total income in 1950; by 1980 it had declined to 0.1 percent. (See Table 15.) The large proportion of income derived from endowments in the private schools in 1940 was the result of philanthropy by private donors, which, according to Robinson (1957), amounted to $500 million during the twenty-five years following Flexner's 1910 report.

Gifts and grants—that is, contributions—from all sources were significant sources of income in 1940 and 1950; since those years, however, they have declined in proportion to the total budget. Included in this category are contributions from the alumni of the schools. The variation in amounts of contributions from the alumni of different schools indicates that some schools have developed very effective ways of garnering support from their graduates; other schools seem to have failed to recognize that their alumni constitute a potentially rich source of continuing income. From 1954 to 1965, the National Fund for Medical Education solicited contributions to the nation's medical schools from corporations; in 1965, corporate gifts to the schools declined as federal funds became available for the support of medical education.

Drucker (1982) has proposed that professional schools be supported by voluntary contribution based on the value added by the professional education of their graduates. He believes that the professional school alumnus should pay 5 percent of his earnings over the national median income, at least until the full cost of the education the alumnus received has been repaid.

Income from Sale of Services. A modest amount of income for most schools is derived from the "sale of services." These services may take the form of teaching efforts by the faculty in other institutions, the operation of special diagnostic facilities by the medical school, or other similar activities.

Income from State and Local Governments. During the 1940s and 1950s, appropriations by the states were the source of approximately half the total income of the nation's state-owned medical schools; thereafter, this source decreased to the level of approximately one third of the total income of the state-owned schools. Some states now provide less than 20 percent of the total income of their school(s), leaving the faculty to generate the bulk of the income needed to pay for the cost of operations.

In many states, the organizational framework for the financing of higher education (including medical education) is provided by state agencies; during the 1960s and 1970s, these bureaucratic structures became more and more complex, often leading to the establishment of state coordinating boards of higher education. In order to obtain one third (or less) of the annual budget for the medical school, the dean of a state medical school often must negotiate with the university administration, the university's regents, the state coordinating board of higher education, the state education agency, the governor's budget staff, and the budget committees of the state legislature. Stirring the annual (or biannual) budgetary stew, these many hands have often produced considerable contraints on the operation of state medical schools. Arcane formulas for faculty/student ratios abound; some are valid and some are not. Several states underwrite the salaries of a specified number of medical faculty members and occasionally specify not only the total number of faculty but also the number of faculty members within each rank and within each grade of each rank (see Savoy, 1977b).

In the past, regional compacts—for instance, the New England Board of Higher Education, the Southern Regional Education Board, and the Western Interstate Commission for Higher Education—provided for the transfer of state funds to out-of-state public and private schools in partial support of the cost of educating residents of the states providing the funds (Savoy, 1977a). The activities of these programs have diminished due to the establishment of new schools in all but six of the fifty states. As noted previously, of the six states that do not operate medical schools, three are involved in the University of Washington's Washington/Alaska/Montana/Idaho (WAMI) consortium. Wyoming, Delaware, and Maine have direct contacts with out-of-state schools to subsidize portions of the cost of educating specified numbers of their state residents.

During the 1960s, when national attention was focused on the need to expand educational programs for physicians, some states enacted legislation that provides for the transfer of tax revenues to private medical schools, usually with the requirement that increased numbers of state residents be enrolled in those schools. With the exception of Texas, most states limited their payments to an annual capitation in the range of $2,000 to $10,000. Other states have attempted to develop similar programs but have encountered constitutional barriers. Although this flow of tax revenues to private schools has been stable and effective in some states, in others the amount of capitation has been subject to political manipulations during every cycle of legislation appropriations. As the states continue to encounter the fiscal constraints that became widespread during the late 1970s and early 1980s and as the supply of practicing physicians increases, the stability of these transfers of state funds from states to private medical schools will surely be subject to increasing scrutiny.

In addition to receiving financial support from the states, a few medical schools receive annually budgeted support from one or more municipalities. For example, Eastern Virginia Medical School receives income from several municipalities, and the University of Cincinnati School of Medicine has received support from the city of its location.

Sponsored Programs and Recovery of Indirect Costs from Grants and Contracts. Until the mid-1900s, sponsored programs of research, teaching, and training for special purposes were small in size in most schools and nonexistent in a number of them. In a few of both the best-endowed private schools and the best-funded state schools, private sources provided irregular financial support for research projects or a modicum few fellowships for advanced study. University endowments, foundations, corporations, and private individuals have provided modest sums of money to finance the equipment, technical support, and supplies used by salaried faculty members in their efforts to develop new scientific knowledge. The development of a massive effort in biomedical research did not begin until Congress started to appropriate annually increasing sums to be used by the National Institutes of Health in underwriting selected research projects by medical faculty members.

In 1940, federal support for research was wholly lacking in the state schools; in private schools, federal support for this activity amounted to only $33,000 (Dietrick and Berson, 1953). In 1950, federal support of research in seventy schools totaled $14.4 million and thereafter grew rapidly. In 1970, the state schools received 51.8 percent of their total income from grants and contracts from all sources, and the private schools received 63.2 percent. By 1980, research grants and contracts were the source of 29.9 percent of the total income in the state schools and 42.4 percent of the total income in the private schools. (See Table 15.)

In reviewing the aggregate data on this source of income for all schools, we must avoid certain misconceptions. In 1979, 40 of the 126 accredited schools received 74 percent of the total amount of funding for biomedical research; this was a relatively steady state for this group of schools from 1963 to 1979 (Perry, Challoner, and Oberst, 1981). The range of the funding for sponsored programs among these 40 schools is quite striking. In 1980, the first-ranked school of these 40 spent more than $52 million on restricted research; the hundredth-ranked school (of the total 126 schools) spent $1.7 million. The remaining schools spent considerably less. As one would expect, the most recently developed schools ranked below the hundredth-ranked school.

Each research grant or contract received by a medical school specifies in its budget the categories in which specific amounts can be expended. The granting agency holds the school responsible for administering the grant or contract, and auditors periodically determine whether the terms and stipulations of the grant have been upheld. Each grant received by a school provides for the expenses incurred by administrative, personnel, purchasing, and payroll services, as well as the rental or leasing of equipment and space. Appropriate allocations for utility and maintenance costs are also included. The rate of these indirect costs incurred in fulfilling the objectives and stipulations of federal grants is negotiated between the school and the federal government at intervals. Most university fiscal officers and medical school deans are convinced that the indirect cost rate does not reimburse the school for costs arising from the administration of grants. Every now and then, government agency administrators or members of Congress attack the overhead rate; in 1982, for example, the federal Office of Management and Budget (OMB) arbitrarily proposed a 10 percent reduction of overhead rates. The OMB also has threatened to impose an exceedingly stringent system of reporting and accounting on each faculty member who receives a fraction of his salary from a grant. Each regulation imposes administrative costs, and the school must rely on other sources of income to meet these unreimbursed costs.

Faculty members, who usually rejoice in receiving a grant from a source external to the school, frequently have difficulty in comprehending the nature, and certainly the magnitude, of the overhead charges. The dean and the principal fiscal officer of the school should maintain a program to educate the faculty on the expenses incurred in providing the administrative infrastructure for each accepted grant.

Faculty Practice Plans: Income from Hospitals and Clinics. During the last two decades, the amounts of income derived from programs of self-support have increased. These programs include faculty clinical practice plans, which provide a substantial part of the salaries of the clinicians active in the plans; payments by the hospitals of all or part of the salaries of full-time faculty members who are assigned to them; and the operation of a variety of health care systems, such as health maintenance organizations. In the state schools, income from faculty practice plans amounted to 3.2 percent of their total income in 1961, 7.5 percent in 1970, and 13.7 percent in 1980. In the private schools, these plans provided 2.7 percent of their total income in 1961 and 4.6 percent in 1970; in 1980, this source amounted to 17.6 percent of the total income (see Table 15). With respect to all sources in this category, the percentage of total income derived from programs of self-support increased from 12.2 percent in 1970–71 to 37.1 percent in 1980–81 (Jolly and Smith, 1981).

The statistical evidence suggests that the medical schools are relying increasingly on the income received from medical practice plans. In 1979–80, one school received 55 percent of its total income from its practice plan; the school that ranked seventieth (among the 126) received 10 percent of its income from this source (Hilles and Fagan, 1977). In a survey conducted in 1981, eighty-seven schools reported the operation of an organized medical practice plan (Schmidt, Zieve, and D'Lugoff, 1981). The plans are as varied as the schools that have them. But there appear to be common objectives to control the volume and the time expended in faculty practice, to provide competitive compensation for the faculty of the clinical departments, and to retain a portion of the net earnings for the benefit of educational and research programs of the clinical departments and the institution at large. Here we need to point out that all university faculty members add an average of 21 percent of their basic, college-derived salaries to their total income through professional activities external to the school (Margarell, 1980).

Total Income

During the 1979–80 academic year, 119 fully developed medical schools reported incomes totaling $5.701 billion; in state schools, the total income was $3.178 billion, and in private schools it was $2.523 billion. In the same year, an additional $773 million became available to support the expanded functions of the medical schools through affiliated institutions, but these funds were not included in the fiscal records of the schools.*

In interpreting these income totals for the 1979–1980 academic year, several considerations should be kept in mind. Since these figures were compiled, the schools have lost the federal capitation as a source of income (see Chapter One for a description of the evolution of this source). Although the dollar amounts derived from federal research grants *appear* to be increasing slightly, the *real* value of this source of income has been declining for several years due to the escalation of all the costs involved. The number of new grants approved annually by the National Institutes of Health has declined in the early 1980s, and some older grants that received funding for a number of years have been discontinued. The recession of the early 1980s has imposed stringent financial constraints on some state budgets; these states, as a result, have forced their state universities to reduce their budgets by 5 to 7.5 percent, instead of providing them with an increase in their annual budgets to offset the effects of inflation. As a further result, the medical schools in these states have been required to reduce or eliminate certain programs and activities. A continuation of the recession through the mid-1980s will probably result in further cutbacks in the programs and activities of the state medical schools. At the same time, some private schools have been forced to draw on their meager fiscal reserves and limited endowments to pay for operating deficits. Several medical schools have been identified as likely prospects for fiscal insolvency by the mid-1980s, unless expenditures can be reduced and new sources of income can be found.

Note: These and other data that follow in this chapter, if not cited specifically, are derived from the LCME Annual Questionnaire completed by all medical schools.

The troubled fiscal circumstances of many of the nation's medical schools have been matters of fact for several years. In 1970, in testimony before the U.S. Senate and House of Representatives Committees on Appropriations, John Cooper, president of the AAMC, reported that sixty-one medical schools—more than half of the total in that year—had been awarded special projects grants on the basis of financial distress. During the 1970s, the federal government gradually reduced the funds for this purpose, but several schools were still receiving annual distress grants due to their financial plights in 1982.

It is clear from the preceding review of income sources that most medical schools faculties, through their own efforts, are paying a substantial part, if not the majority, of the annual expenditures of the medical schools. Perhaps the time has come to bury the common perception, held throughout university circles, that "the medical school is bleeding the university dry." Indeed, numerous university-based policies state, in effect, that "the medical school must sit on its own fiscal bottom"; in other words, the university may not participate in the financing of the medical school. In other institutions, the collected tuition and fees and sometimes the overhead costs recovered from external grants and contracts flow right through the financial books of the medical school and end up in the university or state treasury, sometimes without equivalent, reciprocal appropriation to the medical school faculty members who actually earned these often substantial sums.

Expenditures by the Medical Schools

The data in Table 15 indicate a shift in the distribution of expenditures between 1970 and 1980. In 1970, the public schools expended 48 percent of the total on general operating expenses and 51.9 percent on sponsored activity, which includes research and research training; in 1980, these schools expended 64.4 percent and 34.6 percent, respectively, on general operating expenses and sponsored activity. In the private schools, general operating expenses absorbed 36.8 percent of the total in 1970 and 46.5 percent in 1980; 63.3 percent was expended on sponsored activity in 1970 and 50.8 percent in 1980. Because all expenditures for sponsored programs

**Table 16. Distribution of U.S. Medical School Expenditures
by Department, 1979–80.**

Department	Total	General Operating	Sponsored and Restricted
Total Expenditure, Millions of $	5,592	3,206	2,386
%, Total	100.00	100.00	100.00
Total Basic Sciences	14.91	11.25	20.14
Anatomy	1.77	1.86	1.69
Biochemistry	2.48	1.70	3.57
Microbiology	2.13	1.59	2.90
Pathology	1.84	1.66	2.13
Pharmacology	2.11	1.53	2.94
Physiology	2.25	1.68	3.06
Other	2.33	1.23	3.83
Total Clinical Science	53.28	46.51	61.90
Anesthesiology	2.48	2.90	1.92
Dermatology	0.51	0.38	0.70
Family Medicine	1.93	2.03	1.86
Medicine	12.90	9.84	17.15
Neurology	1.79	1.39	2.34
Obstetrics/Gynecology	2.97	2.80	3.22
Ophthalmology	1.43	1.21	1.73
Orthopedics	0.78	0.81	0.74
Otolaryngology	0.58	0.61	0.54
Pathology	2.21	2.18	2.27
Pediatrics	5.24	4.17	6.73
Physical Medicine	0.58	0.35	0.91
Psychiatry	4.87	4.38	5.61
Public Health/Preventive Medicine	0.93	0.50	1.53
Radiology	3.57	2.92	3.36
Surgery	6.05	6.57	5.40
Urology	0.32	0.34	0.31
Other	4.14	3.12	5.58
Total Other Academic	1.88	1.79	2.04
Allied Health	0.42	0.52	0.32
Nursing	0.25	0.32	0.16
Dentistry	0.03	0.02	0.05
Other	1.18	0.95	1.51
Interdisciplinary Centers and Institutes	3.74	2.23	5.81
Dean's Office	2.81	2.97	2.63
Library	1.04	1.71	0.15
Other Academic Support	2.86	3.28	2.32
Student Support	0.81	1.29	0.17
Institutional Support	6.23	10.38	0.69
Operation and Maintenance of Plant	5.51	9.53	0.09
Scholarships and Fellowships	0.92	0.74	1.17
House Staff	3.86	5.85	1.16
Other	2.14	2.46	1.74

Note: This table is based on data reported by 119 medical schools.
Source: Journal of the American Medical Association, 1981c, 246, 2925.

are restricted, each school can do nothing other than follow the terms of each grant or contract. The funds available for the payment of general operating expenses are divided among the administrative units of each school, a division that is determined by the local authorities. Although some variations are to be found from school to school, it is possible to calculate the average amounts in the distribution of expenditures; this analysis is provided in Table 16.

Regular operating expenditures vary considerably from school to school. During the 1979–1980 academic year, the largest general operating budget was $84 million; each of the top ten schools (in terms of general operating budgets) expended more than $50 million. The median operating expenditures of 110 fully developed schools amounted to $26.8 million. The lowest total for operating expenditures by an established school, which funded the usual cluster of programs and activities in undergraduate medical education, was $8 million. The characteristics of a school with an annual operating budget of $8 million and sponsored program expenditures of less than $1 million are vastly different from those of a school with total expenditures of $140 million.

Experience with Expenditures by New Medical Schools, 1960–1980. In its careful surveillance of the forty new medical schools established between 1960 and 1980, the LCME has collected considerable data on the financial operations of these schools during the early years of their development. The following analysis is based on a representative and varied group of new schools; all dollar figures have been converted to their 1980 equivalents.

For this group of schools, the average total expenditures by year were $5 million for Year One, the first year of instruction of the charter class, $6 million for Year Two, $8.5 million for Year Three, and $12.2 million for Year Four, the year the first M.D. degrees were awarded. The median expenditures for general operating purposes were $3 million for Year One, $3.3 million for Year Two, $5.2 million for Year Three, and $7.6 million for Year Four. The differences between the two sets of figures arise from expenditures for sponsored research, which always develops slowly in new schools, one-time capital expansions or renovations of physical facilities, purchases of a vast amount of equipment and material for teaching purposes, books and journals for the library, and the nonrecurrent costs of recruiting and relocating new faculty members.

No new medical school can achieve complete development during the first four years of operation; most schools experience continued growth in their fiscal operations for at least the first ten years of operation. Furthermore, no proposal for the development of a new medical school in the near future can be considered viable unless the proponents of the new school can demonstrate a secure source of income in the amounts related to the median figures listed above (in 1980 dollars).

Cost of Medical Education. During the 1979–80 academic year, United States medical schools expended a grand total of approximately $5.75 billion; this figure included about $2.4 billion expended for the support of sponsored programs. The expenditures for the operation of the educational programs and all other activities of the schools totaled $3.35 billion. During that year, 65,497 medical students, 13,364 graduate students in the biomedical sciences, 3,485 postdoctoral fellows, 42,266 resident physicians in programs of graduate medical education, and 92,596 students in other programs were enrolled in the schools. In addition to these, a large but unknown number of physicians were enrolled in brief courses in continuing medical education.

Those responsible for the sponsored program activity (including research) and for all the educational and medical care programs consisted of 50,536 full-time and 9,550 part-time faculty members and 89,077 volunteers. Faculty members are assisted in these wide-ranging activities by technical support staffs, clerical employees, and numerous other people who provide administrative, managerial, and building maintenance services. Within a single week, a typical, well-rounded faculty member may devote time to working on a definitive research project for which he is the primary investigator and on other research projects in which he is a participant; to seeing patients, to which he may devote two full afternoons in an office or clinic setting; to teaching freshman or sophomore medical students one or two hours and making patient rounds with junior medical students for three mornings; to participating in major problem-solving clinical conferences involving residents and fellows and in one or two seminars for graduate students; to attending meetings of the admissions, promotions, or curriculum committees; and to addressing the local Lions Club at a noon luncheon meeting. He may also devote time to preparing for formal presentations and studying various sources of new knowledge, such as scientific and clinical journals in "hard" copy or retrieved by electronic means.

These data on the total expenditures of the medical schools and the numbers of students enrolled in the various programs of medical education, along with an approximate accounting of the average faculty member's time, may appear to provide the basis for a precise accounting of the cost of educating a physician. Such an accounting, however, is not a simple undertaking. Only an intricate time-and-motion study of the activities of each faculty member performed by an informed observer, in addition to a study of the cost of using the physical facilities and of the library and operational expenses incurred by the M.D. program, could provide an accurate estimate of the costs of educating one medical student for one year. Yet, in 1974, such an estimate—based on the study of the costs of medical education in fourteen medical schools in 1972—was reported by the Institute of Medicine (IOM). According to the IOM study, *Costs of Education in the Health Professions,* the average net educational cost per student for one year was $12,650 in 1972; in the sample schools, the cost per student ranged from $6,900 to $18,650.

In 1974, the AAMC Committee on the Financing of Medical Education reported its findings on the unit cost of medical education: the range of costs in six private and six public schools was from $16,000 to $26,000. If the average cost and the range of costs computed in the IOM study are converted to 1980 dollars, the average cost increases to $24,916 and the range of costs becomes $13,591 to $36,734. When converted to 1980 dollars, the range of costs computed in the AAMC study becomes $31,515 to $51,211. In both the IOM and AAMC studies, attempts were made to define the cost of the M.D. program, but the consensus is that the studies represent reasonable cost estimates rather than exact calculations.

Forecasting Next Year's Budget. Preparing a budget of expenditures for the next fiscal year for a branch plant of a large manufacturing corporation appears to be a relatively uncomplicated procedure when compared to preparing such a budget for a medical school. *On A Clear Day You Can See General Motors* (Wright, 1979) provides a good summary of corporate budgeting. In the commercial setting, the process involves an extrapolation of cost-of-living and merit increases with respect to personnel salaries and wages (which are often fixed by contracts with several labor unions); of the costs associated with management and plant maintenance; of all other operating expenses, raw materials, depreciation of physical assets, insurance, taxes, Social Security payments, contributions to pension funds; and of allocations to contingency funds. The sum represents total expenditures, which are then scrutinized by the board of directors and officers of the corporation in the corporate board room. Here, the price of next year's manufactured product is set after the advertising costs are added, the total earnings from sales are forecast, and some worry is expressed concerning the potential amount of the dividends the shareholders of the corporation can expect to receive. Income from product sales is transferred to the branch plant executive, who disburses the funds in direct accordance with the approved budget. If sales fall below forecasts, the dividends paid may amount to little or nothing. Product prices may be raised or lowered during the year, in accordance with sales trends. If a loss results at the end of the year, capital reserves are drawn upon, loans are sought, and capital assets are sold; if the losses continue to mount up, then the corporation may ultimately fail.

In contrast to this example drawn from the corporate world, the medical school—which is a kind of educational and service "branch" of the university—pays neither property nor income taxes; it is not involved in dividend payments to shareholders because its activities do not generate a profit. Although the medical school collects tuition in payment for its product, education, the payments contribute only a minor fraction of the operating costs and, in some schools, the university or state treasury pockets this form of income. Of course, other differences between the corporate and educational worlds arise from the faculty's receipt of funds for research and training grants and payments for the delivery of medical care to patients. Even in this respect, the universities may take from the medical schools the income they derive from the retrieval of indirect costs. Distinguishing the medical school from the corporation is the fact that the medical school dean, the "branch plant" manager, has to acquire the medical school's income for the next budget from, for the most part, the efforts of the faculty and the support staff; contributions from the sponsoring university or the state government account for, at the most, one fourth of the total revenues. General Motors was never like this!

As I noted in Chapter Three, the medical dean reigns but does not rule; unlike the manager of a corporate branch plant, he does not occupy the commanding position in budgetary projections. The earnings by the faculty members are largely organized within each department; the chairman and the ranking members of each department have a vested interest in the disposition of their earnings through grants, contracts, and fees for services rendered. The dean of the medical school, therefore, must be intellectually and diplomatically adroit in developing a consensus on the disbursement of the income generated by the faculty members and, in the process, must endeavor to build the strength of the entire school rather than permit the pooling of resources in affluent departments.

On Reducing the Budget. For several decades prior to the 1980s, most schools were able to expand their annual operating budgets on the basis of increases in a variety of sources and amounts of income. The spiraling inflation of the 1970s and the resulting fiscal constraints of the early 1980s have required some schools to hold their expenditures level for one or more years, and in some instances the medical schools have been required to reduce their expenditures. In those schools with expanding faculty practice plans, reductions mandated by the sponsoring universities or state governments have been absorbed, either completely or partially. Those schools that have not been able to offset the reductions in one way or the other have developed various methods of reducing their budgets (see Weston, 1982).

The first method commonly used to reduce expenditures is to cause "the rain to fall on the just and unjust": in other words, reductions across the board for each department, division, and administrative cost center of the school. When faced with shrinking fiscal resources, the medical school dean usually proposes this method once, but only once, before considering other means of economizing. A much tougher approach is to persuade the members of the faculty to accept eleven months of salary instead of the usual twelve.

Because most operating costs arise from the salaries paid to faculty members, attempts can be made to reduce expenditures for the faculty by freezing or delaying the appointment of successors to those members who retire or resign to go elsewhere. Incentives to induce early voluntary retirement of senior faculty members could be developed; these incentives could take the form of cash settlements or part-time salary arrangements to supplement retirement plans. One founding dean established a policy that enabled him to shift the funds for the salary of a vacated position to a department where another position was needed. Senior faculty members who are nearing retirement age could receive salaries that are either entirely or partially paid from "soft-dollar" sources, such as short-term grants or contracts, rather than from "hard-dollar" sources.

Programs and activities that are funded by hard dollars could be eliminated if they are poorly justified. Attempts to eliminate entire departments, institutes, or other major educational programs should be planned very carefully; some of these programs and activities are supported by large numbers of people who are quite capable of mounting fierce political campaigns on behalf of the program or activity slated for elimination—an experience to which several former deans can testify bitterly.

A period of financial retrenchment often has provided the medical school dean and the university president with justification for insisting on evaluations of the effectiveness of every academic department, especially if periodic reviews are not the local custom. The Institutional Self-Study Program of the LCME offers a general outline for such a review; the LCME's program can be supplemented by external reviews of the departments, departmental chairmen, and dean.

Lessons Learned

1. *Inadequacy of Tuition Income Alone.* No medical school can expect to develop the full constellation of resources necessary

to achieve national standards of quality in its educational program if its principal source of income is tuition.

2. *Very High Tuition Rates and Possible Limitation of Enrollment to the Affluent.* In the early 1980s, increases in the tuition charged in some private schools, along with cuts in the financial aid available to needy students, will inevitably restrict enrollments in those schools to members of affluent families; applicants of limited financial means will be excluded unless special provisions are made to support and assist them.

3. *Improving Fund Raising.* For the most part, the medical schools have not devoted enough attention to soliciting permanent endowments or to organizing fund-raising efforts aimed at corporations and the medical alumni. Every medical school dean should explore this potential source of income for his school, and departmental chairmen should accept substantial responsibility for raising funds for their domains from private sources. The private schools have been more effective in raising funds than the state schools; however, both private and public schools may have grown overly dependent on federal and state aid during 1965 to 1980, when this form of assistance for medical education was widely available. Steven Beering, director of the medical center and dean of the Indiana University School of Medicine, a state-supported school, has established twenty-four endowed chairs during his ten years in office; this striking accomplishment illustrates the potential for increasing private support of the programs in any medical school. To establish an endowed chair at the Indiana University School of Medicine, a private source must donate a minimum of $250,000. Private universities may require two to three times this amount to endow a chair.

4. *Deferred Payment of Full Costs by Students.* The dean and faculty should make every possible effort to encourage and facilitate the participation of the students in paying for the actual costs of their education. This can be done by deferring part of the cost to the student until the completion of all training. Drucker's proposal for repayment of educational costs by professional school alumni based on their earnings over the national median income should be evaluated.

5. *State Government as Only Stable External Source of Income.* Until the 1980s, state support of medical education was

the most stable and dependable source of income for the state schools and, to a lesser extent, some of the private schools. Some state governments regulate their educational institutions excessively and thereby place great administrative burdens on the officials of their medical schools. The federal government seems unlikely to fund anything on a continuing basis.

6. *Faculty Understanding of Overhead Charges to Research Grants.* Misunderstanding about the significance of overhead costs involved with research grants and contracts are so prevalent among faculty members, government administrators, and members of Congress that every medical school dean should develop ongoing programs to justify systems for the fair and equitable retrieval of the expenses incurred in conducting programs that receive external support.

7. *Increases in Earnings by Faculty.* Increases in the income derived from faculty earnings may represent a response by the schools to the loss of federal capitation and to the relative decline in federal support of sponsored programs and research projects. Those medical schools that have not yet developed some form of faculty practice plan to regulate individual earnings should do so promptly, even if some full-time faculty members with high incomes from clinical practice object. The dismal financial circumstances most medical schools face in the early 1980s justify the adoption of draconian reforms in financial management. It is patently unfair for an individual faculty member to retain all practice or consultation earnings he receives while he holds a full-time position on the faculty of the school. Comparable rules should be imposed on the clinicians and on the basic scientists; in future, the latter may become involved in new ventures in biomedical engineering.

In the effort to moderate, if not completely satisfy, the ever-present public demands for the clinical and scientific services of the faculty member, the traditional triad of functions of the faculty member—teaching, scholarship, and professional service—must be kept in balance. Younger faculty members, who are increasingly scarce and subject to pressures to expand their commitments to the care of patients, may be deprived of the opportunity to achieve the rigorous standards required for academic promotion by their peers on the faculty.

8. *Operating Funds for New Schools.* The experience accumulated in the development of the forty new schools between 1960 and 1980 demonstrates that approximately $3 to $5 million will be needed to attain the prevailing national standards of quality during the first-year enrollment of the charter class. By the fourth year of operation, total expenditures should be in the order of $7 to $12.2 million (in 1980 dollars).

9. *Zero-base Budgeting.* The system of zero-base budgetary planning may have a role in any effort in financial retrenchment, but it seems that judgments of the quality of educational activities should be based on much more than an analysis of the use of the budget dollar. The founding dean of a new medical school is the master of the only real zero-base budget.

The Faculty

The members of the faculty of the medical school are certainly its most important living resource. Through organized departments and committees, they determine the quality of the teaching and learning environment, the nature of the curriculum, and the academic standards by which the achievements of students are judged. They are responsible for the development of scholarly activities of all types, including organized programs of research. Through the evaluation of candidates for appointment and of their current colleagues who are seeking promotions in rank, faculty continually strive to improve the quality of the school. Furthermore, in addition to their educational and scholarly activities, the faculty provide substantial services to the public in the form of the clinical care of patients; as a result, they play a major role in elevating the prevailing standards of medical practice and care. And, finally, faculty also serve the public by providing expert advice and consultation to agencies of federal, state, and local governments and to many organizations within the private sector.

The preceding description of the duties and activities of the medical school faculty of today reflects the extensive replacement of the part-time faculty by the full-time professorial system in the United States. During the late 1800s, the full-time system achieved outstanding success in the major universities of Europe at the same time that significant discoveries of new knowledge in the biomedical and clinical sciences were proceeding at a rapid pace. This system was first extended into the clinical departments of Johns Hopkins University in 1913 and of Washington University in 1914. The change from a part-time to a full-time faculty at these two universities was partly financed by generous endowments from the General Education Board established by the Rockefeller family (Robinson, 1957; Chesney, 1943). By 1950, the full-time members of the medical school faculties in the United States numbered 5,420; they were nearly evenly distributed between the basic and clinical sciences. By 1980, there had been a tenfold growth in the ranks of the full-time medical faculty—to 50,536; 37,696 of these were clinicians. Chapter Six described the financial sources of support for this sizable national professoriate and highlighted the fact that the activities of the faculty generate a large pool of income for each school.

General Qualifications of a Faculty Member

In order to participate effectively in a modern medical school faculty, the full-time member is expected to possess the following general qualifications:

- General mastery of the body of knowledge of his generic specialty (for example, physiology or pediatrics) and a detailed mastery of his area of subspecialization.
- Diligence in maintaining that mastery of his field of specialization as new knowledge is added.
- Intellectual capacity to contribute to that body of knowledge through a variety of scholarly activities, including organized research.
- Motivation, ability, and skills to impart knowledge and understanding to beginning and advanced students and a specific interest in facilitating the efforts of beginning students to learn.
- Capacity and desire to use his knowledge and abilities to attain and further the goals of the university and of organizations external to it, such as nonprofit agencies under university rules and regulations.

With the increasing complexity of the biomedical and clinical sciences, it may no longer be possible for a single faculty member to excel in each area of the classic triad of education, research, and service. Yet as Petersdorf and Wilson (1982) suggest, each faculty member should be proficient in teaching and in at least one of the other two areas, either in research or in service in the clinical setting or administration. Many biomedical scientists and physicians undoubtedly could qualify for membership on the medical school faculty, but not all are motivated to pursue a life which involves teaching beginning students.

If he is a true scholar, the productive faculty member will possess a singular devotion to his subject and to scholarship within it; mastery of the body of medical knowledge and continual efforts to enhance and expand that mastery are characteristics of the true medical scholar. Along with the personal rewards derived from these characteristics, the medical scholar can obtain benefits from collaborating with his colleagues on the faculty and with others, anywhere in the world, who share his interests. And, finally, through self-criticism and constructive criticism by others, the scholar's ideas and efforts can be refined and strengthened (see Highet, 1972). The current challenge in medical education is to arrange for researchers/scholars to devote increased intellectual attention to the problems of learning by young as well as older learners.

Size and Organization of Medical School Faculties

The number of full-time faculty members varies considerably from school to school; the size of the faculty is usually a function of the range of fiscal resources available to the school and of the number of programs and activities maintained by it. During the 1979–80 academic year, the mean number of full-time faculty members in the 116 schools that reported data was 415; 108 of these were basic scientists. In established schools with a stable enrollment, the ratio of medical students to full-time faculty members was 1.3 to 1.0; from 1976 to 1981—a period when student enrollments reached a maximum—this ratio remained unchanged. Calculations of student/faculty ratios are meaningless during the early years of development of new schools: the early classes are small in size and well below the targeted enrollment to be attained once the full constellation of resources is assembled.

The majority of the medical schools in North America have followed the European university system of organizing the faculty into departments centered around well-established specialties. The German universities, which profoundly influenced the reorganization of American medical education during the early 1900s, organized their faculties of medicine into administratively separate institutes. Each institute was presided over by a director, whose title was *Geheimrat*. This individual held almost absolute power over the teaching, research, and clinical activities of his institute, including the original and continuing appointment of faculty members. Furthermore, he retained his remarkable powers for life. With significant modifications, the German model has been adopted in all but a few of the North American schools.

The Chairman. The chairman of a medical school department is usually selected by a search committee that functions in a manner similar to the search committee for a dean (see Chapter Three). Continuation in the administrative position of chairman may be at the pleasure of the dean; usually, a chairman's tenure in office is extended annually by the dean, the university president, and the board of trustees. A few schools have appointed individuals to the chair of a department for terms of five to seven years; two thirds of the North American schools have established a mechanism to review the performance of an incumbent chairman after a period of five years in office (Smythe and others, 1978). The powers of the chairman of a department vary from school to school; however, the strong chairman (whose powers do not quite match those of the German *Geheimrat*) is the prevailing custom. The chairman usually controls the allocation of space within the departmental territory. He is responsible for presenting the budget for salaries of faculty and support staff for the next year and for recommending faculty members for promotion. The chairman approves all proposals for research grants before they go forward to the dean, and he approves or rejects proposed publications by the members of his department. The manner in which the chairman exercises these elements of his authority determines whether the intellectual talents of the faculty are developed and facilitated or stifled. It is fortunate that the custom of reviewing the department on a periodic basis provides oppressed faculty members with a mechanism to rid themselves of a petty tyrant. On the one hand, according to Petersdorf (1971), the chairman is here to stay, and the powers of his office should be increased. On the other hand, Strauss (1973) thinks that departments have become power bases of excessive strength and as such resist the inevitable and continuing changes in the disciplinary boundaries of research and teaching.

Number of Faculty Members in Each Discipline. In both the basic science and clinical fields, the majority of potential faculty members have been educated on a fairly narrow base; that is, they have spent most of their time in the formal study of a progressively narrower band of knowledge. As a result of this subspecialization, a major generic course—for example, physiology—may require a subspecialist to teach each segment in the course. If the course is divided along organ system lines, a cardiac physiologist will be responsible for instruction on the functioning of the heart and circulatory system; however, this individual may claim to possess little knowledge concerning the functioning of the central and peripheral nervous systems, the domain of the neurophysiologist. Thus, the faculty of each discipline should include representatives of each subspecialty so that they can collectively cover the general field of instruction in each generic course offered to medical students. As a faculty is being organized in a new school or revised in an established institution, it is essential that each departmental faculty contain that number of individuals adequately qualified to cover the subject. Furthermore, in most situations, the members of the faculty will discover that one subspecialist for each subspeciality is not enough; the subspecialist usually finds that he is quite alone in his field with no one with whom to discuss his ideas, inspirations, analyses of the current body of knowledge, or proposals for additions to that body. Thus, experience has demonstrated that a "critical mass" of faculty in each speciality is essential for the well-rounded development of the medical faculty.

The size of each departmental faculty should be determined by the number of students from the various degree programs enrolled in the courses offered by the department; the size is also determined by the magnitude of the professional services offered by the department (such as patient care or the operation of diagnostic laboratories) and by the size and number of organized research programs. As one would expect, there is a wide range in the numbers of full-time faculty members in each department.

Table 17 displays data on the size of the principal departments of the medical school. The first column of this table lists the average strength of the departments during 1966 through 1969 in twenty-five schools: these data were developed by Smythe (1970) in a study of departmental development. The next column lists the average numbers of full-time faculty members in thirty-five of the schools established before 1960; these schools were surveyed by the LCME during the 1980–81 academic year. The final three columns list the average numbers of full-time faculty members in major departments of the schools established between 1960 and 1980. The first of these three final columns lists data for the first year of instruction of the charter class in these schools, for the fifth year of instruction, and for the tenth year of instruction. Data for the first year of instruction are based on analysis of forty new schools; for the fifth year, twenty-eight schools are analyzed; and, for the tenth year, only fifteen schools are analyzed (some new schools had not been in operation long enough to reach the fifth or tenth year of instruction, for which these data were obtained). Blank spaces in the columns are due to unavailability of data.

Although all the schools established before 1960 are organized into departments, several of the forty new schools have developed different systems. At Michigan State University College of Human Medicine, faculty members who teach basic science courses to medical students are drawn from the departments of the university and other health professional schools. The dean of the medical school budgets funds for each generic discipline of the M.D. degree curriculum, and these funds are then transferred to the appropriate departments of the university in what appears to be a "fee for teaching services" arrangement. The Brown University Program in Medicine has established a flexible arrangement whereby faculty members who share common interests in a subject organize themselves into compatible groups for teaching purposes. A faculty member may change groups if his interests change, and each course is taught by individuals with the appropriate qualifications. The

Table 17. Average Number of Faculty Members by Departments.

Department	Established Schools		New Schools		
	1965–66 (35 schools)	1980–81 (35 schools)	Year 1 (40 schools)	Year 5 (28 schools)	Year 10 (15 schools)
Anatomy	10.0	16.0	4.2	8.0	11.6
Biochemistry	11.0	16.0	4.6	7.3	9.7
Physiology	10.0	15.0	5.7	8.0	10.4
Microbiology	8.0	14.0	4.0	7.0	9.0
Pharmacology	7.9	13.0	4.5	6.6	10.5
Internal Medicine	36.0	93.0	6.4	17.0	4.2
Neurology	8.6	13.0	—	—	—
Family Medicine	—	14.0	3.9	5.7	12.6
Pediatrics	16.0	43.0	3.7	10.0	18.0
Psychiatry	23.0	45.0	6.0	12.0	21.0
Obstetrics/Gynecology	7.6	17.0	3.0	4.9	8.4
Surgery	17.0	32.0	3.3	9.0	24.7
Anesthesiology	8.3	21.0	—	—	—
Dermatology	4.5	3.0	—	—	—
Ophthalmology	4.6	8.0	—	—	—
Orthopedic Surgery	3.4	6.0	—	—	—
Otolaryngology	6.3	5.0	—	—	—
Physical Medicine and Rehabilitation	7.6	6.0	—	—	—
Preventive Medicine	9.7	10.0	—	—	—
Radiology	11.9	30.0	—	—	—
Urology	—	2.0	—	—	—

Sources: 1965–66 data from Journal of Medical Education, 1966, 42, 798; 1980–81 data for new schools from Liaison Committee on Medical Education, Confidential records.

University of Nevada School of Medicine has no separate basic science departments; all faculty members belong to a common basic science division, but each major discipline has a designated leader.

The University of California at San Diego School of Medicine is another school that relies in part on the university departments for instruction in a limited group of basic science subjects. The members of the university's departments of chemistry and biology provide instruction in molecular biology and cell biology; other contributions come from social scientists in university departments. Most of the instruction in the basic science fields is undertaken by members of the clinical departments who also possess the Ph.D. degree in a basic science field related to their clinical specialty. From the viewpoint of the medical students, the instruction in the basic science subjects is entirely satisfactory. Yet the question arises whether long-term contributions to the basic sciences can be made by faculty members whose first and primary responsibility is to their clinical specialties. In some circumstances, the clinician/basic scientist undertakes fundamental research in a basic biomedical subject and applies the results of his studies in the clinical setting. In a situation of this kind, due concern should be given to the adequate development of the biomedical sciences. In the development of the Mayo Medical School, individuals from the very large staffs for the clinical fields were solicited to provide instruction in the basic science subjects. The founders of this school may have had little desire to develop baronial basic science departments and, indeed, may have decided to leave the full control of the M.D. degree program in the hands of the clinicians.

Management Within the Department. As the departments have expanded in size and developed complex programs and activities, the burdens on management have grown to such a degree that some highly competent individuals have refused chairmanships because they assumed that they would have to abandon their professional activities for concentrated "paper pushing." Most departmental chairmen in the traditional schools complain about the magnitude of the managerial work expected of them and about the common failure of the university to provide a salary for an adequate administrative assistant. One major contributor to the burden and complexity of modern medical school management is the budget. Since 1950, many medical school departments have reached the point where their annual expenditures range from a half million to several million dollars; a significant number of renowned departments spend more money than some of the smaller medical schools. Research grants require administration and management; and patient care, if it is a service provided by a department, also requires oversight by reliable individuals. In fact, it could be said that each department has become a small specialty college with a large number of beginning, intermediate, and advanced students who take courses, either on a part or full-time basis, within the department's generic specialty.

Solutions to the problems of departmental management have been slow to emerge. Often, they take the form of promoting an efficient secretary to the position of administrative assistant; the results of even this minor measure have been varied. Richard Moy, founding dean of the Southern Illinois University School of Medicine, anticipated the usual plight of the overburdened departmental chairman. In January 1972, at two planning sessions with his newly appointed departmental chairmen, Moy took measures to define and treat the problem:

> The overall responsibilities of departmental chairmen were discussed in light of three major functions: executive, administrative, and managerial. The executive function entails advocacy and explanation for the departments' programs that cannot be delegated. The administrative function is defined by the needs of departmental faculty members (those to whom one ministers—another function which cannot be delegated). Managerial functions including such things as business matters, assemblage of data, preparation of reports, handling of general business correspondence, preparation of departmental budgets, control of expenditures of state and contractural funds, supervision of financial records, business negotiations with external agencies, analysis of internal operating procedures, and other similar functions can be sizeable but also can be delegated.

At a subsequent planning session in May 1972, Moy made the following statement of intent with regard to the management of the new school:

> While many people in academic medicine rise to high positions of management and administrative responsibility, they usually have no specific training for these positions, and I suspect that none of them entered medicine with administration as an expected career goal. In my experience, many competent administrators and teachers have been bogged down by management problems which make them unproductive and cause them to work at things they do not do well or, at best, do grudgingly. Thus, my goal is to have effective management personnel available to all parts of the school of medicine as quickly as resources allow, so that our chairmen and section chiefs can spend most of their time doing those things they are best qualified to do.

During its first ten years, the Southern Illinois University School of Medicine recruited fifty-three professional managers; five held doctoral degrees, thirty-three held master's degrees, and thirteen held baccalaureate degrees in management and other fields. Some of these individuals had experience in the civil service and/or in university management. Only three of the fifty-three managers had had previous medical school experience, but forty of these are now employed by health institutions (Moy, September 1982).

Petersdorf (1980a) has discussed the problems that arise in the management of departments of internal medicine, which continue to grow in size and complexity; he has stressed the need to provide the chairman with adequate managerial support and assistance. Braunwald (1975) suggests that the chairman's chief administrative manager should receive a salary of at least half that of the chairman himself.

Faculty Ranks, Salaries, and Benefits

Medical school faculty members are usually appointed to the rank of instructor (a rare phenomenon in recent years), assistant professor, associate professor, or full professor. Most institutions follow the general rules of the American Association of University Professors; thus, most local bylaws state that an assistant professor who does not achieve promotion to the rank of associate professor within seven years must leave the department and seek employment elsewhere.

During the late 1970s and early 1980s, most of the medical school faculties have aged, and very few younger individuals have received appointments. In this period when few or no appointments have been made, the younger M.D. and Ph.D. graduates have been discouraged from seeking careers in academic medicine. This can only be viewed as an ominous development for the not too distant future.

The AAMC publishes an annual report on the salaries of members of the medical school faculties. According to the 1982 report, the mean compensation for full-time basic scientists for the 1981–82 academic year was as follows:

Instructors	$21,000
Assistant Professors	$28,000
Associate Professors	$35,000
Full Professors	$47,000
Chairmen	$62,000

In the clinical departments, the mean compensation for faculty members was as follows:

Instructors	$30,000
Assistant Professors	$50,000
Associate Professors	$62,000
Full Professors	$77,000
Chairmen	$104,000

Fringe benefits for members of medical school faculties ranged between 5 and 22 percent of the base salary, with a mean of 10.24 percent. Teachers Insurance and Annuity Association/College Retirement Equities Fund (TIAA/CREF) and state retirement plans were the most favored plans in the schools (Taksel, 1982).

Tenure

Tenure is usually assigned to those who hold the ranks of associate professor and full professor; however, in some schools, there may be a waiting period before tenure becomes effective. The basis for promoting faculty members continues to generate discussion, debate, and expressions of dissatisfaction. The "purists" refuse to promote the younger faculty members until they have made "significant contributions to the body of knowledge," the quantity and quality of which often are determined by the departmental chairman rather than according to any general standard. Although lip service is given to the need of the individual to demonstrate adequate teaching skills, in reality the appropriate credit is not usually given to this important component in the overall performance of the faculty member. Also, credit may not be given for the nonteaching activities of the medical faculty. For example, some faculty members become deeply involved in administration, and the clinicians are usually pressed into the care of patients in the hospital setting or in the medical school's practice plan. Also, both basic scientists and clinicians are frequently tapped for contributions to external agencies, such as the National Institutes of Health.

Smythe and his associates (Smythe, Jones, and Wilson, 1982) have written of the problems of tenured faculty members in the medical schools during the early 1980s. They point out that many schools have become "overtenured" because they have not maintained a balance between the number of individuals appointed to tenured positions and the actual resources of the institution. During the early 1980s, some schools have experienced marked reductions in their fiscal resources; as a result, their ability to sustain their support of every tenured faculty member has been threatened.

Tenure was originally devised to protect members of the professoriate from politicians and others so that they could search for truth and speak it in complete freedom without suffering threats to their positions. As the years have passed, more and more people have concluded that tenure can produce "deadwood" and stifle initiative on the part of faculty members who have reached upper middle age. The situation has been exacerbated by the recent enactment of federal statutes that permit a professor to continue in employment until the age of seventy. It is highly questionable whether the universities can continue with the promiscuous appointment of their faculty members to tenure without the security provided by guaranteed resources, such as endowed chairs or a general institutional endowment of considerable magnitude. The problem of "deadwood" among the faculties is so extensive that some schools have instituted periodic reviews of the performance of every faculty member, tenured or not; such review is customary with departmental chairmen and deans, who do not enjoy tenure in their administrative positions. Debates continue to rage over the potential abuse of tenure by faculty members, especially in those institutions that have developed faculty unions with formal bargaining mechanisms and full-time agents who are employed to represent the union members in their negotiations with the university administration. (See the select bibliography for articles and books on the controversial issue of tenure and faculty unions.)

Faculty Governance

The dean of the medical school, the other officials of the deanery, and the departmental chairmen constitute the administrative structure of the institution. Nearly every medical school has an administrative committee composed of the departmental chairmen. The authority of these committees varies from school to school; in some they simply give advice to the dean, and in others they have the authority to select the dean and either extend his term of office or request his resignation.

Governance of the faculty is quite different from administration of the medical school. Early in the history of American medical education, when the total faculty of a medical school numbered two dozen people at most, it may have been possible to arrange meetings of the entire faculty on the format of a town meeting and to address the problems of the institution at those meetings. In the very large contemporary medical school, faculty meetings usually consist of little more than a description of the school's activities; in any event, only a small number of the faculty members attend such meetings. Consequently, faculty meetings are not appropriate for policymaking. Instead, medical school policies are usually defined and refined by an academic policy council. The composition of this council varies from school to school. At one unusual school I visited several years ago, policy was developed by the five most senior members of the faculty. This school had no mandatory retirement policy, I should add; the most senior member of this school's policy council was ninety-two years of age, and the most junior member was a mere seventy-nine.

In the past, many schools appointed every departmental chairman and several people elected by the faculty to serve on the academic policy council; at still others, all full professors serve on the policy-making council. Another system is to seat one elected representative from each department, twelve at-large representatives elected by the faculty, one representative from each affiliated institution, and one representative from the faculty (Liaison Committee on Medical Education data); students may or may not be included on these councils. At some schools, the dean serves as a council member; at others, he is the permanent chairman.

The typical academic policy council entrusts most of its work to standing committees whose members are nominated by an ad hoc committee on committees; the dean and his associates in the deanery often prepare a roster of nominees for this purpose. These standing committees usually include some senior faculty members but do not always include younger faculty members. Student members are judged appropriate for some committees and inappropriate for others. All committees need staff support, if not active oversight by the administration. Effective committees submit an annual report to the academic policy council so that compliance with the policies of the council can be assured. Standing committees are typically formed for the following policy areas: curriculum, student admissions, student promotions and graduation, faculty appointments and promotion, library and learning resources, and research facilities (with subcommittees on the vivarium, the use of radioactive materials, the handling of dangerous substances, computer resources, and other research facilities).

An experimental approach to governance based on the principles of matrix management has been employed at the McMaster University Faculty of Medicine (Evans, 1970). Other schools have examined this method of governance and have decided not to adopt it.

Several universities do not permit separate colleges and schools to develop independent bylaws. Instead, each college or school—such as the school of medicine—is governed by the general bylaws of the university. If this is the local rule, then the academic policy committee could develop a faculty handbook that governs medical faculty affairs in some detail. Newly developed medical schools often operate during their early years without bylaws and, instead, depend entirely on the authority of the dean in governmental affairs.

Lessons Learned

1. *Faculty Duties and Self-Determined Priorities.* At any particular time, most members of the medical school faculty may be at their duty stations in the medical center; however, a significant number of them will be away, serving as visiting speakers, attending professional meetings, acting as consultants, or visiting other medical schools as ad hoc representatives of accrediting agencies. If a faculty is composed of a large number of prominent researchers, the ebb and flow of faculty members from the home base can be extensive and constant. (Sometimes, a medical school dean will encounter a virtual quorum of his departmental chairmen in the late afternoon at one of the airports serving Bethesda, Maryland, the location of the National Institutes of Health.) One chairman, who had become a legend in his own mind, was absent from his post so often that the members of the graduating class asked the dean to arrange a special meeting between themselves and the chairman, whom they had not encountered once during their four years in the school. The request to the deam was prompted by comments about the great man from college mates enrolled at other medical schools, where the peripatetic chairman had been a visiting speaker.

In addition to the problems caused by such extensive absences, activities at the home base may also suffer neglect if the faculty members provide consultations to external agencies for fees. Clinical activities are controlled and organized through faculty practice plans; if they are not, they should be. In recent years, the basic scientists have been sought out by commercial concerns that desire expert advice and opinion in the basic science fields.

The university and medical school should develop policies governing activities that require the faculty member to be absent from the duties for which he is employed. The schools should foster participation in public affairs, but not at the expense of the primary duties in a faculty member's area of professional concern. Fees earned through external consultation should be shared with the medical school in accordance with well-defined guidelines developed by the faculty policy committee. Potential conflicts of interest and unethical relationships should be anticipated and forestalled.

2. *Academic Freedom: Use and Abuse.* The university and the medical school should guard and preserve the academic freedoms of each faculty member. However, each faculty member should be quite circumspect in carefully separating his personal exercise of free speech from any activity that is performed under the auspices of the school. For example, no faculty member should be barred from speaking out on a public issue or from participating in a public rally concerning a controversial issue; but no faculty member should march in a parade with a sign that says "Podunk University Opposes the X Amendment" unless Podunk University has indeed developed such a position through its usual due process. In the same vein, a faculty member should not write a letter to a newspaper editor and sign it with the name of the university rather than his personal name and address. Academic freedom should never be interpreted as academic license.

3. *Appointment Letters.* When an individual is appointed to both faculty and administrative positions, the letters of appointment should be carefully prepared. One letter should cover faculty rank, the question of tenure, compensation and fringe benefits, and the established age of retirement; it should also include a copy of the bylaws and the faculty handbook. A second letter should specify the nature of the administrative assignment and its term, if any. If the administrative appointment is to be at the pleasure of the dean, this should be stated in the letter.

4. *Need for Clinicians to Have Legal Licenses.* No individual should be appointed to a clinical position unless he holds or can readily obtain a license to practice medicine within the state jurisdiction of the medical school. It is very embarrassing when a dean discovers that he has appointed to the faculty a physician who cannot obtain a license to practice medicine.

5. *Communication Within a Department.* A major problem within a departmental faculty concerns communication between the chairman and the members of the department; this problem is usually found in the flow of information from the dean, executive faculty, or other administrative body through the departmental chairman and to the members of the department. For example, I once heard a senior professor at a medical school in the nation's capital say that if his chairman heard in a meeting of the executive faculty with the dean that the Russians were disembarking battle troops at the port of Annapolis and that the Red Chinese were landing paratroopers in the Blue Ridge Mountains of Virginia, it would never occur to him to impart this information to the members of his department. Many faculty members feel that they are neglected and left out and that the fault lies with those who are responsible for middle-level management in the faculty. It is inexcusable for a member of the faculty to go without necessary institutional information; if this occurs, it should be noted whenever the performance record of the chairman is examined.

6. *Faculty Rank for Essential Medical Specialists.* A medical school sometimes finds that individuals who are proposed for faculty membership before they are assigned to service areas of the university hospital have difficulty in earning faculty rank when the traditional criteria for promotion are used. For example, if a university hospital is to be operated, it is essential that the hospital employ radiologists and pathologists, along with other medical specialists, in order to deliver professional services. The hospital cannot function without these individuals and the services they provide. The director of the hospital and the dean of the medical school, however, will soon discover that they cannot hire these specialists unless they offer them faculty rank and recognition on a par with all other members of the faculty. If the dean of the school presents the credentials of a service pathologist to a university-based committee on appoint-

ments that is composed of academic purists with degrees in literature, history, and so on, he may encounter difficulties.

In response to this dilemma and similar problems, several solutions have been offered. One solution involves the establishment of varying tracks for appointment to the faculty and for promotions. One track is designed for the full-time scholar in the traditional sense; this individual usually possesses the time and the resources to convert his efforts into contributions to the body of knowledge in his field. In most instances, he is called on to perform limited educational services; instead, he demonstrates his qualifications for appointment and promotion through the publication of books and articles. A second track is designed for the individual who spends a portion of each working week in clinical activities or in other areas, such as administration; an individual in this track is not expected to make substantial contributions to the body of knowledge in his field; thus, decisions to appoint or promote him are based on judgments of his work in other areas. A third track is reserved for those individuals who contribute to the educational program or some other activity on a part-time basis; most of their income is derived from sources external to the school, which provides them with a small stipend for their part-time services. These three differentiated tracks permit members of the faculty to choose the category that fits their skills and desires.

7. *Developing Bylaws in a New School.* The dean of a new medical school should direct the effort to develop bylaws as soon as the new institution is well launched. During the first years of development, it is better for the school to use the university bylaws or to rely on the benign despotism of an earnest and able founding dean. If the bylaws are developed by a small group of faculty members in the very beginning, they probably will be considered skewed and unacceptable by faculty members who arrive later. This advice is not meant to be a recommendation for long delays, however; once each of the conventional academic disciplines is represented by at least one faculty member who is actively involved in the development of the school, the preparation of the bylaws should proceed. If a dean does not agree to share his originally absolute powers through the development of the appropriate bylaws, he may

find himself losing the enthusiastic support and following of his faculty.

8. *Increased Use of Visiting Professors.* The new schools and some of the older, established ones have not made sufficient use of visiting professors, particularly of those faculty members who are senior but still very active as teachers or clinicians. A visiting professor who is appointed to a term of six to nine months can strengthen the school and permit it an extended period of time to recruit a much-desired appointee for a permanent position. In turn, the visiting professor is often intellectually stimulated by the change of environment.

9. *Need for Basic Science Departments in the Medical School.* During the early 1980s, most educational institutions have been plagued by increasingly stringent financial constraints. In this widespread situation, one often hears rumblings about the possible economies to be achieved through the abolition of the basic science departments and the reassignment of basic science teaching to the science departments of the university. As limited as the experience is in this respect, it raises serious doubts that the educational services required by the medical school can be provided at less expense by the university departments. Other functions, such as biomedical research, are dependent upon massive resources of the fully developed medical school, and these functions cannot be undertaken by the university departments unless they are provided with the necessary major equipment and space. Although basic scientists frequently engage in abstract, pure research, more and more of them are becoming involved in the search for solutions to problems found in the setting of the university hospital. There is a long-standing claim that the new knowledge discovered during one decade by biomedical scientists becomes part of the skills of the practicing clinicians a decade or so later. If the basic scientists on the medical faculty were eliminated or relocated in university departments, then the surviving clinical departments would be forced to employ their own biomedical scientists in order to maintain the quality of their resources.

8

Physical Facilities for Students and Faculty

In the late 1940s and early 1950s, the growth in the expanded medical faculty's educational, research, and clinical care activity created a need for additions to or replacements of the physical facilities in all existing medical schools. By 1960, these facilities were showing signs of age, since most had been built before the "bottom" years of the Great Depression; some buildings had been constructed at the turn of the century. In the early 1940s, the needs of World War II diverted funds and resources from civilian construction projects; none could be undertaken until after VJ day. In the years immediately following World War II, a booming economy was the setting for spiraling inflation and escalating construction costs, as every economic sector rushed to catch up by expanding manufacturing plants, building office buildings, and creating new public and private housing.

Medical School Construction, 1950–1980

In the 1950s, state governments and private donors began to make large contributions to medical schools to defray either the entire cost of new buildings or those amounts needed to qualify for federal matching grants. In 1956, Congress recognized the need to support the construction of facilities to house federally funded research projects by enacting P.L. 84-835. The federal contribution was usually less than 50 percent of the cost of a research building.

Between 1960 and 1980, the forty new medical schools expended $838.7 million for the construction of multipurpose school buildings (LCME, confidential records); of this total, $251.65 million came from U.S. Public Health Service construction grants for educational facilities. In the same period, the eighty-six older schools spent $1.324 billion on new construction; of this amount, the federal contribution was $549.9 million. Thus, the medical schools reported total expenditures of $2.163 billion for the construction of teaching and research facilities (excluding teaching hospitals) during the period from 1960 to 1980.

National Efforts to Assist Planning

In 1959, anticipating the expected surge in medical school construction, the AAMC and AMA established a Joint Ad Hoc Committee on Medical School Architecture; the committee was chaired by George T. Harrell, who had planned and built a modern medical school and hospital at the University of Florida in the mid-1950s. This committee worked closely with staff members of the U.S. Public Health Service, who produced two companion guides to the planning and construction of new medical schools, *Medical School Facilities: Planning Considerations and Architectural Guide* (1964) and *Medical School Facilities: Planning Considerations* (1961). Since their publication, these guides have become somewhat dated, but they still contain useful material.

Two valuable papers by Smythe (1967, 1972) analyzed the resources used by the earliest developing schools; his data were derived from the construction activities of twenty-two new schools established between 1960 and 1970. In 1974, Harrell published *Planning Medical Center Facilities,* his definitive reference guide on the design of new facilities for a medical school and teaching hospital complex at Pennsylvania State University; it includes useful information and assessments of various features of other school buildings constructed in the 1960s and early 1970s. During these years, the U.S. Department of Health, Education and Welfare wisely maintained a central Bureau of Health Manpower Facilities to consider applications for construction grants from the schools. The bureau's professional staff acquired much experience as they monitored construction plans by the schools. Charles Wagner, an architect with the bureau, has shared with me his unpublished notes and a number of letters to various deans advising them about good and bad features of medical school design and construction.

As I have written the bulk of this chapter, I have drawn on the sources mentioned above, on contributions from reviewers of this book and from my peers, and on my own observations gained through visits with accreditation inspection teams to most of the United States and Canadian medical schools. Some founding deans contributed their judgments of and experience with certain features of the buildings they designed; these valuable comments can be found in the papers and articles listed in the select bibliography for Chapter Five. Rather than attempting to write a description of the numerous and varied medical school buildings constructed at a cost of $838.7 million between 1960 and 1980, I have chosen to summarize the experiences various deans have recorded during this fruitful period of twenty years. Thus, the "Lessons Learned" section of this chapter is intended to provide medical educators of the future with some hard-earned insights into the problems of planning and arranging for construction of medical school teaching facilities. The section concludes with some specific recommendations.

Lessons Learned

1. *Relationships Between Programs and Space.* Winston Churchill is credited with the following observation: "First we shape our buildings and ever afterward they shape us." This is an appropriate and practical warning to those who are responsible for determining the number and size of the programs and activities to be housed in a medical school building during the first ten years of growth and then for the remaining forty- to fifty-year life of the structure. Early and fully mature requirements for space must be calculated for the following programs and activities:

- Education of the physician, including medical students seeking the M.D. degree, hospital residents enrolled in graduate medical education, postdoctoral fellows in the basic and clinical sciences, and practicing physicians in continuing medical education.
- Education of basic medical scientists seeking M.S. and Ph.D. degrees.
- Education of individuals in other health professions and occupations, such as dentistry, nursing, and pharmacy, and numerous allied health fields.
- Research in biomedical and behavioral sciences.
- Clinical care of ambulatory patients.
- Amenities for students, faculty, and support staff.

In the United States and Canada during this century, all medical schools have adhered to the responsible policy of enrolling only the number of students in each entering class that can be accommodated in the available lecture rooms and student laboratories. The LCME has also enforced this policy through its authority. Thus, student enrollments in the various educational programs are limited by the design and size of the schoolhouse, which, in turn, are dependent upon the funds available for capital construction and subsequent operation and maintenance. Academic program planners have to project current and future enrollments and define the functions to be housed in a new building from the early years of occupancy through its expected life of forty to fifty years; then they have to join forces with an architect in formulating the definitive plans for the new building.

The need for a careful and comprehensive accounting of the physical resources for a school's programs *cannot be emphasized enough.* If the planners of a school do not set forth their requirements in detail and thereby guide the architect in his work, then the resultant building may be based on a formulaic design of dubious validity, or the architect may indulge himself by following some aberrant fad. Obviously, the degree of detailed planning required demands a significant amount of time on the part of a dedicated group of faculty members and at least one administrator/coordinator who has had extensive experience in medical education, research, clinical care, and the management of medical school personnel.

The task is of such consequence for the future of the medical school that it should not be rushed to completion. Once a contract has been let for construction, any alteration of the design may be either impossible or very expensive.

2. *Size of Required Buildings.* In 1961, the U.S. Public Health Service staff, with the assistance of the AAMC/AMA Joint Ad Hoc Committee on Medical School Architecture chaired by George Harrell, estimated that facilities for basic science instruction, the library, and administrative and support staff space for a class of ninety-six undergraduate medical students require approximately 260,000 gross square feet. Clinical departments were estimated to require approximately 81,000 gross square feet, an area that later proved to be much too small for the clinical faculties that expanded so rapidly during the 1960s and early 1970s. Fourteen years later, Harrell reported that the medical school at Pennsylvania State University allocated 200,170 gross square feet to the basic sciences and 211,640 gross square feet to the clinical sciences (Harrell, 1974). The facilities for the Uniformed Services University of the Health Sciences, which were occupied in 1977, totaled 843,000 gross square feet for a maximum class size of 180 medical students. In 1977–78, the medical school facilities at Texas Tech University, designed for an entering class of 100 students, amounted to 500,000 gross square feet. Other new medical school buildings designed to house the customary cluster of educational programs (excluding the clinical programs housed in a teaching hospital) fall with the range cited here.

An office and a research laboratory for each full-time faculty member require 640 to 1,000 square feet (Harrell, 1974), and additional space must be provided for graduate students and post-doctoral fellows. At least two lecture rooms are needed for undergraduate medical students. Each should contain enough seats for the projected maximum-sized class, along with 25 percent of that number for graduate students, clinical residents, faculty members, and guests. In my opinion, each lecture room also needs old-fashioned blackboards made of slate, twenty feet in width, and extending from three to seven feet from the floor. A simple, nearly infallible system for projecting slides in standard sizes should be permanently installed near a screen, which can be raised and lowered from the ceiling by motor. I have not been impressed by the more technologically elaborate systems for audiovisual presentations that seem to fail frequently and require some immediately unavailable electronic wizard to repair. Although an auditorium is expensive and occupies a large amount of space, if a hall with 500 to 800 seats is not available in the academic health center, one should be built. If possible, the entrance to this auditorium should be at the exterior of the building so that persons attending a function there during the evenings and weekends there need not pass through the security controls usually located at the primary entrance to the school building.

3. *Architects and Architecture.* During the third quarter of this century, architects in the United States (and elsewhere) enjoyed many opportunities to pursue their profession in designing a vast number of new buildings for all purposes, including new medical school buildings built between 1960 and 1980 at a cost of $2.163 billion. Wolfe (1981) has traced the movement of American architects away from the dictum "form follows function" to the experimental principles of architecture fostered by the European Bauhaus school of the 1920s. The ubiquitous solid-glass exterior walls of many buildings—including the uninhabitable Pruitt-Igoe housing project in St. Louis, which the U.S. Department of Housing and Urban Development built in 1955 and abandoned and partly demolished in 1972—are signs of the Bauhaus influence on American architecture. Other dominant features of the Bauhaus cult are small rooms with bare white walls, numerous naked light bulbs, the complete absence of the detailed ornamentation that characterized the earlier Beaux-Arts style, and an apparent scorn for creature comforts. Other wild trends in modern architecture have given us buildings like the Pompidou Center in Paris (which has all of its structural "guts" exteriorized) and the fantasy-like church and apartment houses that Gaudey designed and built in Barcelona.

There is nothing wrong per se in applying modern principles of architecture to the design of a medical school; however, such a facility is highly utilitarian in purpose. Its design should be dictated by the functions to be housed in the facility, and the external appearance should be subservient to those functions; it should not dictate them. The selection of an architect, therefore, poses some hazards, and the following is intended to alert the planners of a new medical school building to these problems.

The modernists have left their mark on some medical school facilities that were designed and built between 1960 and 1980. An architect's prize-winning research building in Philadelphia has laboratories with three walls of floor-to-ceiling glass, which admitted so much light that few scientific activities could actually be undertaken until aluminum foil was glued to the transparent walls. An educational building close to the Canadian border lost so much heat through its glass skin that a costly plastic film had to be applied to the exterior to provide some insulation. In Houston, where air conditioning is required nine to ten months of the year, the interior walls of a similar glass building have to be insulated with heavy, lined draperies, at considerable expense.

Some faults in the design of new medical school facilities are not attributable to the fads of modern architecture. For instance, the original design of one very large school building, constructed at considerable cost, included no provisions for lecture rooms that could seat more than forty people. Wagner (1974) observed numerous auditoriums that were fully equipped to show Cinerama but could not handle a simple slide show. I have found students squeezed into auditorium seats a narrow eighteen inches in width—not the twenty-two inches usually found in the coach section of an airline with a monopoly. Elsewhere, high-velocity air conditioning emitted so much noise that a good lecturer could not be heard, and in another building the blasts of cold air were so humid that some people in their pathways developed an exacerbation of ethmoid sinusitis that had long been latent. Some architects are notoriously parsimonious in providing space for adequate sanitary facilities near large lecture rooms or auditoriums. One suspects that the same architects are responsible for the janitor's-closet-sized facilities that you find in large airline terminals into which wide-body jets disgorge hordes of coffee-laden passengers. Drinking fountains, which should be located near elevators, principal entrances, and areas where people congregate, are often scarce.

At several schools, the programs planned and the facilities designed were so grandiose that the available funding could not carry the project to completion. The projected cost of operating a university hospital approaching completion at one state school was so enormous that the newly elected governor of the state attempted to sell the hospital; ultimately, its opening was delayed for a year. In another instance, the actual construction of a building was finished, but no funds were available to complete the grading and landscaping. In New York, a new academic health center under construction for many years was finally completed, but the capital cost was so great that the annual debt service on the construction bonds alone amounts to $14 million for forty years.

There are other obstacles to be encountered by medical school facility planners and architects. If a medical school is to be built on a university campus where a particular architectural style, such as Gothic, is dominant, the structure may require three to five times the usual time to build and the construction expense itself may be frightful in proportion. Such a building may last 500 years rather than the usual fifty years. Beyond the requirements imposed by a dominant architectural style, such as Gothic, Georgian, Greek, or Baroque (or a derivative thereof, which students may refer to as "Late Bastardian"), some medical school builder/deans have had problems with the constraints imposed by university campus architects or those similar functionaries of the state government. Local building codes may not permit the construction of an academic health center modeled on comparable buildings that have been constructed elsewhere across the country. At a few private schools, a major donor or benefactor to the construction project insisted on the appointment of his favorite architect; and some states evidently have a very short list of favored architects who receive commissions for every building project controlled by state agencies. Creswell (1972) has written in detail about the problems posed by client-architect relations in a variety of building projects. I would advise medical school planners to become well informed by doing their background studies carefully and thoroughly *before* appointing an architect. J. W. Patterson, dean of the University of Connecticut School of Medicine, has written about the delays in the construction of the new medical school buildings there. A commercial planning firm and an architectural firm were employed without a clear definition and division of the responsibilities for each (Patterson, 1972).

4. *Early Tasks for the Planning Committee.* There are a number of tasks that a dean's planning staff or building committee can accomplish as they prepare to design a new building without the assistance of an architect:

- They can canvass the community and surrounding area to learn the cost per gross square foot of various new buildings that have been completed recently or are now under construction. When they discover the reasons for the variations in cost, they can explain to sorrowful faculty members the Greatest Commandment of Building Construction: *Thou shalt pay for gross square feet of thy building, but thou canst divide among thyselves only the net square feet.* The latter usually amounts to about 60 percent of the total gross square feet after the halls, stairs, elevators, janitors' closets, and large mysterious areas labeled "mechanical" on the floor plans have been subtracted. Committee members also should be prepared to interrogate the architect about the ratio of gross square feet to net square feet during the successive stages of his work.
- They can invite a successful planner/builder of one of the newest medical school buildings to visit for a day or two of consultation and pick his brains.
- They can inspect several new medical school buildings, ask the architect to do the same, and find out what problems the occupants have encountered since construction was completed.
- They can explore the available options in construction, such as marble walls versus walls covered with vinyl or other suitable materials or terrazo floors versus vinyl tile or carpeted floors. The initial construction costs should be compared with life-cycle costs, including the expense of routine maintenance—all of which should be balanced against the cost of simple creature comforts and the functional needs of the programs to be housed in the building under consideration (U.S. General Accounting Office, 1972).
- They can develop a stern policy of restraint with respect to faculty demands for expensive installations and building features, such as fume hoods (which must be vented through the roof), cold rooms, and facilities for handling radioactive mate-

rials. Every effort should be made to promote the joint use of these facilities by several individuals. Exclusive use by one individual may become a very expensive status symbol.

- They can investigate the costs of energy very carefully. If winters are severe and fuel oil is to be used to heat facilities, the long-term economy of installing large storage tanks on campus should be explored. A winter-long supply of oil can be purchased on a competitive basis during the off-season at a much lower cost than that incurred with frequent—sometimes daily—delivery of the fuel. The cost of coal for heating may be competitive with the cost of oil, but stationary engineers may be needed to supervise mechanical stokers twenty-four hours per day and for the life of the system.

- After the rough dimensions of the proposed building have been established, they can determine the local experience with the costs of utilities (including water, electricity, gas, sewage, and trash removal), cleaning, security, and any other regularly recurring operational expenses. As options for construction are considered, the costs of continual use must be included in the decision-making process. I once witnessed the chief executive officer of one school go into temporary shock when he first saw the July electricity bill for his beautiful, massive, and air-conditioned new building.

5. *Site Selection.* The geographical location of a medical school and academic health center is often determined by political, rather than functional, considerations. That is, the selection of a particular plot of land may well be a matter of intense interest to one or several elected officials or politically appointed university trustees or regents. In the case of the Northeastern Ohio Universities College of Medicine, which is supported by a regional consortium of three universities and fourteen hospitals, no one participant's "territory" was acceptable to all others as the site for the basic science facility. It was eventually built on a "neutral," somewhat remote tract of land located in the midst of the region and near an interchange of highways leading to the universities and hospitals in the consortium.

The medical schools at Southern Illinois University and Texas A&M University developed their basic science facilities on their parent campuses, but they had to employ affiliated hospitals located 160 and 75 miles away, respectively, for clinical teaching; adequate clinical teaching resources were lacking near each campus. Faculty meetings at these two schools often are held at country clubs or motels located midway between the locations of their basic science and clinical facilities. Twenty-one of the forty new schools were able to locate their basic science facilities on the parent campuses of their sponsoring universities, but only six of these built a university hospital on the same campus. Five new university-related medical schools built their facilities off campus; nine new schools were chartered as independent institutions.

What is the best location for the facilities of a medical school? In 1965, Wolfe noted that it was impossible to evaluate the quality of the medical schools in relation to their locations. Harrell (1974), however, believes that the site should be related to the university for educational functions and to the public for service functions. He demonstrated his convictions when he developed a complete academic health center (including a university teaching hospital) in a semirural area near Hershey, Pennsylvania; the center is 105 miles from the campus of the parent university and 12 miles from Harrisburg, where affiliated hospitals are located.

It is evident that the separation of the site of basic science instruction and administration from the principal site(s) of clinical instruction by a considerable distance requires a daily, mass migration of clinical faculty members and their students. Public transportation between the two sites is often unavailable or unsatisfactory; faculty and students therefore have to rely on automobiles to rush back and forth. In turn, the parking problem at both sites is exacerbated. As a result, the associated costs for the school, the faculty, and the students escalate; street parking near the two locations invariably becomes bothersome to the neighborhood residents, and parking garages have to be built.

The arrangement that Harrell designed and constructed at Pennsylvania State University Medical Center seems to me to be almost ideal. The entire medical school, including its basic science and clinical components, is structurally connected to the university teaching hospital. One complex structure houses the facilities required for educating all medical students, the offices and research laboratories needed by the faculty, and all the facilities required for the clinical care of patients. The only thing the medical center lacks is location on the campus of its parent university.

As of 1980, only one third of the schools had consolidated the bulk of the components of the M.D. degree program by locating administrative offices, the university hospital, and facilities for basic science instruction and faculty research on the campus of the parent university. However, these schools also employ affiliated hospitals scattered throughout their host cities for clinical programs, and six of these rely on clinical branch campuses in other cities for a portion of their clinical instruction of students.

My recommendation to future medical school planners and builders is to develop an academic health center preferably in the same city in which the parent university campus is located and on a tract of land large enough to accommodate the physical expansion required by this type of institution as it matures. The size of this tract of land should be fifty acres at minimum; two hundred acres or more would be ideal. It should be situated where it can be served efficiently by public transportation, as well as by major expressways or beltways around the city.

In the planning of a new site, early attention should be given to the concerns of municipal officials—concerns about the center's need for electricity, gas, water, sewage services, and waste disposal, which is always a major problem for schools, hospitals, and cities (DuVal, 1975), and about the removal of a large tract of land from the city tax rolls; they need to be reassured and educated about the economic contributions the school will be making to the city's commerce through its payroll and purchasing activities. Although there are reasons to decry deliberate plans to separate the medical center from the campus of the parent university, any actual loss to the medical faculty and its students may be more fancied than real. The sheer size of a fully developed enterprise in medical education is such that its operation and administration are more efficiently accomplished if it is somewhat detached from the typically congested university campus.

6. *Laboratories for Teaching Medical Students.* Until the middle of this century, the tradition was to allocate separate laboratory space and equipment to each of the basic science disciplines: microscopic and gross anatomy, pathology, biochemistry, microbiology, and pharmacology (which often was coupled with physiology). At times, these departmental laboratories were used to instruct dental, pharmacy, and nursing students, as well as medical students; however, it was less common to use them for the instruction of various technicians. Medical students are normally exposed to a tightly packed curriculum in smorgasbord style; as a result, each discipline occupies a relatively brief episode in the time track. Thus, pre-1960 laboratories were actually in use only a small percentage of the total time allotted to the instruction of medical students and stood empty for the bulk of the academic year unless they were used in other educational programs. Space analysts and some architects have questioned the need for designing multiple seating for medical students in several different disciplinary laboratories, lecture rooms, the library, and perhaps the lounge area. In allocating space, academic functions should always be the overriding consideration.

In the early 1950s, the medical faculty at Western Reserve University introduced the first major new experiment in medical education in many decades. Among other features, it included an interdisciplinary approach to pedagogy, at least in the basic science subjects. This approach to teaching the body of medical scientific knowledge does not rely on separate courses for each of the traditional disciplines, which formerly operated separate student laboratories. Instead, the content of the curriculum was organized by anatomical/organ systems or concepts, with an interdisciplinary committee of the faculty responsible for each system or concept. For example, the subject committee on the kidney developed a syllabus for instruction in the various facets of basic science knowledge related to that one organ. Similar faculty committees covered other organs and systems of the human body, including their functions and pathology (Greer, 1980). The faculty at Western Reserve decided that the traditional student laboratories, arranged by separate disciplines, were not suited to the new experimental approach. After much debate, the faculty modified a unit laboratory concept developed at the University of Wisconsin (Leake, 1924) and in 1952–53, with the financial support of the Commonwealth Foundation, built new multidiscipline laboratories. From then on, all the basic science disciplines except gross anatomy were taught in these multidiscipline laboratories (Spilman, 1958).

The experimental curriculum initiated at Western Reserve attracted worldwide attention; by the late 1950s, the merits of the interdisciplinary method had been debated by most faculties of medicine. As noted previously, medical student classes began to grow substantially during the late 1950s and early 1960s. At the same time, medical faculties expanded as rapidly as did federal funds for biomedical research. The popular new model for medical education, demonstrating the utility of multidisciplinary student laboratories, and the newly developing shortage of space for biomedical research undoubtedly tilted some faculty opinion toward the establishment of multidisciplinary student laboratories. Each department could then convert its traditional student laboratory into space devoted to research projects. In addition, as each medical student class increased in size, some basic scientists concluded that traditional laboratory work by students had become archaic; as a result, a substantial part of it was discontinued. Biochemists were prominent advocates of the deletion of the laboratory component from their teaching program for medical students.

Fuhrman (1968), a strong proponent of multidiscipline laboratories, has reviewed the early experience with them. According to his estimates, the cost of constructing them was about 65 percent of the cost of constructing comparable departmental laboratories. Fuhrman also has estimated that the cost of equipping multidiscipline laboratories was less than that of equipping the traditional department laboratories; the same was true of the cost of staffing them. However, one area in which the multidiscipline laboratories have not met expectations is in inclusion of facilities for the dissection of cadavers. Fuhrman's analysis of the comparative costs of multidiscipline versus departmental laboratories and the early fervor surrounding Western Reserve's interdisciplinary teaching model certainly figured in the adoption of the multidisciplinary unit system in many new buildings constructed for the medical schools in the 1960s and 1970s.

Spilman (1966) and Harrell, in his comprehensive book on medical school facilities (1974), have described the advantages and disadvantages of multidiscipline laboratories. In 1974, Marchand and Steward published the results of a survey of the changing uses of the multidiscipline laboratories at twenty-seven schools between 1960 and 1973; according to them, curricular changes were the likely reason for a 32 percent reduction in the time devoted to laboratory exercises in these schools. During the late 1970s, I observed similar reductions in actual "hands on" laboratory work by students in the multidiscipline units; these units, however, have been put to use as meeting places for the small-group teaching conferences that have increased in number. Furthermore, the multidiscipline units that were most recently constructed appear to provide greater flexibility in their use. There are fewer "stand up" and "sit down" work benches that are permanently fixed. Instead, some schools have designed movable work benches, large animal tables, and other facilities that can be stored when open space is needed or preferred; they can be reassembled and connected to utility taps if needed to meet the requirements of a changing curriculum. In retrospect, it is clear that the early versions of the multidiscipline laboratories were too elaborately equipped and, as a result, may have inhibited more flexible uses.

As the multidiscipline laboratories evolved, the medical curriculum and its supporting technology became progressively more diverse. After an initial flurry of imitating the Western Reserve experiment in interdisciplinary teaching, some faculties reverted to the traditional system of teaching separate courses in the basic sciences. By 1980, only 23 percent of the schools had integrated all or part of the second-year subjects (Association of American Medical Colleges, 1980a). Thus, in many schools, disciplinary courses that were taught earlier in separate departmental laboratories are now taught in multidiscipline laboratories.

In summary, the efficiency of multidiscipline laboratories depends on the applicability of their design to the total needs of the students, the effectiveness of the staff operating them, and the attitudes of the faculty members who must teach in them. In my own opinion, an elaborate multidiscipline laboratory system may actually constrain pedagogy. It is clear, for instance, that gross anatomical dissection should be done in separate facilities designed and adequately ventilated for that express purpose. I also think that more faculty members are needed to operate the multidiscipline units efficiently than are needed in the traditional, single-discipline laboratories. A multidiscipline unit containing sixteen or more students needs a senior faculty supervisor; a larger number of students per faculty member may be acceptable in one large laboratory, but only if the work of the students has been well planned, so that faculty members function on call rather than actively supervising and directing the observations of the students. If the "home base" concept, wherein medical students have exclusive use of the multidiscipline units, is adopted, then each department must contain student laboratory facilities for use in the instruction of other health profession students enrolled in the school.

7. *A Place to Study.* For more than three decades, I have been curious about the study habits of high academic achievers in the premedical and medical student populations in various colleges and universities. It is clear that the successful premedical student devotes much more of his daily time to study than do his companions with other occupational goals. When he begins medical school, the student discovers that the study load is considerably heavier than he experienced in college. In the late 1960s, I surveyed the study habits of the medical students at Baylor and found that 89 percent of the first- and second-year students spent three to six hours per night in study; 87 percent maintained this schedule for five to six nights per week. Only 10 percent studied less than three hours per night. In the early 1980s, I visited many of those medical schools known for the high academic achievements of their students and found similar study habits. However, there can be no doubt that patterns vary widely among the diverse United States and Canadian medical schools in which students cope with a course load that usually ranges up to forty contact hours per week during the period of basic science studies.

It is well known that serious study is difficult to undertake in noisy dormitories, fraternity or sorority houses, or even most off-campus housing. Some libraries are designed to facilitate student study, but many employ large, open reading rooms that are usually filled with distractions. Some student union buildings contain quiet nooks and crannies ideal for concentration and study, and they are often occupied by serious premedical students. Frequently, the high academic achiever makes an arrangement with supportive faculty members for the use of departmental offices for distraction-free evening study. On the whole, however, colleges and universities have not really addressed the problem of places to study on campus. Therefore, no one should be surprised to learn that most undergraduate students study very little until a periodic exam approaches.

Harrell (1974) has described his innovative employment of student study cubicles at the University of Florida during the 1950s and later at Pennsylvania State University. During the 1960s, a number of the new schools imitated Harrell's design with variable results. Pannill (1972) has reported that the individual study cubicles built by the University of Texas at San Antonio in 1968 had low utilization by students, probably due to the absence of adequate student housing in the vicinity of the medical center. Other schools have designed multidiscipline laboratories that contain individual study spaces for the sixteen to twenty-four students housed in each unit. Some medical school librarians have found space for study carrels inside the library; these can be ideal for study, but the library rules for their use have often led to problems.

Before new medical school facilities are designed, the planners need to analyze thoroughly the ecology of studious students in each medical center setting. Study space for both individual and small-group use should be given a high priority in the allocation of space in a new building or in the renovation of an old one. While an isolated, individual home base for student study seems most desirable, this is difficult to justify if students typically do not return to the school building for evening study because of the lack of student housing in the vicinity, the extremely tight security in the buildings, or the hazards posed by rising crime in the neighborhood. At the very least, each student should be assigned a full-length locker in which street clothes, books, and other valuables can be secured. Numerous unassigned study carrels in the library and the vicinity of student laboratories would be a practical arrangement. In the future, multimedia computer console carrels may be provided, but their high cost may prohibit their assignment to each student.

8. *Amenities and Services.* The need to provide sizable restrooms at appropriate locations near lecture rooms and a locker

for each student has been mentioned. Individual lockers also should be provided adjacent to the anatomical dissecting room for the storage of smocks, aprons, and other odorous protective clothing. There should be a comfortably furnished lounge area in the building for the exclusive use of medical students and doctoral students in the basic medical sciences; these facilities are of particular value to students who reside at some distance from the medical center. The registrar or student affairs office should maintain an individual message/mail box for each student enrolled. Mail should be received in bulk from the post office and letters and packages sorted by school personnel, not by the employees of the postal service. If a commercial bookstore is not located near the school, one should be developed. Although most departments may need individual copying machines, the school may require technically sophisticated printing services for the production of annual reports, lesson plans, laboratory guides, and the syllabi routinely ordered in large quantities by the faculty. Students should have access to copying machines that are either coin operated or activated by auditron counters, which compute the number of copies. Copying machines are needed outside, as well as inside, the library.

A food service for the use of students, faculty members, and employees is indispensable. If a cafeteria or fast-food service is not justified, then a variety of coin-operated vending machines with fresh sandwiches, candy, and soft drinks may be marginally satisfactory. Microwave ovens should be available to warm vended food or sandwiches brought from home by the "brown baggers." The facility planners also should consider the installation of kitchenette units adjacent to departmental conference rooms and administrative offices. Finally, a medical faculty with appropriate concern for the prevention of disease will not permit the installation on campus of vending machines for cigarettes.

Automobile parking is a formidable problem on all school and hospital grounds; when the two facilities are located on the same campus, considerable short- and long-term planning is needed to cope with the problem. In an urban setting, the emerging custom is to construct subsurface parking areas under a new building, courtyard, or other area, with access from streets external to the campus. When the original parking facility is planned, provision for future expansion should be made, perhaps through an above-surface parking garage. Where the space is available, surface parking is usually satisfactory. The construction costs involved with parking garages or paving parking lots are substantial and should be borne by the automobile operators, not by the institution. Some state-operated schools are prohibited from using funds derived from tax revenues for parking facilities. Schools caught in this bind usually have been successful in borrowing construction funds and have amortized this indebtedness through collections from the parking facility users. Even when the parking is subsidized, it is an error to provide free parking; experience has shown that eventually a need will arise for revenues to defray the cost of maintenance, repair, replacement, security, and other unanticapted expenses.

A new medical school and hospital center should be designed for access by city buses, taxis, and an unbelievable number of delivery trucks, as well as automobiles belonging to both regulars and visitors. When the planners discuss this matter with the architect, they should instruct him to plan and design for a volume of traffic comparable to that usually found in front of the Eastern Airline shuttle service at Washington, D.C.'s National Airport.

9. *Recreation Facilities for Students and Faculty.* Although universities and colleges often are faulted for excessive expenditures on varsity athletics, most campuses should and do have considerable resources for student recreation and physical activity. A medical school located on its university campus usually can and should arrange for its students to use the campus facilities. However, since most medical schools are located off the university campus, special provisions should be made for the recreation of undergraduate and graduate medical students, as well as the overworked corps of hospital residents.

Until recent years, few medical schools have adequately met this obligation to student health; some schools still ignore the matter. An increasing number of schools, however, have begun to provide some means for their students and faculty to engage in conveniently arranged physical activity, with the costs ranging from modest outlays to major capital commitments.

If the space is available on the medical center campus, a flat grassy area can be devoted to unstructured recreational activities, such as frisbee tossing, touch football, soccer, or rugby. Some students may desire a softball diamond more than anything else. Tennis courts with the proper enclosures are expensive to install, but they are often the particular delight of medical professionals; courts with lighting permit their use in the evening hours when scheduled duties are less demanding. A basketball court or even a hoop installed next to a paved parking area may appeal to many students. An outdoor swimming pool can be used most of the year in the sunbelt states. Joggers can be assisted in their compulsive pursuit of that exercise by the development of a safe track; in urban settings some schools have installed a running track on the roof of a large building. The Northeastern Ohio Universities School of Medicine has developed a highly successful par cours for graded exercise.

Indoor pools and courts for basketball, volleyball, handball, squash, and racquetball require substantial expenditures to construct, but these facilities are heavily used in those schools that have provided them. Some students will demand wrestling mats. Indoor facilities for recreation should include showers and lockers for men and women.

Except for jogging and the graded exercises found on a par cours, most of the indoor and outdoor activities mentioned above involve groups or teams and some element of competition, both of which are very beneficial. However, most organized sports or games require scheduling with partners and, frequently the reservation of the playing area. The burdensome duties of the medical student, resident, and practicing physician make this requirement difficult to meet. The dedicated physician golfer is well known, but I imagine that many physicians gave up weekly team-based physical activity long ago, due to the difficulties of arranging it. Medical students should be encouraged to develop lifelong habits of physical exercise that can be performed several times a week, regardless of the prevailing climate, the season of the year, the weather, or whether free time in the midst of heavy work falls during the day or the night. The next several pages describe a type of facility for exercise which I strongly recommend for use by physicians as a means of improving their health and extending their longevity.

A relatively inexpensive solution to the problem of physical recreation in the medical school is available if space can be provided in the medical school facility or in a student residence hall. The most practical facility for unscheduled physical recreation is the modern version of the weight lifting gymnasium. Prototypes have been successful commercially and are available for inspection in most cities. During the mid-1960s, I developed such a facility in a low-priority storage area in the school building complex at Baylor. Approximately 3,500 square feet of unfinished vault space were given a spartan finish to accommodate various types of progressive weight resistance equipment, sit-up boards, exercise cycles, rowing machines, motorized treadmills, and other items. Air conditioning and heating ducts were extended into the area, and showers, benches, lockers, and simple wall pegs for clothing made the area quite usable. After the project proved successful, several faculty members contributed the cost of installing a steam room and sauna. Maintenance of the area was handled as it was for the rest of the building. Repairs and the replacement of equipment were funded by student health fees. Faculty members interested in using the facility were charged an annual membership fee.

The commercial success of the modern gymnasium indicates the general acceptance of this approach to physical conditioning. A twenty-minute workout, followed by ten minutes in the steam room and sauna, can do wonders for soma and psyche (an added benefit would be an oversized hot tub or whirlpool tank). Repeated several times a week, this simple regimen for physical conditioning would likely meet a cardiologist's standards for preventive care of the coronary arteries. If practical habits of physical exercise are established during the medical school years, they are easier to maintain and continue later in the years of medical practice. Although a gymnasium of the type described here can be located in a student residence hall, there is something beneficially symbolic about allocating space in the medical school building to a facility that promotes good health.

In his discussion of recreation facilities, Harrell (1974) mentions most of the facilities described above, but he also gives attention to the musical bent of many medical professionals. One or more soundproof rooms just large enough to accommodate an upright piano and its player will be well received. A somewhat larger room could be used by other individual musicians or the inevitable student combos playing rock, jazz, dixieland, or chamber music.

10. *Student Housing.* By 1980, 95 of the 126 schools (that is, 75 percent) reported the availability of some form of school-owned or operated housing for their students (Liaison Committee on Medical Education data). The types of available housing varied considerably, from space in a predominantly undergraduate student dormitory to residence halls on the campus for the exclusive use of medical students to apartment houses located in the vicinity of the center. Of the 40 new schools, 23 provided some form of housing to some of their students as of 1980. This indicates that some of the founding deans gave the housing needs of their future students some priority while faced with the necessity of finding financial resources to construct other aspects of the physical plant.

Because of the increasingly high cost of living for everyone, including the medical student, investments in student housing facilities are not difficult to justify. In the United States during the 1981–82 academic year, the average cost of living for the medical student was approximately $6,150. The high end of the cost range was $8,500 in public schools and $10,600 in private schools. These figures include modest expenditures for lodging, food, books, supplies, personal expenses, and transportation. In the same period, tuition for residents at public schools averaged $2,684; in the private schools, tuition averaged $9,545, and the maximum was $18,000 per year. With the costs of medical education at these levels and increasing annually, medical students would benefit from the availability of on-campus housing if it can be provided at a cost that offers substantial savings in comparison with the costs of housing in the commercial market. This need is particularly great where schools are located in the inner core of large cities.

Experience with medical student housing has varied according to the types of facilities. The least suitable arrangement has been the attempt to assign medical students, who spend a considerable amount of their time studying, to dormitories used by undergraduates, who seem to concentrate on noise-producing activities rather than study in the evening hours. Anyone who doubts this observation should spend a night or two in the guest room

of an undergraduate dormitory. These facilities often consist structurally of a long, very noisy hallway into which small rooms open.
No food preparation is allowed in most university dormitories;
occupants must eat their meals in a central dining room at a fixed
time. In spite of the availability of frozen foods and the miracles
of microwave cookery, the meals quickly become boringly repetitive
and thus facilitate the proliferation of numerous fast-food outlets
near the campus.

Some schools have acquired apartment buildings near the
campus, or an umbrella arrangement for student rentals has been
made with the owners of existing apartment complexes. Such
apartments are usually best suited for married students, especially
those who become parents. Standard one-bedroom apartments
shared by two single students are useful, but less so then well-
designed facilities located on campus. Attempts to crowd three
persons into a small, one-bedroom apartment have not been particularly successful. Several older on-campus residence halls have
unfortunately followed the standard design of the college dormitory:
long narrow hallways and central restroom and shower facilities.
Dormitories with these features and small, single-person rooms were
obviously designed to enhance personal privacy, probably the result
of numerous complaints about the problems of two people occupying the same small space during long periods of intense study.
Occupants of a residence hall with single rooms did like the privacy,
but they often reported feelings of isolation as well as discomfort
with the central restroom and shower facilities.

In the mid-1960s, I assisted with the design of a residence
hall for Baylor medical students at the Texas Medical Center. We
attempted to achieve several desirable objectives with this design:
privacy and quiet for the occupants of each unit, modest accommodations for an overnight visitor, private toilet and shower
facilities, cooking facilities, and, in general, a more pleasing
atmosphere than that usually found in the standard dormitory. Each
unit is occupied by three single persons, each of whom has a private
sleep/study cubicle that opens into a comfortably furnished sitting
room with good external fenestration. The furniture in this room
includes a couch (seven feet in length and adequate for overnight

sleeping by a visitor), a dropleaf dining table, and one lounge chair. A kitchenette unit with a sink, gas burners, oven, small refrigerator, and wall cabinets is located behind a folding accordian panel. The bathroom is equipped with a shower, a toilet, and two basins in front of the wall mirror, which is six feet wide and suitable for simultaneous use by the three occupants. Each sleep/study cubicle contains a closet with high shelves, a bed (eighty inches long with a firm foam rubber mattress and with storage space beneath it), a desk with one pedestal of drawers and a top, six feet wide, that extends over a chest of drawers. Bookshelves are located on the wall above the desk, which also comes equipped with a sturdy armchair. To provide a maximum of window area in the sitting room and to facilitate quiet study, each cubicle is windowless (it was necessary to obtain a waiver of the section of the building code requiring a window in each bedroom). As with most buildings in Houston, each unit is continuously air conditioned; air drains are located in each sleep unit and in the sitting room.

The students who have occupied these three-person apartments have found them to be generally comfortable. Each of the occupants can find privacy by entering his bedroom and shutting the door, but each can also find companionship with one or both of the other occupants in the sitting room. Food for some or all meals can be prepared at less cost than that of purchasing meals in a restaurant or cafeteria, and the units permit modest entertainment of friends. At first the students had to adapt to the unusual windowless sleep/study units, but the experience, in the long run, has contradicted the negative reports on windowless space found by Wilson (1972) and Taylor (1979) in their studies of the problems of stimulus deprivation in intensive care patients.

In designing and developing any physical arrangement of space and furnishings for housing, laboratories, or lecture rooms, the planners should require a full-sized mock-up of the proposed design. If students are to be the principal users of the space, they should be asked to try out the mock-up and to participate in the selection of key furnishings, such as chairs, lecture room seats (with writing arms), beds, laboratory workbenches, and other like items that people will have to use for many years in the future.

11. *Animal Facilities: The Vivarium.* The biomedical sciences constitute the dynamic component of the body of medical knowledge. Most new information is derived from the careful observation and analysis of data yielded by experiments involving various biological systems. Under exceedingly stringent controls, a few experimental studies can be undertaken with humans, but the bulk of biomedical research is dependent on humane, controlled experimentation with many different animals. Thus, the planners of a medical school facility have to provide for the care and housing of a variety of experimental animals, preferably in one central location in the medical school building complex. Decentralized animal facilities should be discouraged, except for short, transient holding purposes for specimens that are to be used for student laboratory exercises or research studies. All animal care should be supervised by an experienced director, usually a well-trained veterinarian, who must be given suitable authority by the dean and a faculty committee to maintain high standards for the care of the animals.

The animal care and housing facilities of a medical school are subject to accreditation by the American Association for the Accreditation of Laboratory Animal Care, as well as certain governmental constraints that have been on the rise in recent years. Public opinion regarding the actual or alleged misuse and abuse of experimental animals can be very negative and can result in punitive reactions from municipal or state officials. The dean and a standing committee of the faculty should demand adherence to very high standards and policies for the use of animals in medical research.

The animal care facilities should be secured for access by restricted personnel only. Employees of the facilities should be screened carefully, since there have been numerous episodes in which members of antivivisection groups have sought employment for the purpose of exposing alleged cruelty to animals. A well-operated facility will have nothing illegal to expose.

The subject of animal care facilities has been discussed by Lang and Harrell (1972). Harrell (1974) has also described in some detail his excellent experience with the design of animal care facilities for a medical school complex and in the use of an animal research farm.

12. *Specific Recommendations for Physical Facilities.*

- The planning and designing effort should focus on the need for a design that will support the functions to be housed in the medical school complex. As long as it is durable and avoids transient fads in design, the external appearance of the building(s) is not particularly consequential.
- Flexibility should be built into every component of the building design. A detailed, novel scheme for academic activity conjured up by the faculty planning committee may not be acceptable to future faculty members and other occupants of the building. A building designed to house an unproven scheme may cause many problems to future users.
- Long-span construction should be considered. During the 1970s, favorable experience was accumulated with buildings constructed with long spans that provide obstruction-free space of usually more than fifty feet between support columns. This structural feature reduces the number of weight-bearing columns and internal walls and permits a relatively practical rearrangement of rooms when needed. Walls that do not bear any weight can be constructed of either concrete block or some varient of drywall materials. Harrell (1974) reported that the movable metal partitions built in the clinical center at the National Institutes of Health have been moved very little, thereby providing little justification for their high initial cost.

    Long-span construction has usually been combined with the use of interstitial spaces between primary floors that contain all the utility lines, communication wiring, and air ducts required for the operation of service functions on adjacent floors. A new medical education building at Washington University is designed with vertical chases, external to the building wall, that provide space for the utility lines, pipes, and ducts extending from the basement level to all floors. At the Northeastern Ohio Universities School of Medicine, Stanley Olson designed an internal utility/service line corridor on each floor. Improvements with these particular design features are sure to continue as experience with their use accumulates. Careful study of current information should be made in order to compare initial construction costs and operating maintenance costs between conventional systems of construction and newer ones.

- The process of planning the academic programs of a new medical school and the design of the building(s) to house them should not be rushed. For example, Harrell (1974) has chronicled the long process involved with his design and planning for the new medical center at Pennsylvania State University. He was appointed dean in November 1964, applied for federal construction funds in June 1965, and let the first construction contracts in June 1966. In October 1967, the first three floors of the teaching wing of the complex were occupied by the charter class of forty students. The complete phase-one teaching building was accepted from the contractor in September 1968, along with a steam plant. Animal research facilities were completed just before phase one. Construction on the clinical sciences wing began in March 1967 and was completed, floor by floor, in time for some teaching of the second class. The teaching hospital was built on a "fast track" schedule. In July 1967, excavations and foundation construction began under a contract including the erection of structural steel; a second contract for general construction was awarded in April 1968, and in October 1970 the hospital's lower floors were occupied. In retrospect, Harrell concluded that this entire schedule, although it was followed as planned, was much too compressed.

The Medical Library

ᴊᴊᴊᴊᴊᴊᴊᴊᴊᴊᴊᴊᴊᴊᴊᴊᴊᴊᴊᴊᴊᴊᴊᴊ

As the twentieth century draws toward its close, computer science appears ready to create a major revolution in the technology of library operations. A comparable revolution has occurred several times since the Sumerians, in approximately 2700 B.C., created the first known library, which consisted of cuneiform impressions on clay tables. Around 530 B.C., the Greeks used scrolls of Egyptian papyrus to develop libraries; papyrus was replaced by parchment, or vellum, which was replaced by paper, an early Chinese invention, in thirteenth-century Europe. Gutenberg's invention of movable type made possible the printing of the first book, the Bible, about 1455 A.D. (Durant, 1939). Now, the Gutenberg era may be phased out and replaced by computer-based systems of retrieval of literature stored on tapes and discs.

Growth of Medical School Libraries

In the United States during the eighteenth century, the first medical school libraries were developed at the older, university-based medical schools and the local academies of medicine located in the larger, older cities. When Flexner visited the proprietary schools in 1908 and 1909, he found that there were few to no books at all for use by the students and faculty members. After Flexner published his report in 1910, some schools improved their libraries, but not rapidly enough to keep pace with the increase in the number of publications. In 1960, in a survey commissioned by the National Library of Medicine (NLM), Bloomquist (1963) found that eighty-six medical schools possessed library holdings consisting of a median number of 54,770 bound volumes and 992 serial titles. Bloomquist consulted the medical librarians at Harvard, SUNY-Downstate, and the NLM, who recommended that a medical library of good quality should contain 100,000 bound volumes and from 1,200 to 1,500 current journals. In 1960, only 25 percent of the medical libraries met the standards of this recommendation.

In the early 1960s, with the financial support of the NLM, the AAMC and the Medical Library Association formed a joint committee to study the needs of medical libraries. Composed of medical librarians, the committee published 166 "Guidelines for Medical School Libraries" in 1965. In 1967, a committee composed primarily of deans appointed by the AAMC and supported by an NLM contract published a second study of the health sciences library and its role in the education of health professionals. The 1965 and 1967 studies were used extensively by the planners of the forty new medical schools established between 1960 and 1980, as well as by the librarians of the eighty-six older schools in planning new library facilities to serve expanded activities in education, research, and the clinical care of patients (see Joint Committee . . . , 1965, and Library Study Committee . . . , 1967).

In 1963, Bloomquist reported that the libraries had either exceeded their book-holding capacities or were about to reach that level. Furthermore, many of the library buildings were inadequate, somewhat antiquated structures; more than half of the library facilities on the campuses of the eighty-six older medical schools had been built before 1930. In the 1950s, when the activities and programs of the medical schools began to expand, financial expenditures for the support of library facilities and holdings remained at low levels, a situation deplored by Deitrick and Berson (1953) in their study of American medical education at mid-century. Meanwhile, every area of science was experiencing a veritable explosion of new information and discoveries; by 1960, this was evident in the publication of nearly 100,000 journals in sixty-five different languages and containing more than one million articles per year (de Solla-Price, 1961). In 1960 alone, the National Institutes of Health gave $715 million in grants to support research that resulted in the publication of approximately 70,000 scientific papers (Bloomquist, 1963).

Development of the National Library of Medicine

While many medical school libraries were foundering from neglect, a national treasure house of medical literature was gradually emerging. From its beginnings as a single row of books behind the desk of the U.S. Army's surgeon general in 1836, the Army Medical Library grew to become the nation's major medical library. In 1956, Congress transferred control of this collection to the Public Health Service and renamed it the National Library of Medicine (NLM) (Wasserman, 1972). In 1965, while this institution was flourishing, Congress passed the Medical Library Assistance Act, P.L. 89–291. This law authorized the expenditure of federal funds for the improvement of medical libraries, the construction of new library facilities, the creation of regional medical libraries, and support for research and publications (Crawford, 1977). The NLM was designated as the agent to administer the act. By 1980, under the leadership of director Martin Cummings and his able staff, the NLM had increased its holdings to 1.545 million volumes and 22,753 current serial titles. It also implemented elaborate systems for bibliographical searches of its vast collections and made these available to the medical school libraries. Between 1965 and 1980, the NLM gave extramural grants and contracts totaling $11,632 million to 4,152 recipients.

One early program of the NLM was the development of a network of eleven regional libraries; these are located in Boston, New York City, Philadelphia, Bethesda (home of the NLM), Detroit, Atlanta, Chicago, Omaha, Dallas, Seattle, and Los Angeles. Eight of these are medical school libraries, and two belong to professional societies. The network was completed in 1975. Each library serves as a reference and interlibrary loan resource for its region and as a link between its local libraries and the NLM. Using federal funds authorized by P.L. 89–291, the NLM awarded grants for the

construction of facilities, the enhancement of collections and additions to staffs, and other improvements in these regional libraries
(Crawford, 1977).

One objective of the regional library network, to eliminate
wasteful duplication of informational resources, has met with only
partial success. Between 1960 and 1980, some medical school libraries
and several separate governmental medical libraries in close prox-
imity continued to enlarge their holdings; such increases involved
a duplication of holdings within the same geographical area. (For
further discussion of this topic, see Miles, 1982.)

Medical Libraries in the 1980s

By 1980, two thirds of the 126 schools reported holdings of
100,000 or more bound volumes; the new schools established after
1960 comprise the majority of the remaining third. The median
number of bound volumes in the holdings of the medical school
libraries is 125,000. Ninety percent of the 126 schools receive 1,200
or more current periodicals; the median number received is approximately 2,100 (Liaison Committee on Medical Education, Confidential Records). A survey of most of the forty new schools shows that
the average holdings for each in the year that it admitted its charter
class were 33,000 volumes and 1,187 periodicals. After ten years
of operation, those schools founded early in the period from 1960
to 1980 had acquired holdings comparable to the average holdings
of the eighty-six older schools. If the standards by which the medical
school library is judged are purely quantitative, then several libraries
have surpassed them: six libraries now possess holdings in excess
of 400,000 volumes, and nearly a dozen now receive more than 4,000
periodicals each. The librarians in these schools appear to be
emulating the book-hoarding habits of the Ptolemaic dynasty in
their attempts to acquire as much of the available medical literature
as possible.

By 1980, more than 90 percent of the libraries were able to
replace, expand, or substantially renovate their physical facilities
with funding provided by a combination of federal, state, and private
sources. Personnel and operating budgets were increased between
1960 and 1980. Thus, after twenty years of remedial action, the

principal problems of the medical libraries appear to have been solved; the goals for the "ideal" medical library that were widely promoted in the early 1960s seem to have been realized (Huang, 1976; Liaison Committee on Medical Education data). Yet even though book and journal collections have been increased, staffs and budgets have been expanded (but not enough, according to some librarians), and the schools have acquired new or improved facilities, new problems of major consequence have arisen and new crises in the operation and maintenance of medical school libraries may be forming.

Rising Cost of Books and Journals. For example, the cost of books and journals has escalated at a consistently rapid pace over the years. The average yearly price of a medical periodical has increased: $7.74 in 1950, $10.28 in 1960, $23.44 in 1970, $42.38 in 1975, and $73.37 in 1980 (Bloomquist, 1963; Perry, 1980). Medical school textbooks have followed the same alarming trend. In 1981, I visited medical schools that recommended texts with these prices: anatomy, $84.00; biochemistry, $32.95; physiology, $79.30; microbiology, $45.00; pathology, $47.00; internal medicine, $80.00; pediatrics, $62.50; psychiatry, $45.00; surgery, $80.00; obstetrics, $52.00; gynecology, $17.95; and, a medical dictionary at $33.50. Rarely is a medical textbook priced at less than $20.00. The impact of the higher prices of books and journals on the library budget (not to mention the student budget) is obvious from this accounting.

Excessive Publishing. The sheer volume of information flowing through the various medical journals can overwhelm both the beginning learner and the experienced academic bibliophile. Medical journals were first published in France in 1679 and in England in 1684, but most of these early publications were short lived. In 1823, the oldest English-language medical journal, *Lancet,* began publication; it is still widely available today. Since that time, the journals have multiplied rapidly; some new periodicals seem to have been developed to accommodate the numerous members of the professional ranks who must publish in order to avoid perishing in their effort to climb the academic ladder to promotion. As long as the publishers of journals can sell them to librarians who are not restrained from purchasing everything available, the volume of paper will continue to flow in ever-increasing quantities.

If every article published in every journal made an original contribution to research and scholarship, the deluge of paper would
be justified. However, many articles and reports are simply reruns
of earlier publications, or they have been printed without the benefit
of the prior peer criticism that is customary in the best-edited
journals. Thus, the researcher is faced with time-consuming sifting
and sorting as he searches for accurate data and valid interpretations
of the same.

Retrieval of Literature by Subjects. The problem of retrieving
relevant writings on a given subject has been with us for a long
time. The Library of Congress, founded in 1815 with the purchase
of 6,487 books from Thomas Jefferson, first used Jefferson's classification of books, which he had derived from Francis Bacon and
Jean d'Alembert. By the end of the nineteenth century, the library
had accumulated so many volumes that a new classification system
had to be devised. The Dewey Decimal System was not considered
adequate for such a large collection. Therefore, in 1904, a new
cataloguing system was devised, and the catalogue cards were made
available for purchase by libraries everywhere. These cards were
never used extensively, but the new system did bring a measure
of order to library research. Eventually, the growth of the collection,
along with the abundant cross-referencing such growth required,
made the use of the card catalogue impractical. By 1979, the Library
of Congress had twenty million cards in its catalogue; these recorded
the volumes occupying approximately 270 miles of shelves. In 1981,
the library "froze" its card catalogue and adopted a new system
of storing cataloguing information and making it available to users.
The system, called SCORPIO, is available for use on site to anyone
at the computerized card catalogue center at the Library of Congress
(Gay, 1979–80).

Professional societies were the first groups to develop comprehensive indexes of scientific literature. The products of their
efforts—for example, *Biological Abstracts* and *Chemical Abstracts*—
form an integral chapter in the history of access to knowledge and
were the first library tools to be automated. In 1879, the indexing
of medical literature was launched with the development of *Index
Medicus* by John Shaw Billings, who combined an intellect of genius
with a remarkable capacity for work. Among his many achievements

were the development of the Army Medical Library (which later became the NLM), the design of the original Johns Hopkins University Hospital, the development of the New York Public Library, and the plans for Peter Bent Brigham Hospital in Boston. In 1879, *Index Medicus* listed about 20,000 articles; one hundred years later, it contained almost 250,000 articles (Kunz, 1979). Due to irregular fiscal support, the *Index's* history was often troubled, and in 1927 it was merged with the *Quarterly Cumulative Index* of the American Medical Association. In 1960, after the NLM was founded and provided with adequate funding, it resumed publication of *Index Medicus* in time for computerization and the adoption of the computer-based MEDLARS. Before the advent of the computer, the researcher had to pore through large tomes that listed journal articles by year and author or medical subject heading. A thorough search of any topic required much time and sustained concentration.

With the development of the MEDLARS system, the conditions for research improved. In response to written or telephoned request, the MEDLARS staff at the NLM would perform computerized literature searches on any subject or author listed in *Index Medicus;* a printed list of references would then be mailed to the researcher. In 1971, MEDLINE was activated, replacing the MEDLARS system and providing direct, on-line access to the computer data base of citations at the NLM. Using a terminal located in any library connected to the NLM, a researcher can call for a visual display of the list of journal articles the computer has stored on the subject of inquiry. A set of citations can then be ordered, as can reprints of selected citations; or abstracts can be viewed on the screen (McCarn and Leiter, 1973). MEDLINE has become a heavily utilized and popular resource for the medical researcher; during 1979–80, 682,802 searches were performed. The staff of the NLM has continued to refine its capabilities and during the past decade has added a number of specialized programs, such as CANCERLIT and AVLINE, which lists audiovisual educational materials.

In 1971, with the support of the NLM, the AAMC published a report of a biomedical communications network steering committee appointed by its Council of Academic Societies (Stead and others, 1971). The report traces the establishment of the Lister Hill

Center to develop networks and information systems to improve
health education, medical research, and delivery of health services
under P.L. 90-456, enacted by Congress in August 1968. The
committee report urged the staff of the Lister Hill Center to develop
educational methods that would render obsolete the current systems
of libraries, textbooks, and medical school curricula and dependence
on memory and pattern recognition in clinical decision making
and problem solving. The center has been active in developing a
series of knowledge bases on hepatitis, peptic ulcer, and human
genetics; and today it continues research on electronic document
storage and retrieval and other aspects of advanced computer
technology. In 1980, the center occupied new facilities adjacent to
the NLM in Bethesda.

In 1980, the National Medical Audiovisual Center of the NLM
moved from Atlanta to Bethesda and was integrated, organization-
ally and physically, with the NLM. The consolidation of the NLM's
programs, which took place during the early 1980s, has facilitated
its primary activities in the production and distribution of materials
and in advanced research concerning the storage and retrieval of
information.

The different programs currently conducted by the NLM are
too numerous to review here in detail. An example of a major
program of timely, direct importance to the academic community
is AVLINE; it provides standardized bibliographical and critical
information concerning audiovisual materials in both on-line and
printed catalogue forms. Faculty members and others can submit
a film, tape, cassette, or other educational teaching aid; the item
is then reviewed and evaluated by experts on the subject of the
item. If the item is accepted, it is purchased and made available
for loan; an interested person can then locate it through an on-
line search by computer or a catalogue containing evaluations of
each item. The AAMC has coordinated the evaluation system and
has enlisted faculty members from various health education schools
and professional specialty societies to provide the evaluations (Suter
and Waddell, 1982).

The Revolution in Library Operation. Recognizing the
changing circumstances of the printed word and the availability
of electronic transmission of information, in 1982 the AAMC and

the NLM published *Academic Information in the Academic Health Sciences Center: Roles for the Library in Information Management,* the results of a fourth study of the status and future of the medical library (Association of American Medical Colleges, 1982a). The report argues that, even though academic health science centers are facing a period of increasing financial constraints, they should invest scarce funds in the control and management of their information support systems—that is, in electronic systems of information management. The future of the library and its use is predicted through three stages—the following five to ten years, the next ten to twenty years, and beyond the next twenty years. During this time span, the medical scholar will move away from reading journals in the open stacks of the library and toward using computer terminals ultimately tied to library collections stored on video discs located on campus or in the NLM network. The printed word of books and journals will be replaced by information retrieved by electronic means. In the future, according to the study, even house calls by physicians may be effected by satellite through long-distance systems that permit two-way audiovisual and digital conferences between the physician's office and the patient's home.

Audiovisual/Multiple-Media Learning Materials. In 1980–81, 90 of the 126 medical school library directors reported inventories of more than 100 audiovisual items for teaching and learning, and 3 schools owned more than 10,000 items each. Some libraries simply check out the audiovisual materials to the borrower; others have provided areas in which slides, films, and videotapes can be viewed on small screens or monitors and heard through earphones. In other schools, audiovisual resources are housed and managed separately from those of the library. Those medical schools with a curriculum heavily based on the use of audiovisual and multiple-media materials have usually developed learning resource centers.

Hampton and his colleagues (1979) have described the learning resource center at the Medical College of Virginia. Software is checked out at a counter and is used in one of twenty carrels for individual study or in one of seven carrels constructed to accommodate six to eight students. The center, which occupies an area of 2,700 square feet, contains approximately 2,000 items of printed material, including books, reprints, and past examinations;

about 40 percent of the total circulation is in these printed materials. The facility is located in the building in which medical students attend classes and laboratories; it is open ninety-six hours per week. During the 1976–77 academic year, 15,042 people visited the learning resource center each month, a number approaching the average monthly use of the medical library. Reports received in 1982 indicate that the center is still heavily used (Steinfeld, 1982). The management policy at the center is student oriented; the two staff members make a deliberate effort to see medical students as future professionals who place a premium on time: users may study during lunch and dinner; food and drink are permitted. The staff also relate closely to the faculty and the dean of curriculum, with whom they review the relationship between the center's functions and the goals, needs, and future activities of the curriculum.

Lessons Learned

1. *Budget and Space Use.* In 1979–80, the average operating budget for the medical school library was $519,999; this amounted to 1.71 percent of the schools' average total general operating budget. In the same year, the average area occupied by the medical school library was 39,500 square feet; this amounted to an average of about 5 percent of the total space available, excluding that occupied by hospitals and clinics. Forty-four of the 120 libraries studied occupied more than a full acre of space—that is, 43,560 square feet (Liaison Committee on Medical Education, Annual Questionnaire).

A significant amount of this space is used to shelve the bound volumes of journals that date back many years. Most studies, as well as my own direct inquiries, indicate that most journals receive their heaviest usage during the first five years after publication; as the old volumes age, they slowly deteriorate due to the type of paper and printer's ink used. A significant number of journals bought by the libraries receive little to no use whatsoever. Given these problems and the increasingly stringent fiscal constraints under which most libraries operate, I recommend that the dean or chief academic officer study the library's holdings and develop new policies controlling the acquisition of new materials and the continuation of presently held items; careful attention should be given to the circulation record of each item, especially the journals. Since acquisition expenditures are the second-largest component of the library budget (the largest is personnel salaries), some reductions in this area may be acceptable so that other budgetary needs can be met.

There appear to be few reasons for holding rarely used, older journals in primary space. Everything older than five or perhaps ten years could be stored in less expensive space or be deleted entirely. If a journal has not been used for two or three years, then a justification for continued subscription is required. Considerations of this sort would clear primary space for the storage of items that are needed and used regularly. Very little browsing is done in the older journals, which are consulted only when an article has been located through a bibliographical search. A copy of such an article can be obtained from the NLM network within a few days. Is it really necessary, then, to permanently bind all journals? Could not each volume or issue be held in a shelf box for the five- to ten-year period of its heaviest usage? If volumes were not permanently bound, they would not be absent from circulation for several months while being bound; they would be on the shelves during the period when they were most heavily used and needed. And, with the availability of computer-based inventory systems, each article in each journal could be located easily. Furthermore, increased coordination of collections between the main medical school library and branch libraries could reduce the duplication of materials and the high cost of storage and primary space.

2. *Student Study Facilities.* One of the primary purposes of this expensive resource, the library, is for study by students. In my inspections of medical schools, however, I still encounter an occasional librarian who frowns on the use of the library as a place for students to study. Individual carrels for students are the most suitable facilities for study, but their number is often inadequate to meet the demand for them. Study cubicles for students could be placed elsewhere in the medical school building if the library is congested or if the librarian discourages its use as a place to study. Programs of instruction in the use of the library that are conducted soon after the first year students arrive on campus often leave much to be desired. A new medical student requires some

time to recognize the need for library research; after all, he or she has just purchased six to eight very large and expensive textbooks and also may have been furnished with a comprehensive syllabus for each course. These materials alone tend to overwhelm the new student; the materials and resources described in the typical library orientation program may not seem very significant in comparison. After the student has had an opportunity to adjust to the flow of materials and information, the chief academic officer or a prominent faculty member should conduct the orientation to the use of medical literature.

3. *Faculty Rank for Librarians.* While it is clear that the library is a service institution, I suggest that each professional librarian be considered for appointment to the faculty on an individual basis. Those who have earned a master's degree could be appointed as instructors or assistant professors. Only those individuals holding doctoral degrees should be appointed to higher rank. The standards for appointment and promotion should be comparable to those in other traditional academic departments; thus, scholarly achievement should be demonstrated before academic rank is granted to anyone. Individuals occupying positions that are primarily service oriented probably should not be granted tenure. For example, deans do not receive tenure in that office. In rare circumstances, there may be justification for granting tenure to a scholarly, senior librarian who has a long record of outstanding service and is nearing retirement. If the school has developed a department or division of medical education chaired by the chief academic officer, then faculty rank for librarians could be assigned in that unit.

4. *Shifting from Gutenberg to the Computer.* From 1960 to 1980, the medical school library received financial support for increases in all kinds of holdings and, in most schools, for the construction or renovation of facilities. Only in a few instances have investments been made in the technology that many predict will be the basis of library operations in the future. The transition to the new computer-based library information systems will require capital investments for hardware and software and funds for the salaries of those technicians needed to operate and maintain the new gadgetry. Budgetary constraints during the mid to late 1980s,

when the new technology will be needed, will probably force the traditional library to alter the nature of its expenditures by deleting questionable and outmoded holdings in order to make space for and pay for the new technology. The widely touted urgency to adopt the new technology could also be used as leverage to correct the fiscal excesses found in the operation of many traditional libraries. Even though it will be reduced, the demand for hard-copy books and journals will continue for several years following the advent of the new technology; yet accommodations must be made for the use of fiscal resources and valuable space in the new era.

5. *Problems Caused by the Computer.* Every medical school library is now connected to the computers of the NLM; on-line bibliographical searches can be performed through the use of the MEDLINE program, which has incorporated references from January 1966 to the present for 3,500 of the 30,000 journals cited in *Index Medicus.* In the medical center library I use for research, a MEDLINE bibliographical search costs twenty-five dollars, in addition to fifteen dollars per hour and five cents for each citation. The faculty and the students of the center are not required to pay the flat fee of twenty-five dollars, but they are charged according to the other rates. The bill for a single research, then, can be considerable. If the researcher has narrowed his subject search according to the NLM's medical subject heading terms, MEDLINE is not complicated or difficult to use (although some, including myself, have problems in scanning the list of citations rolling across the display screen—perhaps because the type font used by computer experts is quite different from that used in most books). If the researcher is not accustomed to the NLM's system for listing subjects of interest to him or if more than one subject is involved in the search, he may need professional help from a librarian trained in the Boolean logic-based ELHILL computer program (McCarn and Leiter, 1973; Horowitz and Bleich, 1981). Dependence on this type of assistance increases the cost of a bibliographical search and limits access to the system to those hours when technical assistance is available. There are proposals to simplify other computer programs of the NLM so that an individual can follow instructions and gain access to the system without assistance and at any hour.

Horowitz and Bleich (1981) have reported on their development of a simplified, computer-based literature retrieval program for locating articles in the 400,000 references shelved in the library of Beth Israel Hospital in Boston. Simpler than the MEDLARS-MEDLINE-ELHILL program, this program, known as "Paperchase," employs a microcomputer that has been programmed with the NLM's MEDLARS indexing for the past five years of about 250 journals in the library. Normal vocabulary can be used to search for a desired journal article at any time, day or night. A similar system could be established in comparable settings, especially where clinical care is delivered and where information may be needed quickly at any hour.

Since antiquity, most scholars and beginning learners have wanted to possess a personal copy of every writing of lasting interest to them. Until recently, purchasing an entire book or subscribing to a journal was the only way to obtain a personal copy, unless reprints of a single article could be obtained. With the advent of the ubiquitous photocopying machine, this is no longer the case. On the basis of the report of the Association of Academic Health Sciences Library Directors (1980–81), I have estimated that over 128 million single photocopies were made in the 126 medical school libraries in one year. This number does not include reprints of single journal articles for distribution to an entire class of medical students or for inclusion in course syllabi. The lesson is obvious: Most people want a hard copy of the whole article on the spot; this would be the case even if the bound volumes were replaced by journals stored on video discs or by other means of electronic transmission. The heavy use a photocopying machine receives justifies a modest price for one copy, preferably around five cents.

6. *Central Coordination by the Chief Academic Officer.* The modern medical school library is facing a period of adaptation and transition in the foreseeable future. On the one hand, there is the new technology to be incorporated into the library's resources; on the other, there is rising competition from the advocates of multiple-media materials found in the typical learning resource center and from other experts in biomedical communications and educational methods. Under these circumstances, school-wide competition for finances and space is likely. I recommend that the chief academic

officer carefully supervise those involved in any manner with the collection, storage, retrieval, and programmed usage of the traditional and newer resources in order to coordinate the management of such resources for use in the educational program involving the faculty and students.

7. *Facilities for Beginning Students and Scholars.* The different needs of the beginning medical student and the seasoned academic scholar for learning materials and informational services should be addressed. For example, the learning resource center at the Medical College of Virginia is obviously of great value to the younger medical students, while the more advanced systems for literature retrieval are more likely to be needed by the advanced students and faculty. As the new technology is adopted, the wisdom of squeezing the beginning learners and advanced scholars in the same facility—heretofore called the library—needs careful examination.

Furthermore, the chairperson of each academic department involving significant teaching responsibilities should explore the possibility of expanding or developing a departmental library and learning center for the relevant specialized subject material. The principal journals in the specialty, the current textual and reference materials, and a basic collection of multiple-media learning resources could be assembled, maintained, and evaluated by the departmental faculty members, the best authorities to judge such materials. This local, specialized learning center should have an appropriately selected microcomputer that is compatible with the more elaborate systems found in the central library. Each department could emulate the "Paperchase" system described by Horowitz in developing a simple, English-language retrieval program to local references available in the departmental center. Such a program could be expanded to include the larger specialized literature collection in the central library; direct access to the NLM's network could be realized later. If departmental libraries are developed, however, the materials held there must be catalogued in the central library.

This proposal is based on the theory that learning entails two steps: first, the appropriate information must be obtained, preferably in the form of a "take-home" hard copy; second, that information needs occasional to frequent evaluation and interpretation from someone who is qualified to give them—that is, the faculty member, who is rarely accessible in the library but is usually found in the department. If the journals of the future are published electronically (Broad, 1982), members of the departmental faculty may subscribe to them directly and use the departmental micro-computer as the receiving instrument.

The needs of the beginning learner deserve special attention. As the central libraries move to place everything on video discs and other electronically retrievable systems, the departmental librar-ies and the learning resource centers could emerge as facilities particularly suited to the beginning learner. As they progress through their educational program, the medical students will need to learn to use the electronic library of the future; when motivated, they usually learn very quickly and well. The faculty member of yesterday and today probably will have the most difficulty in changing his habits of research and scholarship; accustomed to the use of card catalogues and journal abstracts, he will have to adjust to reading electronic blips on a cathode-ray screen. The development of a departmental facility such as the one I have described will help the faculty make the difficult adjustment to the new technology that will dominate the central library of the future.

10

Hospitals
for Teaching
Clinical Medicine

The resources essential for the operation of a medical school that I have described thus far are somewhat similar to those needed in any other program of advanced instruction in a scientific field, such as biology. The teaching hospital—the setting for more than half of the M.D. educational program—is unique within the broad spectrum of resources for higher education. For several millennia or more, medical students have learned their profession by being associated for a period of time with experienced physicians, whom they assist in providing medical care to patients. In the modern teaching hospital, the best forms of therapy known to medical science are administered to patients by medical faculty members who have received superior educational training in leading medical centers. Medical students assigned as clinical clerks for a period of study in a teaching hospital become members of a functioning health care team headed by one or more faculty members and consisting of several recent M.D. graduates enrolled in programs of graduate medical education, one or more fellows (who have completed their

209

graduate medical education), members of the nursing staff, and other
health professionals, including social workers, pharmacists, various
specially trained therapists, medical librarians, and technicians.

The Hospital: A Short History

Some form of hospital has existed for a very long time. The
priest physicians of early Egypt, the Buddhists in India, the Greeks,
the Muslims, and the early Israelites all maintained medical or
nursing care centers, particularly for use by travelers. The beginnings
of the modern hospital, however, are usually traced to an action
by the Council of Nicaea in 325 A.D. instructing the Catholic bishops
to establish hospitals in every cathedral city as acts of Christian
charity. Ten years later, Emperor Constantine closed all pagan
healing temples. Medical care also was available in the monasteries
or in hostels for healing; most of the care rendered in these
institutions was to the incurable, particularly the poor. In the
seventh century, the Hotel Dieu was established in Paris. Like all
medieval hospitals, the Hotel Dieu was crowded; often several
patients were placed in the same bed, and cross-infections resulted.
During the eleventh century, crusaders and pilgrims were cared for
in hospices operated by the Knights of Malta. In England, St.
Bartholomew's Hospital was founded in 1123, and St. Thomas's
was established in 1215; after Henry VIII broke from the Roman
Catholic Church and closed the monasteries in 1549, these hospitals
were rechartered as secular institutions. The oldest hospital in North
America is the Hotel Dieu de Québec, which was chartered by Louis
XIV in 1639. The Pennsylvania Hospital was founded in 1751, the
New York Hospital in 1771, and the Massachusetts General Hospital
in 1811. Until the end of the nineteenth century, however, people
with the money to pay for health care were treated in their homes
by physicians (Vogel, 1980; Siegerist, 1966).

After her experiences in the Crimean War of 1853, Florence
Nightingale's path-breaking work in nursing care led to marked
improvements in that field. It was not until the beginning of the
twentieth century that the hospital became the center for modern
therapeutic medicine, the origins of which can be traced to the
biomedical scientific discoveries of the late nineteenth century

(Knowles, 1973; Garrison, 1966). Around 1900, after the germ theory of disease was understood and accepted, hospitals began to organize patient care in large, open wards, which usually contained forty widely separated and well-ventilated beds. Gradually, the economic circumstances of hospitalized patients began to change, and by 1910 a few single rooms were made available to the affluent; by the late 1920s and 1930s, semiprivate rooms for two to four patients were established. To a great extent, the large open wards have disappeared, except in a few obsolete municipal charity facilities.

Levels of Medical Care

There are four different levels of medical care available to patients today. The kind of nursing care that is mainly palliative can be rendered in the patient's home or in an organized nursing home. Therapeutic medical care is usually divided into three levels. Primary medical care is most frequently administered to patients who are able to walk into the diagnostic and treatment office of a physician; in the early 1980s, however, some physicians once again began to render this type of care to the patient in the home.

Secondary medical care, involving surgery that is elective and fairly simple and the repair of minor trauma, is usually too complex to be delivered in the physician's office and, in many instances, is provided in community hospitals in the suburbs of towns and cities. Ordinarily, the community hospital is small and has an entirely voluntary medical staff, members of which may practice in several such hospitals. More specialized services, such as radiology and pathology, may be directed by part-time specialists who are active in other small hospitals. Nurse anesthetists, rather than anesthesiologists, may provide anesthesia. Family medicine specialists who treat people of all ages usually admit their patients to the community hospital where secondary medical care is provided; they may be joined by other physicians who render some form of general primary care, such as general internists, pediatricians, and obstetricians. With few exceptions, educational programs for undergraduate and graduate medical students are usually not found in the community hospital of less than two hundred beds.

Tertiary medical care encompasses the diagnosis and therapy of complex disease and the repair of extensive trauma. Usually the province of specialists, the tertiary referral hospital often receives patients who have been seen initially in the physician's office or in the small community hospital. The tertiary hospital usually has four to five hundred beds, a large medical staff of well-trained specialists, a well-organized nursing service, and a large cadre of technically trained support personnel directed by physicians who are employed for this purpose. This type of hospital maintains the most modern diagnostic and therapeutic services, which are technically intricate and very expensive.

Types and Characteristics of Teaching Hospitals

Although medical students are often taught in doctors' offices, group clinics, nursing homes, public health service facilities, and secondary care/community hospitals, the bulk of the physician's clinical education takes place in the tertiary hospital that has been specially organized and designed for teaching purposes. The system of medical care and education found in the United States is highly diverse, but the following general characteristics apply to the "flagship" teaching hospital that is used most effectively for the clinical education of medical students (adapted from Butler, Bentley, and Knapp, 1980):

• The hospital is accredited for residency training in most or all of the available programs in graduate medical education. Each educational program is directed by the chairperson or designee of the respective academic department of the related medical school. Extra faculty resources have been allotted to the residency programs in specialties in which medical students are assigned to serve as clinical clerks. Residents have been selected, in part, for their effectiveness in instructing undergraduate medical students. Fellowships are available in selected specialties; fellows divide their time between the study of clinical problems and relevant research in the laboratories operated by the faculty of the related medical school.

- All members of the hospital medical staff who participate in educational programs have been appointed to the faculty after the customary scrutiny of their qualifications. The administrative director of each hospital service is selected by the appropriate academic department chairman if the hospital is owned and operated by the medical school. If the hospital is an independent affiliate of the medical school, the directors of clinical services are usually selected by representatives of the hospital and the school.

- In order to meet the needs of patient care and the objectives of the educational programs, the hospital maintains the full spectrum of modern diagnostic and therapeutic services, unless certain expensive resources are located in another related institution by mutual agreement in order to avoid duplication. In the latter situation, such agreements should also include arrangements for the education of medical students, residents, and fellows, whose work may involve the use of the shared resources. The education of physicians in these institutions also involves the delivery of secondary medical care.

- The patients in a teaching hospital are admitted under the general expectation that each may be included, in some manner, in the educational programs for physicians and other health professionals. A well-staffed and well-equipped teaching hospital usually attracts a diverse mix of patients with a wide variety of diseases and trauma.

- The physical layout of the teaching hospital includes space to be used by students in their educational activities. At each nursing station, space should be provided where medical students can review patients' charts and write their descriptions of the patients assigned to them. A small conference room equipped with a blackboard, X-ray view boxes, slide projection equipment, and, in the future, a terminal for a microcomputer connected to the medical school library should be located on each floor of patients' rooms or in a large wing on each floor of the building. The hospital should contain at least one auditorium for staff meetings, seminars, or other educational functions, as well as several smaller meeting rooms large enough to accommodate thirty to forty people. The hospital cafeteria

should contain several small- to medium-sized rooms for use
by the medical staff during working luncheon or dinner
meetings.

- The teaching hospital must have a working library of clinical
texts and journals; by an uncomplicated administrative arrangement, it should be accessible to staff physicians and residents
at all hours. The library should be a branch or close affiliate
of the medical school. Unless the hospital is near the medical
school library, the hospital library should consider the development of a microcomputer-based system for the retrieval of
articles from its journal collection. Such a system is in operation
now at Boston's Beth Israel Hospital (Horowitz and Bleich,
1981).

    The preceding description of a teaching hospital is broad
enough to encompass hospitals of all types of ownership. Privately
owned, nonprofit hospitals include those operated by self-
perpetuating boards of trustees, religious organizations, and various
associations. Proprietary hospitals organized for profit making
traditionally have belonged to individuals, sometimes physicians;
however, a recent trend is the formation of national chains of
proprietary hospitals owned by corporations. Public hospitals are
institutions controlled by municipal, county, state or federal authorities. Many hospitals have elected to expand their traditional
provision of medical care to patients through participation in some
elements of the education of the physician, either as an independent
venture or in close relationship with a medical school. In the United
States, residency training programs may be accredited and approved
in independent hospitals; in Canada, however, all post-M.D. residency training programs are controlled by the medical schools.

    University-Owned Teaching Hospitals. Before fiscal con-
straints emerged as a general phenomenon in the United States
during the mid-1970s, the goal of most medical school deans seems
to have been the development of a university-owned teaching
hospital. By 1980, there were seventy-three teaching hospitals owned
by the 126 medical schools and/or their sponsoring universities.
Eleven of these were built or acquired by the 40 new medical schools

established between 1960 and 1980. Twenty-six of the teaching hospitals belong to private universities; the remainder belong to state universities or are under the professional control of a state university with ownership vested in some level of government (Association of American Medical Colleges Council on Teaching Hospitals, n.d.).

In the university-owned teaching hospital, essentially all medical staff members are appointed to the medical faculty. The medical care delivered to patients is controlled and regulated by the faculty, who demonstrate expert medical care through teaching programs and perform some clinical research in this setting. Historically, university-owned hospitals have been the locus of the very expensive diagnostic and treatment technology. By the mid-1970s, the escalating costs of operating hospitals of any kind had become a major fiscal problem. The teaching hospital has been particularly burdened by the burgeoning operating costs because of the complexity of the diagnostic and treatment facilities required for patients with illnesses and injuries more serious than those found in hospitals focusing on the delivery of secondary medical care. In particular, the teaching hospital's financial operations have been adversely affected by the diminishing state and local revenues that ultimately provide partial coverage of the care needed by patients who are seriously ill and indigent. Such state and local government revenues declined from an average of 31.6 percent of total operating revenues in 1971 to 11.2 percent in 1978 (Isaacs, 1980; Butler, Bently, and Knapp, 1980).

Federal legislation enacted in the early 1980s and the concomitant development of administrative regulations have reduced the amount of reimbursements to teaching hospitals that provide medical care to patients who are eligible for medical benefits under the Medicare and Medicaid programs. The fiscal constraints affecting hospitals will be exacerbated even more by the tighter Medicare controls established by a new program adopted September 3, 1982 (Iglehart, 1982). In view of these fiscal constraints, it is clear that the teaching hospital will have to adjust to the difficult financial environment by changing some of its organizational and operating characteristics in order to survive. As an example, Berger and Roth (1984) have described their experiences with the new forms of hospital cost containment in New Jersey and the impact on management of university hospitals.

The university hospital needs a director who possesses the knowledge and ability to manage the institution's fiscal affairs and relate empathetically to its educational programs. This kind of hospital is subject to external regulations and forces that can affect revenues immensely and sometimes abruptly; large operating deficits often result during a brief time span. Some principal fiscal officers of the university now also scrutinize carefully the financial status of the university hospital, so that deficits can be recognized and dealt with effectively when they are imminent.

Medical School/Teaching Hospital Partnerships. Many medical schools have formed partnerships with major teaching hospitals that function under the trusteeship of independent boards of directors. Although the nature of these time-honored relationships and contracts between a school and a hospital may vary from case to case, the functional result is that the medical school faculty provides the same general supervision of the standards of patient care and the same control of the educational programs found in the university-owned teaching hospital. Some examples of a partnership between a medical school and an independently controlled teaching hospital are Harvard Medical School with Peter Bent Brigham and Women's Hospital in Boston; Johns Hopkins Medical School with Johns Hopkins Hospital in Baltimore; the University of Pennsylvania Medical School with Philadelphia Children's Hospital; Baylor College of Medicine with Texas Children's Hospital in Houston; Washington University School of Medicine with Barnes Hospital in St. Louis; and the University of Southern California School of Medicine with Los Angeles County Hospital. Some partnerships are supervised by an official joint operating board consisting of trustees or directors appointed by both the school and the hospital. These teaching hospitals are also subject to the fiscal problems arising from inadequate third-party remuneration of the costs of medical care.

Medical School/Veterans Hospital Relationships. Immediately after World War II, veterans' service organizations and the press severely criticized the quality of the medical care being provided in veterans hospitals, which, at the time, were heavily used. In view of the criticism, Congress enacted P.L. 79-293 in January 1946. The new law established the Veterans Administration Department of Medicine and Surgery and placed it under the direction of a physician/chief medical director. Veterans Administration (VA) hospitals were also authorized to become involved in graduate medical education.

The first chief medical director, Major General Paul R. Hawley, and his associate and successor, Paul B. Magnuson, issued Policy Memorandum No. 2 entitled "Policy in Association of Veterans Hospitals with Medical Schools" and dated January 30, 1946. This directive instituted the "deans committee" of senior members of medical faculties to help recruit the full-time medical staff members of affiliated VA hospitals and to supervise the educational programs. This arrangement has allowed the medical schools to recruit medical staff members of high quality for the VA hospitals. Good physicians are attracted by the opportunity to obtain faculty appointments and to engage in educational and research programs sponsored by the schools and the VA hospitals (Cooper, 1976); as a result, the veterans who are patients in VA hospitals now commonly enjoy medical care comparable to that rendered in university teaching hospitals. Many medical schools participate in the partnership through the assignment of both residents and undergraduate medical students for rotations at "Dean's Committee" VA hospitals. Without the partnership with the medical schools, the VA hospitals would have difficulty in recruiting medical staff of high quality (as was the situation prior to 1946). It could be anticipated that without affiliation the quality of medical care for veterans would decline abruptly. Furthermore, the affiliations with the VA hospitals enabled the medical schools to expand their enrollments of medical students during the years from 1960 to 1980 to levels that would not have been possible without the partnerships (Cooper, 1976).

In 1980, 137 VA hospitals and 41 outpatient clinics were affiliated with 104 medical schools through the "Dean's Committee" mechanism (Veterans Administration, 1981). In 1972, P.L. 92-542 extended the VA/medical school partnerships by direct sponsorship for seven years of the following newly established state-owned and operated medical schools: Texas A&M University, University of

South Carolina, Wright State University, Marshall University, and
East Tennessee State University. During 1979–80, VA hospitals
participated in part of the educational programs for 20,427 medical
students and 24, 286 residents. During the same year, the VA hospital
system spent $137.7 million for research activities on the part of
hospital staff members, admitted 1,359,271 inpatients, and provided
treatment to 17,971,407 ambulatory patients in outpatient clinics
(Worthen, 1981; Veterans Administration, 1981).

The relationships between the medical schools and the
"Deans Committee" VA hospitals have not always been entirely
placid. Political influences and pressures emanating from other
forces have impinged on the relationships from time to time. It
is fortunate, however, that the position of chief medical director
has been occupied by a series of physicians who, sometimes by
heroic efforts, have been able to maintain the general principles
of Major General Hawley's Policy Memorandum No. 2; thus, a
standard of medical care worthy of their services to the nation has
been preserved for the veterans.

Affiliated Hospitals Used in Teaching Programs. During the
early 1980s, no medical school in the United States or Canada has
been able to implement the full spectrum of its educational programs
for the physician in a single teaching hospital. From approximately
1950 until 1980, the increase in affiliations between hospitals and
medical schools paralleled rapid growth in the numbers of medical
students, interns, and residents. The largest group of hospitals
involved in the clinical education programs of the medical schools
are those independent institutions, of considerable variety, that are
affiliated under a contract or written agreement or a long-standing
custom establishing an educational relationship ranging from an
affiliation of a limited nature (for example, in a single department)
to a comprehensive interface involving the entire institution. The
hospitals have sought the affiliations in order to improve the quality
and range of patient care, to respond to community needs (for
example, for a new medical school), and to facilitate the recruitment
of young M.D. graduates to fill residency training positions in the
hospitals. The schools have sought affiliations with the hospitals
in order to provide increased numbers of students with the clinical
experience gained by supervised, limited participation in the medical

care of an adequate number and variety of patients and by witnessing forms of medical care different from those rendered in the univerity hospital. A successful affiliation depends upon a good working relationship between the hospital management team and the respective departmental chairmen.

Charity Teaching Hospitals. Many early affiliated hospitals, where an earlier generation of physicians learned clinical medicine, were municipal or county institutions founded to care for the indigent sick. Early examples of these were Boston City Hospital, Bellevue in New York City, Philadelphia General, Baltimore City, Charity of New Orleans, Cook County of Chicago, Parkland Memorial in Dallas, Denver General, and San Francisco General. In some charity hospitals, there is a tradition of affiliating with more than one medical school within the same city. Despite the need for charity hospitals, their use is made difficult by irregular fiscal and professional management by politicians. Some mayors and other officials have used employee positions—even medical staff appointments—for political patronage. The operating expenses of government-owned charity hospitals are often inadequately funded; as a result, the quality of care rendered to patients and demonstrated to students is often less than ideal. The traditional charity hospitals are characteristically burdened with an excessive number of seriously ill patients; frequently, the emergency rooms are filled with patients in staggering quantities. In 1965, with the advent of Medicare and Medicaid, many patients eligible for reimbursement of their hospitalization costs began to seek care in private hospitals. A few charity hospitals closed. The patient loads in charity hospitals were thus somewhat reduced. If the Medicare and Medicaid programs are revised by Congress so as to increase the cost of care borne by the patient, then many indigents will be forced to return to the charity hospitals, some of which have recently reduced their services and numbers of beds.

The uncertainties found in relationships with public charity hospitals undoubtedly induced the medical schools to seek affiliations with private hospitals, some of which had no prior history of involvement with medical education. This was the prevailing attitude and situation in the period between 1960 and 1980, when the forty new medical schools began to develop their teaching programs.

Numbers and Variety of Patients Needed for Clinical Teaching

A general hospital is staffed and equipped to deal with most of the diseases and injuries afflicting people of both sexes and of all ages. Veterans hospitals may limit patient admissions largely to adult males and children's hospitals to children only, and some hospitals may provide only psychiatric care or some form of multidisciplinary care, such as rehabilitation. Thus, medical schools may need to form affiliations with more than one type of hospital, since the medical school dean and the clinical chairmen must make arrangement for demonstrations to students of expert medical care of patients of diverse ages and both sexes who exhibit the full range of disease problems in each recognized specialty of modern medicine. The quantity of patients in each category—that is, medical specialty—must be large enough so that each medical student and each post-M.D. trainee will have the opportunity to study an optimal number of disease problems during an assigned interval in the curriculum.

Formerly, a single, large general hospital with 700 to 800 beds was adequate to provide clinical learning experiences to a medical school class of approximately eighty students. However, the enrollment expansions detailed in the earlier chapters of this book forced the schools to seek additional affiliations. A school affiliated with a large but poorly financed municipal charity hospital, a modest-sized VA hospital, and a small university hospital may have needed to affiliate with one or more general hospitals, a children's hospital, and a psychiatric care facility in order to meet the educational needs of its larger classes. Since not all patients admitted to the hospital are suitable for assignment as "teaching cases," the raw number of beds required should not and cannot be calculated with simple methods. An acceptable but crude standard is eight to ten beds for each clinical clerk in a single class.

Lessons Learned

Medical schools in the United States enrolled 7,177 first-year students in 1950; 8,298 in 1960; 11,348 in 1970; and 17,204 in 1980.

Although a few of these schools were able to accommodate the student increases through existing arrangements for clinical teaching, most had to expand their affiliations to include additional new hospitals. All forty new schools have relied heavily on affiliated hospitals; twenty-nine own no university hospital and are thus entirely dependent on affiliated hospitals. In 1977, Keyes and his associates published a detailed study of the clinical teaching hospital networks utilized by six selected medical schools. This publication, *Medical School-Clinical Affiliation Study,* contains much information about the patterns of affiliation. Drawing upon this study and upon my experience with the process of accrediting all schools, old and new, from 1960 to 1980, certain observations can be presented.

1. *Problems with New Affiliations.* The hospital that has never been affiliated with a medical school has developed over time a set of dynamic relationships among the principal components of its power structure. The hospital relates to the public most commonly through its legal owners of record, the board of directors. These individuals may be self-perpetuating, or they may be appointed to a term of office by some sponsoring organization, which may or may not make financial contributions to the operating budget. The directors may become deeply involved in the affairs of the hospital. (In one famous case, the chairman of a hospital board resided in an office tower of the hospital building complex and from that vantage point sallied forth day and night to superintend the activities of the hospital!) Most directors properly elect to remain somewhat aloof from daily operations and instead concentrate on the formulation of policy and other matters of governance; they depend on their employed executive, the hospital's chief executive officer, to manage the complex day-to-day operations. Another component is the professional staff, consisting of physicians of every conceivable specialty and personality type. They arrange for the hospitalization of their patients, and those who admit large numbers of patients are considered very significant by the director, whose principal technique for operating without a deficit is to maintain a high rate of occupancy of the beds. During the 1970s, the United States became "overbedded" in most urban settings; that is, more hospital beds were maintained in service than were actually needed to handle the aggregate flow of patients.

A demonstrated capacity to cope with responsibility is a standard for the selection of physicians entering the profession as students. Their educational experience fosters the acquisition of strong feelings of self-reliance as their professional competence grows. All of this means that a mature hospital staff is composed of rugged individualists of various ages who expect benign handling by the fiscally minded director and his staff. The usual sociological forces found in group behavior have led to the development of some sort of "pecking order" among physicians, usually structured and divided on the basis of specialties. In many cities, a physician holds staff memberships in several hospitals. If his status in one hospital leaves something to be desired, he can always take his patients elsewhere. Yet, at time passes, an uneasy but relatively stable equilibrium develops in the power structure.

Entering this arena is a medical school seeking an affiliation with one or more hospitals. Initially, several hospitals may jockey for designation as the "flagship" teaching hospital. An older medical school may find that a hospital it is cultivating for affiliation has a number of staff physicians who work there precisely because it has no educational programs. I have been told in several areas of the country that, as the proposed relationship is spelled out in detail, 15 percent of the physician staff bitterly oppose the affiliation, another 15 percent are delighted at the prospect, and the remaining 70 percent are relatively neutral or benign toward the proposal— —as long as their personal prerogatives in the hospital are not disturbed.

When a new affiliation is successful, the dean and his cadre of clinical professors and specialists have usually devoted substantial time and effort to communicating the principles of the proposed affiliation agreement to the medical staff. A harmonious and productive relationship between the school and the hospital is enhanced by communication between the university president and his trustees on the one hand and the hospital's trustees on the other. The latter must provide leadership to assure the director that the new arrangement justifies modest rearrangements in well-established habits. The role of the hospital director is pivotal. My studies reveal several situations in which an affiliation with a major hospital failed—to the jeopardy of a new medical school—because the hospital director felt that his ability to manage the hospital and to fulfill its mission was threatened. The planners of an affiliation should expect many hospital staff members to receive incomplete information; fundamental facts may be exaggerated or distorted unless assiduous diplomacy is exercised through consistent and constant verbal and written communications between the dean and the power structure of the hospital.

2. *Problems Caused by the Medical Faculty.* During the period from 1960 to 1980, some deans and full-time faculty members who had long previous experience in a university-owned hospital occasionally rebuffed the physician staff of a hospital being wooed for affiliation; often the faculty failed to understand the staff's fears of loss of status, as well as uncertainties about the potential economic loss under a new administrative arrangement. Many faculty members who grew up in the hierarchical organization of the classic university-owned hospital—where the clinical chairman expects to be treated like a Prussian field marshall of the eighteenth century—have had difficulty in adjusting to the modified form of leadership appropriate in the new arrangements. By the 1970s, the reflex-like disdain of the medical center academician for the quality of medical care rendered in the average "outside hospital" of the mid-1900s (or earlier) was not justified. The excellent education gained by physician-specialists in the medical school centers after 1950 brought to many well-organized private hospitals of the 1970s capabilities rivaling those in the university-owned hospitals.

3. *Town-Gown Disputations.* Out of the poor flow of information, the delicate sensibilities, the misunderstandings, and the overbearing behavior on the part of both the academicians and town-based physicians, a number of "town and gown" disputes developed; physicians in private practice in that town challenged the efforts of the academic professors/physicians to affiliate with a private hospital or to contract with a city or county to provide staffing and professional control for public hospitals. In one of the latter circumstances, a contract, several decades old, between a school and a city hospital was discontinued when private physicians used political pressure to break it—because the school had made arrangements for the construction of a state hospital to care for non-city-resident indigents and some private patients of the faculty. As

a result of the break in this affiliation contract, the hospital's entire staff of interns and residents was lost, and the care for the patients involved severely deteriorated. In a similar situation, a private medical school affiliated with a municipal/county hospital sought to have a replacement building, for which bonds had been voted, relocated from an inner-city area to an attractive site in a newly developed medical center. Local physicians opposed this move, stating that the medical school would "gain too much power" from the relocation. The wily politicians in power held a public referendum on the issue. The voters balloted heavily in favor of the new medical center location. These two examples illustrate the need for careful planning and actions by a school seeking an affiliation with any kind of hospital.

4. *To Teach or Not to Teach.* A hospital that has not been affiliated with a medical school but that does have experience with independent programs in graduate medical education will have little difficulty in identifying physician staff members who are willing and competent to serve as volunteer instructors in a new program of clinical clerking for medical students. The hospital with no history of educational activity presents a different situation. Here the arrival of medical students on the scene has often been greeted with pleasant anticipation upon the announcement of the plan, with some anxiety in the months just before the students arrive, and with rejection by some physicians who, one or two income tax quarters after their arrival, discover that the investment of time in teaching has reduced their personal incomes. Not all physician staff members are interested in teaching; some are temperamentally ill equipped to become teachers, and all require some planned guidance for efficient discharge of teaching assignments.

The assignment of faculty rank to nonpaid volunteers has been the cause of much dispute. Every physician who is assigned teaching responsibilities should be appointed to the faculty through the usual due process procedures. The oldest tradition is to appoint volunteer teachers to an academic rank modified by the designation of "clinical," which distinguishes them from full-time, paid faculty members. What follows this designation in the academic title has usually been the source of the disputes. If at all possible, a grading of volunteer faculty into various ranks should be avoided, and a general category of rank should be devised instead. For example, in developing the new school at the University of Arizona, DuVal used the designation "clinical associate" (DuVal, 1972).

5. *The Patient in the Teaching Hospital.* A patient admitted to a nonteaching hospital by his private physician can expect to see that physician an average of two times a day for brief visits, unless his illness is grave and life threatening. Medical care, diagnostic tests, and other related procedures are delivered by the physician staff and various technologists according to the orders written in the patient's chart by the admitting physician or a resident physician to whom he delegates that authority. In the teaching hospital, the patient may be admitted by a private physician on the staff or referred to a "consultant" physician on the hospital staff/faculty.

In an older hospital with a well-established teaching program, patients have usually grown accustomed to the various participants in a medical care team and are often pleased with the amount of attention they receive. Indeed, it is not unusual for a patient to become so attached to a medical student assigned to him that he refuses the ministrations offered by a distinguished departmental chairman making an uncommon appearance in the patient's room until "My own doctor says it is okay." Often the medical student sees the patient soon after he arrives in his room; the resident becomes involved early with the patient, certainly if the patient is very ill. If the illness is particularly severe, the supervising physician sees the patient early; even if it is not, this individual will devote substantial time to the patient and his problems during evening rounds or early morning general rounds.

In a hospital that has recently become involved in a teaching relationship with a medical school, there is no tradition to aid the patient in understanding the role played by medical students, residents, clinical fellows, admitting physicians, teaching physicians, faculty member consultants, and all the others who provide medical care. Thus, efforts must be made to communicate to the patient the values of his participation in the program. In a newly affiliated hospital, a period of transition may be required to allow the private physicians and their patients to adapt to the new order. The involvement of private patients as "teaching cases" should be discussed thoroughly with the hospital staff during the negotiations and development of the affiliation agreement.

6. *The Medical Student in a Newly Affiliated Hospital.* The sudden arrival of several dozen third-year medical students in a newly affiliated hospital has been known to create much disruption if little or no definition of their functions has been communicated to the hospital personnel. The clinical clerks are usually assigned in groups of two to four students to a single specialty service; each student is allotted two or three new patients per week for the intense study of the diagnostic and therapeutic procedures determined by responsible, ranking physicians, who are assisted by residents. The clinical clerks often accompany the residents on their working rounds as various services are provided to the patients; they also attend special conferences held for their benefit in the hospital or medical school and, either daily or several times a week, are required to describe their patients in infinite detail to a faculty member on "teaching rounds."

If the affiliated hospital is located some distance from the medical school, as many are, and if public transportation is unavailable, as it often is, then the students may need to use automobiles, which, in turn, require parking space. Students should be instructed to submit to established rules to prevent them from using the parking areas reserved for the physician staff. If possible, the hospital should contain a student locker and lounge area where outer clothes can be stored, along with books and other valuables. Rules about the students' use of the doctors' lounges should also be promulgated. If the resident staff and the physician staff enjoy free meal privileges, decisions should be made concerning whether no meals, a midnight meal (when on all night duty), and/or others are to be provided for students.

In the nursing stations, students should be provided adequate space in which to write up histories of the illnesses of the patients assigned to them—although these areas usually are too small to accommodate all the nurses of varying degrees, the aides, and the clerical assistants, much less the medical students. Students and nurses need to have immediate access to patients' charts; thus, all concerned need to be considerate of the needs of others. Several new hospitals contain the best arrangement: the nurses' station is located adjacent to the students' work area, and the patients' charts are displayed on a carousel rack between the two areas. During the period from 1960 to 1980, I visited many hospitals in which these unsolved problems have been the cause of unnecessary antagonism toward the medical students.

In my opinion, the medical school administrators should analyze the factors in the clinical ecology of their students and provide appropriate arrangements that are satisfactory to all concerned. In particular, deans and departmental chairmen should develop a clinical dress code and require students to adhere to it unless they want to court dismissal. The physicians who staff an affiliated hospital can be expected to object to the presence of any medical student with a slovenly appearance or unprofessional behavior.

Part Four

ๅ๕ๅ๕ๅ๕ๅ๕ๅ๕ๅ๕ๅ๕ๅ๕ๅ๕ๅ๕ๅ๕ๅ๕ๅ๕

Educational Programs for Physicians

ๅ๕ๅ๕ๅ๕ๅ๕ๅ๕ๅ๕ๅ๕ๅ๕ๅ๕ๅ๕ๅ๕ๅ๕ๅ๕

In Chapter One, I described the evolution of medical education in the United States during the eighteenth and nineteenth centuries. The apprenticeship system that had been imported from England during the eighteenth century was gradually succeeded by a system centered largely in the propietary medical schools. During the middle decades of the 1800s, these schools usually offered a curriculum consisting of sixteen to eighteen weeks of study, and the student repeated this course of study once. By the late 1800s, the prevailing curriculum gradually shifted to a partially graded two- to three-year M.D. curriculum to which high school graduates were admitted. During the early twentieth century, the reforms that followed in the wake of Flexner's (1910) report were enforced by the AAMC and the AMA Council on Medical Education; as a result, by mid-century the majority of medical schools in the United States had adopted the requirement that entering students must complete three or four years of premedical collegiate study before undertaking the four years of study involved in the M.D. degree curriculum; in 1980, 95 percent of all medical school entrants had completed four years of college.

Figure 3. Comparative Length of the Education

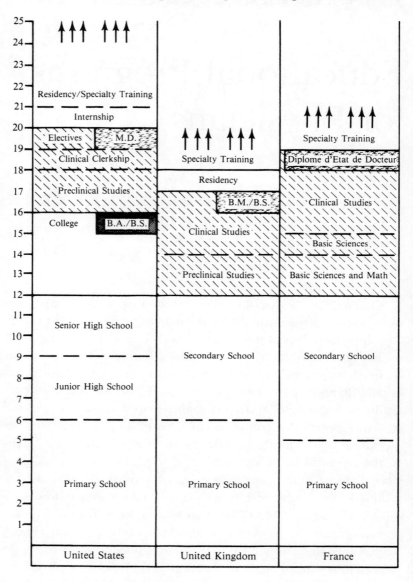

Key: ▅▅▅▅ Degrees required for formal admission to medical studies.
     ◩◩◩◩ The period of medical studies in each country.
     ▨▨▨▨ The medical degree received after the successful completion of the period of medical studies in each country.

of the Physician in Various Countries.

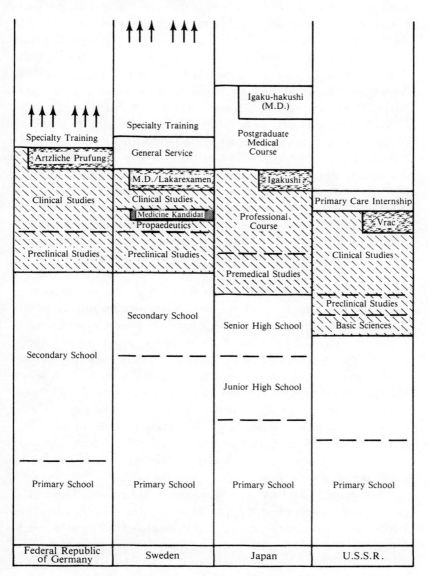

Source: World Health Organization, 1979.

Although the new M.D. graduate of the nineteenth century usually went directly into practice, in the early 1900s M.D. graduates began to seek internship training in hospitals for one year; by 1923, the number of internship training positions had expanded to match the size of the annual crop of new M.D. graduates and after that year exceeded the number of new M.D. graduates (Curran, 1959a). Although "house physicians" were on staff at the Pennsylvania Hospital as early as 1773, formal specialty training in the form of residencies in a teaching hospital did not begin until the founding of Johns Hopkins Hospital in 1891. Opportunities for residency training expanded very slowly until World War II; thereafter, they multiplied rapidly and by the 1960s exceeded the annual number of M.D. graduates. Now, in the early 1980s, before entering medical practice, the aspiring physician must first complete twelve years of primary and secondary school, four years of college, four years of medical school and usually three to six years of residency training. Thus, with the exclusion of the precollege school years, the duration of the formal education of most of those who prepare for the practice of medicine is eleven to fourteen years. After the completion of residency training, a small number of physicians pursue one to three years of fellowship training, usually in a subspecialty area.

After the completion of these formal programs of general and professional education, the physician needs to engage periodically in various forms of continuing medical education to renew old knowledge and acquire new information and skills. The physician should pursue these programs of continuing medical education throughout the period of the active practice of medicine. In a few states, the annual renewal of a physician's license to practice is contingent on the completion of a specified number of continuing medical education courses.

Figure 3 displays a comparison of the typical duration of the formal education of the physician in the United States, the United Kingdom, France, the Federal Republic of Germany, Sweden, Japan, and the Soviet Union. As Figure 3 shows, the period of medical education in the United States (which is comparable to that in Canada) is longer than that in several other highly developed countries. The high standards of secondary school education in the leading European countries may contribute to the differences in the total time involved in the education of the physician. Furthermore, four years of premedical studies usually are required for entrance to medical school in the United States, whereas premedical studies in other countries are incorporated into their medical degree programs.

In the United States, the aspiring physician can pursue premedical studies at one or more of a great number of colleges; the M.D. degree can be pursued at a medical school of another university and residency training can be undertaken at a teaching hospital in a different medical center. A minority of physicians complete their premedical and medical education at one university; most shift the site of their education at least once, and many do so two or three times. Some students choose a different institution for each component of their preprofessional and professional studies; if they follow their residency training with one or more years of advanced fellowship studies, a fourth site may be chosen. The current organization and sequence of education for the physician in North America is the result of a series of evolutionary changes that came about *without* either coordination or regulation by the federal government or by a single national organization in the private sector. In fact, each component is managed separately; sometimes, unilateral modifications of a single component have led to undesirable effects in an adjacent component.

Chapters Eleven through Fourteen describe the several components of medical education in the United States, including a brief account of how each component has evolved to its present state. Following these descriptive chapters, which constitute Part Four, I offer a number of suggestions for improving the education of the physician during the next several decades.

11

The Period Prior to Medical School: High School and College

High School

This significant component of American mass education has fallen on hard times in many communities. Able young people in many public schools frequently fail to find any intellectual challenge and drift with the herd into self-destructive habits instead of acquiring personal discipline while gaining the rudiments of a general education. The widespread decline in educational standards in many high schools is well illustrated by the Herblock cartoon that depicts high school students, literate or not, mounting the educational escalator and then falling off, diplomas in hand. The report of the National Commission on Excellence in Education (1983) gives elaborate details of the quarter-century decline in high school standards. In September 1983, the Carnegie Foundation for the Advancement of Teaching published the results of a major study of American secondary education (Boyer, 1983). The latter report

ESCALATOR EDUCATION

From *Herblock On All Fronts* (New American Library, 1980).

gives additional insight into the dreary daily experiences of students in many high schools.

A few of the intellectually able, energetic, and motivated young people who aspire to become physicians are able to attend academically rigorous private high schools, and an additional small number are able to enroll in special honors or talent public high schools located in some of the large cities. These fortunate students receive instruction from teachers who have acquired a good education and who are highly motivated to facilitate learning by their competitively selected students. In contrast, the bulk of aspiring physicians-to-be must attend the high schools roundly criticized in the two 1983 studies of secondary education. Here, a small minority of bright, well-motivated, and studious young people headed toward college and later toward graduate or professional school take classes with a large majority of students of widely varied intellectual abilities and usually faint or poor motivation for learning (Boyer, 1983).

During the past thirty years, I have made diligent inquiries into the high school experiences of successful medical students. Amid a large amount of sociological information I have collected about these high achievers, I have learned that those who were enrolled in the type of high schools under current criticism seem to possess recognizable characteristics: All are well above the general average in intellectual ability, and most were able, early on, to perceive that they were capable of achieving at a higher level than most of their classmates. This significant finding was made independently by many of the students; others had their special abilities pointed out by an unusual teacher or by insightful parents who induced them to depart from the wasteful behavioral patterns of their heterogeneous classmates. Most of my respondents reported that their early attempts to deviate from the anti-intellectual patterns of peer behavior were met with limited tolerance by their peers. Unfortunately, in American society, elitism is highly regarded in athletic activities at all levels, but intellectual elitism is usually suspect among the general population—especially among the school-aged population.

These successful medical students (who now are all physicians) all gave evidence of above-average energy and drive. This finding is based on the nearly universal history of significant learning experiences—all self-initiated—which supplemented their routine classroom activity. Also, nearly all reported having held a variety of jobs before or after school hours and during summer vacations. Their innate curiosity equipped them to learn from all of their experiences, however mundane, during their youthful years. Obviously, the students who began to develop their independent intellects during high school years and continued the process during their subsequent years in college were able to present attractive candidacy for enrollment in medical school.

College

In the United States and Canada, the general education of the physician begins after the completion of twelve years of non-specific primary and secondary studies. Thus, after graduating from high school, the aspiring physician enrolls in one of approximately 1,100 liberal arts colleges and universities with the general objective of completing the institution's requirements for the baccalaureate degree and the specified course requirements for admission to one or more medical schools.

History of American Colleges. The North American college was originally modeled on the early English institutions for post-secondary education, the Universities of Oxford and Cambridge. In 1639, graduates of Emmanuel College, Cambridge, sought to develop a college for the Massachusetts Bay Colony; several years later, the institution they founded was named Harvard College. William and Mary was founded in 1693, Yale in 1601, and Princeton in 1746; these and other early colonial institutions were nurtured, for the most part, by the clergy of those various religious denominations that played such a central role in seventeeth- and eighteenth-century America (Schmidt, 1957). These "copies" of the original models—and the multitude of copies of the copies—did not replicate all the characteristics of Oxford and Cambridge in frontier America. For instance, in England, from the early days until very recently, a college education was the privilege of a small, elite group. The number of students who complete compulsory secondary school in England has increased, but in 1979 only 33 percent entered Oxford, Cambridge, or other university colleges (British Information Service, 1979).

Although the colonists of the eighteenth century looked to English institutions as models for their own schools of higher education, Americans eventually evolved an approach to higher education that was and is different from its English counterpart. The Revolutionary War and the ongoing hostilities between the new states and Mother England that lasted through the War of 1812 effectively blocked the migration of faculty members from the English institutions to the new colleges founded in America. The affluent student who could afford the fine education one could acquire in England found it either unavailable or too uncomfortable to pursue. Thus, the original American colleges were forced to go it alone; although they were immature in terms of their resources, customs, and standards, these institutions became the model for the new schools that sprang up with the expansion of United States territory. Jefferson's purchase of the Louisiana territory in 1803, Jackson's conquest of the Florida-Alabama territories from 1819 to 1827, the annexation of Texas in 1845, Polk's Mexican conquest in 1848, the rush to the Rockies in 1859, and the completion of the railroad to California in 1869—all these events opened up a vast expanse of land whose inhabitants would need little red schoolhouses, academies, female seminaries, and, ultimately, universities and colleges (Harlow, 1959). By 1980, the number of universities and colleges had grown to 3,134 (National Center for Education Statistics, 1981). These are very diverse institutions that were developed by a fiercely pluralistic society whose citizens have generally rejected federal control of education.

Levels of Preparedness for College. In the following discussion, I am not concerned with describing in detail the contemporary American college with baccalaureate degree programs; instead, I want to focus on the quality of the preparation for professional studies that an aspiring physician receives during his premedical education.

Most colleges annually enroll a heterogeneous cohort of students; the quality of the secondary education received by these new college students ranges from poor to excellent. Some of the oldest and best-endowed private colleges and the strongest of the public institutions (at least in terms of their honor programs) have been able to attract students with respectable academic records and to enable these students to maintain a high level of academic achievement. This much is clear from the SAT scores of their students at entrance and from the scores they receive on the Graduate

Record Examination and the other specialized measures, such as the Medical College Admissions Test, at the time of graduation from college.

In general, however, Scholastic Aptitude Test (SAT) scores have declined sharply since 1973, and the mean scores on any nationally administered entrance exam indicate striking variations in the academic standards of the secondary schools (College Entrance Examination Board, 1980). Newspaper articles decrying the illiteracy of the American high school graduate are daily occurrences. Thus, the colleges have no choice but to build on the scholastic attainments of their students in secondary school.

Changing Campus Attitudes. Not only have recent years seen wide fluctuations in student preparation for college, but the attitudes of students (and professors as well, in some cases) have undergone drastic metamorphoses. With the beginning of the 1960s, the maturing cohorts of college and graduate school candidates waxed in size while traditional respect for the authority of parents, police, parsons, and professors waned. During the 1960s and early 1970s, many colleges and universities were disrupted by dissident students, sometimes aided and abetted by ambivalent faculty members and poorly managed by pusillanimous administrators. In addition, during the Vietnam War, some professors who opposed the military draft succumbed to an academic malaise manifested by a creeping inflation in the grades they gave their students. Ravitch (1983) has described in detail how this widespread campus unrest caused a decline in college entrance and graduation standards.

During this period, when opportunities for college and medical education expanded to the greatest point in American history, relevance, a somewhat utilitarian word, acquired an almost religious meaning. I know a few basic science professors who are still suffering profound shock from being told by freshman medical students during the 1960s that "biochemistry is not relevant—it has nothing to do with real medicine." Also during the 1960s and early 1970s, competition for slots in the professional schools began to gain momentum; some highly competitive premedical students reportedly cheated on examinations and sabotaged laboratory experiments in the hope of enhancing their own chances for entrance to medical school (Tittle and Rowe, 1974).

Education for Everybody. The democratic ideal that underlies the American educational system has been pursued so assiduously during the twentieth century that enrollment in the colleges and universities has included a higher percentage of the appropriate age cohort than in any other nation ever. In the United States, about 55 percent of all who finish high school now enroll in college (National Center for Educational Statistics, 1981). This is in contrast to 33 percent in the United Kingdom, 21 percent in France, 16 percent in the Federal Republic of Germany, 33 percent in Sweden, and 32 percent in Japan (Information Officers, respective embassies, in Washington, D.C., 1979). Although the democratic ideal does encourage a more equitable distribution of the benefits to be gained from a college education, one result has been that the colleges are now packed each year with several million freshmen of varying intellectual ability and with varying academic achievements in high school; many possess little motivation for serious, self-directed study. Robert Hutchins was not far from the mark when he asserted on many occasions that "Every citizen of the United States at birth should have conferred on him/her a baccalaureate degree, so we can get that over with."

Forces Influencing the Premedical Student in College

Although an occasional chap claims that he had fully committed himself to a career in brain surgery by the age of nine, most young people do not feel the urge to enter medicine until late in high school or early in college; they tend to move faster toward the decision when faced with the regulations concerning the selection of a major for the baccalaureate degree.

After choosing medicine as a career goal or after sliding into that choice following enrollment in a series of science courses, beginning premedical students come under the influence of several potent forces:

- Requirements for the baccalaureate degree.
- Requirements or recommendations established by premedical advisors.
- Requirements for admission to various medical schools.

- Requirements for specific courses and specified duration of premedical studies under some state medical licensure laws.
- Rumors of all kinds, originating with older premedical students and with alumni who are now first-year medical students.

The Baccalaureate Degree. Many believe that the baccalaureate degree signifies the achievement of a general liberal arts education. Oxford and Cambridge were originally established as institutions in which an elite group of young gentlemen, in isolated environments, could obtain such an education from excellent tutors who would teach them to think through problems and arrive at solutions, to understand something of the world, and to use their leisure time wisely.

In general, medical educators support the concept of the liberal arts education as the first phase in the formal education of the physician. The problem is that many colleges have difficulty defining what a liberal arts education is: furthermore, many proceed to foul their general requirements by condoning the development of easy courses that become well known and heavily sought by the gregarious undergraduates. For example, the science requirement for many baccalaureate degrees can be met by a somewhat philosophical course in the elementary aspects of geology, properly called "Rocks for Jocks." Many other illustrations of this type can be drawn from colleges from the Ivy League to the far West. In this respect, it is encouraging to know that the Association of American Colleges launched a major project to redefine the meaning and purpose of the baccalaureate degree in 1983 (Association of American Colleges, 1983).

In choosing a major, the college undergraduate usually consults the bulletin of courses. This document may be cast in a comprehensible form, or it may have been edited by a retired registrar and designed for understanding by professors emeriti only; thus, the novice learner is left to the mercy of the advisory system, the fraternity counseling program, or feedback from anybody who has had experience with the major or a particular course in it during the past several semesters.

Most college advisors believe that medicine is based on scientific principles, and there seems to be an easy acceptance of the theory that someone who plans to go to medical school should study some of the prevalent scientific disciplines en route to this goal. If one looks at most requirements for a major in chemistry, one may find that the four years are loaded not only with all kinds of chemistry but also with high-level mathematics and physics (in this respect, see, for instance, the 1983 undergraduate catalogues for Pomona College, Princeton University, Haverford College, and the University of Illinois at Urbana-Champaign). As a result, the student has little time for the liberal arts offerings of the college after he has completed all the mathematics, physics, chemistry, and so on. Therefore, many premedical students reject chemistry and elect biology as a major. The members of the biology faculty are usually less demanding than are the chemists with regard to supplementary studies in mathematics and physics; thus, the student with a major in biology can pursue special interests in the social sciences or the arts.

Thus, the requirements for the baccalaureate degree dominate the thinking and plans of the premedical student in the beginning, at least while he is in the hands of the general advisor or of the rule makers in the several departments granting the baccalaureate degree. Afterward, the premedical student may find that his college has someone called a "premedical advisor."

The Premedical Advisory System. The characteristics and duties of the premedical advisor vary significantly from school to school. In the smaller colleges, this individual is likely to be a biologist or chemist. Occasionally, the student health service physician or someone from the social sciences, such as a psychologist, serves in this capacity. In the larger institutions, there may be a committee composed of all these individuals in addition to a few others; in some instances, the premedical advisory committee is chaired by a representative of the dean's office. The current organization of this system is the same as the one that Severinghaus, Carman, and Cadbury studied in 1953.

In my search for current information about premedical student advising, I asked for a review of the situation by medical students. Phillip Wackym, a sophomore medical student at Vandervilt University School of Medicine, surveyed his classmates during late 1982 and found that 11 percent of the respondents, who received their baccalaureate degrees from forty different colleges, were not satisfied with the information concerning medical school that was provided by their premedical advisors. Thirteen percent were the subjects of recruiting efforts on the part of their advisors, who pressured them to major in the scientific disciplines from which the advisors had been drawn. Forty-two percent were advised to major in the sciences; however, some of these had made that decision before consulting their advisors. Ninety-two percent of the respondents majored in biology, chemistry, or physics, and 4 percent pursued doubled majors in science and the humanities; the remaining 4 percent majored in the humanities. In thirty-eight of the forty colleges attended by the students in the sample, letters of recommendation for each candidate were drafted by a member of the premedical advisory committee of the college (Wackym, 1983).

Having read thousands of letters of recommendation from premedical advisors and advisory committees, I have concluded that these letters often provide little assistance to the admissions committee of the medical school. A letter from a premedical advisory committee often gives a rather homogenized view of each applicant; confronted with hundreds of these letters, the admissions committee is often unable to distinguish one applicant from the other. Most, if not all, applicants from a single school may receive apparently inflated ratings of "superior" or "good," and an admissions committee is usually quick to note this. If the premedical advisory committee uses a formulaic rating scale to evaluate each student, descriptions of personal character and special achievements of each application, in which admissions committees are very interested, may be omitted entirely. There is also the ever-present danger that personal biases against a premedical student may enter the composition of a letter of recommendation by the advisory committee or its secretary. Some advisors have a distinct aversion to the medical profession and may allow this opinion to interfere with the discharge of their institutional responsibilities to premedical students.

In some institutions, faculty members from diverse disciplines provide extremely significant advisory services to premedical students and often devote a great deal of time to advising without adequate secretarial or budgetary support. The work load of the premedical advisor varies from school to school. In 1980, the largest colleges produced 300 to 500 applicants; an estimated 400 colleges produced fewer than ten applicants (Association of American Medical Colleges data).

The effective premedical advisor has a well-established tradition of inviting representatives of the medical schools to visit the campus for the purpose of making presentations to an assembly of premedical students and interviewing students; anything that can be done to facilitate communication between the medical schools and premedical students should be a priority for the premedical advisor. A college that does not provide this kind of preliminary interaction between the premedical student and the medical school leaves its students to the mercy of whims, fancies, and rumors from various sources.

If the medical school publishes a clear and comprehensive bulletin of its programs, if the premedical advisor and his advisees become well acquainted with the Association of American College's annual publication *Medical School Admissions Requirements* (now in its thirty-third year of publication, with an annual sale of 31,000 copies), and if the interface between colleges and medical schools is strengthened through regular exchanges and communication, then the actual requirements for admission to various medical schools will become well known to the premedical students and their advisors. It seems astounding that effective communication is not a routine matter of course; yet it is a common problem today as it was thirty and forty years ago.

Requirements for Admission to Medical School. What are the admissions requirements the medical schools impose on prospective candidates for the study of medicine? Table 18 indicates that the medical schools tend to require that applicants complete studies in inorganic and organic chemistry, biology of several varieties, general physics, English (grammar in particular), mathematics (if not previously studied), and other subjects, such as the humanities and the social sciences. Many educators believe that a significant number of these studies should be included in the colleges' specifications for granting the baccalaureate degree to anyone, regardless of career goal.

Table 19 displays data on admissions to medical school by undergraduate majors. The data suggest that the medical schools

Table 18. Subjects Required by Ten or More U.S. Medical Schools,
1983–84 Entering Class.[a]

Required Subjects	Number of Schools[b]
Organic Chemistry	120
Physics	120
English	89
Inorganic Chemistry	76
Biology (unspecified)	69
General Biology or Zoology	51
General or Inorganic Chemistry	33
Calculus	25
College Mathematics	25
Humanities (unspecified)	15
Chemistry (unspecified)	11
College Algebra	10
Social Science (unspecified)	10

[a]Figures are based on data provided in Fall 1981.

[b]Six of the 126 medical schools (University of Arkansas College of Medicine, Southern Illinois School of Medicine, University of Illinois College of Medicine, University of Missouri–Kansas City School of Medicine, University of North Carolina School of Medicine, and Northeastern Ohio Universities College of Medicine) did not indicate specific course requirements and are not included in the tabulation.

Source: Association of American Medical Colleges, 1982c, p. 8.

are eclectic in their selection of applicants; they do not seem to be guilty of the allegation that they automatically exclude students who have not majored in biology or chemistry—the fact is that the overwhelming majority of students who apply to medical school have selected majors in those fields. This unfounded allegation is rooted in the mistaken perceptions of the premedical student, aided and abetted by premedical advisors who have a scientific orientation, inflamed by rumors spread by undergraduate juniors and seniors who are applicants to medical school, and driven to panic by the commentary of last year's graduates, who this year are enrolled in the first year of medical studies. A typical quote from the latter would be: "Medical school is really tough! My class is full of chemistry majors—even Ph.D.s. I wish I had taken a lot more courses in science." It is easy to understand how the premedical student

Table 19. Acceptance to Medical School by Undergraduate Major, 1980–81 Entering Class.

Undergraduate Major	Total Applicants		Accepted Applicants	
	No.	% of Total	No.	% of Major
Biological Sciences				
Biology	13,609	37.7	6,107	44.9
Microbiology	936	2.6	424	45.3
Physiology	289	0.8	123	42.6
Science (other biology)	148	0.4	64	43.2
Zoology	1,957	5.4	885	45.2
Subtotal	16,939	46.9	7,603	44.9
Physical Sciences				
Biochemistry	1,519	4.2	915	60.2
Biomedical Engineering	258	0.7	167	64.7
Chemical Engineering	267	0.7	148	55.4
Chemistry	4,291	11.9	2,327	54.2
Chemistry and Biology	598	1.7	290	48.5
Electrical Engineering	169	0.5	77	45.6
Mathematics	369	1.0	208	56.4
Natural sciences	401	1.1	226	56.4
Physics	238	0.7	132	55.5
Science (general)	195	0.5	103	52.8
Subtotal	8,305	23.0	4,593	55.3
Nonscience Subjects				
Anthropology	147	0.4	71	48.3
Economics	171	0.5	99	57.9
English	313	0.9	154	49.2
Foreign Language	193	0.5	90	46.6
History	220	0.6	118	53.6
Philosophy	135	0.4	72	53.3
Political Science	110	0.3	51	46.4
Psychobiology	273	0.8	130	47.6
Psychology	1,423	3.9	659	46.3
Sociology	119	0.3	56	47.1
Subtotal	3,104	8.6	1,500	48.3
Other Health Professions				
Medical Technology	425	1.2	116	27.3
Nursing	331	0.9	120	36.3
Pharmacy	555	1.5	198	35.7
Subtotal	1,311	3.6	434	33.1
Mixed Disciplines				
Double Major (science)	557	1.5	293	52.6
Double Major (science and nonscience)	539	1.5	283	52.5
Interdisciplinary Studies	114	0.3	64	56.1
Premedicine	1,221	3.4	621	50.9
Preprofessional	182	0.5	106	58.2
Subtotal	2,613	7.2	1,367	52.3
Other	3,828	10.7	1,649	43.0
Total	36,100	100.0	17,146	47.5

Source: Association of American Medical Colleges, 1982c, p. 10.

can fall into the trap of thinking that, since the medical schools require some study at the introductory levels of chemistry, biology, and physics, the best way to win admission to medical school would be to immerse oneself in the study of science at the expense of the humanities.

When an applicant is interviewed by the admissions committee of a medical school, it is likely that he will be questioned about his course records in organic chemistry, advanced biology, and the like. The members of the committee are justified in thinking that medicine is a science and that the foundation for successful pursuit of medicine as a science is the general accumulation of a scientific base in the form of chemistry, biology, and physics. The medical faculty will and must build on this foundation by applying it to human anatomy, physiology, biochemistry, and similar courses that constitute the bioscientific education of the physician. If the premedical student has studied chemistry for two years and biology for one or one and one half years and has proved to be competent in these studies, the members of the admissions committee will not take a dim view of the applicant if his undergraduate major was in a nonscientific field. Unfortunately, undergraduate premedical students and their advisors often do not believe this and think that the more science the student has, the better.

Thomas (1978) thinks that the premedical curriculum, the problem area in this respect, can be "fixed" by requiring premedical students to concentrate on the study of Latin and classical Greek during the baccalaureate years. He thinks that the term "premed" should be abolished, that premedical advisors should be banished from the campuses, and that the college faculty should select those students who are to enroll in medical school. It seems unlikely that these suggestions will receive wide acceptance among faculty members in either the colleges or the medical schools.

Legal Requirements for Licensure of the Physician. Often hidden away from the premedical students, their advisors, and even some medical school officials are laws or regulations for the licensure of the physician in a number of the states. These laws or regulations often stipulate the completion of certain courses by the premedical student as a prerequisite for the receipt of a license to practice medicine; in some instances, the duration of these studies is specified. Each medical school admissions officer is duty bound to explore the licensure requirements of the state in which his medical school is located and of those states from which the school draws the majority of its students; on this basis, he should act to protect the interests of the students. Although these legal requirements have caused only a few problems in the past, any proposal to alter the design of premedical students should be studied with these legal requirements in mind (Page and Littlemeyer, 1969). During the 1980s, licensure authorities are likely to pay more attention to the laws and regulations of their states as they attempt to cope with the sensitive problem of evaluating the credentials of foreign medical graduates.

Application to Medical School

There has existed for several decades a relatively constant relationship between the number of twenty-two-year-olds and the number of persons applying to medical school (see Figure 4). The number of applicants to United States medical schools began to increase in 1960, reached its apogee in 1974, declined during the next few years, stabilized briefly, and in 1982 appeared to be declining further.

The number of applicants far exceeds the available spaces in the medical schools, in spite of the doubling of enrollments between 1960 and 1980; thus, during the last two decades applicants have often assumed that it is next to impossible to gain admission to medical school. This inaccurate view of the situation has produced a general state of panic, fueled the rumors that circulate with electronic-like rapidity through the campuses, and consumed unnecessary amounts of energy.

The fact is that, during the late 1970s and early 1980s, there was a marked increase in the number of available spaces in the first-year classes of the medical schools; of those who applied for those spaces in 1980, an estimated 1.1 persons per available space

Figure 4. Trends in the Number of Twenty-Two Year Olds, Medical School Applicants, First Year Students, and Graduates.

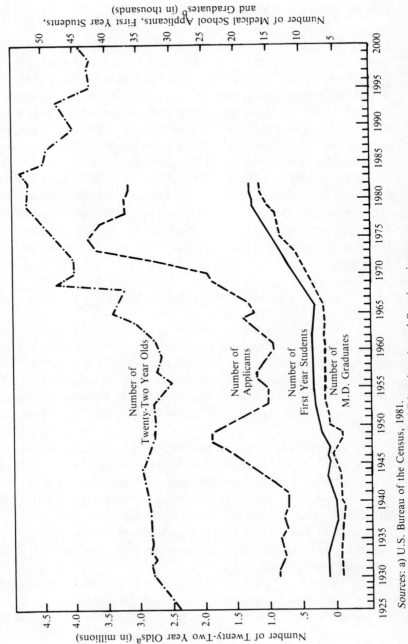

Sources: a) U.S. Bureau of the Census, 1981.
b) Liaison Committee on Medical Education, Annual Questionnaires.

were prime candidates for admissions to medical school; this prime candidacy was defined by their status as fall-term senior undergraduate students seeking admission to medical school for the first time. The remaining applicants were those who were rejected in the previous year (or two years) and those ambitious junior undergraduates who made a long-shot attempt to be admitted to medical school after only three years of premedical studies (often the latter were advised by someone in the collegiate arena to make the attempt "just for the experience of it") (Johnson, 1983, p. 58).

The data in Figure 4 indicate that we can expect a further decline in the number of applicants to medical schools during the remainder of the 1980s due to demographic trends: Whopping increases in tuition and fees, the uncertain economic future of the nation, and other influences will reduce the size of the pool of future applicants. Now that federal laws mandating the enrollment of specified numbers of students have lapsed, the medical schools may reduce the size of their entering classes, and predictions will be more difficult to make. It seems logical, however, to assume that the period of intense competition for the available spaces in the first-year classes of the medical schools is over; indeed, in certain sections of the country, particularly in those states in which only resident applicants are considered for admission, there may be an actual shortage of qualified applicants by the middle to late 1980s. This prediction represents such an abrupt departure from the experience of the last twenty years that it has been very difficult to sell to the premedical students and their anxious parents, who are in constant contact with the admissions officers of the medical schools.

The mechanics of applying to medical school have been streamlined and made more efficient by the development of the American Medical College Application Service (AMCAS) program under the sponsorship of the AAMC. The AMCAS program enables the applicant to complete only one set of application forms. After receiving this set of forms, AMCAS makes duplicate copies of the forms and of everything received from the registrar of the applicant's college(s), verifies the authenticity of the student's records, and forwards a copy of the student's application materials to each of the medical schools to which he is applying. After receiving the materials from AMCAS, the medical schools may send the applicant a second packet of application materials that seek more personal and specific information about the applicant for use by the admissions committee. The AMCAS system, which now involves 100 of the 127 accredited medical schools, saves the student much time and numerous filing fees.

In recent years, there have been other proposals to streamline the application process. For instance, in 1972 the AAMC conducted an extensive and expensive study of the feasibility of using a computer-based program to match applicants and medical schools. Eventually, this proposal was rejected. Also, from time to time there has been discussion of employing a lottery system for the final selection of applicants for enrollment in the medical schools. The admissions committee of a medical school would canvass its entire pool of applicants; on the basis of its admissions criteria, it would then decide which applicants were acceptable. Finally, a drawing or some other form of lottery would be used to select from those in the acceptable category enough applicants to fill the available spaces in the entering class. This proposal has usually been rejected on the grounds that the younger American population is likely to be very suspicious of a lottery system and would prefer to leave the decision to the wisdom of the admissions committees. Such a system has been tried in Europe, however. In 1980, medical schools in the Federal Republic of Germany and in the Netherlands implemented a lottery system as the final stage in the selection of medical students (Bowers, 1980; Burn, 1978).

Selection of Students by the Medical School

The Admissions Committee. Each medical faculty designates a representative number of its members (and often of its students) to serve on the official Committee on Admissions. Sometimes the full-time basic scientist and clinician members of the medical faculty are joined on this committee by volunteers from the local practicing profession, by an occasional representative of another discipline of the university, and, in a few circumstances, by lay individuals.

In the last decade or more, the admissions committees of the medical schools have been composed of exceedingly hard-working individuals. The hard work has been generated by the large number of applicants for the number of spaces available as well as by the custom of each applicant applying not to just one medical school of interest but to a whole cluster. Indeed, it is common for an applicant to apply to an average of nine medical schools, and some students have applied to fifty or more (Gordon, 1979). This behavior of the anxious applicant produces in each medical school a very large number of applications. For example, in the 1980–81 experience, the 36,100 applicants filed 330,888 formal applications to the 126 schools of medicine—for the 16,590 spaces available (Liaison Committee on Medical Education data). To illustrate the workload of individual admissions committees, Table 20 shows the number of applications received in 1980 by various medical schools.

Clearly, it is the duty of the admissions committee at each medical school to consider all the applications received and to make every attempt to select and recruit the best-qualified persons available to fulfill the objectives of their school. The process of selection begins in the early autumn and can require concentrated effort for more than six months; the work load lightens somewhat for the next three or so months, as students who have been granted acceptances by several medical schools make their final decision to settle on a single school, thereby freeing the duplicate appointments for assignment to others waiting in the applicant pool. This acceptance of students by the schools and subsequent selection of a single school by the student consumes inordinate time; the strongest students by all criteria win the majority of the acceptances available, leaving their peers in the same applicant cohort to wait with increasing feelings of desperation until final appointments are made for the national class to begin studies sometimes after the mid-point of the calendar year, usually August or September. On the average, each school offers each of its first-year places to two or more applicants. Most-favored schools fill their classes by offering acceptances to less than 10 percent of their applicants; less-favored schools have offered places to 40 to 50 percent of their applicants (Liaison Committee on Medical Education data).

Grade Point Average. The AAMC publication *Medical School Admissions Requirements* lists the statement made by each of the

Table 20. Medical School Applications Received by Selected Universities,
1980–81.

Medical School	Entering-Class Size	Applications 1980–81	Applications per Position
Georgetown University School of Medicine (P)	205	7,320	35
George Washington University School of Medicine and Health Sciences (P)	150	7,224	48
Johns Hopkins University School of Medicine (P)	120	3,091	26
Stanford University School of Medicine	86	5,711	66
University of Michigan Medical School (S)	187	3,010	16
Indiana University School of Medicine (S)	302	1,287	4
University of Illinois College of Medicine (S)	348	2,034	6
University of Texas Southwestern Medical School at Dallas (S)	203	2,277	11

Key to Symbols: P = Private, S = State.

Note: Most premedical students apply to several schools; thus, the large number of applications received can be quite deceptive. Usually, each applicant is interested in enrollment at any one of the schools to which an application is sent. A more accurate accounting of the quantity of applications received can be obtained from considering the following: in 1980 Johns Hopkins received 3,091 applications; if this total is divided by 9, the average number of applications one premedical student makes, then 344 students applied for 120 positions at Johns Hopkins. In the same year, the University of Texas Southwestern Medical School at Dallas received 2,277 applications; thus, an estimated 275 people applied for 203 positions. Finally, it is likely that the private schools receive more duplicate applications than the average and that the state schools receive fewer.

Source: Association of American Medical Colleges, 1982c, pp. 99, 107, 109, 131, 141, 157, 173, and 301.

medical schools for its criteria for selection of students. There really is not much significant variation. All the schools are interested, first of all, in students who have earned superior or very good grades in the subjects of the collegiate period of study. Often the grade point average for nonscience as well as science subjects is considered significant.

The admissions committee members, through years of experience, acquire considerable sophistication as to the value of the grades from one college to another. Applicants from a college that is well known for inflation of grades are given less attention than are those from an institution that is known to have very demanding standards. While there may not be mathematical precision in these attempts to estimate the merit of the collegiate experience (and the meaning of grades earned in specific courses), the members of the admissions committees do have before, during, and after exposure to the products of the colleges and universities from which they commonly draw their students and should be well informed about these colleges' relative academic standards.

Medical College Admissions Test Scores. Next, the admissions committees have particular interest in the scores earned by the candidates on the Medical College Admissions Test (MCAT). *Medical School Admissions Requirements* contains descriptive information about this test, which attempts to measure (1) students' academic achievement in the introductory level of subjects in the biomedical and physical sciences and (2) their capacity to utilize such information in problem-solving circumstances. The medical schools have used some type of admissions tests since the 1930s. The current test (MCAT) has been in operation only since 1978, but it has been worked through sufficient experience that the members of the medical school admissions committees rely heavily on it in sorting out their candidates.

To illustrate one use of the MCAT scores: If a candidate has a very high grade point average from a college that is suspected of having inflated grades and weak academic standards for promotion and graduation, and if this student's MCAT scores are well below the national mean of scores on the MCAT, then this candidate, in the interview, would be questioned with greater sophistication than might ordinarily be employed. Additionally, superior scores on the MCAT occasionally have been used as justification for accepting a candidate whose grade point average is marginal, especially if the low grades were received mainly in the first year of collegiate study.

Noncognitive Criteria. In selecting medical students, most admissions committees rely considerably on limited cognitive criteria—that is, grade point averages (adjusted in accordance with the standards of the college—or even of individual professors in small colleges) and MCAT scores. This reliance on "numbers," while often criticized, is expected by the applicants (who quickly learn the comparable "numbers" of their competitors), by the premedical advisors, and by the legal counsel retained by disappointed applicants possessing higher "numbers" than those of one or more accepted applicants. Noncognitive criteria also are used, but with guarded confidence and with concern about the hazard of bias in subjective judgments. Applicants presenting "high numbers" are rejected occasionally on the basis of noncognitive criteria involving concerns about personal character, stability, and reliability.

Limited reliance is placed on the evaluations sent in by the premedical advisors, who may be reluctant to be negative when writing about their charges now that such written opinions cannot be kept confidential. However, comments from a well-known advisor usually can be evaluated accurately and are considered useful.

The employment history of the applicant, use of leisure time, literature read, and actual store of knowledge possessed (irrespective of the grades on the transcript) are all of interest to the members of the admissions committee; these personal features commonly are examined during the interviews extended by most medical schools to applicants who have presented "high numbers" in the cognitive criteria. In my experience, not all interviewers have proven to be skilled in conducting interviews, but some experienced committee members develop an uncanny ability to detect latent, undeveloped talent in many applicants—a form of intuitive "clinical judgment" which also can detect humanistic values in the applicant.

Thus, the selectors select those applicants who have used well their personal talents and often quite varied opportunities for learning and maturation during their college years—expecting that what young adults have done in the recent past is likely to be repeated in the near future as they enter medical school (see *Medical School Admissions Requirements* for additional details).

Composition of Entering Class of Medical Students

The composition of the enrolling class in recent years has changed markedly from that of twenty years or more ago. For many years, relatively few women applied for entrance to medical schools; in 1960, 1,044 women applied (7.2 percent of all applicants) and 600 were enrolled (7 percent of the total, nationally). Table 21 shows the experience of the past few years. Minority persons also have been enrolled in the study of medicine in much larger numbers in recent years. In 1970, there were 1,250 black applicants, of which 697 were enrolled (8.7 percent and 6.1 percent). Table 22 presents the data on a broad spectrum of minority persons, 1976–1981.

Most medical schools engage in some form of recruitment of and special financial support for minority students; but, despite some gains, the number enrolled remains relatively low. Andrew Young, speaking at an AAMC annual meeting in 1979, emphasized the heavy recruitment of still scarce young black college graduates into corporate positions at excellent beginning salaries, a move that effectively removes many of these people from application for enrollment in graduate and professional schools. The pool of applicants to medical school is restricted to persons who have

Table 21. Comparative Acceptance Data for Men and Women Applicants, 1976–77 to 1980–81.

First-Year Class	Number of Applicants		Number Accepted		Percent Accepted	
	Men	Women	Men	Women	Men	Women
1976–77	31,911	10,244	11,852	3,922	37.2	38.3
1977–78	30,374	10,195	11,896	4,081	39.2	40.0
1978–79	27,075	9,561	12,352	4,175	45.6	43.7
1979–80	25,919	10,222	12,156	4,730	46.9	46.3
1980–81	25,436	10,664	12,196	4,950	47.9	46.4

Source: Association of American Medical Colleges, 1982c, p. 23.

Table 22. Application and Acceptance Rate of Selected Minority Group Applicants to First-Year Classes in U.S. Medical Schools, 1976-77 to 1980-81.

Black Americans

First-Year Class	Applicants Number	Applicants Percent of All Applicants	Acceptees Number	Acceptees Percent Accepted
1976-77	2,523	6.3	966	38.3
1977-78	2,487	6.4	966	38.8
1978-79	2,564	7.3	970	37.8
1979-80	2,599	7.4	1,024	39.4
1980-81	2,594	7.4	1,057	40.7

Mexican Americans

First-Year Class	Applicants Number	Applicants Percent of All Applicants	Acceptees Number	Acceptees Percent Accepted
1976-77	460	1.2	223	48.5
1977-78	487	1.3	227	46.6
1978-79	433	1.2	241	55.7
1979-80	457	1.3	267	58.4
1980-81	449	1.3	240	53.5

American Indians

First-Year Class	Applicants Number	Applicants Percent of All Applicants	Acceptees Number	Acceptees Percent Accepted
1976-77	128	0.3	39	30.5
1977-78	122	0.3	43	35.2
1978-79	133	0.4	54	40.6
1979-80	151	0.4	64	42.4
1980-81	147	0.4	62	42.2

Mainland Puerto Ricans

First-Year Class	Applicants Number	Applicants Percent of All Applicants	Acceptees Number	Acceptees Percent Accepted
1976-77	212	0.5	85	40.1
1977-78	203	0.5	93	45.8
1978-79	191	0.5	92	48.2
1979-80	173	0.5	92	53.2
1980-81	191	0.5	102	53.4

Source: Association of American Medical Colleges, 1982c, p. 24.

finished high school and completed up to four years of college. In 1980, the dropout rate of fifteen- to nineteen-year-olds during high school was 35 percent for whites, 45 percent for blacks, and 59 percent for persons of Spanish/Hispanic origin. Fifty-five percent of whites aged fifteen to nineteen enrolled in college, while 39 percent of blacks and 30 percent of persons from Spanish/Hispanic origin in this age group entered college (Grant and Eiden, 1982). The data for twenty- to twenty-four-year-olds graduating from college in 1980 is as follows: whites, 23 percent; blacks, 11 percent; Spanish/Hispanics, 6.3 percent. From these numbers, only a small percentage opt to apply for admission to medical school. I hope that necessary remedies for the small number of minority persons enrolling in medical schools will be applied in the future, beginning at the level of the junior high and high schools as well as in the colleges. The medical schools, through various recruitment methods, can assist in the enlargement of the pool of minority applicants, but they cannot be expected to solve this major problem of society alone.

In any discussion of the selection of medical students, it is essential that care be taken not to fix on a generalized stereotype as the ideal. There are many kinds of physicians who practice enormously varied types of medicine or apply a medical education to widely ranging occupations. Most seasoned admissions committee members deliberately seek to enroll, in a single class, a wide variety of students whose backgrounds—as well as education and experience—are also varied. A classroom full of premedical clones would represent total failure on the part of the committee on admissions.

Medical School: The M.D. Degree

Early History of the Medical Curriculum

The American colonies of England were lacking in medical schools until the College of Philadelphia was established in 1765. Therefore, colonists who were unable to finance a medical education in England or Scotland, particularly at the popular University of Edinburgh, had to rely on the apprenticeship system, which was copied after that in Europe. Instead of the seven years of legal indenture to a preceptor that were required in the European guild system, however, the colonial apprenticeship was rarely longer than three years and binding indenture became uncommon. For nearly 200 years, more than 90 percent of American physicians entered practice after an apprenticeship. As late as the mid-1800s, more than half of the medical practitioners gained their training in this manner (Arey, 1959; Norwood, 1957).

Only ten medical schools were established before 1780 and thirty-three were in operation when the American Medical Association was organized in 1847 (Norwood, 1957, 1965). Through the first half of the 1800s, the schools offered a single course of lectures which lasted no more than sixteen weeks; the student sat through the same lecture series the next year and, if all fees had been paid, was thereupon graduated. Some schools required a period of practical experience with a preceptor; only those schools in the largest eastern cities required any hospital experience.

The movement of the pioneers westward created a need for physicians, and a chronic shortage of them on the frontier caused the development of more than 400 unregulated proprietary schools, some of which were still functioning when Abraham Flexner visited all of the schools in operation in North American in 1908–1909. Many proprietary schools admitted students without any entrance requirements and most dropped any requirement for experience as an apprentice; few offered hospital experience. Some students signed on with a physician as an apprentice to "read medicine" for a year, then attended one term of lectures in a local or regional school but failed to return for the repetition and were never graduated. Licensure of physicians by the state governments was abandoned during the populist movement launched during the Jacksonian presidency of the 1820s and was not resumed until quite late in the century. Under these permissive circumstances, the standards of the curriculum became the despair of leaders of the profession and helped motivate the founders of the AMA in 1847 (Norwood, 1957; King, 1983).

Origins of the Graded Curriculum

Arey (1959) has described the formation in 1859 of the Medical School of Lind University with the first three-year graded curriculum for the M.D. degree in the United States. This school was succeeded in 1868 by the Chicago Medical College, which became the "medical department" of Northwestern University in 1870 and was fully absorbed by the university in 1891. The reform-minded founders of Lind, who included N. S. Davis, also reinstated some measure of entrance requirements and lengthened the school year from the prevailing four to six months.

Harvard adopted a graded curriculum in 1871 and simultaneously extended the annual session to nine months; a few other schools followed this trend for improving the curriculum. Twenty-two schools founded the first Association of American Medical

Colleges in 1876, but this organization encountered difficulties in enforcing its membership requirements for a fully graded three-year curriculum. The opening of the Johns Hopkins School of Medicine in 1894 established a new model of a four-year graded curriculum into which only baccalaureate graduates were admitted. Variations in the curriculum persisted until the beginning of the twentieth century. In 1902, the AMA Council on Medical Education began classifying the schools according to the performance levels of graduates on the state's licensure examinations, and in 1904 the AAMC began inspecting the schools. These efforts bore some desirable results, but not until after publication in 1910 of Flexner's report of his survey of 155 schools in the United States and Canada was there a universal movement to the four-year graded curriculum (Gray, 1961).

The reforms that changed the circumstances of American Medical Education following the Flexner Survey of 1910 may be summarized as follows:

- Gradual development of the full-time faculty system, first in the basic sciences and more slowly in the clinical areas.
- Establishment of universal requirements for entry into medical school (for example, at least three years of college, including the study of biology, chemistry, and physics).
- Emphasis on the basic science subjects, with instruction based heavily on laboratory work.
- Use of university-controlled hospitals for much-improved clinical teaching.
- Universal adoption of a graded program of studies extending for a minimum of eight months per year for four years (Jarco, 1959; Chapman, 1974; Lippard, 1974).

The "Flexner 2 Plus 2" Schedule

Reform can be very useful, but it also may produce some undesirable rigidity; by mid-century, almost all the medical schools offered an M.D. curriculum consisting of two years devoted to the basic sciences and two years to clinical studies—that is, the "Flexner 2 Plus 2" schedule. When this form of curriculum was first adopted by Johns Hopkins in the 1890s and later copied almost universally after the Flexner survey, the available body of scientific and clinical medical knowledge possibly could be presented, in a general treatment, within the allotted four years. However, from 1910 to mid-century the advances in the sciences basic to medicine and in their application to clinical therapy were of such great magnitude that the faculties gradually made major increases in the content of all courses in the curriculum as they attempted to cover the full body of knowledge. The result was that by mid-century the students and their faculties found themselves attempting to carry an insuperable burden of learning. Wearn (1956) described how a bad situation grew worse due to the disruptions of the medical schools during World War II. As part of the war effort, many voluntary physician faculty members were called into active military service and medical scientists and educators were asked to take part in emergency research and development activities. As a result, most medical students were selected by the army and the navy. The curriculum was accelerated, involuntarily, even though it had to be enhanced by new material deemed necessary by medical officers who served in exotic areas of the world. After VJ Day in 1945, biomedical research in the schools began to receive annually increased governmental support; further enlargement of the curricular body of knowledge was anticipated. Thus, the "Flexner 2 Plus 2" curriculum, which attempted to digest the full body of knowledge in four years, had reached the point of diminishing returns by mid-century. Before proceeding with my narrative about the evolution of the curriculum, I shall describe the typical (though not universal) World War II to mid-century M.D. program.

The Typical Curriculum at Mid-Twentieth Century

At mid-century, the first two years of medical school study were tightly packed with basic science courses, taught as separate disciplines, which were scheduled from 8:00 A.M. to 5:00 P.M. Monday through Friday and until noon on Saturday. Occasionally, the students were allowed a free afternoon mid-week, sometimes beginning at 3:00 P.M. The total clock hours for each of the first two years ran as high as 1,200 (Deitrick and Berson, 1953). Anatomy, in its several forms, was assigned as many as 800 to 1,000 clock hours in the first year; most of this time was consumed by a complete dissection of a cadaver according to the method developed at Edinburgh through the prior two centuries. Biochemistry and physiology usually were pitted against anatomy in the schedule, and both generally lost the attention of the students whenever the anatomists gave their frequent tests. Biochemistry laboratory was dominated by numerous test tube experiments of the cookbook variety. Sophisticated instrumentation was being developed at that time for use in biomedical research but was rarely available to students. Physiology, as well as pharmacology, operated interesting laboratory experiments involving small animals, but the nemesis of the experience was the smoked drum kymograph, a grossly inefficient gadget the students attempted to use to record physiological events.

Pathology dominated the second year with its hundreds of microscopic slides of diseased tissues and its complete autopsies. Microbiologists were still called bacteriologists, as the viruses were then vaguely known but largely unseen. Bacteriology laboratory concentrated on germ morphology, which was based on extensive culturing of the organisms on agar plates or in other media. Pharmacology, then as now, was given only a small slice of time. Preventive medicine, with its field trips to public health installations, took the students out of the schoolhouse but often bored them in the process. Laboratory diagnosis was a major exercise in the study of blood, urine, feces, saliva, and stomach juices, while physical diagnosis, scheduled late in the second year in most schools, gave the students their first authentic, personal encounter with human patients. Infinite detail was droned out in lectures and through laboratory studies; all faculty members recommended supplemental areas of study "to obtain complete coverage." Tests were frequently administered in all courses; such multiple measurements allowed the students to memorize considerable detail and to regurgitate it promptly, thereby gaining a series of grades which most people felt indicated suitable mastery of the courses. Some schools used the "block" schedule, in which the courses were offered serially, in heavy concentration, in order to avoid competition among the departments.

The third and fourth years of study were in the hands of the clinical departments. In many schools, the third year was divided between four to six hours of lecture per day and several hours of clinical clerking rotated through internal medicine, pediatrics, psychiatry, obstetrics-gynecology, surgery, and the surgical specialties. The fourth year often was a repetition of the third-year clerking series with additional assignments to multiple specialty outpatient clinics; in some schools, small groups of juniors and seniors were assigned to a single clinical service simultaneously. The quality of supervision of the clinical clerks varied considerably among the schools. Prior to 1950, many hospitals used for teaching students depended heavily on interns for first-echelon care of patients; the great growth of residency training programs did not begin until mid-century. If only interns were present on the teaching services, the senior students often were pressed into direct care of patients—sometimes prematurely.

Discipline of medical students was severely enforced. Seniority of the faculty was equated with authority, and authority could never be questioned. Despite the intrinsic fascination well-motivated medical students (then as now) held for human biology and clinical diagnosis and therapy, the curriculum of mid-century was oppressive in many schools; and one should not be surprised to learn that, after the passage of several decades, graduates of the period often speak of their experiences in medical school with resentment. Powers, Darley, and Littlemeyer reported in 1965 that during the period from 1959 to 1963 the M.D. graduates of 1925 through 1963 made a median average contribution of $28.00 to private schools and $10.00 to public schools. These findings indicate that an entire generation of M.D. graduates, despite their ultimately favorable economic situation, was unwilling to give support to an unloved medical alma mater.

The Experiment at Western Reserve University

Widespread adherence to the traditional curriculum was shattered after 1952, as the faculty of medicine of Western Reserve University introduced a fresh new plan for the instruction of medical students. The essence of this plan was to introduce the beginning students to a curriculum designed as a logical continuum by the faculty as a whole. Teaching was to be interdisciplinary rather than departmentalized; basic scientific material was to be combined with clinical material whenever possible; teaching was to be based on problem solving rather than limited to memorization of facts; students were to accept responsibility for self-education; and it was accepted that it was impossible to learn all of medicine in four years (Williams, 1980). The new M.D. program at Western Reserve was supported generously by the Commonwealth Fund, which made available grants totaling $3.6 million between 1950 and 1978. Substantial additional funds controlled by the university were committed to the development of facilities and personnel needed for the program.

Williams (1980) has described eloquently the difficulties Dean Joseph Wearn encountered in obtaining approval from the medical faculty at Western Reserve for revision of the traditional curriculum. Some senior chairmen never accepted it fully, as a result, a majority of them were replaced between 1945 and 1952. As is the usual experience with radical new programs in education, this one was modified by the faculty in 1968, after a number of its originators had been replaced by new people. In 1982, the Committee on Medical Education of Case Western Reserve announced its intent to change the curriculum once again so that it would reflect recent major developments in medicine (Case Western Reserve School of Medicine, 1983; "Case" was added to the school's name in 1972).

Other Experiments with the Medical Curriculum, 1952–1980

The activities at Western Reserve attracted much attention throughout North America and much of the rest of the world. Within a few years, many faculties began to consider adoption of some of the features of the Western Reserve plan; or, stimulated by the intellectual ferment it engendered, faculties began to devise their own curricular modifications. The thirty years between 1952 and 1982 were filled with changes in the older schools; the forty new schools established after 1960 were able to choose from a variety of experiences elsewhere and were free to attempt even greater modifications in newly created programs leading to the M.D. degree.

Rise and Fall of the Organ System Teaching. The most radical component of the 1952 curriculum at Western Reserve was the abolition of separate disciplinary courses taught by a single basic science department faculty, usually without any organized communication with the other departments. In the new plan, the total subject material previously offered by the basic scientists was reclassified according to organ systems; each segment was assigned to an integrated committee of basic scientists and clinicians. A number of medical faculties adopted this approach in whole or in part; the idea was enthusiastically accepted by some faculty members and vigorously opposed by many others. In 1980, from an analysis of the entries of the 126 schools in the *Association of American Medical Colleges Curriculum Directory, 1980–81* (Association of American Medical Colleges, 1980a), I find that only 8 schools now offer all the basic sciences in an integrated manner, 3 offer some integrated courses in the first year, and 21 offer integrated courses in the second basic science year. This tally in 1980 shows reduced adoption of the scheme for integrated teaching from higher levels observed during the 1960s.

Why was there a rise and fall of interest? Most faculty members who were enthusiastic early on were highly motivated (as are most pioneer-innovators) to make the new approach work effectively. After some time went by, however, many of the pioneers were replaced by others who found that the integrated subject approach required massive amounts of time for planning each presentation to the students, and motivation decreased. The traditional disciplinarians found that an organ system plan was not able to include certain significant concepts considered highly significant for the education of medical students. Rapid developments in intracellular biology were sometimes difficult to integrate into a series of such subjects as the kidneys, lungs, heart, gut, and the like. Territorial disputations between the members of, say, the Committee on the Lungs and the Committee on the Heart disenchanted some faculty members. The students complained about numerous faculty members who appeared before them briefly to give an overwhelmingly comprehensive presentation somewhat out of synchrony with related presentations and who then disappeared. Inconsistent methods of evaluation of achievement by students in numerous segments were criticized by faculty and students alike. Some schools which early on had adopted the fully integrated system moved to a system which returned some time in the curriculum to the departments while retaining a diminished integrated sequence; others reverted to the disciplinary sequence of basic science courses but gave a large block of time in the second year to "Introduction to Clinical Medicine," a course variously defined but usually consisting of a series of presentations on clinical disease syndromes.

Early Introduction of Clinical Subjects. Abraham Flexner was so intent on increasing the content of basic science instruction in the curriculum that he expressed vigorous opposition to the inclusion of any clinical subject material within the first two years of the curriculum. This was the pattern for most of the years from 1910 until the beginning of the Western Reserve experiment. With the exception that the latter part of the second year usually included some work in physical diagnosis, the introduction of clinical experiences within the first year at Western Reserve opened up a new area for experimentation. This idea was widely accepted in both the old and the new schools by 1980. Of the 126 schools surveyed in the AAMC's *Curriculum Directory, 1980–81,* I can identify only 25 schools that have no labeled separate clinical course offered during the first year of the curriculum. All the other schools include a definitive clinical experience, which sometimes takes the form of clinical correlations, emergency medicine, introduction to patient care, or the principles of physical diagnosis. The amount of time devoted to one or more of these subjects ranges from 20 clock hours to over 200 clock hours. In 1980, only 4 schools showed no identifiable clinical experience in the second year, and 2 of these must be excluded, since they have an all-elective curriculum; the final 2 separate the basic science years of study from the clinical clerking years by a well-developed clerkship in the methodology of physical diagnosis and history taking and other related skills.

Multidiscipline Laboratories for Students. Western Reserve was among the early pioneers in the use of multidiscipline laboratories for instruction of the basic science subjects. This topic has been discussed in some detail in Chapter Eight.

Decline of Laboratory Instruction in the Basic Sciences and the Elective Fourth Year. As the 1960s departed and the 1970s appeared, the increasing enrollment of students created considerable administrative and logistic problems for the arrangement of their education. Some of the basic science departments adopted the view that the traditional laboratory had become archaic (the biochemists were principal in this movement); as a result, most of the basic science laboratory exercises were markedly diminished, if not entirely abolished. Revisions in the curriculum, which took place gradually around this time, also modified the arrangement of the clinical clerkships. Reemphasis on bedside teaching was responsible for the deletion of extended lectures in the third year of the four-year curriculum; when this occurred, many schools adopted the completely elective fourth year, in which the students were permitted to select several studies from a specified list prepared by the faculty. Many senior students seized the opportunity to migrate to other schools for the purpose of becoming familiar with the program directors of highly desired residency training programs. A probable negative result of these changes was the movement of a large amount of clinical lecture time into the second year in the course called "Introduction to Clinical Medicine" or "Pathophysiology" or something similar.

The Three-Year M.D. Curriculum. During World War II, the federal government, in an effort to produce as rapidly as possible an increasing number of physicians to become medical officers, accelerated the M.D. program to a total of three calendar years by deleting the usual summer holidays traditional for medical and other kinds of college students. Later, during the widely accepted physician shortage of the 1960s, the federal government offered certain inducements called "special projects incentives," which, among others, included financial bonuses for medical schools that developed a three-year M.D. program. At one time, 23 percent of the schools of medicine were offering a mandatory three-year M.D. curriculum, and a number of other schools offered a three-year option. At the beginning of the 1980s, no school offered a mandatory three-year M.D. program, although fifteen schools continued to offer the three-year scheme as an option to medical students.

Beran (1978) has reported the results of a thorough study of this experiment, which lost favor as soon as both faculty and students became well acquainted with the problems it presented.

These problems included substantial fatigue for the students, who found themselves deeply immersed in the over-detailed medical curriculum for a continuous thirty-five to thirty-six months. Minority students, in particular, encountered problems with the tightly packed schedule, which had no vacation time available for use in remedial study. The members of the faculty found that they were engaged in teaching far more months of each calendar year than they were accustomed to doing. Students who completed the three-year program were found by many residency program directors to be somewhat deficient in maturity and in the development of clinical judgment, which often comes with a slightly less frenetic form of study. From this extended experiment, I think it can be concluded that the three-year curriculum is not suitable for the majority of students pursuing the M.D. degree. While the three-year program may be a viable option in some of the medical schools, it would appear folly in the future to reinstate this program, which has had negative experience twice in this century.

Self-Learning in the Basic Sciences. One of the most innovative programs for treatment of the basic sciences was that established at the McMaster University School of Medicine in Hamilton, Ontario, beginning in 1969. In this program, the students were provided with all the learning materials required for a series of units of study, the objectives of which had been outlined in detail. The students were expected to use the learning materials and the descriptive syllabi provided by the faculty and to learn at their own pace without organized didactic presentation by the faculty, except by invitation from the students. In the beginning of the program, achievement of students was measured by a number of tutors, each of whom supervised a small group of students (Spaulding, 1969).

Docent-Directed Instruction. At the University of Missouri-Kansas City, another quite radical departure in pedagogy to medical students was installed in 1971. In this curriculum, students were accepted for medical studies out of high school and were enrolled in a six-year program leading to the M.D. degree. The students were organized in units of fifty to include students in each of the six years of study; this cluster of students was under the direct supervision and guidance of a clinician who was called a docent, a sort of mini-dean. The docent was responsible for guidance of the student through their series of organized studies in the basic sciences and in a series of encounters with patients over an extended period (Sirridge, 1980).

Criterion-Referenced Instruction. Other institutions developed elaborate sets of objectives for each of the courses in the curriculum and, indeed, for each of the specific hourly presentations within each course. At Southern Illinois University School of Medicine, the program of studies was criterion referenced and the students were required to learn the specified material before they could be promoted or graduated (Silber, 1978).

Computer-Assisted Instruction. A number of schools have experimented with computer-instructed subject material. For example, in the 1960s Ohio State University School of Medicine developed a computer-instructed program in the basic sciences, which has had some favorable responses but which apparently has had some difficulty in being transferred to another institution (Liaison Committee on Medical Education data).

Problem-Based Instruction. Concern about the poor response of students to an overpowering series of formal lectures has led to some experiments with instruction through the assignment of a series of problems to be solved by small groups of interacting students. Barrows (1982), during the early 1970s at McMaster University, developed a method of instruction in the neural sciences by assigning to a group of students the protocol of a clinical-pathological conference, the subject of which had a neurological disease. The students, early in their first year of medical studies, were able to make an accurate diagnosis of the patient's complaint; while doing so, they learned much useful information about neuroanatomy, neurophysiology, neuropathology, and clinical neurology (Liaison Committee on Medical Education data). Similar attempts to convert students from passive to active learning have been tried at McMaster (Canada), Newcastle (Australia), Limburg (the Netherlands), and Southern Illinois University (Barrows, 1982). It is not clear to me whether these methods of instruction are efficient enough to replace older methods entirely. However, any method of pedagogy that enlivens the existence of medical students and converts them into independent thinkers/researchers needs to be encouraged.

Use of Simulated Patients in Clinical Instruction. For many years, some faculty members have illustrated their presentations about various diseases by demonstrating clinical manifestations in a cooperative patient. If a suitable patient was not available, the instructor might simulate a characteristic physical posture or imitate a locomotor gait found in a neurological disease. Barrows (1971), while at the University of Southern California during the 1960s, trained several actors to simulate such clinical signs. This method has been adopted in many schools.

Instruction in the performance of a pelvic examination has gradually incorporated the use of trained models who agree to submit to medical examination by a series of medical students. Adoption of the use of models in instruction in gynecology has reduced the necessity for students to learn how to do these vital examinations on actual patients.

Use of Family Medicine Clinics for Teaching Ambulatory Medicine. During recent years, the medical schools have increased their use of facilities used by departments or divisions of family medicine. To illustrate, of 111 schools offering the M.D. degree, 7 required students to enroll in a mandatory clerkship in family medicine during 1973-74 (Association of American Medical Colleges, 1973). In 1982-83, 36 of 125 M.D.-granting schools required family medicine clerkships, and 18 additional schools required a clerkship called "Primary Care" and a number of other clerkships listed as "Community Medicine" during the final two years of study (Association of American Medical Colleges, 1982b). Such experiences appear to have replaced the outpatient experiences that were a major feature of the senior year at mid-century.

Use of Prepaid Health Care Plan Facilities for Clinical Teaching. The proliferation of health maintenance organizations (HMOs) since the late 1960s has induced a significant number of medical schools to explore the use of these facilities for the instruction of undergraduate medical students. In 1983, Isaacs and Madolf reported that 26 medical schools had formal educational arrangements with HMOs and that 35 other schools planned or were seriously considering such arrangements or would make arrangements for their use if facilities were available. Hudson (1981) has published the proceedings of a national conference on HMOs and their interaction with academic medical centers.

The combination of HMOs and Family Medicine Clinical Centers for clinical teaching of medical students appears to be present in most of the medical schools in the early 1980s. This form of teaching clinical medicine is quite different from the traditional focus on instruction inside the teaching hospital.

Research Projects Required for the M.D. Degree. Another innovation in the Western Reserve experiment was to require each student to develop a research project during the course of enrollment in the medical school. Other schools adopted this requirement, some with separate projects for the first and second years, followed by a thesis to be presented at the time of graduation. This thesis could either be on one of the first two topics or on a third topic to be selected by the students under the guidance of both a primary sponsor within the faculty and the associate dean. This was the plan I organized with the faculty at Baylor University College of Medicine during the 1960s. Other schools adopted the requirement for a research project but abandoned it—probably because of the substantial increase in enrollment of medical students that began to occur in the late 1960s and early 1970s.

General Internship Discontinued. As the medical schools moved gradually toward nearly universal adoption of the fully elective fourth year, the Council on Medical Education of the American Medical Association, which then was responsible for supervision of graduate medical education (GME), decided to discontinue the rotating internship, which normally followed immediately after the M.D. degree and before the onset of the residency program. While not all fresh M.D. graduates enrolled in rotating internships (some took a specialized straight internship leading into the specialty residency), the combination of the loss of a rotating general experience in the first GME year along with the less-structured elective fourth year produced, in the opinion of many experienced clinicians and medical educators, a certain void in the clinical experience of the medical student. The rule deleting the general internship became effective in 1975.

Decentralization of Instruction. The next innovation that took place was geographical in nature. By that I mean that an existing medical school that had conducted the majority of its educational activities for the M.D. degree program in a single academic health center or in the hospitals of a single city attempted to expand its enrollments by decentralizing its educational programs. Indiana University, for example, began to offer basic science instruction in the subjects typically found in the first year of the curriculum in some nine satellite campuses over the state of Indiana. Students entered the study of medicine at one of the several campuses or in the academic health center in Indianapolis, the second and third years of study took place in Indianapolis and the fourth year gave freedom for choice of electives in any of the involved sites where the university provided fiscal subsidy to medical education. Michigan State University School of Medicine, when it was organized, conducted its basic science instruction on the main campus in East Lansing but developed a series of clinical branch campuses scattered over the state. The same arrangement was used at the University of Alabama, Birmingham, which developed clinical teaching programs at Tuscaloosa and in Huntsville. The University of Kansas extended clinical teaching to a new site in Wichita. Texas Tech University, situated in Lubbock, attempted to comply with the mandate in its charter granted by the Legislature of the State of Texas, which required that the school operate some of its educational programs in Amarillo, El Paso, Midland, Odessa, Abilene, and Wichita Falls. During its first decade of experience, it confined its undergraduate activity to Lubbock and to clinical branch campuses in Amarillo and El Paso. The State University of New York in Syracuse developed a clinical branch campus in Binghamton. The University of Florida developed first-year-level basic science instruction at Florida State, following which the students transferred to the principal campus of the University in Gainesville; there they joined a larger cohort of students who had begun their original studies in that setting.

Regionalization of Medical Education. The principle of regionalization was adopted by several schools, each in a different manner. The University of Illinois divided itself into two parts in Chicago and developed a second site for basic science instruction in Urbana, as well as clinical branch campuses in Peoria and Rockford. The University of Washington in Seattle formed regional governmental pacts with the states of Alaska, Montana, and Idaho. In these settings, the school developed instructional programs in certain of the basic sciences for small numbers of students, following which the students shifted to the principal campus in Seattle; they then found clinical options available to them in the numerous far-flung areas in which the university had made cooperative arrangements for clinical instruction. Other school-state governmental pacts were developed at the University of Vermont with Maine and New York, Jefferson Medical School with Delaware, and the University of Utah and Creighton University with Wyoming. One of the new schools, Northeastern Ohio Universities, carried the principle of regionalization to a somewhat more elaborate degree. Here, three universities compacted to sponsor a new medical school, which accepted students to a six- or seven-year premed plus medical school program; basic science instruction was offered in a single setting in the midst of the three universities and clinical instruction was arranged in fifteen affiliated hospitals in the northeastern quadrant of the state of Ohio (Liaison Committee on Medical Education data).

Failed Experiments. Experiments that were tried and failed or that were proposed but never instituted include the various proposals for a "medical school without walls." In this proposal, which was never developed, the intent was to assign medical students to practicing physician/preceptors for several years in the expectation that the revival of the preceptorship popular during colonial America would suffice as a medical education. In another experiment, one or more of the schools experimented with the combination of medical, dental, graduate, nursing, pharmacy, and allied health students all in a common class in the basic sciences and in some of the clinical activities. This effort failed totally, probably because the medical, dental, and graduate students, at least, all had the benefit of four years of completed undergraduate study while other students came to the common experience directly from high school.

In another school, an arrangement was made for a small cluster of students to be given all of their basic science instruction by family practitioners. This was not considered to be a satisfactory experience by the Liaison Committee on Medical Education, and it was discontinued after a few years of experience. In some of the revised older schools and in several of the schools established since 1960, curricular planning and control of the academic program of the school was left to professional "educationalists," who introduced an elaborate jargon and various methodologies largely unknown to the content people—that is, the members of the traditional disciplines of the faculty. This experiment has had only modest success and, in recent years, dominant educationalists appear to have left the scene.

Western Reserve made an unusual experiment in the instruction of anatomy within the second year of studies. This move has seen very little adoption in the other schools, which have retained anatomy in its traditional position early in the first year of medical studies. Another failure was commonly experienced in the enrollment of educationally deprived premedical students into highly competitive medical schools before such students were fully prepared to accept that level of responsibility.

Combined Degree Programs

In 1960, Cooper reported the details of a new program in medical education at Northwestern University into which highly selected students were admitted after completing high school. Since 1960, a number of other schools have developed similar programs; in 1982, twenty schools reported operation of a six- or seven-year sequence of studies first leading to the granting of the baccalaureate degree and then to the M.D. degree. In 1980, other schools appeared to be considering adoption of the scheme partly due to the availability of financial support by the Commonwealth Fund. Daubney, Wagner, and Rogers (1981) have published a review of the literature on this experience.

For decades, many medical schools have been able to make special arrangements for the enrollment of Ph.D. graduates in one or another of the sciences in the study of medicine. It has been customary to grant advanced standing to such persons by recognizing their earlier achievements. Ordinarily, one to several persons per class have been enrolled in the M.D. program after completion of the Ph.D. degree. In 1971, the University of Miami began a formal program that provided accelerated medical qualifications to candidates with Ph.D. degrees in the natural, physical, and engineering sciences (Awad, Harrington, and Pepper, 1979).

Structure of the Curriculum in the Early 1980s

At mid-century, it was possible to write a single description of the typical M.D. curriculum that, with some exceptions, was accurate for most of the schools. Now, after about thirty years of experimentation and modification, it would be difficult to find more than a few examples of any single curriculum; there are many versions in use today. However, with some limited exceptions, the variations from school to school are manifested in the temporal arrangement of the content of each curriculum and the nomenclature of its components; a detailed analysis of subject content would reveal only modest variations. To illustrate, Table 23 gives a general outline of the generic subject content of the medical curriculum; a careful review of this outline will prepare the reader for an examination of various schedules and weekly time tracks that illustrate the curricular plan devised by a number of medical faculties.

In addition to the generic courses or subjects listed in Table 23, the following subjects are commonly included in the generic courses of a typical undergraduate medical curriculum but are not necessarily offered separately.

Additional Topics Not Included in the Generic Subjects

Alcoholism	History of medicine
Biomedical engineering	Human sexuality
Community preventive medicine	Human values in medicine
Cost containment	Medical hypnosis
Drug abuse	Medical jurisprudence
Emergency medicine	Nutrition
Environmental health hazards	Occupational health
Ethical problems in medicine	Office management
Genetic counseling	Patient education
Geriatrics	Population dynamics
Health care delivery	Primary care

Table 23. An Outline of the Generic Subjects of the Medical Curriculum.

I.   Basic Science Subjects
    A.   Anatomy (including gross, microscopic, neuro-, and embryological anatomy)[a,b]
    B.   Biochemistry[a,b]
    C.   Physiology[a,b]
    D.   Microbiology[a,b]
    E.   Public Health (including epidemiology, biometry, and preventive medicine)[a,b]
    F.   Pathology[a,b]
    G.   Pharmacology[a,b]
    H.   Behavioral Sciences (including psychology, sociology, and anthropology)[a]
II. Introduction to Clinical Skills[a]
    A.   Taking the History of a Patient's Illness
    B.   Physical Diagnosis
    C.   Laboratory Diagnosis
III. Pathophysiology
IV. Clinical Clerkships
    A.   Internal Medicine[a,c]
    B.   Pediatrics[a,c]
    C.   Psychiatry[a,c]
    D.   Obstetrics/Gynecology[a,c]
    E.   Surgery (including surgical specialties)[a,c]
    F.   Family Medicine
V.   Electives[a,d]

---

[a]These subjects are specified by the LCME.

[b]These subjects are components of Part I of the National Board of Medical Examiners examination.

[c]These subjects are components of Part II of the National Board of Medical Examiners examination.

[d]Since the 1960s, most schools have offered a block of time, which may extend through the fourth year, to be used by a student for the study of freely chosen subjects or electives; they have also offered another block of time for "selectives," freely chosen subjects on a short list of fixed, required subjects. Since 1970, the trend toward in increase in the required subjects in the final years of the curriculum has reduced the time available for the choice of electives in a number of schools.

Special-interest groups often lobby the medical faculties, the deans, and the LCME to give additional time to one of the subjects listed above. For example, former Senator George McGovern, past chairman of the U.S. Senate Select Subcommittee on Nutrition, demanded that special attention be given to the subject of clinical nutrition within the medical curriculum. A former chairman of

the LCME and I were summoned to give testimony on this issue
before this subcommittee in 1979; the members of the panel were
unwilling to accept our assertion that every medical school curriculum includes substantial consideration of the science of nutrition
and its application to clinical dietetics. Deans frequently receive
poorly designed questionnaires that ask whether the curriculum
contains a particular course. Apparently, the presence of a distinct,
separate course must be demonstrated or the questioner will conclude
that the subject material is entirely missing from the curriculum.

The Medical Student's Weekly Schedule. In most schools,
first- and second-year students follow a fixed schedule of courses.
Usually, the entire class is expected to attend each course. In a
particular course, the entire class may be subdivided into laboratory
sections, small group tutorials, or special field trip units.

In the first two years devoted to the study of the basic sciences,
the work week of the medical school student is much more
burdensome than is that of the college undergraduate; the amount
of time spent in class each week in the early 1980s extends from
twenty-two clock hours to forty clock hours. This range also includes
some assigned laboratory time, but some students may not need
to use all this time to complete their laboratory experiences.

The rapid growth in the body of biomedical and clinical
knowledge has exerted pressure on the members of the faculty to
present their subject material in highly concentrated increments
and at a high velocity. The LCME has often criticized the weight
of the work week that the first- and second-year medical student
must bear; the faculties have to be reminded constantly of the need
to provide the students with a modicum of free time for independent
study and recreation during the work week. Even so, some schools
still hold classes on Saturday morning. The reaction of students
to this course overload is predictable: Lecture note services have
sprung up, sometimes without the approval of the faculty, and
in some schools class attendance has significantly declined. In some
instances, faculty members have attempted to force class attendance
by holding frequent—sometimes weekly—tests, often undertaken
for what seem to be punitive reasons.

In the third year, the medical student becomes a clinical clerk.
Small groups of four to six clinical clerks are assigned to a series

of rotations through specialized clinical care services in a teaching hospital. The clinical clerk joins the patient care team composed of interns, residents, and attending physicians; he is expected to be in the hospital for a very long day of observation and participation in the care of patients. Night duty and weekend responsibility are frequent; usually, the clinical clerk alternates with others in the group in scheduling these work periods.

The actual hours spent on duty at the hospital vary according to the specialty. Psychiatry often operates on "banker's hours" (that is, from 9:00 A.M. to 5:00 P.M.). The surgeons, who characteristically require little sleep, may expect their clerks to report to the operating room at 5:00 or 6:00 in the morning for a day that often lasts twenty hours. Obstetrics is another specialty that often requires a twenty-four-hour commitment on the part of the clerk. Internal medicine and pediatrics are very demanding, but they tend to be the most variable of the specialties in terms of work load. This glance at the effort required of the clinical clerk makes it clear that he is expected to adapt to the working life-style of a very busy practicing physician.

To a large extent, the study load of the fourth year is determined by the student, but, as noted before, a number of schools have begun to specify certain required courses for study during this year.

Variations of the Medical School Curriculum. Tables 24 through 35 provide illustrations of the weekly work loads in various programs and the time devoted to subjects leading to the M.D. degree at selected medical schools.

Methods of Teaching

The Basic Science Subjects. In the basic science subjects, lectures, demonstrations, and small group conferences and discussions are used most frequently. Laboratory studies, which have diminished in recent years, vary from subject to subject and from school to school.

Traditional anatomical dissection of cadavers is still a facet of the teaching methods in most schools, but this ancient practice in medical science does not receive the allotment of time that it

Table 24. Typical Curriculum Year with Saturday Classes.

First Year Fall Semester   *Schedule of Courses*

HOURS	MONDAY	TUESDAY	WEDNESDAY	THURSDAY	FRIDAY	SATURDAY
8:00–12:00	Biochemistry	Anatomy		Anatomy	Biochemistry	Anatomy
1:00–2:00	Biochemistry	Psychiatry				
2:00–4:00		Anatomy		Anatomy	Biochemistry	
4:00–5:00				Dean's Hour		

First Year Spring Semester   *Schedule of Courses*

HOURS	MONDAY	TUESDAY	WEDNESDAY	THURSDAY	FRIDAY	SATURDAY
8:00–12:00	Anatomy	Physiology		Physiology	Anatomy	
1:00–4:00	Anatomy	Physiology		Physiology	Anatomy	
4:00–5:00	Medical Statistics	Psychiatry		Dean's Hour		

Note: Elective time is blank. Most freshmen should take 4-5 elective hours each semester.
Sources: The Bulletin of Vanderbilt University School of Medicine, 1980–81.

Table 25. Typical First- and

FRESHMAN SCHEDULES— 1982-1983

1982 Fall Quarter (12 Weeks + Examination Week)

	8	9	10	11	12	1	2	3	4	5
M	Microanatomy			Biochem.			Gross Anatomy			
T	Gross Anatomy						Independent Study Time			
W	Microanatomy			Biochem.			Gross Anatomy			
TH	Microanatomy			Biomath.			Gross Anatomy			
F	Microanatomy			Biochem.			Independent Study Time			

1983 Winter Quarter (10 Weeks + Examination Week)

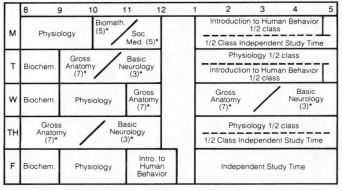

	8	9	10	11	12	1	2	3	4	5
M	Physiology		Biomath. (5)*	Soc. Med. (5)*			Introduction to Human Behavior 1/2 class — 1/2 Class Independent Study Time			
T	Biochem.	Gross Anatomy (7)*	Basic Neurology (3)*				Physiology 1/2 class — Introduction to Human Behavior 1/2 class			
W	Biochem.	Physiology		Gross Anatomy (7)*			Gross Anatomy (7)*	Basic Neurology (3)*		
TH	Gross Anatomy (7)*	Basic Neurology (3)*					Physiology 1/2 class — 1/2 Class Independent Study Time			
F	Biochem.	Physiology		Intro. to Human Behavior			Independent Study Time			

*weeks

1983 Spring Quarter (10 Weeks + Examination Week)

	8	9	10	11	12	1	2	3	4	5
M	Physiology		Basic Neurology				Introduction to Human Behavior 1/2 class — 1/2 Class Independent Study Time			
T	Physiology	Intro. to Human Behavior	Biochemistry				Introduction to Human Behavior 1/2 class — 1/2 Class Independent Study Time			
W	Physiology	Biochemistry — Basic Neurology					Biochemistry 1/2 class — Physiology 1/2 class (3 afternoons during quarter)			
TH	Biochem.	Biochemistry — Basic Neurology					Biochemistry 1/2 class — Physiology 1/2 class (3 afternoons during quarter)			
F	Physiology		Basic Neurology				Independent Study Time			

Second-Year Curriculum.

SOPHOMORE SCHEDULES — 1982-1983

1982 Fall Quarter (14 Weeks + Examination Week)

	8	9	10	11	12	1	2	3	4	5
M	Path.	Microbiol. & Immunol. ----------- Pathology					Microbiol. & Immunol.	Microbiol. & Immunol. -------- Pathology		
T	Microbiol. & Immunol.	Pharm.	Epidemiol. (10)* Pharmacol. (4)*			Independent Study Time				
W	Pharm.	Microbiol. & Immunol. ----------- Pathology					Microbiol. & Immunol.	Microbiol. & Immunol. -------- Pathology		
TH	Microbiol. & Immunol.	Pharm.	Epidemiol. (10)* Pharmacol. (4)*			Independent Study Time				
F	Pharm.	Microbiol. & Immunol. ----------- Pathology					Microbiol. & Immunol.	Microbiol. & Immunol. -------- Pathology		

*Weeks

1983 Winter Quarter (First 3 Weeks, January 3-19)

	8	9	10	11	12	1	2	3	4	5
M	Microbiol. & Immunol.	Microbiol. & Immunol. ---------- Pathophysiology of Disease (PPD)					PPD	Microbiol. & Immunol. ----------- Pathophysiology of Disease		
T	Microbiol. & Immunol.	Pharmacology				Independent Study Time				
W	Microbiol. & Immunol.	Microbiol. & Immunol. --------- Pathophysiology of Disease				Pharm.	Microbiol. & Immunol. ----------- Pathophysiology of Disease		
TH	Microbiol. & Immunol.	Pharmacology				Independent Study Time				
F	Microbiol. & Immunol.	Microbiol. & Immunol. --------- Pathophysiology of Disease				PPD	Microbiol. & Immunol. ----------- Pathophysiology of Disease		

1983 Winter (Last 7 Weeks) and Spring (9 Weeks + Examination Week) Quarters

	8	9	10	11	12	1	2	3	4	5
M	Pathophysiology of Disease (PPD)			Psycho-pathology			Clinical Fundamentals Medicine Surgery Psychiatry Pediatrics Neurology Obstetrics & Gynecology Ophthalmology A schedule will be prepared including Independent Study Time.			
T	Pathophysiology of Disease			Pharm.						
W	Pathophysiology of Disease			Psycho-pathology						
TH	Pathophysiology of Disease			Pharm.						
F	Pathophysiology of Disease			Psycho-pathology						

Table 26. Traditional Disciplinary Courses with a General Clerkship Preceding Rotation of Primary Clerkships: University of Rochester School of Medicine and Dentistry

Total weeks of instruction: 146

First Academic Period: Begins September. Duration: 36 weeks.
Hours per week: 28 scheduled/12 unscheduled.

Required Courses	Lecture	Conference	Lab	Other	T
Overview		3			
Human Biology (Gross Structure and Function)	30		200	10	
Cell Biology (Biochemistry, Endocrinology, Nutrition, and Histology)	236	14	65		
Human Genetics	42	6			
Regulatory and Adaptive Mechanisms	82	92	82	34	
Psychosocial and Community Medicine	64	57	38	27	
Total	454	172	385	71	1,

Elective Program

Electives may be taken on 2 free afternoons or Saturday morning during the second semester of first year and throughout the second year.

Second Academic Period: Begins September. Duration: 36 weeks.
Hours per week: 27 scheduled/13 unscheduled.

Required Courses

Medical Microbiology, Immunology, and Parasitology	111	25	116		
Pharmacology	78	23	36	52	
Neural Sciences	32	24	88		
Psychosocial and Community Medicine	36	174			
Pathology	82	15	102	35	
Pathophysiology	36				
Total	375	261	342	87	1,

Third Academic Period: Begins September. Duration: 44 weeks.

Required Clerkships ... We

General Clerkship ....
Medicine ....
Surgery ....
Psychiatry ....
Obstetrics/Gynecology ....
Pediatrics ....

Fourth Academic Period: Begins October. Duration: 30 weeks.

Required Clerkships

Surgical Specialties ....
Emergency ....
Ambulatory Care (given ½ day per week throughout the year)

Students must select two of the following 4-week clerkships: Musculoskeletal Medicine, Rehabilitation, and Neurology.

Elective Program

14 weeks of electives are taken by each student. All departments participate.

Source: Association of American Medical Colleges, 1982b, p. 158.

Table 27. Heavy Interdisciplinary Presentations: Case Western Reserve University School of Medicine

Total weeks of instruction: 152

First Academic Period: Begins August. Duration: 36 weeks.
Hours per week: 24 scheduled/12 unscheduled.

Required Courses	Lecture	Conference	Lab	Other	Total
		Hours			
Cell Biology	94	11	20	14	139
Tissue Biology	72	11	24	10	117
Metabolism	58	17	29	9	113
Tissue Injury and Disease	63	14	28	4	109
Cardiovasculary-Pulmonary-Renal	96	9	26	20	151
Biostatistics	15			2	17
Fundamentals of Therapeutic Agents	25	4	9	16	54
Mechanisms of Infection	59	3	27	6	95
Clinical Science		96			96
Total	482	165	163	81	891

Elective Program—2 afternoons per week (8 hours) are used for curricular options program. Curricular options consist of independent study, research, courses, and programs designed by departments in the medical school and courses offered by other units of the university.

Second Academic Period: Begins August. Duration: 36 weeks.
Hours per week: 24 scheduled/12 unscheduled.

Required Courses					
Hematology	34		31	3	68
Respiratory	32	12	8	2	54
Urinary	21	19	6	10	56
Cardiovascular	43	7	24	4	78
Biometry	12				12
Integument	9				9
Gastrointestinal	53		16	3	72
Endocrine	48		2	2	52
Reproduction	60		20	4	84
Mind	69			3	72
Musculoskeletal	49	7	36	6	98
Nervous System	96		76	4	176
Legal Medicine	9				9
Clinical Science		86		38	124
Total	535	131	219	79	964

Elective Program—1 afternoon per week (4 hours) is used for curricular options program. (See above explanation of curricular options.)

Third Academic Period: Begins June or September. Duration: 50 weeks.

Required Clerkships	Weeks
Introductory	2
Medicine	8 or 12
Pediatrics	8 or 12
Surgery	8
Psychiatry	8
Obstetrics/Gynecology	8
Ambulatory Medicine	8

Fourth Academic Period: Begins, Varies. Duration: 32 weeks.

Entirely elective and designed by the student with 1 month the minimal elective block.

Source: Association of American Medical Colleges, 1982b, p. 178.

Table 28. Heavy Interdisciplinary Presentations:
University of Southern California School of Medicine, Structured Fourth Year.

Total weeks of instruction: 156

First Academic Period: Begins September. Duration: 36 weeks.
Hours per week: 31 scheduled/9 unscheduled.

Organ System or Clerkship Topic	Lecture	Conference	Lab	Other	Total
Human Biology	171½	33½	103½	73	381
Neurosciences	54	8	51	23	13⦀
Respiratory/Renal/Skin	56	4	42	2	10⦀
Blood/Gastrointestinal/Liver	66	10	50	15	14⦀
Endocrine/Reproduction	48	2	32		8⦀
Introduction to Clinical Medicine (ICM).				176	17⦀
Family and Preventive Medicine	58				5⦀
Behavioral Science	45				4⦀
Total	498½	57½	278½	289	1,12⦀

Second Academic Period: Begins September. Duration: 36 weeks.
Hours per week: 36 scheduled/7 unscheduled.

Organ System or Clerkship Topic					
Mechanisms of Disease	155	20	102½	26½	30⦀
Renal	25	15½	10	5	5⦀
Cardiovascular	21	16	6	21	6⦀
Neurobehavioral	18	17	13		4⦀
Musculoskeletal	22	15	4		4
Respiratory	20	14	4	10	4⦀
Gastrointestinal/Liver	28	8	18	18	7⦀
Endocrine/Reproduction	36	37	17	10	10⦀
Blood	23	13	13	15	6
Introduction to Clinical Medicine				180	18⦀
Total	348	155½	187½	285½	97⦀

Third and Fourth Academic Period

Required Clerkships   Wee⦀

Medicine, Part I ....
Medicine, Part II ....
Psychiatry ....
Pediatrics ....
Obstetrics/Gynecology ....
General Surgery ....
Basic Science ....

Selective Clerkships

Two 3-week clerkships are required and must be chosen from the following: neurosurge⦀
ophthalmology, orthopedic surgery, otolaryngology, or urology. Three 6-week clerkships must⦀
scheduled in affiliated hospitals, with the consent of the faculty advisor. Free electives, total⦀
weeks, may be scheduled in modules of no less than 3 weeks and also require the consent of ⦀
faculty advisor.

Source: Association of American Medical Colleges, 1982b, p. 26.

Table 29. Interdisciplinary Presentations with Clinical Tracks: University of Washington School of Medicine.

Total weeks of instruction: 148

First Academic Period: Begins September. Duration: 34 weeks.
Hours per week: 28 scheduled/12 unscheduled.

Required Courses	Lecture	Conference	Lab	Other	Total
Microscopic Anatomy	16		29	3	48
Gross Anatomy and Embryology	33	17	50		100
Mechanisms of Cell Physiology	36	10	4		50
Introduction to Clinical Medicine	8	6			14
Molecular and Cellular Biology I	41				41
Ages of Man	30	6			36
Cell and Tissue Response to Injury	51		14		65
Natural History of Infectious Diseases and Chemotherapy	55	13			68
Introduction to Clinical Medicine	26				26
System of Human Behavior I	24	6			30
Molecular and Cellular Biology II	19				19
Epidemiology	20				20
Head, Neck, Ear, Nose, and Throat	36		30		66
Nervous System	42	7	26	4	79
Introduction to Clinical Medicine	10	25	20		55
Cell Biology	22				22
Total	469	90	173	7	739

Second Academic Period: Begins September. Duration: 34 weeks.
Hours per week: 28 scheduled/12 unscheduled.

Required Courses	Lecture	Conference	Lab	Other	Total
Endocrine System	16	16			32
Cardiovascular and Respiratory System	66	28	10	12	116
Gastro-Intestinal System	8	40	5	3	56
Introduction to Clinical Medicine	32	6		20	58
Principles of Pharmacology I	40				40
Introduction to Clinical Medicine	10	10		40	60
Skin System	16			2	18
Reproductive Biology	40				40
Musculoskeletal system	20	28	12		60
Genetics	26				26
Medicine, Health, and Society	34	6			40
Introduction to Clinical Medicine	20	20		45	85
Hematology	15	15	6		36
Urinary System	20	17	9	3	49
System of Human Behavior II	28				28
Principles of Pharmacology II	30				30
Systemic Pathology	20			2	22
Total	441	186	42	127	796

Third and Fourth Academic Period: Begins July. Duration: Varies.

Clinical Curriculum (120 Credits)

The clinical curriculum is pursued predominantly in the third and fourth years of medical school. It includes three elements: prescribed clerkships to be completed by all students (72 credits or 36 weeks in Medicine, Obstetrics/Gynecology, Pediatrics, Psychiatry, Surgery); a clinical selective requirement that all students complete in a variety of ways—a minimum of 20 credits in three clinical areas (family medicine, rehabilitation medicine/chronic care, and emergency care/trauma); and 28 credits of clinical clerkships elected by the student.

Source: Association of American Medical Colleges, 1982b, p. 256.

Table 30. Disciplinary First Year, Interdisciplinary Second Year, Clinical Tracks: University of Minnesota Medical School at Minneapolis.

Total weeks of instruction: Varies
(minimum 36 weeks full-time clinical study for completion of graduation requirements)
First Academic Period: Begins September. Duration: 40 weeks.
Hours per week: 28 scheduled/12 unscheduled.

Required Courses	Hours				
	Lecture	Conference	Lab	Other	Tot.
Gross Anatomy........................	60		150		2
Histology............................	40		60		1(
Embryology..........................	40				∠
Biochemistry.........................	80		51		1≀
Physiology...........................	82		56		1≀
Pathology	60		60		1≀
Pharmacology........................	65	24			8
Psychological Medicine	45				∠
Introduction to Clinical Medicine	20			60	8
Microbiology	80		60		1∠
Neuroanatomy	20		10		≀
Total.............................	592	24	447	60	1,1≀

Elective Program—Optional: interaction discussion groups.

Second Academic Period: Begins September. Duration: 45 weeks.
Hours per week: 28 scheduled/12 unscheduled.

Required Courses	Lecture	Conference	Lab	Tot.
Pathology				30-5
Cardiovascular	25	10-20		≀
Respiratory	25	10-20		≀
Endocrine/Metabolism	40	10-20		∠
Reproduction	30	10-20		≀
Eye	15	10-20		▮
Ear, Nose, and Throat.................	23	10-20		≀
Fluid and Electrolyte..................	29			≀
Human Genetics	13	4		▮
Human Sexuality......................	18			▮
Blood	29	10-20		≀
Kidney and Urinary Tract	27	10-20		≀
Skin	17	8-15		▮
Psyche	44	30-40		∠
Nervous System and Muscle Disorders....	44	10-20		∠
Gut	34	10-20		≀
Bone, Joint, and Connective Tissue	38	10-30		≀
Student as Physician Tutorials			475	4≀
Laboratory Diagnosis			16	▮
Total.............................	451		496	977-99

Elective Program
Special programs in medical ethics, humanistic medicine, and nutrition.

Source: Association of American Medical Colleges, 1982b, p. 118.

Table 31. Mixed First and Second Year, Above-Average Requirements in the Fourth Year: University of California–Davis School of Medicine.

Total weeks of instruction: 160

First Academic Period: Begins September. Duration: 30 weeks.
Scheduled hours per week: 30

Required Courses	Lecture	Conference	Lab	Other	Total
Anatomy	109	3	188		300
Biological Chemistry	115	10			125
Physiology	127	39	44		210
General Pathology	27	2	11		40
The Life Cycle	23	17	7		47
Diagnostic Process	83	20	16	9	128
Total	484	91	266	9	850

Elective Program
Optional.

Second Academic Period: Begins August. Duration: 36 weeks.
Scheduled hours per week: 30–35.

Required Courses					
Human Sexuality	18	2			20
Systemic Pathology	41	23	81		145
Microbiology/Immunology	90		38		128
Pharmacology	65	46	16		127
Preventive Medicine	32	28			60
Psychopathology	24		20		44
Organ Systems Medicine	316	101	51		468
Diagnostic Process	59	4	18		81
Total	645	204	224		1,073

Elective Program
Optional.

Third Academic Period: Begins July. Duration: 48 weeks.

Required Clerkships	Weeks
Surgery	12
Internal Medicine	12
Obstetrics/Gynecology/Neonatal	8
Pediatrics	8
Psychiatry	8

Elective Program
Optional.

Fourth Academic Period: Begins July. Duration: 40 weeks.

Required Clerkships	
ENT/Eye	4
P M & R	4
Selectives (Track I—Surgical Specialties; or Track II—Medical Specialties; or Track III—Family Practice and Behavioral Specialties)	20
Electives	12

On exceptional occasions, fourth-year requirements may be met by special arrangement for students with strong research/academic interests who have already demonstrated superior performance.

Source: Association of American Medical Colleges, 1982b, pp. 124–125.

Table 32. Docent System: University of Missouri at Kansas City School of Medicine.

Six- Year Combined Baccalaureate-Medical Degree Program
Total weeks of instruction: 272

First Academic Period: Begins September. Duration: 48 weeks.

Required Courses	Lecture	Conference	Lab	Other	Tot
General Chemistry	96		128		2:
Human Biology	128		96		2:
General Psychology	48				4
Sociology	48				4
Total	320		224		5

Required Clerkships—Introduction to Medicine is 36 weeks.

Second Academic Period: Begins September. Duration: 32 weeks.

Required Courses				
Elementary Organic Chemistry	64		48	1
Human Biochemistry I	64			6
Life Cycles	48			4
Human Physiology	67	13		8
Introductory Pharmacology (Self-Study)				
Total	243	13	48	32

Required Clerkships	Week
Introduction to Medicine:	
The Child and Development	16
The Woman	16

Third Academic Period: Begins June. Duration: 48 weeks.

Required Courses	Hour
Medical Microbiology	144
Human Biochemistry II	64
Saturday Morning Correlative Medicine Series	90
Required Clerkships	Week
Docent Team/Internal Medicine	8
Pathology/Anatomy	12
Family Practice Preceptorship	4
Continuing Care Clinic (4 hours once per week)	48

Elective Program—4-12 weeks available for electives in basic and clinical sciences.

Fourth Academic Period: Begins June. Duration: 48 weeks.

	Hour
Required Course—Saturday Morning Correlative Medicine Series	90
Required Clerkships	Week
Docent Team/Internal Medicine	8
Geriatrics/Family Practice	4
Pediatrics	8
Psychiatry–Mental Health	4
Continuing Care Clinic (4 hours once per week)	48

Elective Program—4-12 weeks available for electives in basic and clinical sciences.

Fifth Academic Period: Begins June. Duration: 48 weeks.

Required Clerkships	Week
Docent Team/Internal Medicine	12
Pathology	8
Surgery	8
Obstetrics–Gynecology	8
Continuing Care Clinic (4 hours once per week)	48

Elective Program—8-12 weeks are open for electives.

291

Table 32. (Cont'd)

Sixth Academic Period: Begins June. Duration: 48 weeks.

Required Courses
Assigned to College of Arts and Sciences to complete baccalaureate degree

Required Clerkships — Weeks

	Weeks
Docent Team/Internal Medicine	8
Pediatrics	8
Family Medicine	4
Emergency Medicine	4
Continuing Care Clinic (4 hours once per week)	48

Elective Program—8-16 weeks are open for electives.

Source: Association of American Medical Colleges, 1982b, pp. 124-25.

Table 33. Largely Elective Curriculum, Third and Fourth Years: Duke University School of Medicine.

Total weeks of instruction: 153

First Academic Period: Begins August. Duration: 41 weeks.
Hours per week: 36 scheduled/8 unscheduled.

	Hours				
Required Courses	**Lecture**	**Conference**	**Lab**	**Other**	**Total**
Microanatomy	32		64	7	103
Gross Anatomy	20		74	5	99
Neuroanatomy	17	8	24	2	51
Biochemistry	59	40		6	105
Physiology	55	46		10	111
Neurophysiology	17	11		2	30
Genetics	21	14		3	38
Pathology	61		140	12	213
Microbiology (includes Immunology)	98		50	12	160
Pharmacology	72	36		13	121
Human Behavior	28	30		4	62
Introduction to Clinical Medicine	91		104	6	201
Total	571	185	456	82	1,294

Second Academic Period: Begins September. Duration: 48 weeks.

Required Clerkships — Weeks

	Weeks
Family Medicine	8
Medicine	8
Obstetrics/Gynecology	8
Pediatrics	8
Psychiatry	8
Surgery	8

Third Academic Period: Begins September. Duration: 32 weeks.
Entirely elective. Students usually choose basic science electives or study programs.

Fourth Academic Period: Begins September. Duration: 32 weeks.
Entirely elective. Students usually choose clinical electives.

Source: Association of American Medical Colleges, 1982b, p. 170.

Table 34. Criterion-Referenced Curriculum: Southern Illinois University School of Medicine.

Total weeks of instruction: 138

First Academic Period: Begins August. Duration: 50 weeks.
Hours per week: 31½ scheduled/29½ unscheduled.

Required Courses	Hours				
	Lecture	Conference	Lab	Other	Total
Introductory Block I	65	56	7	66	19
Locomotor...........................	43	35	100	31	20
Neuroscience.........................	46	71	16	30	16
Cardiovascular	30	50	24	57	16
Gastrointestinal	42	56	30	26	15
Respiratory	34	58	10	23	12
Renal	24	24	6	24	7
Endocrine	24	22	9	43	9
Reproduction	24	22	9	43	9
Behavioral, Social Sciences, and Humanities	40	40		16	9
Introduction to Clinical Medicine I	22	21	16	9	6
Total...............................	394	455	227	368	1,44

Second Academic Period: Begins June. Duration: 38 weeks.
Hours per week: 20 scheduled/50 unscheduled.

Required Courses	
Microbiology	25
Immunology..	15
Pharmacology..	40
Pathology	51
Radiology	11
Clinical Medicine...	25

Third Academic Period: Begins January. Duration: 52 weeks.

Required Clerkships	Week
Surgery..	10
Medicine	11
Obstetrics/Gynecology	7
Pediatrics	7
Family Practice..	4
Psychiatry	4
Anesthesiology	1
Medical Education, Society, and the Humanities	4

Fourth Academic Period: Begins January. Duration: 24 weeks.

Entire period devoted to electives.

Source: Association of American Medical Colleges, 1982b, p. 76.

Table 35. Self-Study in Basic Modules: McMaster University School of Medicine.

Total weeks of instruction: 133

First Academic Period: Begins September. Duration: 24 weeks.

This period consists of Phases I and II of the program. Formal courses are not scheduled, but the content of Phase I emphasizes the behavioral and biological aspects of growth, aging, and development. Phase II content emphasizes the chemical, functional, and structural characteristics of the cell and maintenance of cell integrity, stimuli, and changes in the cell, tissue, organs, and the organism.

Second Academic Period: Begins March. Duration: 40 weeks.

This period is Phase III, which focuses on the study of body systems in health and disease.

Third Academic Period: Begins March. Duration: 32 weeks.

Required Clerkships	Weeks
Medicine/Surgery	16
Family Medicine and Psychiatry	8
Obstetrics/Gynecology/Pediatrics	8

Elective Program and Revision

There are 26 weeks open for electives and 9 weeks of revision during the total program.

Source: Association of American Medical Colleges, 1982b, p. 280.

once did. In two schools, plaster models have replaced cadavers. Films, videotapes, and other media are employed more and more. Although there is no shortage of cadavers, there is an acute need for anatomists who can relate the structure of the human body to human disease and the repair of trauma; in one school, this link is made through the surgeons, who have total responsibility for the teaching of gross anatomy. Radiologists and orthopedists often visit the dissecting room and participate in teaching anatomy to medical students.

Biochemistry, which once was taught with the assistance of many test tube type experiments, has been changed through improvements in the technology of this rapidly changing science. Now, elaborate equipment is used and the emphasis has shifted away from direct laboratory work to demonstrations and to the interpretation of experimental results. The same is true of microbiology; it, too, employs many techniques that are characteristic of biochemistry. Usually, one can find some agar-agar around, but not much. The teaching of physiology and pharmacology is extensively dependent upon lectures and demonstrations; in some schools, no "hands on" animal experiments are offered at all.

The pathologists and microscopic anatomists still issue slide sets for microscopic study, but multiple pictoral media are now in wide use. Gross pathological specimens are commonly held in a deep freeze or encased in plastic envelopes awaiting the student's examination. Autopsies are still observed but, as in gross anatomy, the biochemical evidence of disease receives more emphasis than do the structural changes brought about by disease. The clinical pathological conference, the big weekly event for students and faculty thirty years ago, has disappeared almost everywhere, except in the pages of *The New England Journal of Medicine*.

The behavioral scientists expend a lot of effort trying to attract the attention of the students during their first and second years; however, the results have been disappointing, with poor class attendance in many schools. Wilson and Smythe (1983) have described changes in the curriculum since 1960 in much greater detail.

Introduction to Clinical Skills. Most schools introduce first-year medical students to the care of patients in a variety of ways. This is usually done to illustrate the relevance of some science the new students are currently studying. For instance, when the students are learning about the microscopic layers of the skin, a friendly dermatologist may demonstrate some of his (willing) patients who suffer from basal cell carcinoma of the facial skin in order to provide the students with direct observation of the effect of this disease on the normal structure of the skin.

A few schools begin to instruct their students in the techniques of eliciting the history of the patient's illness as early as their first year. Except for one or two, the schools complete this instruction by the second year, during which it is combined with practical exercises in physical diagnosis. The use of two-way screens and videotaping techniques facilitates the learning of interviewing and history taking by the students in many schools.

The medical schools at the University of Rochester and Yale University use a general clerkship, which precedes the rotation through the specialty clinical clerkships of the third year, to bridge the study of the basic sciences and the clinical material. In the elaborate program at Rochester, specially trained faculty members in large numbers work "one on one" with the students as they acquire sophisticated hands on diagnostic skills. Every school in the United States and Canada strongly emphasizes applied clinical skills and, in one way or another, prepares students to assume the responsibilities inherent in the clinical clerkship.

Clinical Clerkships. As noted before, in this exceedingly significant phase of the education of the physician, third-year students are divided into small groups of four to six clerks; for a specified block of full-time study, the group is assigned to a particular specialty, which is usually confined to one geographical area of the teaching hospital. There patients receive medical care from the advanced students in graduate medical education, from the residents who assist the faculty members, and from volunteer physicians who constitute the professional staff of the teaching hospital.

In the typical situation, the clinical clerk is assigned two or more patients per week. Ideally, the clerk contacts the new patient upon his arrival at the hospital or soon thereafter to elicit the history of the illness and to perform a preliminary physical examination and some minor laboratory tests. The patient is actually in the direct care of the resident, who is responsible to the attending faculty member/physician, the ultimate authority in the hierarchical team approach to the delivery of medical care to the patient. Nurses, technicians, social workers, specialist physician consultants, and, in some cases, the hospital chaplain are active participants in the health care team. Table 36 displays the types of diseases of patients studied by clinical clerks in internal medicine.

The first responsibility of the clinical clerk is to try to establish a diagnosis of the patient's illness and to outline a regimen of therapy. In most circumstances, a patient who is admitted in the late afternoon or evening must be "presented" in elaborate detail to the attending faculty member/physician at teaching ward rounds early the next morning. The student is expected to know every

Table 36. Patient-Related Experience of 165 Medical Students
in 42 Medical Schools, 1980–1982: Clerkship in Internal Medicine.

System	Number of Patients	Percentage of Patients
Heart	422	14
Oncology	402	14
Respiratory	313	11
Alimentary	228	8
Metabolic	212	7
Infectious Disease	207	7
Central Nervous	166	6
Vascular	158	5
Genitourinary	119	4
Hepatobiliary	116	4
Drug Abuse/Intoxication	102	4
Hematology	82	3
Immune	70	2
Bone/Joint	51	2
Endocrine	51	2
Pancreas	50	2
Behavioral/Psychiatric	49	2
Neuromuscular	35	1
Critical Care/Accident	28	1
Skin	20	0.7
Nutritional	10	0.3
Total	2,891	100.0

Source: Bradford and Schofield, 1983.

detail about the patient and to defend his provisional diagnosis and his recommended therapy under questioning by the presiding faculty member/physician. The other clinical clerks in the group and the residents assigned to the team are present during this interrogation of the student. If the student cannot respond to the faculty member's questions in a thorough manner, the faculty member will direct his questions to other clerks in the group. If the students fail to deliver the answers sought, the residents move into the line of questioning as the faculty member fulfills his traditional role of establishing very demanding standards for clinical education.

The residents are very important participants in the learning process each clinical clerk undergoes. Ordinarily, the student and one or more residents examine the patient together and, as a team, they discuss initial procedures for the care of the patient. In some hospitals, the clinical clerk and the resident work with the patient's private physician through the completion of the admission routine and as diagnostic examinations are performed. The clinical clerk participates in the care of the patient as much as is safe and always under supervision. Acute, serious problems are handled by senior physicians and residents. If the patient is not acutely ill, the student is given a larger role and may be able to establish an excellent rapport with the patient, a close relationship that often continues until the patient is discharged. A student who is paired with a well-informed resident who enjoys teaching as well as learning is likely to profit immeasurably from the association.

Improving the Faculty Teaching Skills

Many schools have experimented with an "Office of Research in Medical Education" or a similar unit devoted to the study of teaching skills in the medical sciences and staffed by persons trained in educational methodology. These units have been established to provide training for the faculty in methods of lecturing, the use of visual aids, the design of examinations, and other pedagogical techniques. Although the general concept of this effort has been successful, many faculty members have been reluctant to seek or to accept a critical review of their long-used practices in pedagogy by "foreign" or unfamiliar experts. The concept has been most successful in those schools in which the educational technologists are attached to the staff of the chief academic officer and to the faculty committees on curriculum and student promotions; problems have arisen when the experts in educational methodology function in administrative isolation. Miller (1980) has reviewed the movement to improve the teaching skills of the faculty.

Part of the problem with improving the faculty's teaching skills is that many medical students are critical of the small amount of attention the faculty members devote to the teaching aspects of their responsibilities. And although the dean and departmental chairmen may pay lip service to the need to pursue each faculty function in the classical triad of teaching, research, and patient care, every faculty member feels the weight of the heavy mantle of the originally Germanic emphasis on the discovery of new knowledge through research—an emphasis that has pervaded American medical schools for some time. Few medical school faculties actually reward and recognize the highly effective, devoted teacher, whereas most pay profound homage to the creative researcher. The criteria for promotion and tenure are thus unsettled issues. A new concern is the fact that clinical faculty members, especially the younger ones, are increasingly being pressured to devote more time to the clinical services that generate income for the schools; as a result, the time available for research activity, the publication of papers, and direct contact with students has been reduced.

Although it is widely criticized, the lecture continues to be commonly employed as the primary means of transmitting information to the students. Faculty members acquire the ability to give a decent lecture by accident; most have no instruction whatsoever in instructing students through oral presentations. Poor lectures stifle the curiosity of the students, often impede learning—and often leave students feeling cheated. For example, a class of 100 medical students, each member of which pays an average of $15,000 per year in tuition for about 900 clock hours of instruction, collectively pay $1,666 per hour for their scheduled educational program. Thus, each individual in such a class pays an hourly rate of $16.66, the average cost of a good seat at a symphony in a major city. At this price, a medical student has good reason to expect an hour of well-prepared and delivered instruction from the faculty member.

In the clinical setting, a physician/preceptor often takes a small group of third-year clinical clerks on patient rounds, during which the professor pauses by each patient for a bedside discussion of the patient's illness with the students and residents. This type of teaching can be either quite stimulating or hopelessly dull. In fact, a class of medical students, many of whom have been reared on a steady diet of television for at least twenty years, is a sophisticated and critical audience for any performance by a medical faculty member—in a lecture, a small-group conference, a demonstration of laboratory technology, clinical examinations and conferences, and ward rounds.

In 1953, I attended the First World Conference on Medical Education, at which I heard a very senior French medical educator exclaim: "Giving a lecture is like tossing a bucket of water on a large pile of empty bottles—a little water gets into some bottles." For some time now, medical students have applied the term "shifting dullness" to the boring, unstimulating bedside lecturer. *Shifting dullness* is a term usually applied to the clinical signs of dullness that are revealed when a chest or abdomen containing fluid is thumped with the finger; when the patient shifts position, the fluid—and the dullness—shifts. In short, the boring clinical professor may show signs of shifting dullness to the students as he moves from patient to patient on teaching rounds. A steady, daily fare of this professorial syndrome for a curricular block of six to eight weeks can stifle the minds of some very intelligent twenty-two- to twenty-four-year-olds.

Evaluating Student Achievement

Most medical educators would agree that the undergraduate medical student must: (1) achieve a general understanding of the organization of the body of medical knowledge at the introductory level; (2) acquire the skills needed to apply that knowledge to the care of patients; and (3) learn the methods and acquire the habits required to renew that knowledge throughout the years of clinical practice. The achievements of the students in these respects are measured by various tests and procedures devised by the course directors, the departmental faculties, and interdisciplinary committees of the faculties.

A large number of medical schools rely on external examinations for these student evaluations. The series of tests prepared by the National Board of Medical Examiners (NBME) is the best known and most commonly used. The NBME is an independent body sponsored by the AMA, the AAMC, the Federation of State Medical Boards, and other organizations. It has developed a bank of well-designed questions on all the generic subjects usually presented in the undergraduate medical curriculum. The questions are created and maintained by subject committees composed of faculty members drawn from the medical schools of the United States; these committees thus constitute a sort of "national" medical faculty. Table 37 displays data on the methods of grading and testing those employed in United States medical schools and on the use

Table 37. Number and Percentage of U.S. Medical Schools with Methods of Evaluation of Students.

	1978–79 (N = 124)		1979–80 (N = 125)		1980–81 (N = 125)		1981–82 (N = 126)		1982–83 (N = 126)	
	No.	Percent	No.	Percent	No.	Percent	No.	Percent	No.	Percent
Grading and Testing										
Pass/fail or equivalent										
Basic sciences	29	23.4	27	21.6	28	22.4	27	21.4	25	19.8
Clinical sciences	25	20.2	23	18.4	23	18.4	21	16.7	21	16.7
Electives	39	31.5	36	28.8	39	31.2	38	30.2	40	31.7
Honors/pass/fail or equivalent										
Basic sciences	62	50.0	61	48.8	58	46.4	60	47.6	60	47.6
Clinical sciences	67	54.0	66	52.8	63	50.4	63	50.0	63	50.0
Electives	66	53.2	65	52.0	63	50.4	62	49.2	63	50.0
Letter/number										
Basic sciences	37	29.8	42	33.6	45	36.0	45	35.7	46	36.5
Clinical sciences	35	28.2	40	32.0	44	35.2	44	34.9	46	36.5
Electives	16	12.9	22	17.6	24	19.2	22	17.5	23	18.3
Use of NBME exam, Part I										
Exam optional	30	24.2	30	24.0	31	24.8	32	25.4	31	24.6
Student must record score	25	20.2	30	24.0	35	28.0	33	26.2	34	27.0
Student must record passing total score	59	47.6	57	45.6	58	46.4	62	49.2	57	45.2
Student must record passing score in each section							3	2.4	4	3.2
To determine final course grades	34	27.4	33	26.4	31	24.8	29	23.0	11	8.7
Use of selected sections of NBME exam, Part I, by departments to evaluate students										
Anatomy	13	10.5	13	10.4	12	9.6	10	7.9	8	6.3
Behavioral sciences	6	4.8	6	4.8	7	5.6	5	4.0	5	4.0
Biochemistry	17	13.7	16	12.8	14	11.2	12	9.5	10	7.9
Microbiology	21	16.9	24	19.2	23	18.4	20	15.9	15	11.9
Pathology	20	16.1	21	16.8	21	16.8	17	13.5	12	9.5
Pharmacology	20	16.1	20	16.0	19	15.2	16	12.7	10	7.9
Physiology	18	14.5	19	15.2	18	14.4	15	11.9	11	8.7
Use of NBME exam, Part II										
Exam optional	30	24.2	33	26.4	36	28.8	39	31.0	38	30.2
Student must record score	35	28.2	35	28.0	37	30.4	36	28.6	42	33.3
Student must record passing score to graduate	51	41.1	49	39.2	47	37.6	46	36.5	44	34.9
To determine final course grades	17	13.7	15	12.0	16	12.8	17	13.5	14	11.1

Note: Compilation for 1978–79 includes data from 124 schools; compilations for 1979–80 and 1980–81 include data from 125 schools; compilations for 1981–82 and 1982–83 include data from 126 schools.

of Parts I and II of the NBME examination, which cover the basic science subjects and clinical subjects respectively.

Although many believe that each medical school faculty is responsible for its own educational program and for the measurement of the achievements of its students, there is also a general consensus that an external examination, such as Parts I and II of the NBME examination, can play an important role as *one* indicator of the students' progress; for one thing, such an examination provides a comparison with national standards. The LCME has found an external measure to be valuable in assessing the quality of the educational programs of newly developing schools, which have not yet produced several cohorts of graduates whose performance can be judged. Some medical educators, however, find the style of questioning on the NBME examination and the time constraints on the administration of the examinations to be bothersome. Others believe that the use of the NBME tests tends to force the curriculum into a constricted mold containing only those subjects covered in the NBME question banks. Since the tests are entirely objective in nature, they measure regurgitation of recently memorized facts, leaving absent any assessment of accomplishments of skill in the application of facts to the solution of problems of patients.

In the 1960s and 1970s, some students have balked at the requirement that they submit themselves to any examination. The pass/fail system found in less than 20 percent of the schools during the 1982–83 academic year may be the result of these protests. Most schools have abandoned the practice of ranking each student in the class on the basis of examination grades; instead, they have adopted expanded systems of recording evaluations of students' performances in small-group sessions, in laboratories, and in the clinical setting. Such evaluations are or should be discussed with the students in a timely fashion in order to give them an opportunity to improve their skills or knowledge. Only the Uniformed Services University of the Health Sciences grades its students to the third decimal point.

The mastery of clinical skills must be measured during the intimate association of the clinical clerk with the supervising faculty member and residents with whom the clerk works for extended hours, night and day, in the care of patients. In the American system of clinical education, in which bedside teaching and learning is heavily emphasized, the student can attain a full mastery of the customary and required clinical skills. Not every foreign medical school possesses the resources available for clinical teaching commonly found in the United States and Canada; thus, before they are admitted to programs of graduate medical education or are licensed to practice medicine in the United States, foreign medical graduates should be required to demonstrate achievement in the mastery of clinical knowledge, especially in the possession of "hands on" clinical skills.

Electives

During the 1960s, many medical educators became aware of the awesome magnitude of the body of medical knowledge; as a result, most faculties reduced the clock hours and/or the weeks of clerkship required of students and left the entire fourth year open for the free choice of electives by the students. This substantial block of time has been managed differently from school to school. On the average, the fourth-year student enjoys considerable latitude in deciding how to use this time. Although electives in both the basic and clinical sciences are available, most students have chosen to gain more experience in the clinical sciences than in the basic sciences.

After fifteen years or more of experience with the elective senior year, I observe that a large number of students do not broaden their medical education through election of learning experiences that complement their chosen specialty. Rather, much of the senior year is used as "political time," as they speak of it. A senior who desires to be appointed to a highly competitive residency program in another academic medical center is likely to seek an elective at that school/hospital so that he can advance his chances for selection to the residency there. Sometimes several programs in different parts of the country are given comparable investment of the senior's valuable time. The result is a narrowing of education toward the specialty—with neglect of the opportunity to gain knowledge and skills in subject areas that complement the primary choice for several years of study as a resident. This artifactual disease of the curriculum is iatrogenic in nature.

As the faculties have acquired more experience with the elective system and as the body of medical knowledge has continued to grow, some medical schools have begun to replace fourth-year electives with specified, required courses. Elsewhere, the process of selecting studies has been tightened, and most of the electives are now being subjected to increased scrutiny by the faculties.

Problems of the M.D. Curriculum in the 1980s

Constantly Enlarging Body of Knowledge. Wearn (1956, p. 517) in his justification for the precedent-shattering change in the curriculum at Western Reserve in the early 1950s, described his faculty's assumptions as follows:

> From the beginning, we faced the fact that the accumulated mass of knowledge had reached such proportions that no medical student's mind could absorb it, nor could any faculty present it. Therefore, we abandoned all thought of total coverage. Instead, we agreed that emphasis must be placed upon the basic concepts, the mechanisms of disease, continuing self-education, the development of a scientific critique, the development of powers and skills and the inculcation of ideals. It was realized in this (latter) connection that the example set by the faculty would play an important role.

These words describing the mass of medical knowledge of thirty years ago aptly characterize the dilemma of the faculty of today. However, the intervening three decades have included the golden age of medical research, during which clinical and biomedical scientists have reported their new factual discoveries in some 27,000 medical journals around the world. Thus, the problem of pedagogy for the medical student by a faculty faced with a constantly increasing mass of knowledge has risen to an overwhelming level. While most deans and faculty members admit that total coverage in the medical curriculum is no longer possible (and may not have been possible even in Flexner's day), few effective plans for solving the problem have yet emerged. During 1981 and through 1984, the AAMC has a Commission on the General Professional Education of the Physician studying the problem; perhaps the results of this effort may be useful to the medical faculties as they face up to their responsibilities.

As evidence that the medical faculty has not solved its continuously growing problem of dealing with the mass of medical knowledge, Anderson and Graham (1980) performed an analysis of the medical curriculum in the United Kingdom—a curriculum quite comparable to that in the United States and Canada. They found that the basic science subject material contained 47,900 facts and 29,900 concepts. The authors concluded that a student who studies 40 hours per week for 2 years must assimilate approximately 24 new facts or concepts per hour. The clinical subjects, including pathology, were found to contain 27,000 facts and 25,500 concepts. A student who studies the clinical subjects for 50 weeks a year for 3 years must absorb 9 facts or concepts per hour. Anderson and Graham estimated that a modern language course requires a learning rate of 6 facts or concepts per hour. They recommend that this learning rate be applied to medical students. Adoption of this recommendation would require revolutionary change in the process of education of the physician.

Changed Status of the Physician at M.D. Graduation. What is the professional status of the physician at the time the M.D. degree is received? Until early in this century, possession of an M.D. degree was the final requirement for receipt of a license to practice medicine, despite the largely didactic nature of the curriculum of those times. Gradually, after the Flexner Survey of 1910, opportunities for post-M.D. graduate medical education developed to the point that each new recipient of the M.D. degree could obtain a general internship and later residency training in a clinical specialty. By mid-century, most of the states required a year of graduate medical education prior to granting licensure. Currently, we expect that an estimated 94 percent of new medical students of 1980 (M.D. Class of 1984) will enroll in and complete most or all of the requirements for clinical specialty training, ranging from three years in Pediatrics and Family Medicine to six years for Neurosurgery (Association of American Medical Colleges, 1980c).

Thus, the historic timing of the granting of the M.D. degree now falls at the interface between studies in medical school and the continuation of advanced clinical education in a selected specialty. In 1957, in recognition of the changing customs, the national accrediting authority for programs of physician education, the Liaison Committee on Medical Education, formalized the limited purpose of the M.D. curriculum as follows. "The undergraduate period of medical education leading to the M.D. degree is no longer sufficient to prepare a student for independent medical practice without supplementation by a graduate training period which will vary in length depending upon the type of practice the student selects" (Liaison Committee on Medical Education, 1973a).

Discontinuity in the Programs of Physician Education. If the period of undergraduate medical education is no longer adequate to prepare the recipient of the M.D. degree for independent medical practice, as the LCME has declared, then the altered objective for the M.D. program must be to prepare the student of medicine for an orderly transition into the period of graduate medical education—which is sometimes defined as a period of supervised medical practice under the direction of a qualified faculty. A few universities have attempted to give structure and organization to the continuum of physician education—as a premedical student, medical student, and hospital resident enrolled in a specialty program of graduate medical education. However, the long-established custom is that each segment goes its own way with inadequate reference to activities by the others.

Expansion of Total Time Unacceptable. If mastery of the entire body of knowledge is not set as the objective of the M.D. curriculum, what part is to be included and what is to be excluded? Here indecision reigns and concensus in any faculty is elusive. The usual result, in many traditional schools, is that it is rare for a specialty departmental faculty to think that the allotment of teaching hours for its disciplinary course in the curriculum is adequate; its spokesmen usually seek an opportunity to increase their portion of time with the students. Under these circumstances, the students' "free" study/recreation time is vulnerable, as is any block of time intended for elective study. A strong dean, a nonpartisan curriculum committee, and periodic admonitions from the LCME (the accrediting authority) are needed to enforce a truce regarding territorial raids among the barons who occupy the traditional departmental chairs.

The remedies used in the past to tame the increasing body of knowledge have been to extend the total time involved in the education of the physician and to organize specialized educational programs. Following is a periodic rough approximation of the two-hundred-year evolution of the time required to meet gradually increasing educational standards for American physicians.

1780s to 1870s: Apprenticeship and/or two-year medical curriculum

1870s to 1900: Movement toward the three-year graded M.D. curriculum; four-year graded curriculum at Hopkins, beginning 1894.

1900s to 1930s: Two to three years of college; four-year graded M.D. curriculum; one year of internship

1930s to 1950s: Three to four years of college; four-year graded M.D. curriculum; one year of internship and gradual growth of specialty residency training

1950s to 1980s: 95 percent of students complete four years of college; four-year graded M.D. curriculum; residency programs extending from three to six years for 94 percent of all M.D. graduates

Should the M.D. program be extended from four to five years in the 1980s and to six years by A.D. 2,000, so that the faculty can pack more facts into the curriculum? Should the existing twenty-six medical specialties be splintered into ever-narrower slices of the body of knowledge? Extension of the duration of either the M.D. program or the residency programs does not appear to be practical due to the costs the students must bear.

Increased Cost of Physician Education. During 1982–83, a state-resident student in a public medical school paid an average tuition of $2,697 and average living expenses and fees amounting to $6,891, for an average total of $9,588 per year. The upper end of the range amounted to $21,231. In private schools, tuition averaged $10,721 and expenses $7,489, for an average total of $18,210.

The upper end of the range amounted to $32,243 (Association of American Medical Colleges, 1983). These costs to the medical students have increased rapidly in the early 1980s, as many medical schools have had to struggle with declining operating income from the federal government and from some of the states. The result has been the accumulation of quite large debts by many graduating seniors; indebtedness of as much as $80,000 has been reported by some individuals (Tonesk and Nelson, 1981; Winslow, 1981). My colleague, Davis Johnson, has written a detailed analysis of the methods used by medical students to finance their medical education (1983). The perception of an impending surplus of physicians by the mid-1980s, in the view of the Reagan Administration, has led to a reduction of financing of federally sponsored programs to support the cost of medical education.

While residents receive a stipend during their years of training, their income is inadequate to support a spouse and sometimes children; most Americans by their late twenties and early thirties desire to marry and to develop a family. Further extension of time in residency training would extend the financial problems of the aspiring practicing physician. Since there is already much criticism about the pattern of specialism in medicine, any effort for further division is likely to encounter much opposition from both within and without the profession. If we decide to rule out the traditional solution of adding more time to the total period of education of the physician and if further specialism appears unlikely, we are forced to examine critically the efficiency of the educational program of the 1980s to determine if improvements can be made.

Conversion of Students into Passive Learners. Basic scientists who have discontinued laboratory exercises in their courses have caused a deterioration in the quality of medical education by converting their students into passive learners, with some rare exceptions. Use of small group conferences may be palliative but these are a poor substitute for meaningful, carefully planned opportunities for students to expend their capacities to make careful, accurate measurements of biomedical phenomena, using scientific equipment essential to the sophisticated forms of medical care they later shall render to their patients.

13

Graduate and Continuing Medical Education and Other Medical School Programs

Graduate Medical Education

The recent recipient of the M.D. degree bears the title of physician but is no longer considered adequately qualified at that point to embark on the independent practice of medicine. Rather, since the beginning of the 1980s, all but a few M.D. graduates have gone directly from medical school into residency training in a chosen medical specialty.

Specialty training is a comparatively recent form of education of the physician in the United States. In the latter part of the nineteenth century and early in the twentieth century, at least until World War I, specialty training was generally not available in the United States, and those who sought such training found it necessary to travel to the United Kingdom, France, or the German-speaking nations. After World War I, this trend diminished markedly. Residency programs gradually became available in the major hospital-medical school health centers during the 1920s and 1930s; however, a majority of the graduates in medicine of those decades took a single year of internship and then proceeded into independent private practice. The demands for medical services during World War II accelerated the motivation of medical graduates to undertake residency training and the adoption of residency training grew rapidly during the 1950s and 1960s, arriving at the 94 percent level by the beginning of the 1980s.

Residency programs are offered by teaching hospitals, with the bulk of such training institutions being those affiliated with or owned by a medical school. The residency training program for each of the recognized specialties of medicine is regulated by the Accreditation Council for Graduate Medical Education (ACGME), which is sponsored by the Association of American Medical Colleges, the American Medical Association, the American Board of Medical Specialties, the Council of Medical Specialty Societies, and the American Hospital Association. This broadly based organization took over the activities of accreditation performed prior to 1975 by the AMA–CME.

Specialty Boards and Residency Training Programs. While the ACGME assumes national responsibility for certifying to the quality of individual residency training programs, the M.D. graduate of a residency training program has to seek individual certification by the respective American Board of his or her chosen specialty. The first such board, the American Board of Ophthalmology, was developed in 1917; the twenty-seventh recognized specialty board, emergency medicine, was established in 1979. Table 38 lists the residency programs. Each specialty board establishes the general requirements expected of a person who seeks certification by that board. The duration of residency programs varies; in general, the range is from three to seven years, with an additional year or more in some programs for the acquisition of unusual skills. Greater details may be found in the annual publication by the AMA, *Directory of Residency Training Programs.*

Status of the Resident Physician. At the point of entry into a residency training program, the typical recent graduate of an M.D.

Table 38. Accredited Residency Programs by Specialty, June 1983.

Specialty

Allergy and Immunology	Pediatrics
Anesthesiology	Pediatric Allergy
Colon and Rectal Surgery	Pediatric Cardiology
Dermatology	Physical Medicine and
Dermatopathology	Rehabilitation
Emergency Medicine	Plastic Surgery
Family Practice	Preventive Medicine, General
Internal Medicine	Aerospace Medicine
Neurological Surgery	Occupational Medicine
Neurology	Public Health
Nuclear Medicine	Psychiatry
Obstetrics/Gynecology	Child Psychiatry
Ophthalmology	Radiology, Diagnostic
Orthopedic Surgery	Radiology, Diagnostic (Nuclear)
Otolaryngology	Radiology, Therapeutic
Pathology	Surgery
Blood Banking	Pediatric Surgery
Forensic Pathology	Thoracic Surgery
Neuropathology	Urology

Source: Journal of the American Medical Association, 1983, 250, 1542.

program is approximately twenty-six to twenty-seven years old and has completed four years of medical school, which in most cases was preceded by four years of study in college. The economic circumstances of the aspiring physician have changed through the years. Prior to mid-century, some of the most desirable hospitals for internship and later residency training provided no cash stipend to the house officer but may have made room and board available as perquisites. Indeed, early in this century, house officers (residents) were forbidden to marry by a number of the major teaching hospitals. In 1952, the Journal of the American Medical Association, in its annual report on internships and residencies, noted that half of the hospitals affiliated with the medical schools paid stipends ranging from $25.00 to $75.00 per month. Nonaffiliated hospitals offered salaries from $125.00 to $200.00 a month.

The annual survey of resident stipends prepared by the Council of Teaching Hospitals of the AAMC (Association of American Medical Colleges Council of Teaching Hospitals, n.d.)

reported that during 1982–83 the average first-year stipend was $18,930; second-year stipend, $20,238; third-year stipend, $21,412; fourth-year stipend, $22,537; fifth-year stipend, $23,654; and sixth-year stipend, $24,832. All these stipends compare unfavorably with the potential earnings of these persons had they entered the job market after earning a baccalaureate degree or perhaps after completing one additional year of studies (say in the process of earning the Master of Business Administration degree).

The problem of financing graduate medical education continues to be a thorny one. While special provisions for payment of resident stipends have been enacted by a few of the state legislatures, by and large the payment of resident stipends is borne by the hospital sponsoring the program in which they are enrolled. Thus, the maintenance of a series of programs in graduate medical education by a teaching hospital represents no small expense to that institution, not only providing stipends but also through the direct cost of providing the educational experience for the residents enrolled. The hospitals struggle with the means of payment of these costs for graduate medical education, and the most common method is to increase the charges for patient care so as to include much of the cost of graduate medical education. Federal regulations regarding reimbursements from Medicare could be changed so that the hospitals would have to bear the entire cost of residency training.

The resident is classified as a student who, in return for the educational experience of the residency program, provides certain services to the patients admitted to the teaching hospital. During the late 1970s, efforts were made by some residents to organize themselves into unions and to establish bargaining agencies to negotiate with the hospital management in the matter of stipends and other prerogatives. However, the National Labor Relations Board determined in 1979 that resident physicians were to be classified as students rather than as ordinary hospital employees.

Activities of the Resident. The resident physician is engaged in an exceedingly busy activity. In a teaching hospital, the resident may be the first physician a patient sees after his admission to the hospital, although on occasion the patient may be seen first by both the admitting physician and the hospital resident. Depending on the number of residents assigned to a service in a hospital and depending on the number of patients admitted to that service and the degree of severity of the illnesses they present, the residents assigned to such a service may be exceedingly busy in caring for the patients both during the day and throughout the night. It is usually the resident who is expected to respond on an emergency basis to care for a patient who develops a critical complication in the course of his or her illness, day or night.

Through the years, the average length of stay in the hospital by patients has tended to be reduced as the quality of medical care and its efficiency of application have been improved. This means that a hospital that maintains a high percentage of occupancy at all times now receives new patients with greater rapidity than it did at an earlier time, when the average length of stay was longer. More rapid turnover of patients in a typical ward service area increases the number of patients that must be admitted and thoroughly studied by the resident as well as by the supervising physicians of the service. The time consumed in these repetitive "workups" of the many patients may in some circumstances decrease the overall quality and desirability of the educational experience of the resident. Wray and Friedland (1983), in a study of house staff performance, found that older residents made 13 percent errors and first-year residents made 15.6 percent errors in physical diagnosis of patients, as observed by attending physicians. This problem merits constant attention in the future, since hospitals continue to enlarge and the overall number of residents appears to have reached a plateau—and in some hospitals may even be declining—due to the cost of maintaining graduate medical education programs.

There is considerable literature on the physical as well as mental stress experienced by overworked residents; some teaching hospital and residency program directors may have been slow in developing awareness of the potential for excessive stress borne by their residents. There is also a considerable body of popular literature dealing with the stressful lives of hospital residents. Recent examples of such literature, which no doubt are mildly to considerably exaggerated are *The Saturday Night Knife and Gun Club,* by B. P. Reiter, and *The House of God,* by Samuel Shem.

The Resident as Teacher. In addition to the arduous duties of a resident in caring directly for patients and in studying the complications they may present or acquire in the course of an illness, the resident is expected to devote some time to first-echelon supervision of medical student clinical clerks, who may be assigned for periods of four to eight weeks to a hospital service. Since the medical student may be in the geographic hospital service area during the day and by rotation on night call, the student is frequently paired with one or more of the residents on duty continuously through a typical work week. The medical student clerk is fortunate indeed if he is paired with a highly knowledgeable, sympathetic, compassionate, and accommodating resident. If the medical student clerk is paired with a severely overworked resident who has little interest in the needs of the medical student, the interface between the two will be far less than satisfactory.

Although it is clear that the medical student clerk must depend on the paired resident for explanation of many practical matters, most residents are not given any specific guidance or preparation for their role as preceptor to the medical student clinical clerk. The faculty of the medical school or those responsible for the direction of the residency training program in an unaffiliated hospital have very clear responsibilities to foster the education of those who look to them for guidance. By fostering education, I mean that the faculty members are expected not only to provide an excellent example of professional expertise in the management of therapy for the patients attended, but the faculty member also is responsible for demonstrating a general spirit of cooperativeness among the physicians, medical students, members of the nursing service, and all others involved in patient care.

Problems of the Future. During the period from 1950 through the early 1980s, there have been larger numbers of residency positions available than there have been persons annually graduated from the medical schools in the United States. As the annual output of the medical schools in this country has increased, this number has closed on the number of first-year positions in graduate medical education. For example, in 1978, 1.20 positions in the beginning year of graduate medical education were available for each of the 14,393 graduating students who participated in the National Resident Matching Program. In 1982, the ratio was 1.15 positions per graduate, and in 1983 the ratio was 1.14. When this ratio is corrected by removing from the roster of approved residencies the estimated 2,000 first-year spaces which have never received an application from an M.D. graduate of an LCME-accredited medical school, the ratio falls to 1.0 positions per graduate. Until the mid-1980s, the number of United States M.D. graduates will continue to increase before reaching a steady state or declining. However, as of the early 1980s, the number of residency positions funded by the hospitals has stopped increasing and may begin to decline. Under these circumstances, we can predict that competition among M.D. graduates for a first-year residency training position of good quality will increase and that the number of positions may fall below the annual number of M.D. graduates. Foreign medical graduates are likely to have diminishing success in obtaining appointments in graduate medical education from 1984 on (Stimmel and Graettinger, 1984).

Continuing Medical Education: The Fading Body of Knowledge

Medical students and residents enrolled in formal study programs and in daily contact with a faculty consisting of authorities in all the basic scientific and clinical subjects in the existing body of medical knowledge reasonably can be expected to acquire a current fund of knowledge and skills that will equip them, upon completion of the program, to begin a competent independent practice of medicine. However, while his knowledge base and clinical skills may remain stable for a short time after leaving the programs of education, the physician five years or more into practice certainly begins to lose an increasing amount of what was learned during formal studies. Conservation of one's level of competence at the time of completion of formal studies and the enhancement of the knowledge and skills of the practicing physician are dependent on personal initiative. Even in the twenty-five states that require completion of a modest amount of study annually as the price for extension of the license to practice, the physician involved controls his degree of motivation for serious study.

The rapid rate of increase in the body of knowledge, described many times heretofore, severely burdens the very busy practitioner, whose hours are filled with delivery of medical care to his patients. For most, little time is available for serious study either to renew old knowledge or to acquire the new and unknown. Since much of medical practice is of a routine nature and easily mastered, the physician may be lulled into a sense of false confidence in the current quality of his knowledge base and thus may not detect any need for mastering constantly changing and improving clinical skills.

Means of Access to New Knowledge. For the past several decades, a sizable number of physicians have depended largely on briefings about new drugs and new forms of chemical therapy given by itinerant salesmen representing the major drug manufacturers. These amiable "drug detail men" characteristically give the physician a brief, memorized spiel on a new drug and then offer him free samples of it. Some of these drug company representatives are former medical students who failed the course and were then recruited to "detail drugs." During my tenure in the dean's office at Baylor, I frequently was asked by personnel officers of the drug companies to provide the names of recently failed students. This system is not the best means of conveying new pharmacological knowledge to practicing physicians with legal authority to prescribe any drug.

Remedies attempted for the problem of reeducating the physician are old and numerous. Arey (1959) has reported that in 1880 the Chicago Medical College (the medical department of Northwestern University) offered the first purely postgraduate course for M.D.s in the United States; the University of Pennsylvania offered a similar course later the same year. Youmans (1935) has described his experience with a series of four-month-long courses that Vanderbilt began offering during the late 1920s. Shepherd (1960) has chronicled the development of the wave of experience with continuing medical education since 1930.

Problems with "Refresher" Courses. Most earlier and many current methods used to update physicians offer a series of lectures on some cluster of subjects from the recent additions to the body of knowledge. Frequently a "course" is scheduled over two and a half days in a medical center; physicians travel there for the courses. Having monitored many of these experiences, I am able to describe the responses of many of the physicians enrolled. On the first morning, all arrive near the starting time and appear eager to learn. Attention is high for the first and second speakers but lags quickly thereafter. If the third speaker lectures from a long series of projected lantern slides, many of the chronically overworked and underslept physicians drop off to sleep, just as they did as medical students. During the luncheon hour, many of those in attendance telephone locally residing classmates from school or housestaff days; inevitably, they receive (1) an invitation to dinner that evening and/or (2) an invitation to play golf the next afternoon. At the beginning of the program on day two, the audience is much diminished; those who accepted dinner invitations the night before may not arrive or be fully alert until late in the morning. Later on day two, the typical physician in the course receives a telephone call from his office informing him of a serious complication suffered by a patient. He is needed at home and thus he may cut loose from the course before it is completed. Naturally, some course members attend all functions offered quite compulsively, but these are in the minority of the group. Various efforts have been made to increase the efficiency of such courses. Lectures offered on cruise ships or at resorts are other variants, with uncertain efficiency.

It has been difficult to arrange effective medical education in America, at any level, in ways other than the highly suspect lecture method. Houle (1980), who has analyzed systems of continuing learning, believes that the primary responsibility must rest on the individual; he must monitor his own work continually through various systems of self-study, making judgments about the quality of his work and modifying his performance accordingly. Manning (1983) has criticized the older systems of CME and has defined the good expectations for newer forms of self-study when linked with programs developed by medical schools, professional societies, and organizations. Such programs likely will include the use of computers, video disc materials, and television linkages. My colleague Emanuel Suter, of the AAMC staff, has coedited a book treating these matters (Green, Grosswald, Suter, and Walthall, 1984). Haynes, Davis, McKibbon, and Tugwell (1984), in a comprehensive study, reviewed 248 original articles describing CME interventions. The authors conclude that CME can improve physician behaviors, but they report that there is a paucity of data indicating that conventional CME produces automatic improvement in patient outcomes.

Other Medical School Programs that Enrich the
Education of the Physician

Graduate Education in the Biomedical and Behavioral Sciences. During 1981–82, the 13,273 faculty members of the basic science departments of the medical schools in the United States enrolled 3,139 students in master's degree programs, 9,893 students in Ph.D. programs, and 3,669 postdoctoral fellows (Liaison Committee on Medical Education data). The number of Ph.D. degrees awarded in the biomedical sciences by all sources has remained relatively unchanged at about 3,500 annually since 1971 (National Academy of Sciences, 1981). The majority of the graduate students are enrolled in the medical schools or their universities, which receive the largest aggregate amounts of research grant awards.

Bickel and colleagues (1981) have reported that, in the early 1980s, only about 150 M.D.-Ph.D. graduates were produced annually; this number can meet only about half the estimated national need for physician researchers. However, the current production of Ph.D. graduates may be too large for the number of academic positions projected to be vacated during the 1980s, now that Ph.D. faculty members appear to be postponing retirement past age sixty-five and since medical school faculties have ceased the large expansion experienced since 1960. No new medical schools are scheduled to open during the early to mid-1980s and perhaps thereafter for another decade or so. Positions for recent Ph.D. graduates and two-year postdoctoral fellows thus have become scarce; about half of those that were formerly available were absorbed by the clinical departments of the medical schools.

The basic science faculty members provide instruction in the general courses of each discipline in the M.D. curriculum, but all desire the intellectual stimulation that comes from close association with graduate students who progress past the general courses into advanced levels of study and from collaboration in projects of biomedical research. A biomedical science faculty without graduate students and lacking active scholarly pursuits in various areas of research is likely to become stale and inefficient in providing an optimal learning experience for medical students as well as for residents in graduate medical education.

Research. *Research* is ordinarily defined as the process of discovering new knowledge. Since the federal government devised the National Institutes of Health, it has appropriated immense sums annually since the end of World War II for the discovery of new knowledge (Shannon, 1967; Fredrickson, 1982). The benefits to the public of this massive effort in biomedical research have been monumental, and further benefits are likely to flow yet in the future. But, most research projects are by necessity narrow in scope; the researcher must bore a hole of a very narrow diameter into unknown territory in search of an elusive, often slender, fact which, when placed with other similar borings, ultimately may elucidate some previously clouded biological phenomenon. This is a brief approximation of what is usually called "pure" research as contrasted with "applied research," which may be directed toward solving a specific disease problem—such as a clinical trial of a new vaccine to protect humans against a viral disease. The view that the best teaching is done by researchers requires examination. The researcher who spends his life digging into an ever more narrow area of inquiry may be an excellent mentor for his advanced graduate students and fellows, but is he likely to be effective in teaching medical students and residents who must be learners in broad areas? After all, patients present their physicians with many dilemmas of disease that need solutions. Thus, some researchers may be good generalist teachers; but functioning in the role of a generalist is an unusual deviation from the expert pursuit of the narrow research project.

Distribution of Funds for Research. Data derived from the 1979–80 fiscal questionnaire of the LCME indicate that the largest expenditure for research by a single school was $52 million; twenty-three schools expended in excess of $21 million, and the hundredth-ranked school of the 125 reporting expended $1.6 million for sponsored research projects. Perry, Challoner, and Oberst (1981) have reported that 75 percent of federal health research expenditures occur in the "top forty" institutions. They postulate that the heavy resource demands of complex research, combined with shrinking contributions by the federal government, are likely to cause a gradual shift of scarce resources toward the already research-rich schools; this shift may prove disruptive to the quality of medical education in the middle and lower strata of funded research activity.

While most, but not all, experienced medical educators adhere to the idea that teaching and learning of the highest quality should occur in the environment in which substantial amounts of biomedical and clinical research take place, the trends outlined by Perry, if accurate, may force a broad reexamination of this view. The medical students enrolled in the schools ranking 41 through 127 constitute about two thirds of the aggregate national student body; these students are entitled to receive a medical education of adequate or better standards.

Need for High Ethical Standards. Research is a fundamental function of a medical school; however, each institution is obligated to develop stringent means of supervising the researcher so that impeccable ethical standards can be maintained. Unfortunately, during the early 1980s there have been several highly publicized episodes of the faking of data and of their subsequent publication—leading to inaccurate conclusions and inappropriate applications (Broad and Wade, 1983). The AAMC Executive Council in 1982 developed a series of guidelines around which faculties and their institutions can develop processes for promoting ethical standards in research and in dealing with misconduct and fraud.

Scholarship. According to Carter (1980), *scholarship* is possession of an extensive and profoundly thorough knowledge of a subject. The scholar who has mastered his field is best prepared to evaluate the usefulness as well as the validity of original research such as is required of the candidate for the Ph.D. degree; and the well-developed scholar may be an extraordinarily competent teacher without being a researcher of new discoveries. Consider the hypothesis that the body of knowledge late in the 1900s is so voluminous that much of it requires development and testing with the intent of making much more use of it than has been done in the past. So, if the "researching discoverer" cannot in future be accommodated in large numbers in two thirds of the nation's medical schools, perhaps all is not lost. Scholarship may once again return to its former place of great honor, and the quality of teaching might improve.

14

Lessons Learned: Recommendations for Improving the Education of Physicians

Thus far in Part Four, I have reviewed the expanding segments of the North American system of physician education as these have evolved into their present state. As I have described each segment from high school through lifelong continuing education, I have introduced various criticisms of these programs and reviewed some successful and unsuccessful experiments. Also, I have provided data indicating that the circumstances surrounding some of the segments in the early 1980s seem destined to undergo modest to major change at an early date. Now, I shall use the remaining pages of text in this book to detail my recommendations for improving the education of physicians of the future. All recommendations or suggestions

320

for consideration are directed either to the young persons who are climbing or propose to climb the medical education ladder or to those faculty members and educators who are responsible for operating the various programs.

The recommendations I propose have been devised to facilitate achievement of a series of definitional premises on the general functions of physicians and the human characteristics of those who are fully effective in the practice of medicine. These premises have implications for the educational programs for physicians, selection of students, and related matters.

Life-Style of the Physician

The practicing physician traditionally has been expected to give greater priority to the needs of his patients than to the pleasurable activities of his personal life. Demands of patients for service by their physicians are often quite heavy; they may occupy the hours of a long working day and extend to emergency calls during the night, on weekends, or while the physician is attending some public event. Everyone is familiar with the emergency call for a doctor, by name or by prearranged number, over the public address system at a ball game. Similarly, the busy practitioner may be called out of church, the theater, or any other scheduled activity. Many modern physicians carry an electronic "beeper" while on duty to alert them to some summons for their services. These characteristic activities of physicians are rarely, if ever, observed in business persons, bankers, lawyers, civil servants, or persons in most other well-known professions.

Expectations for the Performance of Physicians

1. *Knowledge is Necessary*. Success in the professional performance of the practicing physician is dependent on his mastery of the organization of a considerable body of scientific knowledge; further, he must be able to recall pertinent scientific facts rapidly in order to diagnose and evaluate the problems of patients who are acutely ill or injured. Persons in other occupations or professions generally are not required to mobilize previously learned detailed knowledge on an emergent basis.

2. *Knowledge Must Be Applied.* Knowing the scientific facts alone is insufficient. The physician must be able to apply his rapidly retrieved knowledge in a skilled manner, using previously learned technological procedures to treat the problems of each patient. Further, he must be alert to the presence of variations from the norm in the biological constitution of each patient and know how to adapt his methods of therapy accordingly.

3. *Effective Communication with Patients.* Knowing the facts and knowing what to do about a patient's problem should allow the physician to perform effectively in a controlled situation, such as rendering treatment in an emergency room or writing treatment orders after a patient has been admitted to a hospital. But most of the contacts between a physician and his patient occur elsewhere and usually result in the provision of advice about therapy, often including prescription of medications. Whether the patient complies with the advice received or takes the pills prescribed after going home depends substantially on the physician's capacity to be convincing as he communicates with that patient. Most physicians educated within the past several decades may have command of essential data and may know how to convert their knowledge into useful recommended therapy, but, unfortunately, a significant number of them fail to induce substantial compliance with their instructions (Sackett, 1979; Sackett and others, 1975). If a patient decides to ignore most of his physician's advice or if he takes only half the pills prescribed or fails to take them on the regular schedule specified in his prescription, that patient is failing to utilize his physician's scientific knowledge and skills. While poor compliance by patients may be partly their own fault, the physician is the active agent in all diagnosis and therapy and, if he is to be fully effective, he must acquire the special art of communicating convincingly with patients of all levels of education and varieties of culture. Gardner (1983), defines this ability as interpersonal intelligence.

4. *Compassion and Empathy.* Possession of knowledge, therapeutic skills and the art of convincing communication are still not sufficient to allow the physician to achieve his full potential. The remaining ingredients are compassion and empathy for the patient—that is, warm, humanistic concern expressed by actions as well as by verbal and nonverbal transmission. The American

people are sharp critics of the medical profession because of the failure of many physicians to recognize both the need for and the value of these highly personal characteristics of the fully effective healer of human soma and psyche.

5. *Flexibility for Continuing Medical Education.* The final premise is that the physician, who must expend enormous energy and time to acquire his original educational qualification, must also acquire the flexibility to renew his old knowledge periodically, unlearn techniques and facts that fail the test of time, and replace them with entirely new information that will expand throughout the life of his practice.

The reader is herewith advised that the recommendations that follow are my own, are based on my accumulated experience, and are not to be construed as statements of policy of any of the organizations with which I have been associated for many years.

The High School Period

1. *Insight into the Practice of Medicine.* As early as possible, those who aspire to become physicians need to acquire the insight that will help them, over a period of years, adapt gradually to standards of professional behavior and performance that will make them somewhat different from those who enter many other professions. High school career guidance counselors and college premedical advisors, as well as thoughtful parents, should guide their advisees to accept these basic precepts, which I judge to be prerequisites for a successful career—first as a medical student and later as a physician.

2. *Special Methods of Learning.* Bright young people who exhibit some interest in the biomedical sciences and medicine should be counseled to enroll in the special honors programs or talent schools found in some large cities. If such programs are not available and if the only educational environment is of such poor quality that it is unlikely to produce the desired results, then the aspiring physician must accept personal responsibility for sharpening his own intellect through self-initiated learning. A very old-fashioned but effective method of learning is through reading some of the world's accumulated literature.

Whatever the nature of the high school attended, the aspiring physician should study diligently all of the courses required for graduation. In addition, all the sciences available should be sampled, along with advanced courses in the humanities and a modern language, if they are not required. The final year of high school might be arranged with a heavier than average load of courses as an early test of motivation for the level of study to be expected in college.

3. *Learning Through Work Experience.* Because the physician is in constant contact with many people whom he seeks to serve, the precollege/medical student can profit from the experience of after-school and weekend employment. Jobs involving shared responsibility and contact with a cross section of the human race are most useful. The checkout counter in a grocery store or the order counter in a fast-food restaurant can provide a young person with useful insight into the wide range of human behavior. Summer vacations should be used for constructive experiences. During my twenty years of experience as chairman of a medical school admissions committee, my most productive query about the maturity and education achievement of applicants was to call for a description of how high school and college summers had been used, what jobs had been held, what books had been read, what trips had been taken, and what had been learned while traveling, reading, and working. Needless to say, the applicant who had used adolescent and very young adult years effectively, especially in a poor educational milieu, was the most impressive.

4. *Special Skills Needed. No* student should leave high school (perhaps even junior high) without learning to type; and, in these electronic times, the high school student should make every possible effort to become familiar with computers, both in primary use and in programming. Acquisition of the skills for writing in lucid English, in courses or otherwise, deserves highest priority. During high school or during the early years of college, the aspiring physician should be tested for speed of reading and comprehension. If reading skills are poor, remedial study should be undertaken.

5. *Information About Medical Education.* I recommend that each high school student interested in medicine obtain a copy of the AAMC's annual publication, *Medical School Admissions Re-*

quirements. This booklet, which has been carefully edited by a number of medical educators over a period of thirty-three years, is the best available source of accurate general information about the early education of the physician in the United States and Canada through high school, collegiate premedical studies, and the process of entry into medical school.

The College Years: Students

1. *Selecting a College.* Best results ensue in a college or university that has a reputation for producing a noticeable number of baccalaureate graduates who have been admitted to medical colleges through the years. Such colleges usually provide a well-developed premedical advisory system; an exploratory visit to the campus should include a fact-finding interview with a premedical advisor—sometimes there is only one. Colleges vary significantly in academic standards; if it is difficult to obtain admission to a particular college, it likely has high academic standards. Medical school bulletins usually list the colleges from which their medical students were chosen.

A small college with less than one thousand students enrolled may not have strong science departments or the broad strength of faculty needed to produce a rich academic environment. By the same token, the megauniversities that enroll tens of thousands of students may have quite powerful academic departments offering superior graduate degree programs, but the undergraduate student may receive relatively little attention. Some large state universities offer a special program limited to high-achieving undergraduates who attend small classes conducted by well-motivated faculty members; these "honors programs" usually produce first-rate applicants for the study of medicine. Plan II of the College of Arts and Sciences at the University of Texas at Austin illustrates this very successful means of preparing for the study of medicine.

2. *Selecting Courses and a Baccalaureate Major.* Since 95 percent of those admitted to medical schools in the early 1980s have completed the bachelor's degree, the neophyte premedical student should make his plans accordingly. Table 19 (p. 247) shows that medical schools accept students who have majored in a wide variety

of subjects; indeed, admissions committees seek a variety of backgrounds of education and experience in the cohort selected for each
entering class. Therefore, the premed student should select his major
in the area of study in which he is most interested. Those who
are interested in the "hard" sciences and who may opt for a scientific
career within the broad field of medicine may enjoy heavy concentration in combinations of chemistry, physics, mathematics, or
engineering. Biology, in its most modern form, offers opportunities
for exciting advanced scientific study at some but not all colleges.

Those who plan a conventional practice of clinical medicine
are free to select any field as a major; however, about half of those
enrolled during the early 1980s have majored in some form of
biology. This choice may have been pushed by premedical advisors
or selected by the students because of interest in the field or because
of a desire to anticipate the medical curriculum, which is a major
extension of basic biological principles in the human. The student
should make certain that the specific course requirements of the
medical schools are completed with good results.

Requirements for the bachelor's degree vary considerably
among the major fields and among the colleges that offer them.
However, there is usually some opportunity, even in a major in
the sciences, to elect courses that may provide some insight into
the humanities—which usually contribute to a liberal education.
Studies in the humanities should be sought, not avoided.

I recommend that some electives be chosen from among those
subjects that are not represented or that are treated somewhat scantily
in the usual medical curriculum; examples of such subjects include
statistics, business law, economics, demography, political science,
computer science, public speaking, and, most of all, writing. Every
graduate of a college should possess the fundamental skills of writing
in a clear, understandable manner. Most English departments offer
no advanced courses in the development of writing skills; they prefer
to concentrate on the study of writing by others. Occasionally, a
course in "scientific writing" may be available; a journalism department might be a source of useful studies in writing.

While enrollment in liberal arts courses may be an effective
means of broadening cultural knowledge, independent reading and
study ultimately can accomplish the same goal. An enterprising

college student can collect the recommended reading lists for a selected group of courses that sound interesting but that may not fit into the time available. Reading lists are often posted in the library or in the academic departmental office, or they can be requested from the responsible faculty members. With a set of reading lists in hand, the premedical student, medical student, or graduate physician can expand his education through his own initiative. Those who are curious, self-starting learners always are lifelong students.

Now, I offer a very sturdy personal opinion: Study of the humanities does not automatically induce humanistic behavior in the aspiring physician. Humanistic behavior (compassion, empathy, respect for human dignity, and personal courtesy) must be learned from the examples set forth by other humans, particularly by attractive role models found among parents, teachers, and other mentors. This observation leads me back to my preference for the liberal arts college of high academic standards or for a special program within a large university as the best situation for premedical studies. Humanistic behavioral traits are most likely to flow from teacher to student when the student-to-teacher ratio is small and when the teacher possesses admirable traits of character and demonstrates humanistic values, whatever the subject taught. There is so much confusion between the "humanities" and "humanistic behavior" that it seems appropriate to inset here a definition and historical derivation of the terms; this definition was prepared by Dan Davis (1983), who labored as the researcher/editor for this book while completing requirements for the Ph.D. degree in philosophy and ethics.

> From the philosophical perspective, "humanism" has two meanings. The first is particular and historical and refers to a philosophical and literary movement that originated in the late fourteenth century in Italy and spread from there to other countries of Europe; as a driving force of the Renaissance it became one of the major factors in modern culture. The second is a more general meaning derived from the first: "humanism" in this sense refers to any

philosophy that takes as its central theme the value
and dignity of humankind; that, in one way or the
other, sees human nature as the measure of all things
or takes human nature as such as its primary focus.
Renaissance humanism looked to the classical world
as its guide; it took what Cicero called "humanitas,"
that is, the education of man as such, as its guiding
theme and goal or what the Greeks called "paideia,"
education through the liberal arts, which were thought
to be the instruments or disciplines proper to humankind and which differentiate humankind from other
inhabitants of the animal kingdom. The Renaissance
humanists, with their eyes on the past of classical
antiquity, accorded primary value to humanities—that
is, poetry, rhetoric, history, ethics, and politics—
because these disciplines alone educate the human
being as such and enable the human being to exercise
freedom.

From these two meanings of the term a looser
one has been derived; in this respect, "humanism"
refers to a concern for, devotion to, humankind and
its needs, hopes, and so on. This is the primary link
with "humanistic" behavior, behavior evidenced in
a respect for the dignity of each human being, regardless of race, sex, class, and so on.

3. *Quality of Studies.* Many college students elongate their
adolescence and avoid acceptance of responsibility to learn and to
mature and instead devote themselves largely to fun, foolishness,
and fraternity or sorority life. The medical profession is available
only to those persons who can accept and discharge increasing
amounts of responsibility. Thus, the premedical student needs to
comprehend that his stewardship of the college years will be
measured by the medical school admissions committee when they
review the grades recorded on his college transcript. Students
admitted to medical schools in the early 1980s have earned all "A's"
and "B's" in college courses, with very rare exceptions. The
admissions committee members are usually well informed about

easy courses used by clever students to earn high grades and do not look with favor on applicants who have taken academic shortcuts. On the contrary, the applicant who enrolls in an honors program and achieves highly in his studies is likely to receive special attention.

4. *Collecting Information About Medical Schools.* As early as possible, the premedical student should obtain a copy of *Medical School Admissions Requirements,* published annually by the AAMC, and become familiar with its contents. Next, the student should collect bulletins from neighboring medical schools or from those of interest anywhere. These publications provide much information about each school, its objectives, and its distinguishing features. The medical schools vary substantially; the applicant should seek to enroll in a cluster of schools that offer, in addition to a universal medical education, those special features he seeks. The premedical student should seek guidance from the premedical advisor on his campus, but he ultimately should follow the guidance available from the medical school admissions officers. Using these sources will diminish the deleterious effects of the unfounded rumors that permeate the ranks of premedical students.

5. *Confirming a Commitment to Medicine as a Career.* As the junior year begins, the declared premedical student should assess his motivation to continue the long sequence of studies yet before him, calculate the cost of such study, and attempt to obtain accurate predictions about the economic rewards available to the physician from about 1990 onward. A "C" average earned during the first two years of college nearly always prevents admission to any medical school. The cost of medical studies is increasing and may rise to levels that will prevent many students from completing the extended M.D. program. The probable surplus of physicians from 1985 on may result in much diminished earnings by physicians late in the twentieth century. A college junior should switch career plans if these general principles are negative for pursuit of qualification as a physician.

The College Years: Administrators

1. *Attitudes Toward Premedical Students.* Premedical students in most colleges and universities receive appropriate guidance

and counsel as they endeavor to prepare themselves for entrance to medical schools; in other institutions, premedical students are looked on and treated as academic bastards. In fact, premeds may be openly resented by the departmental barons who logically accept as their intellectual heirs those students who major in their disciplines with the intent of progressing into graduate study.

Much has been written about the "premed syndrome," which is manifested by intense competition for grades among the students involved. Generalities are never accurate for whole categories of persons, so I suggest that many diligent premedical students have been given a bum rap. On many college campuses I have visited, industrious learners in any major are viewed with both contempt and alarm by other students.

2. *Oversight of the Premedical Advisory Program.* I recommend that the dean of arts and sciences of a university or the president of a liberal arts college increase their oversight of the premedical advisory system on campus. The advisor(s) should be chosen carefully and provided with adequate clerical support for the sometimes quite heavy production of letters of recommendation for the annual crop of applicants to medical school. Based on a number of unsavory personal experiences with biased or prejudiced premedical advisors, I urge that each be asked to present a detailed annual report of activities (see the next recommendation) and be subject to audit of his letters of recommendation. Some rotation of advisors may be indicated; a single dominant advisor who retains unaudited power for many years may be providing exemplary services to the premedical students, or he may become a prejudiced tyrant. Special recognition should be given to those advisors who provide strong support to their advisees. One or more advisors should be given fiscal support for annual travel to the medical schools of greatest interest to applicants as well as for attendance at the annual meeting of the AAMC.

3. *The Premedical Advisory System.*

• *Objectives and Organization.* The customary purposes of an advisory system for college students who have opted for a career in medicine are: (1) to provide information about medical schools and guidance for application strategies to gain admission to one of them and (2) to evaluate the applicants for the benefit of the medical school admissions committees. Thus, the premedical advisor is expected to play the sometimes conflicting roles of both coach and referee. This uncomfortable fusion of functions has sometimes caused confusion of roles as well as tension between a single advisor and one or more of his advisees. Use of a committee of advisors for the process of evaluation may diffuse the stress somewhat and usually provides checks and balances that may prevent the development of unfair biases.

• *Collecting and Dispensing Information About Medical Schools and Medical Education.* Each premedical advisor will discover that the best currently published general information he and his advisees need can be found in the following: *Medical School Admissions Requirements* (edited annually by the AAMC); *Association of American Medical Colleges Curriculum Directory,* (edited annually); "Annual Report on Medical Education in the U.S.," in the *Journal of the American Medical Association* (see the September 23, 1983 issue).

Specific information about the medical schools of interest to the advisees is best obtained from an up-to-date collection of their bulletins, circulars, or catalogues. The advisees should have access to such a collection and should be encouraged to obtain their own copies from the schools in which they have an interest. Detailed information and pertinent telephone numbers of officers and faculty of each medical school are published annually in the *Association of American Medical Colleges Directory of American Medical Education.*

Some college premedical advisors have successfully developed a single office in which all pertinent information about medical schools can be displayed for use by interested students. A large bulletin board is essential for use in posting materials provided by the medical schools, the AAMC, and other sources. Thoughtfully prepared displays on a bulletin board can provide necessary information to the students and obviate the necessity for them to seek an appointment with an advisor.

• *Visits to Regional Medical Schools.* Each premedical advisor can improve his factual knowledge about and insight into medical education by a periodic (preferably yearly) visit to one or more of the medical schools that interest his advisees. Such visits should be supported financially in an appropriate manner by the college or university. This recommendation is included in these writings because I have discovered not a few premedical advisors who either never had visited a medical school or had not had that experience for more than a decade. When making personal driving trips across country, the curious advisor usually follows the practice of making a quick visit to medical schools in which he and his students are interested.

• *Identification of Premedical Students.* Ideal advising begins with matriculation of the first-year college student; however, not all entering students are prepared at that time to declare themselves as premeds. The process of decision making seems to spread over the four years. We know that some advisors are surprised to meet for the first time a senior student who reveals his desire to attend medical school within about six months. Assuming that the best evaluation of an applicant for medical school results from serial observations during several years, I urge that each college devise its own system of establishing a roster of declared premedical students—through the use of computerized systems of registration or by other means. Availability of a roster, which is updated at the beginning of each semester, would allow the advisor(s) to develop a card or computerized information file on all known premedical students. A small computer-based record would facilitate the work of the advisor significantly.

Many advisors hold assemblies of their premedical students in order to provide them with needed information; a premedical club or society may provide a forum for advisors, physicians, and visiting representatives of medical schools. Students who ignore such opportunities to learn about their chosen career may have questionable motivation or lack the degree of maturity appropriate at this stage of development. In short, if I were the responsible premedical advisor with a computerized record on all my advisees, I would record their attendance at selected (but not all) assemblies designed to broaden their insight into their chosen profession and the means of access to it.

• *Early Discouragement of Poor Achievers.* In 1982, the national cohort of 16,480 new first-year medical students presented college grade point averages (GPA's) as follows: Where A=4.0, 46.4

percent had earned between 3.6 and 4.0; 41.6 percent had earned between 3.1 and 3.5; 9.3 percent between 2.6 and 3.0; 1.6 percent less than 2.6 percent; and the 1.1 percent remaining had unknown GPA's from schools with irregular systems of grading (Liaison Committee on Medical Education data). Data for the past five years are comparable.

Knowledge of higher mathematics is not needed to conclude that the typical applicant has completed six semesters of study at the point of application and that a GPA below 2.8 to 3.0 earned in the first three semesters likely will preclude selection for enrollment in medical school on consideration of GPA alone. Therefore, I urge that premedical advisor(s), using the small computer I hope the dean/president provides do a systematic analysis of all known premedical students in the spring semester of their second year. All who, in three or four semesters, have achieved no higher than a 2.8 GPA or so should be informed in writing that admission to medical school is a very dim possibility and that they cannot be recommended by the representatives of the college. Admittedly, not all those who receive such a warning will heed it, and they may persist anyway. However, if current trends hold, of one hundred students who apply to medical school, about fifty will be accepted. The remaining fifty are great problems to themselves, to the colleges, and to society in general. If half of those not destined to be accepted could be steered into alternate career pathways as early as their sophomore year, much anguish for both students and their families could be avoided and much useless processing of applications, accumulation of credentials, and other expensive activities could be reduced.

 • *Letters of Recommendation/Evaluation of Applicants.* The premedical advisor should be certain in all communications regarding his applicants that he refers to the credential letter requested for medical school application as a *letter of evaluation* rather than using the word *recommendation* in any context. We have heard of legal complaints against letter writers who evaluated bud did not recommend as stated in some manner.

Since the medical schools have transcripts of the grades earned in the various courses, particularly those schools that belong to the American Medical College Application System, the premedical advisor should concentrate on advising the admissions committee as to whether the applicant took an "easy" sequence of courses or tackled "tough" courses. Further, if it is possible for the premedical advisor to distinguish between courses that require simple memorization of facts and courses that call for the use of basic principles in problem solving, transmission of such information would be very valuable to the admissions committees. The advisor also should be able to tell the admissions committee whether the applicant's educational program was broadly based or whether it was narrowly focused on a single discipline at the expense of a liberal education.

The advisor should assume that the admissions committee knows little about the applicant personally. If the premedical advisor does know his advisees personally and has observed them over several years of development, I recommend that the advisor concentrate on evaluating the following topics: Is the candidate mature for his age and this stage of development? Is the candidate able to accept and discharge responsibility effectively and within established time frames? What is the level of curiosity of the applicant? What is the level of energy and industriousness of the candidate? Is the candidate a self-starting, autotelic learner, or does he merely follow instructions in doing class exercises and the like? What is the estimated quality of social development of the candidate? That is, does the candidate interact effectively with other students who are members of laboratory or study groups? Is the candidate sensitive to and considerate of other humans? Are there other personal features and characteristics that make this candidate different from the bulk of this year's applicants? Do the college records have any notation of disciplinary actions taken against the candidate by the authorities of the college or university?

In a summary paragraph, the premedical advisors should give an estimate of the applicant's projected success as a medical student and predict his ultimate usefulness as a physician. The summary may be able to include comparison of this candidate with previous students of this college who have been accepted by medical schools.

• *Medical School Officials.* Representatives of the medical school should visit the colleges that produce the applicants, and, in turn, they should invite the premedical advisors to visit the medical school for special functions designed to facilitate the work of premedical advisors. In view of the fact that applicants for medical schools in the future may become relatively scarce as compared with the experiences of the 1970s, medical school officials may find it necessary to develop skills for the recruitment of superior applicants rather than merely using a process of selection.

The medical school officials should prepare a catalogue or bulletin designed especially for young readers who are newly enrolled in the colleges as premeds as well as for current applicants to the medical schools.

The medical school academic dean should provide feedback to the advisors on the medical school performance of former college students. Former students who receive any kind of recognition in the medical school should be brought to the attention of the college premedical advisors. At the very least, the medical school should send a copy of each graduation program of the medical school to the premedical advisor. Newsletters and other periodic publications routine for the medical school ordinarily will be welcomed by the premedical advisors, who may see fit to post them on the premedical students' bulletin board.

The director of admissions or the academic dean responsible for admissions should be very alert to the possibility of bias against one or more applicants by a premedical advisor. Such a matter should be explored delicately but persistently, and, if deliberate bias is uncovered, the dean of the college of arts and sciences or the president of the liberal arts college should be informed.

If the applicant pool declines during the 1980s and later as has been predicted, the medical school dean should consider replacing the admissions committee chairman, the director of admissions, and others involved in the process with new individuals who can attack the changing circumstances from a fresh viewpoint. Those who had considerable experience in admissions during the 1970s learned how to operate an admissions program during a period of surplus applicants and might not be able to accommodate different strategies that would be necessary if there were a relative shortage of well-qualified applicants. The experiences of those of us who were active in the admissions programs of medical schools in the 1950s may turn out to be useful as admissions programs are revised to accommodate a declining applicant pool.

The Medical School: Selection of Students

1. *Composition of the Faculty Committee on Admissions.* If the medical school desires heterogeneity in each class of students selected, the members of the admissions committee should be quite varied in their personality characteristics as well as in their actual professional specialities. In my experience, two thirds or more of the members of the admissions committee should be holders of the M.D. degree who are currently involved in clinical medicine. These members should be drawn from a variety of the medical specialties. Those chosen should be serviceable as attractive role models for the young students whom they will be canvassing in the search for those to be enrolled. Other members of the committee should be drawn from the ranks of the biomedical science faculty and should include those who have demonstrated appreciation for medical students and who at the same time adhered to quite high objective standards of performance.

While many medical schools have appointed medical students to the committee on admissions, I have never been certain that this is an appropriate procedure. My concern is that the immense amount of work required of the committee on admissions may be very burdensome to the (usually two or three) medical students selected, who might better be using their valuable time in active pursuit of their own professional education. I have no aversion to the participation of students in this important process; rather, I would report that my experience in about a decade at Baylor might be of some interest to others. During this period, I was able to arrange for the faculty committee on admissions to receive in rotation four or five members of the senior medical class each time the faculty committee processed a group of candidates through a series of interviews. This process took place weekly, beginning in October and extending through February, and involved most of the weekends during this time. The five visiting senior students were asked to participate in one-on-one interviews of students and then sit with the faculty committee and vote on the candidates interviewed during the visitation experience. Using this system, no student was deprived of valuable study time, and the experience was made voluntary to the members of the senior class. A majority of the Baylor seniors elected to participate and signed up for a weekend experience of their own choice as their schedules permitted. The objective for this process of involving students was to equip the medical school graduates to be better informed alumni during their years of practicing medicine.

2. *The Committee and the Administration of the Medical School.* The policies for selecting medical students should be formally adopted by the faculty committee and, in accordance with the bylaws of some colleges of medicine, such policies should be presented for adoption by the academic senate of the medical faculty or by some other policy-making body of the institution. However, proposals for the development of new policies to improve old policies, as well as proposals for the procedures to be used by the committee, should be advanced by the chief academic officer of the college of medicine. In Chapter Four, I described the functions of the chief academic officer, who should be able to serve full time as principal schoolmaster of the educational program of the medical school. The CAO should be responsible for staff support for the committee on admissions through the appointment of an administrative secretary/director of admissions or other administrative support person. It is very important indeed that those employed in the office of the medical school that receives visiting premedical candidates should be courteous and helpful individuals. There is nothing more discouraging to a somewhat shy premedical student who has come to the medical center to seek information than to be greeted by a difficult termagant who verbally and nonverbally communicates contempt for young visitors who want to be physicians.

Policies of institutions vary somewhat; in my experience, either the chief academic officer or a senior faculty member may serve as chairperson of the committee on admissions. I suggest that the CAO is a proper chairman, at least during periods of considerable change in the circumstances of selection of medical students in the college as a part of changes in national trends; even if he is not the chair of the admissions committee, the CAO ought to spend some time visiting the colleges that provide the medical school with its principal supply of applicants. If the CAO has never had direct experience with an admissions committee, I have serious doubts about his capacity to fully exercise the functions of the office as I have defined it. In the event that the CAO does serve as the chairperson of the committee on admissions, the procedure should be established that complaints or appeals be passed on to the chief executive officer for arbitration.

3. *Objectives for the Selection Process.* The members of the committee should be enjoined to look forty years into the future rather than fixing on practices established twenty or so years ago. The members of the committee should note that the state of the practice of medicine has become somewhat fluid in the final years of the twentieth century; they should thus be prepared to adapt their practices in accordance with what best can be predicted for the future professional life of the persons they select to be enrolled in the study of medicine.

The members of the committee also should be kept aware of the potential effect of population demography and economic considerations on the size of the applicant pool. Here again, the chief academic officer may be best prepared to provide this service to the committee. The members of the committee in the mid-1980s and thereafter should be prepared to change or reshape their procedures to fit the possibility of a decline in the size of the national pool of applicants for the study of medicine. In short, the members of the committee should be prepared to shift their emphasis to (1) passive forms of recruitment and (2) active recruitment of the best candidates available in their area of catchment of potential applicants.

In view of the apparent change in the nature of the practice of medicine, I suggest strongly that admissions committees consider whether they should shift from traditional practices of selecting mostly independent-minded rugged individualists to a search for applicants who can be predicted to work more effectively with other physicians and with numerous other professionals involved in medical care delivery. My conclusion is that those students selected to study medicine within the final fifteen years of the twentieth century are more likely to do their professional work in group relationships than was true in the generation I represent.

4. *College Courses Required for Admission.* Having justified the continual use of requirements in the introductory courses in several of the hard sciences, I believe that the committee on admissions should decide whether they wish to enroll only scientists or whether they wish to enroll students who have had a breadth of experience both in the sciences and in the liberal arts subjects commonly known as the humanities. The members of the committee on admissions should be prepared to demonstrate both verbally and in their printed materials the fact that students who major in the nonscience areas not only are welcome but are sought after— provided that they have proven their capacities to manage some of the subject material represented in the required science courses.

The admissions committee, in my opinion, is forced to conclude that physicians must be prepared by the time they leave their formal schooling to use various methods of science: In particular, the physician requires quantitative skills for measurement and observation as he practices medicine. While study of the humanities will undoubtedly enrich the life of the future physician, pursuit of scholarly writings accumulated through the centuries may not necessarily provide the practicing physician with a capacity to deal with the technology already available and constantly emerging. These are matters with which the faculty committee members should come to grips and on which they should develop a cogent general statement that they are prepared to implement in all of their procedures.

5. *Objective Measures.* As has been stated before in this book, a common means of determining the projected behavior of humans in the near future is to look at their standards of performance during their recent past. Thus, the members of the medical committee on admissions will undoubtedly continue their well-establshed practice of examining the grades the candidate earned in the courses of study he followed at his college.

However, the first great lesson that must be learned by new members of the medical school admissions committee is that there is quite a shocking variation in the academic quality among the 1,000 colleges and universities that produce applicants to the nation's medical schools. From my twenty years of experience with the national sample of colleges that produced applicants for Baylor University College of Medicine, and from continuous review of scholastic aptitude test scores and Medical College Admissions Test scores for each of the colleges' applicants, I am forced to conclude that some colleges bestow baccalaureate degrees on students whose academic achievement and intellectual attainment, on the average, is approximately at the same level of an average cohort of students at the point of leaving a good high school. Even the brightest student from a college lacking rigorous academic standards is likely to encounter serious difficulties when matched against medical student classmates from colleges known to be academically tough. At this point, I wish to include a passionate plea that the members of the admissions committee not engage in premeditated institutional cruelty by admitting to the medical school a student who has not yet learned how to make significant achievement in organized courses of study. While the provision of tutors for the educationally deprived upon entrance to medical school may be useful, repair work in intellectual development ought to be done before placing the rookie into scrimmage with powerful professionals who have attended superior places of learning during the past four years.

While great dependence has always been placed on the academic record earned during the college years, caution should be exercised to avoid the blind acceptance of students who present a transcript containing all "A's" (or "A+'s") without further specific examination of the individual. Some individuals have adhesive minds for short-term recollection of digital details such as might be presented in the courses pursued in college and are able to regurgitate such data on the tests given all too frequently in most American institutions. It has been sad indeed to observe some of these pure "A"-average students in the medical curriculum, where no living soul has the intellectual capacity to memorize everything, as they decompensate psychologically because they are unable to be the first in the class and cannot answer all the questions on whatever type of measurement may be administered by the members of the medical faculty.

The Medical College Admissions Text is particularly valuable in sorting out the relative strengths of the colleges that produce applicants and can also be very helpful to the committee on admissions if they, upon examination of a candidate, find that he wasted time during the first year of college only to achieve sudden maturity and henceforth make strong grades in the course of study. Sometimes these late bloomers are very worthy candidates for enrollment but may be missed if pure mathematics is applied as an exclusion factor in grade point average considerations alone. The combination of GPAs and MCATs in understanding hands can be very effective in developing a pool of applicants who are intellectually able to do the work of the medical school and at the same time have given significant demonstration of their capacity to accept and discharge responsibility effectively.

6. *Humanistic Measures.* Most admissions committee members find it easy to focus on the numbers represented in the GPA and in the MCAT. It is much more difficult to make fair and relatively objective estimations of the noncognitive data on the individuals who are applicants and who have made it through the cut-off scores for GPAs and MCATs.

Most admissions committees use some form of interview of the candidates who present strong basic, objective criteria. Interviews can be conducted very effectively or very poorly. But I know of no other way to develop first-hand estimates of the human characteristics of candidates for the highly sensitive responsibilities delegated to the licensed physician. Further, it is highly probable that applicants who are hovering somewhere around twenty-one years of age at the time of application have already developed personal habits of behavior and personality traits that are likely to be reasonably well fixed. The premedical advisor in the smaller colleges probably can assist the medical school admissions committee in these estimates of human values. Admissions committee members should work diligently to develop systems of judgment of human characteristics and should be constantly alert to the possibility that they are making automatic superior ratings of candidates based only on high GPA and MCAT scores.

If the membership of the faculty committee on admissions is heterogeneous in nature, and if the members of the committee are themselves humanistic individuals inclined to demonstrate personal courtesies and considerations and even empathy for earnest

young people who desire to prepare themselves for the responsibility
of the practice of medicine, then I believe that a balanced series
of interviews can elicit the noncognitive measures that are so very
important in the work of the committee. It is very important that
each student accorded opportunity for interview be given several
different interviews by a balanced group of individuals. In my
experience, one tough interviewer should be surrounded by at least
two warm-hearted yet thorough and searching interviewers in the
individual experience of the young applicant to the medical school.

The work of the faculty committee on admissions is a labor
of love and calls for intense concentration and contribution of
valuable time. Not every member of the medical faculty is psychologically equipped to perform these vital functions. One of the
principal tasks of the chief academic officer is to review the
performance of younger faculty members and select for service on
the admissions committee those who are both competent in their
fields and interested in the phenomenon of learning by medical
students. I would go so far as to suggest that service on the admissions
committee should become a desirable criterion for promotion to
senior rank in the faculty or as a chairperson.

The Medical School: Institutional Responsibility
for the M.D. Program

1. *Faculty Constituency for Medical Students.* It is well known
that medical students have no automatic cadre of faculty supporters
or constituency in most of the medical schools. This places the
medical student body in a relationship quite unlike that of the
graduate students in a single department. The latter students are
expected to reproduce intellectually the chairman and his faculty
as they pursue their specialized studies for an extended period of
time. The same is true for residents enrolled in programs of graduate
medical education or for fellows in either the basic or clinical fields.
These individuals remain in their respective departments for three
to six years, usually become closely attached to their mentors, and
are looked upon as junior members of the departmental faculty.
By contrast, medical students take courses of study for limited periods
and appear in a department, either basic science or clinical, in such

large numbers that the members of the faculty generally fail to acquire any personal knowledge of them.

Because of the relative neglect of medical students in some of the medical schools, I suggest that it is now appropriate for each medical faculty to accept its obvious responsibility for first-class commitment to the M.D. program. Medical students in private schools, almost without exception, now pay high tuition and fees to the institution, and they are entitled to reasonable attention to their needs as they tackle the curriculum established by the faculty. In the publicly owned institutions, the taxpayers of the state pay substantially for the operation of the M.D. education program. Indeed, in some states, the legislature has limited the number of faculty members it will support in the budget to the number of professorial positions determined necessary for the operation for the M.D. program. In addition to considering these economic factors, the faculty should demonstrate a sense of honorable responsibility towards students enrolled in the college of which they are participants. I would invite each medical faculty, through its system of organization, to reavow its institutional responsibility for the education of the next generation of physicians. If a faculty decides to give low priority to the education of medical students, it should make a public statement of that policy.

2. *Defining Program Objectives.* In response to the enormous changes that have taken place in the activities of colleges of medicine and in the body of knowledge since the mid-1900s, the faculty needs to reexamine its objectives for the M.D. program. The Liaison Committee on Medical Education in 1957 clarified the purpose of the M.D program somewhat when it stated: "The undergraduate period of medical education leading to the M.D. degree is no longer sufficient to prepare a student for independent medical practice without supplementation by a graduate training period which will vary in length depending upon the type of practice the student selects." Since this statement was made by the LCME in 1957, the body of knowledge has grown unbelievably, and it is clear to all concerned that it is no longer possible to expect a medical student to achieve mastery of the full body of knowledge in four years. Therefore, it is the responsibility of the faculty of medicine to determine what they expect the student to accomplish during his

four years of residence in the college of medicine. For example, perhaps the principal duty of the medical student is to learn the vocabulary of the biomedical and clinical sciences and to learn the systems of organization of the body of medical knowledge. Next I suggest that the medical student be provided substantial assistance in acquiring the skills of accessing the myriad details of the full body of knowledge through some of the modern systems of data retrieval that are already widely available and that can be predicted to become ubiquitous in the near future. The faculty, then, ought to be responsible for developing for the student those organizing principles of each of the various disciplines considered essential for the education of the physician and ought not to expect students to memorize the vast amount of detail available in the full body of knowledge.

I suggest that modified objectives require convincing articulation of purposes and expression by the mentors and directors of each of the courses or units of study. By this I mean that those responsible for particular units of the M.D. curriculum should make plain to their students that the material presented for their immediate consideration and learning by no means represents the full scope of the subject. Rather, each course director should be required by the faculty, as a matter of policy, to make specific and pragmatic recommendations to the student for continuing learning in that discipline and, if possible, in associated disciplines, so that the student may leave the course with full comprehension of the fact that he is by no means a finished authority in that field of study. There is an old feeling on the part of some faculty members— and certainly among many of their students—that once a course is passed that is the end of the matter. I challenge the faculty to treat this natural human tendency by considering their responsibilities as mentors of a course to be twofold: (1) to present principles of current knowledge and its organization and (2) to present the student with practical means and methods of expanding knowledge in that subject through the succeeding forty or so years of work as a physician. This is by no means an original idea; I have encountered numerous departmental chairpersons and course directors who have accepted the second responsibility outlined above for many years.

3. *Improving Administration of the M.D. Program.* In various places in this book, I have described the pressing need for the appointment of a chief academic officer of the faculty of medicine. I believe that the diseases of the M.D. curriculum are to a large measure due to the absence of adequate central organization and attention to improving the management of the components of the curriculum. Therefore, I think of the CAO as the active leader of learning in the academic community of the medical school, who should be instrumental in implementing the general policies for physician education that have been developed by the appropriate bodies of the faculty. Additionally, I believe that the CAO has a responsibility to be a general ombudsman for the cadre of students who constitute each of the four classes or smaller work groups and the like. I have found that there frequently is a clear need for intervention by a ranking dean into the relationship between a group of students and an instructor or one of the departments. If the faculty has not empowered a strong academic dean to attend to the needs of the students as they encounter a variety of masters in their experiences in learning, then chaos can ensue and the morale of the students can be severely damaged. The CAO should be supported by other individuals who are capable of providing staff support to the committees of the faculty responsible for surveillance of the content of the curriculum and of the achievements of the students. Staff support should include means of improving pedagogic performance of the faculty and other related skills.

If the faculty and the institution agree to the appointment of a chief academic officer with appropriate responsibilities and powers of office, then I would suggest that the constiuency in support of medical students be expanded through the designation of departmental counselors for medical students. In some schools, the chairperson performs this role effectively; however, in very large departments, the chair is a mini-dean who is responsible for so many educational programs and activities that he is an executive rather than a suitable academic counselor. I suggest that one or more faculty members, preferably senior, be designated as departmental counselors and that the names of these persons be published in a list made available to faculty and students. The chief departmental counselor for medical education could be the course director and he could be involved in the evaluation of student achievement within the course or unit of instruction. The counselor should be a functional tutor for students who need remediation. Such assistance should be provided early in the progress of each course so that the student may be given the opportunity to rectify any faults in his pattern of learning. Further, the departmental counselor should be the reference person for career guidance for the discipline represented by the academic department. Students who seek guidance in selection of electives or in the development of strategies to obtain appointment to competitive residencies should be welcome in the office of the departmental counselor.

It is obvious that the departmental counselor, or several of them, should be persons of broad scholarship in the disciplines in which they participate. The typical, exceedingly narrow specialist, who has restricted his area of intellectual interests to a very thin slice of research, may or may not be a suitable general counselor. I recommend that those who become counselors be recognized scholars who have become known in the institution for their capacity to synthesize old and new facts derived by specific researchers and who are appreciated for their capacity to evaluate old and new findings in publications printed in both journals and books. In order to be fair to those who might be asked to assume the responsibilities of departmental counselor, I suggest that the faculty develop systems of reward for them as they provide services to medical students that now are substantially lacking in many of our academic departments throughout North America.

4. *Improving the Functioning of Educational Committees.* (a) Curriculum Committee: On many occasions in many medical schools, I have followed the faculty's activities as it came to the conclusion that it was necessary to change the M.D. curriculum. I have observed intense activity on the part of the curriculum committee as changes were made in the distribution of class time to the departments. Also, I have observed that after the considerable effort required to change the curriculum has run its course, the curriculum committee often becomes relatively moribund; somnolence sets in while the new curriculum unfolds in its time track and schemata for a period of years. Occasionally, the curriculum committee may be reactivated due to the demands of some small,

newly emerging discipline that seeks time, space, and turf in the curriculum.

I suggest that the curriculum committee has an ongoing dynamic function: to monitor exactly what happens in each course in each academic year while the plan developed by the committee is being implemented. To be specific, I suggest that the curriculum committee has a clear responsibility to use staff support provided by the chief academic officer to maintain an ongoing inventory of the content of the curriculum. Review by the curriculum committee of proposed lesson plans for each of the courses (even this is not done in many schools) is not sufficient to make certain that what was proposed was indeed implemented in the classroom, laboratories, or clinical services of teaching hospitals. The curriculum committee, therefore, is responsible for scrutinizing the content of each course or unit of instruction so that the densely packed curriculum may not be filled with wasteful repetition of subject material or be guilty of omission of significant matters. Considerable effort is required to maintain active and accurate knowledge of the content of the curriculum; it is obvious that only the students themselves know exactly what happens to them.

In order to develop a coherent plan for the M.D. curriculum, the faculty committee on curriculum should avoid progressive splintering of the body of medical knowledge into multiple courses. Rather, the emphasis should be on fostering generic courses that can include under their umbrellas all related subjects. Failure to develop a system of synthesis and consolidation around a finite number of generic subjects in the past has led to demands for separate time and turf by the partisans of narrow technologies, new knowledge, or recently seceded area of learned technology from a generic subject.

To illustrate, I suggest that the ancient subject of anatomy should be arranged in such a manner that it welcomes a variety of clinicians in the dissecting room or in the neuro- or microscopic anatomy laboratory. It is traditional for radiologists and orthopedists to visit the dissecting room and make displays or formal presentations to the young medical students, who, after all, came to medical school with the intention of becoming practicing physicians. But representatives of the clinical disciplines involving the special senses also have a place under the general umbrella of anatomy. That is, the ophthalmologists and the otolaryngologists can expand the interests of the students from consideration of mere structure to consideration of mechanical problems connected with the structures they are studying. The dermatologists, as noted previously, can present an interesting hour on common tumors of the skin and thereby justify the learning of the composition of the skin.

Similar arrangements can be made in the basic courses of biochemistry, physiology, and microbiology. Participation by clinicians in the basic science courses thus facilitates the application of the traditional content of the basic science disciplines to clinical problems, leaving to the professional faculty of those departments presentations of their studies of modern biomedical science.

(b) Evaluations and Promotions Committee: Just as I believe that a representative committee of the faculty should be responsible for the philosophy of the curriculum and its content, so I believe that another committee of the faculty should be responsible for evaluating the achievements of the students. It is important that there be some crossover in membership between the curriculum and the evaluations committees; however, much of the continuity between these two significant bodies in the education of the physician can be provided by the chief academic officer and his associates, who must provide significant staff support for both groups.

It has been my experience that it is impossible to make improvements and changes in an old curriculum without central supervision of the means and methods of examining students in the various courses and units of instruction. While I believe that the content of each departmental examination should be determined by those who are the most knowledgeable in the discipline, it is essential that the evaluations committee be authorized to supervise the content of the departmental examinations. Simply stated, I believe that peer review in educational matters is at least as important as it is in well-established practices of review of articles submitted for publication in a medical journal or in the process of considering applications for research grants by the very prestigious National Institutes of Health.

Further, I believe that the faculty committee on evaluation should establish some general rules and guidelines to regulate the number of examinations each course director may inflict upon his students. As I have visited medical schools, I have found frequently that it is the custom in some departments to give short tests on a frequent basis—sometimes weekly. The test questions put to the students under these circumstances generally require a quick regurgitation of memorized information that has been encountered in one manner or another within the previous week. The time has come to decide that this is poor pedagogy, certainly at the level at which medical students pursue a doctoral degree. Philosophical consideration of the nature of examinations and the frequency of their use by the faculty will unquestionably have considerable influence on the nature and content of the curriculum presented to the students by that same faculty.

This consideration leads to the conclusion that total dependence on any kind of external examinations, such as those of the National Board of Medical Examiners, is probably quite inappropriate. Therefore, I recommend as the fairest system of measurement of student learning a combination of local examinations and the periodic use of some form of external examinations (not necessarily those of the NBME, unless the NBME improves its methodology).

Having graded a significant number of student examinations myself, I can testify with emphasis that it is very difficult to grade essay questions with equivalent fairness. However, I believe that the faculty is obliged to require students to demonstrate their capacity to use literary language in order to describe the findings of examinations of their assigned patients or any other event that can be described in print. If essay questions are not to be used in examinations, then I suggest that a reasonable requirement for writing papers be considered as a means of inducing improvement in the literary performance of students.

The time may have arrived for the faculty to shift from total reliance on traditional measurements of students' ability to recall recently memorized details. If, in the future, students are to be expected to master a reduced amount of detail and are to be trained to develop expert means of retrieval of the bulk of the body of knowledge, then the faculty should experiment with new systems of measurement that embody the new philosophy.

Finally, I think that the system of measurement of achievement ought not to depend entirely on measurements supplied at the end of each temporal period of instruction. By this I mean that there should be some use of mid-course measurements, preferably not for recorded determination of the final grade in the course but for feedback to the students so that they themselves may then apply necessary remedial actions. If my recommendation for appointment of departmental counselors were adopted, then the students would have a designated individual whom they could consult if they required some guidance by an experienced member of the departmental faculty (see also Eichna, 1980).

5. *Improving Performance by the Faculty.* There is a traditional expectation that a faculty member has a triad of functions: education, research/scholarship, and service. However, the combination of the forty-year euphoria for discovery of new knowledge through research and a much more recent intense concentration on provision of clinical service has resulted in neglect in many medical schools of the educational function. The rules for promotion of faculty members often have been modified so as to require demonstration of excellence in at least two of the three components of the triad. However, the faculty member who demonstrates significant contributions only in education and in some form of service may find that his promotion is delayed, while his peer in the departmental faculty who extends most of his time in a very narrow research field is likely to obtain promotion much more rapidly—and very likely will be assigned larger amounts of space, equipment, technical support, and the like. It is up to the faculty to decide what its priorities are. However, the faculty should be very honest. If it has low regard for the education of medical students, it should clearly state that fact in its bulletin of courses and in its communications with students who might be interested in considering enrollment in the institution.

I suggest that the only way for greater emphasis to be given to education would be for the policies for promotion of faculty to be modified to require each person considered for promotion to demonstrate significant educational contribution to the M.D.

program, to graduate education programs, and to programs of graduate medical education. In short, I believe that before promotion to senior tenured rank, the individual faculty member should be expected to excell in the field of education, which has been accepted as a major institutional responsibility, plus one other component of the triad. If policies are modified along this general line, in the future able members of the faculty may pay greater attention to the problems of undergraduate medical education. Additionally, departmental chairmen and deans should be urged by university presidents, provosts, and the like to reward excellent teachers by providing extra emoluments in the monthly paycheck and by providing such other perquisites as are available to those responsible for administration of the academic community.

The biomedical scientists who staff the basic science departments of typical medical schools, by and large, are interested in the development of new knowledge in their respective fields. This is obviously a very significant function and one that should be appropriately honored and supported in major ways. However, if the modern biomedical faculty is overwhelmingly intent on discovering new information—usually of a very narrow sort—it may find involvement with young medical students who desire to become physicians to be a burdensome responsibility.

In my visits to medical schools throughout North America, I have frequently found basic science departments consisting of eminent scientists, none of whom had any clear knowledge as to the full scope of education of the physician and none of whom had been inside a hospital since the birth of his last child. Such lack of information about the life of a physician has led to feelings of either insecurity on the part of the basic scientists as they relate to medical students or supercilious behavior, including expressions of disdain about either the intellectual ability of the medical students or the merit of the medical profession at large. Whether these feelings are communicated verbally, as they sometimes are, or whether they are communicated through nonverbal actions and expressions matters very little; students quickly determine which of their faculty members are interested in their welfare, and it is quite common to find considerable tension between members of the basic science departmental faculty and their enrolled medical students.

Each basic science department should contain at least one (preferably more) person who has earned the M.D. degree and who has achieved scholarly development in that biomedical scientific discipline. Some departments have recruited persons who hold both a doctoral degree in science and the M.D. degree. Whatever arrangement may be possible, I suggest that a department made up of individuals who have neither interest in medical students nor particular respect for the medical profession at large are not fully suitable for continuing contact with medical students.

In the clinical departments, the medical student is traditionally assigned as a member of the "health care team." This generally means that the student is assigned to close working relationships with several members of the resident staff enrolled in a specialty program of graduate medical education. Often as much as 90 percent of the actual "teaching" interface between a medical student clinical clerk and a faculty person is with one or more members of the resident staff. Students report that their experiences with residents are highly variable; some relationships are unquestionably desirable and provide benefits that have lifelong significance, while in others the resident is not at all interested in medical students and looks upon them as usurpers of his undoubtedly precious time. The student linked to an overly busy or uninterested resident misses an opportunity to learn clinical medicine through the case study system, which we have treasured so highly as it is conducted at the bedside in the teaching hospital.

I suggest that the clinical faculty have very clear responsibilities to see to appropriate supervision of the clinical clerks assigned to a geographic service in any teaching hospital. It is possible for some clinical departments to designate an older resident for a period of time as a "teaching resident." This allows an experienced senior resident to devote adequate time to the teaching of medical students. In any case, I suggest that the participation of the bona fide members of the faculty with clinical clerks may require frequent inspection and criticism by those responsible for the general management of the curriculum. Students should be queried at some length by representatives of the curriculum committee or its agent, by the CAO, or by his designee as to the nature of the supervisory relationship. It is clear that the increase in class size over the last twenty years has contributed to a deterioration of clinical teaching, and this problem not only must be recognized but should be treated appropriately.

In the clinical setting, it is the responsibility of the departmental chairperson/course director to make certain that each clinical clerk receives an adequately balanced variety of experiences with patients assigned for study. In some LCME studies, we have found that a student may be assigned to a single specialty service for the duration of a required clinical clerkship with the result that a single disease is pursued in great depth to the complete exclusion of almost all other organ systems or types of diseases. This is an unacceptable situation which cheats the student out of receiving a balanced educational experience.

Debate about the use and abuse of formal lectures to large groups of students is familiar to all; undoubtedly debate will continue in the future. If a member of the faculty is to give a lecture to a large group of students, great care should be taken to make certain that this use of time is efficient and appropriate. Obviously, the member of the faculty who lectures to 100 or 150 students in a large room is obliged, upon his professional honor as an academic officer of the university, to come to the event fully prepared to give his best possible presentation. The conscientious member of the faculty who desires to meet his commitment to excellence in teaching, and who probably does so in his research endeavors, should avail himself of whatever means of improvement are available in his school. The CAO and members of his staff should have available the various means of making audio and video recordings of the performance of members of the faculty; these recordings should then be studied with the intent of improving methods of delivery, presentation of the data in multiple media, and the like.

Finally, and hopefully, I enter a plaintive plea that experimentation be undertaken with an arrangement whereby students are asked to do basic reading on a prescribed subject prior to a formal presentation on it through lecture, demonstration, or otherwise. If this method is followed (which is rare), the encounter between the faculty member and his group of students can go past elementary delineation of the pertinent facts related to the subject to the second stage of explanation, interpretation, and application of those facts or principles to useful and significant purposes.

6. *Modifying Emphasis and Content of the Curriculum*. For centuries, the medical profession has been struggling to cope with a heavy load of problems connected with therapy of acute diseases and trauma. As a result, enormous achievements have been made in therapy of acute diseases, and the typical medical school curriculum gives much attention to such significant subjects. However, the increasing longevity of the population due to improved control of acute disease problems has predisposed the emergence of many more chronic disease problems—which have never received significant attention in the curriculum. The aged accumulate problems from several diseases; such patients present challenges in therapy to physicians who practice narrow specialties.

Pharmacology and clinical therapeutics need increased emphasis. Performance of difficult and potentially dangerous surgery is generally restricted to surgeons who are well trained in such procedures; also the surgeon operates under fairly public surveillance by his peers. In contrast, any physician with a legal license to practice and a narcotic permit can prescribe any drug or medication available, without any thought of immediate professional peer review. Side effects of drugs, synergistic reactions resulting from use of more than one medication, and potential idiosyncratic reactions of patients to certain drugs need to be well known by every physician with a prescription pad. Students should be assisted in acquiring polished skills in the evaluation of the constant stream of new drugs.

Nutrition, especially in the geriatric group, also deserves higher priority than this significant subject generally receives.

7. *Restricting External Influences on the M.D. Program*. The adoption of the all-elective senior year some fifteen years prior to this writing has led to the use of much elective time by the students for development of strategies to obtain appointment in highly desired residency training programs. This means that many students have abandoned their primary college of enrollment and have migrated—often to several places—during their senior year for the purpose of making themselves known to the directors of desirable residency training programs. I support what I perceive as a trend:

that is, a gradual reintroduction of required courses of study in the fourth year of the M.D. curriculum. Due to the vast and growing size of the body of medical knowledge, it appears highly inappropriate to allow a full year (25 percent of the total) to be substantially ignored by many faculties and misused by many students for premature specialization in the subject of the anticipated residency program.

The other evil that has developed in an artifactual manner during the past twenty years is the requirement by certain directors of residency training programs for the filing of applications by medical students not in the beginning of the senior year, as might be considered appropriate, but early in the junior year and even in some cases while the students are yet sophomores. Everyone who has acted as an academic dean has been visited by a youthful student who at that point has not yet experienced any of the clinical clerking provided in the curriculum yet who has in his hand application materials for a specialty residency program that would begin two years hence. The dean is entreated to write a supporting letter for this medical student at the demand of the director of a residency training program. The most frequent offenders of this practice are the directors of those programs that have a large surplus of candidates for appointment. Under these circumstances, it is impossible to understand the necessity for their demands for early application to their residency programs. The most appropriate remedy to this national problem would be for the deans of the medical schools of this country to rigidly hold their clinical departmental chairpersons (who are invariably the directors of residency training programs) to a time table that would schedule applications for residency programs only after Labor Day of the medical students' final year of study, with the appointment to be made sometime in the early part of the calendar year in which the student is posted for graduation with the M.D. degree. If the deans of the medical school were to strengthen their collective spines and agree on a system of protection of their medical students, the residency program directors would still find it possible to appoint students to their programs sufficiently early to allow orderly planning for the beginning of the first year of graduate medical education. The students would be allowed a much broader opportunity than presently to explore the various forms of medical specialism before they make a rigid commitment to any one. In my experience with more than 2,000 medical graduates, I have seen many medical students change the direction of their application for residency programs not once but two and sometimes three times deep into their senior year. It seems only fair to allow the student to complete the studies required for the M.D. degree without interference from external agents, such as the directors of the residency training programs. I believe that this situation is so scandalous, as viewed in the early 1980s, that severe constraint should be applied as soon as possible.

8. *Increasing Attention to the Personal Development of Medical Students.* Since mid-century, the medical faculties have gradually adjusted to the changing life-style of young adults, some of the best of which are enrolled in the study of medicine. In the old days now forgotten, the medical student was under the absolute authority of the dean and the members of the faculty, and stern discipline was frequently administered for major infractions and for many minor ones. Under this system, young adults were subjected to a prolongation of their adolescence while enrolled in medical school between the average ages of twenty-two through twenty-seven, with some local variation. The adjustment made by the medical faculty is to discontinue the rule of "in loco parentis," a legal phrase which, in my Texian definition, runs something like: "You are crazy if you think you can parent five hundred or more young adults." This change in philosophy, having been described and accepted, leads to the current observation that the medical schools in recent times may have neglected the personal development of their students toward professional maturity at a time when they are learning all of the elements of the profession they will pursue for a lifetime.

While I support the emancipation of medical students from overweaning authoritarian supervision by the officers and faculty members of the medical school, I am nonetheless strongly convinced that the deans, departmental chairpersons, course directors, and all members of the faculty have very clear professional responsibilities to facilitate the performance of their students in all of the curricular exercises required for the M.D. degree. Previously, I have reviewed the problems of some faculty members who are disdainful of medical students and of the medical profession in general; these same individuals often are quite ignorant of the problems of the medical profession and are content to offer philosophical criticisms of it without clear knowledge of the problems faced by the members of the profession. If medical students, upon their arrival at the school of medicine, are greeted by basic scientists, however eminent, who verbally and nonverbally express their dislike for medical students and their chosen profession, then reverse facilitation begins to develop rapidly.

Each academic dean and assistant dean for student affairs should carefully examine their system of orientation of newly arrived medical students and gradually develop a program to blunt the stress and shock of entry into a new, highly competitive learning experience with classmates who have been carefully selected and who have achieved very high levels of attainment in a variety of colleges and universities. Similar stress becomes acute when the students begin their initial encounter with clinical clerkships.

The chief academic officer should have supervisory responsibility over all individuals employed by the college in any sort of service relationship with the medical students. This includes the registrar, the librarian and assistants, the security guards, the departmental secretaries, the loan officers, and all others who have contact with students. It is a clear responsibility of a chief academic officer, aided and abetted by the chief executive officer, to ensure that all of these individuals who have contact with students exhibit satisfactory competence in the performance of their assigned duties. Competence, in my opinion, includes the capacity and motivation for humanistic behavior toward all publics, particularly medical students. The objective is to develop a courteous and helpful service staff. Obviously, the deans must demonstrate personal examples of humanistic behavior if they expect those they supervise to acquire the same characteristics.

After much experience, it is my belief that medical students need empathic support of an unsentimental nature as they pursue high standards of performance—certainly during the first year of adjustment to a level of performance not required of them previously and then again as they make the adjustment to daily participation in the clinical care setting. My rationale for this view is very simple:

If a faculty desires to produce a physician who manifests humanistic behavior in the care of his patients, the program of medical education must be operated by humanistically inclined persons who enjoy facilitating the development of the most noble features of behavior of their students. In short, I believe that medical education can and should be quite the opposite of that of training warriors for close combat, where the object of the training program is to convert the student into an efficient, methodical combat trooper capable of destroying the life of a designated enemy.

There is a developing literature on the stress experienced by medical students, residents, fellows, faculty members, and practicing physicians. The select bibliography included in this book cites various publications that describe sequelae of stress in the medical profession. The best source of authentic advice to medical students and those medical educators who desire to understand their students and their substantial stresses is : *Doctor-To-Be: Coping With the Trials and Triumphs of Medical School*, by J. Knight (1981).

The chief academic officer has a clear responsibility in his role as ombudsman for his students to provide a variety of support services for students who require such. An efficient student health service that has procedures for quick and confidential referral of overstressed students to competent psychiatrists for professional support is essential. Often, the chief academic officer himself, if he is personally interested in students in difficulty, can be very effective in using intellectual discussion to help a student increase his confidence in his ability to cope with the unexpectedly heavy responsibilities most students find upon enrolling in medical school.

If the CAO, the curriculum committee, and the evaluation and promotion committee members perform their functions adequately, as has been discussed heretofore, students will not have to endure a series of harrassments and provocative experiences in the course of their instruction. In many medical schools, a department that offers a course is given such total and independent authority to conduct the course as it sees fit that problems in relationship to students can develop quickly and grow into major confrontations between faculty and students—to the point that a satisfactory solution is relatively impossible to arrange. Any school that would permit such confrontations to develop because of a failure to install a well-known and practiced system of preventive measures needs substantial criticism and probably replacement of those responsible for operating the educational programs.

Medical students need help in building sensitivity to the reactions of patients faced with various diagnostic and therapeutic measures. The typical medical student is physically robust, and most have enjoyed lifelong good health. As such, during student days and when active in the residency training program, the medical student may have acquired only limited insight into the iatrogenic trauma inflicted on patients who are frail and in pain and who usually are very anxious when the physician orders certain diagnostic or therapeutic procedures. For example, a simple venipuncture (drawing blood from the vein of a patient), even if done properly, can be very troublesome to a patient. Having a stomach tube passed down one's pharynx and esophagus is a real ordeal; accepting a proctoscopic tube is also a fearful experience—at least the first time either of these diagnostic procedures is endured. Preparation of a patient for surgery often includes the ignominious experience of having one's private skin shaved and an enema administered.

All such events and numerous others become routine activities ordered automatically by physicians. The more dangerous of these diagnostic or therapeutic procedures are administered by the physicians themselves, but many routine procedures are administered by health aides or attendants in the hospital setting. The point is that the healthy medical student and resident who has never been ill and who may have never been hospitalized may have a very poor, limited perspective of the reaction of the patient to some of these routine experiences. Whether it is possible or in any way practical to provide each medical student with some of these experiences, which cause so much traumatic reaction in patients, is to be determined by those responsible for each medical school. If it is not possible for each student to experience some of these major tests, at least there should be thoughtful explanation of these and other tests and their impact upon the patients.

In concluding this section about facilitating the performance of students and some of the activities that could improve their humanistic characteristics, I would like to offer two open-ended questions directed to academic deans, members of curriculum and evaluation committees, departmental chairpersons, course or clerk-ship directors, and members of the participating faculty. The first question is very general but hits each of the persons outlined above: Exactly what deliberately planned activities have you installed in the routine organization of your educational activities that provide facilitation of learning by students as they are expected to develop into humanistic and responsive, as well as professionally competent, physicians? The second question is the obverse of the first: What activities do you routinely administer at this time that, after careful examination, you judge to be counterproductive and nonfacilitating in the development of your students along desirable lines?

It is my intention to develop another manuscript in the near future that will treat the matter of facilitation of learning in medical students and young physicians. In this volume, I intend to record my own results of numerous experiments that have attempted to facilitate the performance of students in their assigned responsibil-ities and in the accomplishment of supplemental goals that extend beyond routine and ordinary expectations of learning in medical school.

Graduate Medical Education

1. *Report of a Major Study on GME by the AAMC.* The best source for an analysis of the current status of GME and for authoritative recommendations for its improvement can be found in *Graduate Medi-Education: Proposals for the Eighties,* which was prepared by a task force of the AAMC and published by its Executive Council in 1980 (Association of American Medical Colleges, 1980). I refer the reader to this valuable publication for detailed study of GME.

2. *Inappropriate Demands for Early Applications.* Earlier in this volume, I reviewed the disruptions caused by demands by some residency program directors for medical students to place applica-tions for GME programs during their junior or sometimes their sophomore year. This practice is quite unjustified and should be modified.

3. *Overwork and Stress of the Resident.* Residency program directors and faculty members should devise effective means of

recognizing inappropriate stress on residents due to overwork. Recent changes in the flow rate of patients in and out of hospitals have produced substantial modification of the duties expected of many residents. Traditional assignments of duty hours, as well as on-call hours, may require modification.

4. *The Resident as a Teacher of Medical Students.* Conventional arrangements for management of clinical clerkships place medical students in close relationship with one or more residents. If the resident is overburdened with the care of an increasing number of patients due to their short term of hospitalization, the medical students assigned to him are likely to receive less than optimal attention. More institutions should appoint a "teaching resident" who is detached from patient care duties for a time and who is delegated the responsibility of very close supervision of a cluster of medical students. Teaching residents, as well as all residents appointed to GME programs with medical students attached, should be provided with guidance in their teaching responsibilities by members of the faculty.

Continuing Medical Education

1. *Evaluating Current Methods.* Much effort is expended annually in providing "refresher courses" in CME for physicians. Studies of conventional methods have failed to prove that patient care has been modified significantly, even though physician behavior seems to have been modified. Those responsible for the organization of CME activities should devise methods of evaluation of their approaches which can either demonstrate the worthiness of CME or lead to its improvement.

2. *Further Experimentation with Methods of CME.* The rapid and constant change in technology in medicine requires that the practicing physician be provided with efficient, valid means of maintaining professional competence. High priority should be assigned to research in devising improved methods of CME.

Appendixes

 το το το το το το το το το το το το το το το το το το το το το

A. *Accredited Schools*
    That Survived
    The Flexnerian Reforms
    as of 1929

B. *Percentage Increase*
    in Entering-Class
    Enrollment
    of the Eighty-Six
    Pre-1960 Schools by 1980

C. *Classification*
    of Medical Schools
    Based on the
    Carnegie Classification

Appendix A

Accredited Schools That Survived the Flexnerian Reforms as of 1929

Alabama
1. University of Alabama School of Medicine, Tuscaloosa
Arkansas
2. University of Arkansas School of Medicine, Little Rock
California
3. College of Medical Evangelists, Los Angeles
4. Stanford University School of Medicine, San Francisco
5. University of California, San Francisco, School of Medicine
6. University of Southern California School of Medicine, Los Angeles
Colorado
7. University of Colorado School of Medicine, Denver
Connecticut
8. Yale University School of Medicine, New Haven
District of Columbia
9. George Washington University Medical School, Washington
10. Georgetown University School of Medicine, Washington
11. Howard University School of Medicine, Washington
Georgia
12. Emory University School of Medicine, Atlanta
13. University of Georgia Medical Department, Augusta
Illinois
14. Loyola University School of Medicine, Chicago

15. Northwestern University Medical School, Chicago
16. University of Chicago, Rush Medical College
17. University of Chicago School of Medicine
18. University of Illinois College of Medicine, Chicago

Indiana

19. Indiana University School of Medicine, Bloomington and Indianapolis

Iowa

20. State University of Iowa College of Medicine, Iowa City

Kansas

21. University of Kansas School of Medicine, Lawrence-Kansas City

Kentucky

22. University of Louisville School of Medicine, Louisville

Louisiana

23. Tulane University of Louisiana School of Medicine, New Orleans

Maryland

24. Johns Hopkins University School of Medicine, Baltimore
25. University of Maryland School of Medicine and College of Physicians and Surgeons, Baltimore

Massachusetts

26. Boston University School of Medicine, Boston
27. Harvard University Medical School, Boston
28. Tufts College Medical School, Boston

Michigan

29. Detroit College of Medicine and Surgery, Detroit
30. University of Michigan Medical School, Ann Arbor

Minnesota

31. University of Minnesota Medical School, Minneapolis

Mississippi

32. University of Mississippi School of Medicine, Oxford

Missouri

33. St. Louis University School of Medicine, St. Louis
34. University of Missouri School of Medicine, Columbia
35. Washington University School of Medicine, St. Louis

Nebraska

36. Creighton University School of Medicine, Omaha

37. University of Nebraska College of Medicine, Omaha
New Hampshire
38. Dartmouth Medical School, Hanover
New York
39. Albany Medical College, Albany
40. Columbia University College of Physicians and Surgeons, New York City
41. Cornell University Medical College, New York City
42. Long Island College Hospital, New York City
43. New York Homeopathic Medical College and Flower Hospital, New York City
44. Syracuse University College of Medicine, Syracuse
45. University and Bellevue Hospital Medical College, New York City
46. University of Buffalo School of Medicine, Buffalo
47. University of Rochester School of Medicine, Rochester
North Carolina
48. University of North Carolina School of Medicine, Chapel Hill
49. Wake Forest College School of Medicine, Wake Forest
North Dakota
50. University of North Dakota School of Medicine, Grand Forks
Ohio
51. Eclectic Medical College, Cincinnati
52. Ohio State University College of Medicine, Columbus
53. University of Cincinnati College of Medicine, Cincinnati
54. Western Reserve University School of Medicine, Cleveland
Oklahoma
55. University of Oklahoma School of Medicine, Oklahoma City
Oregon
56. University of Oregon Medical School, Portland
Pennsylvania
57. Hahnemann Medical College and Hospital of Philadelphia
58. Jefferson Medical College of Philadelphia
59. Temple University School of Medicine, Philadelphia
60. University of Pennsylvania School of Medicine, Philadelphia
61. University of Pittsburgh School of Medicine, Pittsburgh
62. Woman's Medical College of Pennsylvania, Philadelphia

South Carolina
63. Medical College of the State of South Carolina, Charleston
South Dakota
64. University of South Dakota School of Medicine, Vermilion
Tennessee
65. Meharry Medical College, Nashville
66. University of Tennessee College of Medicine, Memphis
67. Vanderbilt University School of Medicine, Nashville
Texas
68. Baylor University College of Medicine, Dallas
69. University of Texas School of Medicine, Galveston
Utah
70. University of Utah School of Medicine, Salt Lake City
Vermont
71. University of Vermont College of Medicine, Burlington
Virginia
72. Medical College of Virginia, Richmond
73. University of Virginia Department of Medicine, Charlottesville
West Virginia
74. West Virginia University School of Medicine, Morgantown
Wisconsin
75. University of Wisconsin Medical School, Madison
76. Marquette University School of Medicine, Milwaukee

Appendix B

Percentage Increase in Entering-Class Enrollment of the Eighty-Six Pre-1960 Schools by 1980

State	Name of School	Entering Class of 1960	Entering Class of 1980	Number Increase	Percentage Increase
Alabama	Medical College of Alabama	80	170	90	112.5
Arkansas	University of Arkansas	92	145	53	57.6
California	Loma Linda University	103	144	41	39.8
	Stanford University	60	86	26	43.3
	Univ. of California, Los Angeles	71	172	101	142.2
	Univ. of California, San Francisco	103	158	55	53.4
	Univ. of Southern California	69	140	71	102.8
Colorado	University of Colorado	85	136	51	60.0
Connecticut	Yale University	80	102	22	27.5
District of	Georgetown University	117	207	90	76.9
Columbia	George Washington University	102	154	52	51.0
	Howard University	106	138	32	30.2
Florida	University of Florida	53	117	64	120.7
	University of Miami	82	180	98	119.5
Georgia	Emory University	75	116	41	54.6
	Medical College of Georgia	104	189	85	81.7
Illinois	Chicago Medical School	76	138	62	81.5
	Northwestern University	131	172	41	31.3
	Stritch School of Med.–Loyola Univ.	88	147	59	67.0
	University of Chicago	73	105	32	43.8
	University of Illinois	200	357	157	78.5
Indiana	Indiana University	194	323	129	66.5
Iowa	State Univ. of Iowa Coll. of Med. (now University of Iowa)	124	176	52	41.9
Kansas	University of Kansas	105	209	104	99.0
Kentucky	University of Louisville	95	142	47	49.5

State	Name of School	Entering Class of 1960	Entering Class of 1980	Number Increase	Percentage Increase
Louisiana	Louisiana State Univ.-New Orleans	142	188	46	32.4
	Tulane University	133	151	18	13.5
Maryland	Johns Hopkins University	78	121	43	55.1
	University of Maryland	98	176	78	79.6
Massachusetts	Boston University	74	139	65	87.8
	Harvard Medical School	117	168	51	43.6
	Tufts University	115	150	35	30.4
Michigan	University of Michigan	200	247	47	23.5
	Wayne State University	125	256	131	104.8
Minnesota	University of Minnesota	141	247	106	75.2
Mississippi	University of Mississippi	81	161	80	98.8
Missouri	St. Louis University	122	162	40	32.8
	University of Missouri-Columbia	81	110	29	35.8
	Washington University-St. Louis	88	122	34	38.6
Nebraska	Creighton University	77	115	38	49.3
	University of Nebraska	90	155	65	72.2
New Jersey	Seton Hall Coll. of Med. & Dent. (now Univ. of Med. & Dent.-New Jersey Med. School)	80	186	106	132.5
New York	Albany Medical College	64	128	64	100.0
	Albert Einstein Coll. of Med.	98	186	88	89.8
	Columbia Univ. Coll. of Phys. & Surg.	120	148	28	23.3
	Cornell University	85	104	19	22.3
	New York Medical College	128	179	51	39.8
	New York University	130	171	41	31.5
	SUNY-Downstate Med. Ctr.	156	233	77	49.3
	SUNY-Upstate Med. Ctr.	84	154	70	83.3
	University of Buffalo (now SUNY-Buffalo)	88	138	50	56.8
	University of Rochester	72	99	27	37.5
North Carolina	Bowman Gray School of Med.-Wake Forest	55	113	58	105.4
	Duke University	75	117	42	56.0
	University of North Carolina	69	165	96	139.1
Ohio	Case Western Reserve University	87	147	60	68.9
	Ohio State University	151	257	106	70.2
	University of Cincinnati	98	195	97	98.9
Oklahoma	University of Oklahoma	104	179	75	72.1
Oregon	University of Oregon	80	117	37	46.3
Pennsylvania	Hahnemann Medical College	111	196	85	76.6
	Jefferson Medical College	176	230	54	30.7
	Temple University	137	185	48	35.0
	University of Pennsylvania	127	160	33	26.0
	University of Pittsburgh	101	138	37	36.6
	Women's Med. Coll. of Pennsylvania (Now Med. Coll. of Pennsylvania)	63	102	39	61.9
Puerto Rico	University of Puerto Rico	55	150	95	172.7
South Carolina	Medical College of South Carolina	80	166	86	107.5

State	Name of School	Entering Class of 1960	Entering Class of 1980	Number Increase	Percentage Increase
Tennessee	Meharry Medical College	71	162	91	128.2
	University of Tennessee	204	211	7	3.4
	Vanderbilt University	54	104	50	92.6
Texas	Baylor University	85	168	83	97.6
	Univ. of Texas–Galveston	144	211	67	46.5
	Univ. of Texas–Southwestern	100	208	108	108.0
Utah	University of Utah	55	101	46	83.6
Vermont	University of Vermont	51	93	42	82.3
Virginia	Medical College of Virginia	85	168	83	97.6
	University of Virginia	77	142	65	84.4
Washington	University of Washington	77	175	98	127.2
Wisconsin	Marquette University (now Med. Coll. of Wisconsin)	102	205	103	100.9
	University of Wisconsin	92	165	73	79.3
	Sub-Totals	8,101	13,247	5,146	

Accredited Schools of Basic Medical Sciences

State	Name of School	Entering Class of 1960	Entering Class of 1980	Number Increase	Percentage Increase
Kentucky	University of Kentucky	40	114	74	185.0
New Hampshire	Dartmouth Medical School	24	66	42	175.0
North Dakota	University of North Dakota	24	69	27	64.3
South Dakota	University of South Dakota	45	68	23	51.1
West Virginia	West Virginia University	46	88	42	91.3
	Sub-Totals	179	405	208	
	Totals	8,280	13,652	5,354	

Source: Journal of the American Medical Association, 1961, 178, 645–646; 1981, 246, 2974–2976.

Appendix C

Classification of Medical Schools Based on the Carnegie Classification

Appendix C shows a classification by the Carnegie Council on Policy Studies in Higher Education (1976b) of the universities that developed new medical schools before 1980. The criteria employed in this classification are as follows:

Research Universities I: Universities ranked among the 50 leading universities in terms of federal financial support of academic science; awarded at least 50 Ph.D.s in 1973–74.

Research Universities II: Universities ranked among the top 100 universities in terms of federal financial support of academic science; awarded at least 50 Ph.D.s in 1973–74.

Doctorate-Granting Universities I: Institutions that awarded at least 40 Ph.D.s in at least 5 fields in 1973–74 or that received at least $3 million in total federal support in 1973–74 or 1974–75.

Doctorate-Granting Universities II: Institutions that awarded at least 20 Ph.D.s in 1973–74 without regard to field or 10 Ph.D.s in at least 3 fields.

Comprehensive Universities and Colleges I: Institutions offering a liberal arts program as well as several other programs; lacked a doctoral program or had extremely limited doctoral programs but included 2 or more professional or occupational programs with at least 2,000 students in 1976.

Liberal Arts Colleges II: Institutions that failed to meet the Carnegie Council's standards for inclusion within the category of Liberal Arts Colleges I, which encompasses the 200 leading baccalaureate-granting institutions in terms of the numbers of their graduates receiving Ph.D.s at 40 leading doctorate-granting institutions from 1920 to 1966.

Those universities listed below the dotted lines established their medical schools during the period from 1960–1980.

Research Universities I

State	Name of School
California	Stanford University School of Medicine
	University of California, Los Angeles, School of Medicine
	University of California, San Francisco, School of Medicine
	University of Southern California School of Medicine
Colorado	University of Colorado School of Medicine
Connecticut	Yale University School of Medicine
Florida	University of Florida College of Medicine
	University of Miami School of Medicine
Illinois	Northwestern University Medical School
	University of Chicago, The Pritzker School of Medicine
	University of Illinois College of Medicine
Iowa	University of Iowa College of Medicine
Maryland	John Hopkins University School of Medicine
	University of Maryland School of Medicine
Massa-	Boston University School of Medicine
chusetts	Harvard Medical School
Michigan	University of Michigan Medical School
Minnesota	University of Minnesota Medical School–Minneapolis
Missouri	University of Missouri–Columbia School of Medicine
	Washington University School of Medicine
New York	Albert Einstein College of Medicine of Yeshiva University
	Columbia University College of Physicians and Surgeons
	Cornell University Medical College

New York University School of Medicine

University of Rochester School of Medicine and
Dentistry

North
Carolina   Duke University School of Medicine

University of North Carolina School of Medicine

Ohio   Case Western Reserve University School of Medicine

Ohio State University College of Medicine

Pennsyl-   University of Pennsylvania School of Medicine

vania   University of Pittsburgh School of Medicine

Texas   University of Texas Southwestern Medical School at
Dallas

University of Texas Medical School at Galveston

Utah   University of Utah College of Medicine

Washington   University of Washington School of Medicine

Wisconsin   University of Wisconsin Medical School

. . . .

Arizona   University of Arizona College of Medicine

California   University of California, Davis, School of Medicine

University of California, San Diego, School of
Medicine

Hawaii   University of Hawaii John A. Burns School of
Medicine

Michigan   Michigan State University College of Human
Medicine

Pennsyl-

vania   Pennsylvania State University College of Medicine

Texas   Texas A & M University College of Medicine

University of Texas Medical School at San Antonio[1]

University of Texas Medical School at Houston

---

[1]The Carnegie Council classification placed the University of Texas
Medical School at San Antonio within the category of Comprehensive
Universities and Colleges I (see Carnegie Council on Policy Studies in
Higher Education, 1976b, p. 21); for the purposes of this book, this particular
ranking has been modified.

Research Universities II

State	Name of School
Arkansas	University of Arkansas College of Medicine
California	University of California, Irvine, California College of Medicine
District of Columbia	George Washington University School of Medicine and Health Sciences
	Georgetown University School of Medicine
	Howard University College of Medicine
Georgia	Emory University School of Medicine
Indiana	Indiana University School of Medicine
Kansas	University of Kansas School of Medicine
Louisiana	Louisiana State University School of Medicine in New Orleans
	Louisiana State University School of Medicine in Shreveport[2]
	Tulane University School of Medicine
Massachusetts	Tufts University School of Medicine
Michigan	Wayne State University School of Medicine
Missouri	St. Louis University School of Medicine
Nebraska	University of Nebraska College of Medicine
New York	State University of New York at Buffalo School of Medicine
Ohio	University of Cincinnati College of Medicine
Oklahoma	University of Oklahoma College of Medicine
Oregon	University of Oregon School of Medicine
Pennsylvania	Temple University School of Medicine
Tennessee	University of Tennessee College of Medicine
	Vanderbilt University School of Medicine
Vermont	University of Vermont College of Medicine
Virginia	University of Virginia School of Medicine

[2]The Carnegie Council classification placed the Louisiana State University School of Medicine in Shreveport within the category of Comprehensive Universities and Colleges I (see p. 16, *A Classification of Institutions of Higher Education*); for the purposes of this book, this particular ranking has been modified.

West Virginia	West Virginia University School of Medicine

. . . .

Connecticut	University of Connecticut School of Medicine
Kentucky	University of Kentucky College of Medicine
Massa-chusetts	University of Massachusetts Medical School
New Jersey	College of Medicine and Dentistry of New Jersey Rutgers Medical School
New Mexico	University of New Mexico School of Medicine
New York	Mount Sinai School of Medicine of the City University of New York
	State University of New York at Stony Brook School of Medicine
Rhode Island	Brown University Program in Medicine

Doctorate-Granting Universities I

State	Name of School
Alabama	University of Alabama School of Medicine
Illinois	Loyola University of Chicago Stritch School of Medicine
Kentucky	University of Louisville School of Medicine
Mississippi	University of Mississippi School of Medicine
New Hampshire	Dartmouth Medical School
North Dakota	University of North Dakota School of Medicine
Virginia	Virginia Commonwealth University–Medical College of Virginia School of Medicine
Wisconsin	Medical College of Wisconsin

. . . .

Illinois	Southern Illinois University School of Medicine
Missouri	University of Missouri–Kansas City School of Medicine
South Carolina	University of South Carolina School of Medicine
Texas	Texas Tech University School of Medicine

Doctorate-Granting Universities II

State	Name of School
California	Loma Linda University School of Medicine
South Dakota	University of South Dakota School of Medicine

. . . .

State	Name of School
Florida	University of South Florida College of Medicine
Nevada	University of Nevada–Reno School of Medicine

Comprehensive Universities and Colleges I

State	Name of School
Nebraska	Creighton University School of Medicine
North Carolina	Bowman Gray School of Medicine at Wake Forest University
Ohio	Wright State University School of Medicine
Puerto Rico	University of Puerto Rico School of Medicine

. . . .

State	Name of School
Alabama	University of South Alabama College of Medicine
Minnesota	University of Minnesota–Duluth School of Medicine
North Carolina	East Carolina University School of Medicine
Oklahoma	Oral Roberts University School of Medicine
Tennessee	East Tennessee State University, Quillen-Dishner College of Medicine
West Virginia	Marshall University School of Medicine

Liberal Arts Colleges II

State	Name of School
Georgia	School of Medicine at Morehouse College

Independent Medical Schools, Academic Health Centers, and Health Science Universities

State	Name of School
Georgia	Medical College of Georgia School of Medicine[3]
Illinois	University of Health Sciences/The Chicago Medical School
New Jersey	College of Medicine and Dentistry of New Jersey/ New Jersey Medical School
New York	Albany Medical College
	New York Medical College
	State University of New York Downstate Medical Center College of Medicine[3]
	State University of New York Upstate Medical Center College of Medicine[3]
Pennsylvania	Hahnemann Medical College
	Jefferson Medical College
	Medical College of Pennsylvania
South Carolina	Medical University of South Carolina College of Medicine[3]
Tennessee	Meharry Medical College School of Medicine
Texas	Baylor College of Medicine

. . . .

State	Name of School
Illinois	Rush Medical College of Rush University
Missouri	Uniformed Services University of the Health Sciences School of Medicine
Minnesota	Mayo Medical College
Ohio	Medical College of Ohio at Toledo[3]
	Northeastern Ohio Universities College of Medicine[3]
Puerto Rico	Ponce School of Medicine
Virginia	Eastern Virginia Medical School

[3]Indicates a medical school governed by a state-wide board of trustees that, in the majority of cases, is responsible for all higher education in a particular state.

Select Bibliography

‏‏⚬⚬⚬⚬⚬⚬⚬⚬⚬⚬⚬⚬⚬⚬⚬⚬⚬⚬⚬⚬⚬⚬⚬⚬‏

This section consists of a number of references to books and journal articles that have not been cited in the text. These references are arranged according to the general topics treated in the four parts of the book and are divided into twenty-four subjects. The list for each subject can provide the curious, scholarly reader with somewhat greater detail than does the basic text of the book, which is intended for a heterogeneous readership.

Part One: Medical Schools and the Supply of Physicians

I. Supply and Distribution of Physicians: Changes in Medical Care

Bowman, M., and Katzoff, J. "Estimates of Physician Requirements for 1990 for the Specialties of Neurology, Anesthesiology, Nuclear Medicine, Pathology, Physical Medicine and Rehabilitation, and Radiology." *Journal of the American Medical Association*, 1983, *250*, 2623–2627.

Igras, S., and others. "Factors Associated With Retention of Medical
    School Graduates for In-State Graduate Medical Education."
    Journal of Medical Education, 1983, *58,* 733–735.
Petersdorf, R. "Managing the Revolution in Medical Care." *Journal
    of Medical Education,* 1984, *59,* 79–90.
Spencer, D., and D'Elia, G. "The Effect of Regional Medical
    Education on Physician Distribution." *Journal of Medical Ed-
    ucation,* 1983, *58,* 309–315.
Starr, P. *The Social Transformation of American Medicine.* New
    York: Basic Books, 1983.
Tarlov, A. "Shattuck Lecture—The Increasing Supply of Physi-
    cians, the Changing Structure of the Health-Services System, and
    the Future Practice of Medicine." *New England Journal of
    Medicine,* 1983, *308,* 1235–2344.
Williams, A., and others. "How Many Miles to the Doctor?" *New
    England Journal of Medicine,* 1983, *309,* 958–963.

II. History of Medicine

A. Greek Medicine

Adams, F. (Trans.). *The Genuine Works of Hippocrates.* Hunting-
    ton, N.Y.: Krieger, 1972.

B. The Middle Ages

O'Malley, D. *Andreas Vesalius of Brussels, 1514–1564.* Berkeley:
    University of California Press, 1964.
Pachter, H. *Paracelsus: Magic Into Science.* New York: Collier, 1961.
Sarton, G. *Appreciation of Ancient and Medieval Science during
    the Renaissance, 1450–1600.* New York: Perpetua-Barnes, 1955.
Singer, C. *A Short History of Anatomy and Physiology from the
    Greeks to Harvey.* New York: Dover, 1956.

C. Seventeenth and Eighteenth Centuries

Camac, C. (Ed.). *Classics of Medicine and Surgery.* N.Y.: Dover,
    1959.

Kobler, J. *The Reluctant Surgeon.* Garden City, N.Y.: Dolphin-Doubleday, 1962.

Rather, L. *Mind and Body in Eighteenth Century Medicine.* Berkeley: University of California Press, 1965.

Zimmerman, L., and Veith, I. *Great Ideas in the History of Surgery.* Baltimore: Williams and Wilkins, 1961.

D. Ravages of Infectious Diseases

Defoe, D. *A Journal of the Plague Year.* New York: Signet/New World Library of World Literature, 1960.

Hoehling, A. *The Great Epidemic: When the Spanish Influenza Struck.* Boston: Little, Brown, 1961.

Nohl, J. *The Black Death.* New York: Ballantine, 1960.

Rosebury, T. *Microbes and Morals.* New York: Ballantine, 1971.

Slaughter, F. *Semmelweis: The Conqueror of Childbed Fever.* New York: Collier, 1961.

Wilson, F. *The Plague in Shakespeare's London.* Oxford, England: Oxford University Press, 1963.

III. Diseases and Their Influence on History

Henschen, F. *The History and Geography of Diseases.* New York: Delacorte, 1966.

McNeill, W. *Plagues and Peoples.* Garden City, N.Y.: Anchor/Doubleday, 1977.

Sigerist, H. *Civilization and Disease.* Chicago: Phoenix-University of Chicago Press, 1972.

Zinsser, H. *Rats, Lice and History.* New York: Bantam, 1960.

A. Nineteenth Century

Bernard, C. *An Introduction to the Study of Experimental Medicine.* New York: Dover, 1957. (Originally published 1865.)

Bleich, A. *The Study of X-Rays.* New York: Dover, 1960.

Conant, J. *Modern Science and Modern Man.* Garden City, N.Y.: Anchor-Doubleday, 1952.

Curie, E. *Madame Curie.* New York: Pocket Books, 1973.

382 Select Bibliography

Dubos, R. *Pasteur and Modern Science.* Garden City, N.Y.: Anchor-Doubleday, 1960.
Holbrook, S. *The Golden Age of Quackery.* New York: Collier, 1962.
Virchow, R. *Disease, Life, and Man.* New York: Collier, 1962.

B. Nazi Medical War Crimes

Mitscherlich, A., and Mielke, F. *Doctors of Infamy.* New York: Schuman, 1949.
Nyiszli, M. *Auschwitz.* New York: Frederick Fell, 1960.

C. Modern Medical Problems

Lasagna, L. *The Doctor's Dilemmas,* New York: Harper & Row, 1962.
Lasagna, L. *Life, Death and the Doctor.* New York: Knopf, 1968.

Part Two: Medical School Administration

I. Selection of a Dean

Bennis, W. *The Leaning Ivory Tower.* San Francisco: Jossey-Bass, 1973.
Dingerson, M., and others. "Procedures and Costs for Hiring Academic Administrators." *Journal of Higher Education,* 1982, *53,* 63-74.
Jacobson, R. "Curtailing the Cost of Search Committees." *Chronicle of Higher Education,* June 21, 1976, p. 17.
Kaplowitz, R. *Selecting Academic Administrators: The Search Committee.* Washington, D.C.: American Council on Education, 1973.
Petersdorf, R. "The Academic Mating Game." *New England Journal of Medicine,* 1978, *298,* 1290-1294.
Sommerfield, R. "Seek and Ye Shall Find." *Journal of Higher Education,* 1974, *45,* 239.

II. Materials: New Medical Schools

American Hospital Association Guide to the Health Care Field. An annual publication of the American Hospital Association, 444 North Capitol Street, Washington, D.C.

American Medical Association (AMA) publications (for sale at AMA offices, 535 North Dearborn Street, Chicago, Ill. 60610):
Directory of Residency Training Programs. An annual publication.
Journal of the American Medical Association. A weekly publication; each December issue contains an annual report on medical education in the United States.

Association of American Medical College (AAMC) publications (for sale at AAMC offices, 1 Dupont Circle, N.W., Washington, D.C. 20036):
AAMC Curriculum Directory. An annual publication providing details on the curricula of the medical schools in the United States and Canada.
AAMC Directory of American Medical Education. An annual listing of all medical schools in the United States and Canada, including officers, departmental chairpersons, and programs.
Journal of Medical Education. A monthly publication containing articles and studies on all facets of medical education.
Medical Education. A monthly publication containing articles and studies on medical education in the United Kingdom and Ireland.
Medical School Admissions Requrements. A good general description of the nature of medical education, methods of application, and details concerning the programs of study at each accredited medical school in the United States and Canada.

U.S. Census Reports. Available from U.S. Department of Commerce, Bureau of the Census, Washington, D.C. 20233.

World Health Organization (WHO) publications (for sale at WHO Publications Centre, U.S.A., 49 Sheridan Avenue, Albany, N.Y. 12210):
The Planning of Medical Education Programs. No. 566 in the WHO Technical Report Series, 1974.

The Planning of Schools of Medicine. No. 547 in the WHO Technical Report Series, 1975.

III. The Establishment of the Forty New Medical Schools, 1960–1980

This bibliography of select articles, books, and pamphlets on the establishment of new medical schools from 1960 to 1980 is arranged by the name of the institution to which these items relate; the institutions are listed in the order in which their charter classes were enrolled. Each item in this bibliography as printed was provided by either the dean or the librarian of the respective school.

University of Kentucky College of Medicine (September 1960)

Ellis, J. H. *Medicine in Kentucky.* Lexington: University of Kentucky Press, 1977.

Jordan, W. S. "University of Kentucky College of Medicine." *Harvard Medical Alumni Bulletin,* 1959, *43,* 24–30.

"Kentucky's New College of Medicine." *Journal of the Kentucky State Medical Association,* 1960, *58,* 1199–1222.

Ransdall, G. "The University of Kentucky Medical Center Approaches Reality." *Journal of the Kentucky State Medical Association,* 1957, *55,* 301–318.

Talbert, C. G. *The University of Kentucky: the Maturing Years.* Lexington: University of Kentucky Press, 1965.

Brown University Program in Medicine (September 1963)

Galletti, P. M. "Brown University, Division of Biological and Medical Sciences." In V. W. Lippard and E. F. Purcell (Eds.), *Case Histories of Ten New Medical Schools.* New York: Josiah Macy, Jr., Foundation, 1972.

University of New Mexico School of Medicine (September 1964)

Curran, W. S. "The Impact of New School on State and Regional Applications." *Southern Rocky Mountain Medical Journal,* 1968, *65,* 31.

Fitz, R. H., and Stone, R. S. "New Medical Education in the Old Southwest." *Journal of Mount Sinai Hospital,* 1967, *34,* 302–308.

Papper, S. "A New Department of Medicine—Aims, Goals, and Methods." *Archives of Internal Medicine,* 1967, *120,* 504–509.

Michigan State University College of Medicine (September 1966)

Aronson, L. D., and Murray, R. H. "Internal Medicine Clerkship Experience in Community Hospitals." In A. Hunt and L. Weeks (Eds.), *Medical Education Since 1960: Marching to a Different Drummer.* East Lansing: Michigan State University with the W. K. Kellogg Foundation, 1979.

Hunt, A. D. "Medical Education at Michigan State University." *Clinical Research,* 1965, *13,* 375–379.

Richards, R. W., and others. "The Upper Peninsula Medical Education Program: Educating Primary Care Physicians for Rural Areas." In A. Hunt and L. Weeks (Eds.), *Medical Education Since 1960: Marching to a Different Drummer.* East Lansing: Michigan State University with the W. K. Kellogg Foundation, 1979.

Sprafka, S. A., and others. "Patient Centered Problem Solving Evaluation in Undergraduate Medical Education: Development, Management, and Theoretical Perspectives." In A. Hunt and L. Weeks (Eds.), *Medical Education Since 1960: Marching to a Different Drummer.* East Lansing: Michigan State University with the W. K. Kellogg Foundation, 1979.

Walsh, J. "Medicine at Michigan State." Parts I–IV. *Science,* 1972, *177,* 1085–1087; *178,* 36–39, 288–291, 377–380.

University of Medicine and Dentistry of New Jersey, Rutgers Medical School (September 1966)

"The Development of the College of Medicine and Dentistry of New Jersey as a State Resource for Health." *College of Medicine and Dentistry of New Jersey Journal,* November 1981, pp. 4–17.

Fox, T., and others. "Planning a Medical School Teaching Hospital in an Era of Cost Containment: The CMDNJ-Rutgers Medical School Experience." *Health Policy and Education,* 1981, *2,* 59–75.

University of Texas Medical School at San Antonio (September 1966)

Pannill, F. C. "University of Texas Medical School at San Antonio." In V. W. Lippard and E. F. Purcell (Eds.), *Case Histories of Ten New Medical Schools.* New York: Josiah Macy, Jr., Foundation, 1972.

Pennsylvania State University College of Medicine (September 1967)

Harrell, G. T. "The Pennsylvania State University, Milton S. Hershey Medical Center." In V. W. Lippard and E. F. Purcell (Eds.), *Case Histories of Ten New Medical Schools.* New York: Josiah Macy, Jr., Foundation, 1972.

University of Arizona College of Medicine (September 1967)

DuVal, M. K. "Medical Education in Arizona." *Arizona Medicine,* 1964, *21,* 501–504.
DuVal, M. K. "Basic Sciences Building—Planning and Scheduling." *Arizona Medicine,* 1965a, *22,* 471.
DuVal, M. K. "Curriculum Design—Functional and Architectural Considerations." *Arizona Medicine,* 1965b, *22,* 881, 981.
DuVal, M. K. "The Philosophy of Architectural Design." *Arizona Medicine,* 1965c, *22,* 807.
DuVal, M. K. "The Planning Team." *Arizona Medicine,* 1965d, *22,* 639.
DuVal, M. K. "Signs of Progress." *Arizona Medicine,* 1965e, *22,* 715.
DuVal, M. K. "The Timing of Faculty Recruitment." *Arizona Medicine,* 1965f, *22,* 561.

DuVal, M. K. "Clinical Facilities: Functional Design." *Arizona Medicine,* 1966a, *23,* 755.

DuVal, M. K. "A Medical Library: Personnel." *Arizona Medicine,* 1966b, *23,* 199.

DuVal, M. K. "Planning for the First Class." *Arizona Medicine,* 1966c, *23,* 377.

DuVal, M. K. "The Teaching Hospital." *Arizona Medicine,* 1966d, *23,* 597, 671.

DuVal, M. K. "The Curriculum." *Arizona Medicine,* 1968, *25,* 717, 808.

DuVal, M. K. "University of Arizona, College of Medicine." In V. W. Lippard and E. F. Purcell (Eds.), *Case Histories of Ten New Medical Schools.* New York: Josiah Macy, Jr., Foundation, 1972.

Heins, M. (Ed.). *History of the University of Arizona College of Medicine.* Tucson: College of Medicine, University of Arizona, 1980.

Kettel, L. J. "Arizona's Three Year Medical Curriculum: A Postmortem." *Journal of Medical Education,* 1979, *54,* 210–216.

Volker, J. R. *The Arizona Medical School Study.* Tucson: University of Arizona Press, 1962.

University of Hawaii John A. Burns School of Medicine (September 1967)

McDermott, J. F., and others. "Motivation for Medicine in the Seventies." *American Journal of Psychiatry,* 1973, *130,* 252–256.

Rogers, T. A., and Jones, G. B. "Johns A. Burns School of Medicine, University of Hawaii." In J. Z. Bowers and E. F. Purcell (Eds.), *New Medical Schools at Home and Abroad.* New York: Josiah Macy, Jr., Foundation, 1978.

Young, B. B. C. "Medical Training in Remote Areas: The Cultural Component." In A. Hunt and L. Weeks (Eds.), *Medical Education Since 1960: Marching to a Different Drummer.* East Lansing: Michigan State University with the W. K. Kellogg Foundation, 1979.

Mount Sinai School of Medicine (September 1968)

Barka, T., and others. "Proposed Curriculum for Mount Sinai School of Medicine." *Journal of Mount Sinai Hospital*, 1967, *34*, 366–377.
James, G. "Mount Sinai School of Medicine, City University of New York." In V. W. Lippard and E. F. Purcell (Eds.), *Case Histories of Ten New Medical Schools*. New York: Josiah Macy, Jr., Foundation, 1972.
Popper, H. "A Hospital as the Basis of a New Medical School." *Journal of Medical Education*, 1970, *45*, 571–577.
Samuelson, R. J. "Mount Sinai: How a Hospital Builds a Medical School." *Science*, 1967, *158*, 614–618.

University of California, Davis, School of Medicine (September 1968)

Tupper, C. J. "In the Beginning." In M. Merala (Ed.), *Anomalies and Curiosities in Medicine: Yearbook of UCD Medical School*. Davis: University of California, 1972.

University of California, San Diego, School of Medicine (September 1968)

Grobstein, C. "University of California, San Diego, School of Medicine." In V. W. Lippard and E. F. Purcell (Eds.), *Case Histories of Ten New Medical Schools*. New York: Josiah Macy, Jr., Foundation, 1972.
Simon, H. J. "Recruitment, Admission and Retention of Socioeconomically Disadvantaged Medical Students from Racial and Ethnic Minority Groups at UCSD School of Medicine." In A. Hunt and L. Weeks (Eds.), *Medical Education Since 1960: Marching to a Different Drummer*. East Lansing: Michigan State University with the W. K. Kellogg Foundation, 1979.

University of Connecticut School of Medicine (September 1968)

Patterson, J.W. "University of Connecticut, School of Medicine." In V. W. Lippard and E. F. Purcell (Eds.), *Case Histories of Ten New Medical Schools.* New York: Josiah Macy, Jr., Foundation, 1972.

Louisiana State University School of Medicine at Shreveport (September 1969)

Hahn, R., "A Four Year Medical School Curriculum in Family Medicine and Comprehensive Care." In A. Hunt and L. Weeks (Eds.), *Medical Education Since 1960: Marching to a Different Drummer.* East Lansing: Michigan State University with the W. K. Kellogg Foundation, 1979.

Medical College of Ohio at Toledo (September 1969)

Brooks, G. L. "Medical College of Ohio at Toledo." In V. W. Lippard and E. F. Purcell (Eds.), *Case Histories of Ten New Medical Schools.* New York: Josiah Macy, Jr., Foundation, 1972.
Sodeman, W. A., and Kemph, J. P. "Faculty Evaluation in the Community Based Medical School." In A. Hunt and L. Weeks (Eds.), *Medical Education Since 1960: Marching to a Different Drummer.* East Lansing: Michigan State University with the W. K. Kellogg Foundation, 1979.

University of Massachusetts Medical School (September 1970)

Bulger, R. J. "The Medical Center of the University of Massachusetts." In J. Z. Bowers and E. F. Purcell (Eds.), *New Medical Schools at Home and Abroad.* New York: Josiah Macy, Jr., Foundation, 1978.

University of Texas Medical School at Houston (September 1970)*

---

*No available information relating specifically to this school.

Rush Medical College of Rush University (September 1971)

Graettinger, J. S. "History of Rush Medical College." *The Pharos,*
    Summer 1973, pp. 110-112.
"Rush Medical College." *Chicago Medicine,* 1973, *76,* 261-263.

*State University of New York at Stony Brook Health Sciences
Center School of Medicine (September 1971)*

Pellegrino, E. D. "State University of New York at Stony Brook,
    Health Sciences Center." In V. W. Lippard and E. F. Purcell
    (Eds.), *Case Histories of Ten New Medical Schools.* New York:
    Josiah Macy, Jr., Foundation, 1972.

*University of Missouri Kansas City School of Medicine
(September 1971)*

Baydin, L. D. *The Harvard Business School Study of University
    of Missouri Kansas City Medical School.* Boston: Intercollegiate
    Case Clearing House, 1973.
Dimond, E. G. "A Six Year Plan for Medical Education: The Pluses,
    the Minuses, and What Might Have Been Done Differently."
    Paper presented to symposium on "Issues and Challenges: A
    Decade of Experience with Cost Effective Models of Medical
    Education," Kansas City, April 3-4, 1981.
Sirridge, M. S. "The Docent System: An Alternate Approach to
    Medical Education." *The Pharos,* Fall 1980, pp. 25-28.

*University of Nevada, Reno, School of Medicine (September
1971)*

Anderson, F. M. "Nevada's Medical School Comes of Age." *Western
    Journal of Medicine,* 1980, *133,* 526-531.
Baldwin, D. C., and Baldwin, M. A. "Interdisciplinary Education
    and Health Team Training: A Model of Learning and Service."
    In A. Hunt and L. Weeks (Eds.), *Medical Education Since 1960:
    Marching to a Different Drummer.* East Lansing: Michigan State
    University with the W. K. Kellogg Foundation, 1979.

Scully, T. J., and Smith, G. T. "School of Medical Sciences, University of Nevada, Reno." In J. Z. Bowers and E. F. Purcell (Eds.), *New Medical Schools at Home and Abroad.* New York: Josiah Macy, Jr., Foundation, 1978.

University of South Florida College of Medicine (September 1971)

Journal of the Florida Medical Association. Special Issue on University of South Florida College of Medicine. September 1981.
Smith, D. L. "College of Medicine, University of South Florida." In J. Z. Bowers and E. F. Purcell (Eds.), *New Medical Schools at Home and Abroad.* New York: Josiah Macy, Jr., Foundation, 1978.

Mayo Medical School (September 1972)

Pruitt, R. D. "Mayo Medical School." In J. Z. Bowers and E. F. Purcell (Eds.), *New Medical Schools at Home and Abroad.* New York: Josiah Macy, Jr., Foundation, 1978.

Texas Tech University School of Medicine (September 1972)

Steward, C. W., and Tyner, G. S. "School of Medicine, Texas Tech University." In J. Z. Bowers and E. F. Purcell (Eds.), *New Medical Schools at Home and Abroad.* New York: Josiah Macy, Jr., Foundation, 1978.

University of Minnesota-Duluth School of Medicine (September 1972)

Boulger, J. G. "School of Medicine, Duluth, University of Minnesota." In J. Z. Bowers and E. F. Putcell (Eds.), *New Medical Schools at Home and Abroad.* New York: Josiah Macy, Jr., Foundation, 1978.
Boulger, J. G. "Family Practice in the Predoctoral Curriculum: A Model for Success." *Journal of Family Practice,* 1980, *10,* 453–458.

University of South Alabama College of Medicine (January 1973)

Huggins, C. G., and Huggins, P. M. "College of Medicine, University of South Alabama." In J. Z. Bowers and E. F. Purcell (Eds.), *New Medical Schools at Home and Abroad.* New York: Josiah Macy, Jr., Foundation, 1978.

Southern Illinois University School of Medicine (June 1973)

Colvin, R. H., and Taylor, D. D. "Planning Student Work-Study Time in an Objectives-Based Medical Curriculum." *Journal of Medical Education,* 1978, *53,* 393–396.

Kimmich, H. M. *Innovations in Medical Education.* Carbondale: Southern Illinois University Press, 1971.

Moskoff, W., and others. *The Economic Impact of the Southern Illinois University School of Medicine on Springfield and Sangamon County.* Springfield, Ill.: Center for the Study of the Middle-Size City, 1980.

Moy, R. H. "Turf and Illinois's New Medical School." *Illinois Journal of Medicine,* 1973, *141,* 198–206.

Moy, R. H. "School of Medicine, Southern Illinois University." In J. Z. Bowers and E. F. Purcell (Eds.), *New Medical Schools at Home and Abroad.* New York: Josiah Macy, Jr., Foundation, 1978.

Moy, R. H. "Critical Values in Medical Education." *New England Journal of Medicine,* 1979, *301,* 694–697.

Silber, D. L. "The SIU Medical Curriculum: System-Wide Objectives-Based Instruction." *Journal of Medical Education,* 1978, *53,* 473–479.

Strassman, H. D., and others. "A New Concept for a Core Medical Curriculum." *Journal of Medical Education,* 1969, *44,* 170–177.

Eastern Virginia Medical School (November 1973)

Holman, G. H. "Eastern Virginia Medical School of the Eastern Virginia Medical Authority." In J. Z. Bowers and E. F. Purcell (Eds.), *New Medical Schools at Home and Abroad.* New York: Josiah Macy, Jr., Foundation, 1978.

Wright State University School of Medicine (September 1976)

Beljan, J. R. "School of Medicine, Wright State University." In J. Z. Bowers and E. F. Purcell (Eds.), *New Medical Schools at Home and Abroad.* New York: Josiah Macy, Jr., Foundation, 1978.

Lewis, W. J. "A New Concept in Medical Education: The Development of Wright State University School of Medicine." *Ohio State Journal of Medicine,* 1977, *73,* 274–278.

Uniformed Services University of the Health Sciences School of Medicine (October 1976)

Curreri, A. R. *"The Role of the USUHS." Military Medicine,* 1975, *140,* 245–250.

East Carolina University School of Medicine (September 1977)*

Northeastern Ohio Universities College of Medicine (September 1977)

Northeastern Medical Education Development Center of Ohio. *Financing the MEDCO Plan for Medical Education: The Northeastern Ohio Universities School of Medicine.* Akron: Northeastern Medical Education Development Center of Ohio, 1973a.

Northeastern Medical Education Development Center of Ohio. *A Plan for Medical Education: The Northeastern Ohio Universities School of Medicine.* Akron: Northeastern Medical Education Development Center of Ohio, 1973b.

Texas A & M University School of Medicine (September 1977)*

University of South Carolina School of Medicine (September 1977)*

*No available information relating specifically to this school.

Marshall University School of Medicine (January 1978)*

Ponce School of Medicine (January 1978)*

East Tennessee State University, Quillen-Dishner College of Medicine (September 1978)*

Oral Roberts University School of Medicine (November 1978)*

Universidad del Caribe School of Medicine (January 1979)*

School of Medicine at Morehouse College (September 1979)*

The following books are general treatments of recent trends in medical education and the establishment of new medical schools.

Bowers, J. Z., and others (Eds.,). *Medical Schools for the Modern World.* Report of a Josiah Macy, Jr., Foundation conference on "How to Start a Medical School," Bellagio, Italy, October 13–18, 1968. Baltimore: Johns Hopkins University Press, 1970.

Lee, P. V. *Medical Schools and the Changing Times: Nine Case Reports on Experimentation in Medical Education, 1950–1960.* Evanston, Ill.: Association of American Medical Colleges, 1962.

Lippard, V. W. *A Half-Century of American Medical Education, 1920–1970.* New York. Josiah Macy, Jr., Foundation, 1974.

Popper, H. (Ed.). *Trends in New Medical Schools.* (A Mount Sinai Hospital Monograph.) New York: Grune and Stratton, 1967.

Purcell, E. F. (Ed.). *Recent Trends in Medical Education.* New York: Josiah Macy, Jr., Foundation, 1976.

*No available information relating specifically to this school.

Part Three: Essential Resources for a Medical School

I. Tenure of Faculty Members

Carnegie Council on Policy Studies in Higher Education. *Faculty Bargaining in Public Higher Education.* San Francisco: Jossey-Bass, 1977.

Carnegie Foundation for the Advancement of Teaching. *The Control of the Campus: A Report on the Governance of Higher Education.* Lawrenceville, N.J.: Princeton University Press, 1982.

Clarke, C. A. "The *Yeshiva* Case: An Analysis and an Assessment of Its Potential Impact on Public Universities. *Journal of Higher Education,* 1981, *52,* 449–469.

Curran, W. J. "Dismissal of Tenured Faculty in Medicine: Income-Limitation Agreements." *New England Journal of Medicine,* 1979, *300,* 721–722.

Duryea, E. D., Fisk, R. S., and Associates. *Faculty Unions and Collective Bargaining.* San Francisco: Jossey-Bass, 1973.

Ladd, E. C., and Lipset, S. M. *Professors, Unions, and American Higher Education.* Berkeley: Carnegie Commission on Higher Education, 1973.

O'Toole, J. "Tenure: A Conscientious Objection." *Change,* June-July 1978, pp. 22–31.

Oi, W. Y. "Academic Tenure and Mandatory Retirement Under the New Law." *Science,* 1979, *206,* 1373–1378.

"Pandarus." "One's Own Primer of Academic Politics." *American Scholar,* 1973, *42,* 569–592.

Smith, B. L., and Associates. *The Tenure Debate.* San Francisco: Jossey-Bass, 1973.

Smythe, C. M., Jones, A. B., and Wilson, M. P. "Tenure in Medical Schools in the 1980s." *Journal of Medical Education,* 1982, *57,* 349–360.

Tucker, A., and Mautz, R. B. "Academic Freedom, Tenure, and Incompetence." *Educational Record,* 1982, *63,* 22–25.

II. Information and Libraries

de Sola Pool, I. "Tracking the Flow of Information." *Science,* 1983, *221,* 609–613.

Eisenstein, E. L. *The Printing Revolution in Early Modern Europe.*
    Cambridge, England: Cambridge University Press, 1983.
The Management of Information in Academic Medicine. Vols. I
    and II. Washington, D.C.: Association of American Medical
    Colleges, 1983.
Weed, L. *Medical Records, Medical Education, and Patient Care.*
    Cleveland, Ohio: Case Western Reserve University Press, 1969.

III. Teaching Hospitals

Cushman, R., and Perry, S. *Planning, Financing and Constructing
    Health Care Facilities.* Rockville, Md.: Aspen Systems, 1983.
McCullough, L. "Moral Dilemmas and Economic Realities: Ethical
    Issues in Administering a Teaching Hospital." *Journal of Med-
    ical Education,* in press.
Purcell, E. *The Role of the University Teaching Hospital: An
    International Perspective.* New York: Josiah Macy, Jr., Founda-
    tion, 1982.
Rosner, D., and others *A Once Charitable Enterprise: Hospitals
    and Health Care in Brooklyn and New York; 1885–1915.* New
    York: Cambridge University Press, 1982.

Part Four: Educational Programs for Physicians

I. History of Medical Education

Bigelow, H. *Medical Education in America.* Cambridge, England:
    Cambridge University Press, 1871.
Billings, J. "A Review of Higher Medical Education." *Bulletin of
    Institute of the History of Medicine,* 1938, *6,* 287–385. (Originally
    published 1878.)
Flexner, S., and Flexner, J. *William Henry Welch and the Heroic
    Age of American Medicine.* New York: Viking, 1941.
Haller, J. *American Medicine in Transition, 1840–1910.* Chicago:
    University of Illinois Press, 1981.
Hoehling, A. *The Great Epidemic.* Boston: Little, Brown, 1961.
Kaufman, M. *American Medical Education: The Formative Years,
    1765–1910.* Westport, Conn.: Greenwood Press, 1977.

Kevorkian, J. *The Story of Dissection.* New York: Philosophical Library, 1959.

King, L. "The Painfully Slow Progress in Medical Education." *Journal of the American Medical Association,* 1983, *249,* 270-274.

Klett, J. *The Formation of the American Medical Profession: The Role of Institutions, 1780-1860.* New Haven, Conn.: Yale University Press, 1968.

McNeill, W. *Plagues and Peoples.* Garden City, N.Y.: Anchor, 1977.

Moore, F. D. *"In Medicina, Veritas:* The Birth and Turbulent Youth of the Faculty of Medicine at Harvard College." *New England Journal of Medicine,* 1982, *307,* 917-925.

Numbers, R. (Ed.). *The Education of American Physicians: Historical Essays.* Berkeley: University of California Press, 1980.

O'Malley, C. (Ed.). *The History of Medical Education.* Berkeley: University of California Press, 1970.

Pepper, W. *Higher Medical Education: The True Interest of the Public and the Profession: An Address.* Philadelphia: Collins, 1877.

Poynter, F. (Ed.). *The Evolution of Medical Education in Britain.* London: Pitman Medical, 1966.

Puschman, T. *A History of Medical Education.* New York: Hafner, 1966. (Originally published 1891.)

Robinson, G. *Adventures in Medical Education.* New York: Commonwealth Fund, 1957.

Shapiro, H. (Ed.). *Physician to the West: Selected Writings of Daniel Drake.* Lexington: University of Kentucky Press, 1970.

Sigerist, H. *Civilization and Disease.* Chicago: University of Chicago Press, 1962.

Slaughter, F. *Semmelweis: The Conqueror of Childbed Fever.* New York: Collier, 1961.

Starr, P. *The Social Transformation of American Medicine.* New York: Basic Books, 1983.

Virchow, R. *Diseases, Life, and Man.* New York: Collier, 1962.

Welch, W. "The Relation of Yale to Medicine." *Yale Medical Journal,* November, 1901.

Welch, W. "Development of American Medicine." *Columbia University Quarterly Supplement,* December 1907.

II. Premedical Education and Selection of Medical Students

Ahrens, E., and Akins, C. "On the Need to Consider Modifications in the Premedical Education and Selection of Applicants to the Harvard Medical School: Report to the Alumni Council." Harvard Medical Alumni Bulletin, Fall 1981, pp. 21–26.

An Annotated Bibliography of Research on the MCAT. Washington, D.C.: Division of Educational Measurement and Research, Association of American Medical Colleges, 1982.

Bauman, P. "Who Shall Study Medicine?" *Journal of the American Medical Association,* 1981, *245,* 1630.

Bejar, I., and Blew, E. "Grade Inflation and the Validity of the SAT." *American Educational Research Journal,* 1981, *81,* 143-156.

Bernstein, J. "Science Education for the Non-Scientist." *The American Scholar,* Winter 1982/83, pp. 7–12.

Best, W., and others. "Multivariate Predictors in Selecting Medical Students." *Journal of Medical Education,* 1971, *46,* 43–50.

Biemiller, L. "Most Colleges Urged to Reconsider Use of Admissions Test." *Chronicle of Higher Education,* February 10, 1982, p. 9.

Blum, A. "Who Shall Study Medicine in the 1980s? One Solution to the Admissions Predicament." *Journal of the American Medical Association,* 1980, *244,* 779–780.

Bowden, G. "The Fallacy of Equal Educational Opportunity." *Educational Record,* 1981, *62,* 8–12.

Brewer, W., DuVal, M., and Davis, G. "Increasing Minority Recruitment to the Health Professions by Enlarging the Applicant Pool." *New England Journal of Medicine,* 1979, *301,* 74–76.

Bruer, J., and Warren, K. "Liberal Arts and the Premedical Curriculum." *Journal of the American Medical Association,* 1981, *245,* 364–366.

Busse, E. W., "The Interface of Premedical and Medical Education." *Duke University Letters,* April 15, 1980, pp. 1–4.

Busse, E. W. "Impact of Premedical Preparation." In *Report on the Macy Conference on Premedical Preparation and Medical School Admissions, April 24, 25, and 26, 1980.* Durham, N.C.: Duke University School of Medicine, 1981.

Dickmann, R., and others. "Medical Students from Natural Science and Nonscience Undergraduate Backgrounds: Similar Academic Performance and Residency Selection." *Journal of the American Medical Association,* 1980, *243,* 2506-2509.

Dyer, A., and Trent, P. "Noncognitive Criteria for the Selection of Medical Students." In *Report on the Macy Conference on Premedical Preparation and Medical School Admissions, April 24, 25, and 26, 1980.* Durham, N.C.: Duke University School of Medicine, 1981.

Flaherty, J. "What Are Best Criteria for Future M.D.s?" *American Medical News,* February 12, 1982, p. 25.

Friedl, E. "The Humanities and Premedical Education." In *Report on the Macy Conference on Premedical Preparation and Medical School Admissions, April 24, 25, and 26, 1980.* Durham, N.C.: Duke University School of Medicine, 1981.

Geisler, D. "Preprofessional Preparation: An Overview." In *Report on the Macy Conference on Premedical Preparation and Medical School Admissions, April 24, 25, and 26, 1980.* Durham, N.C.: Duke University School of Medicine, 1981.

Gellhorn, A. "Prescription for Premed Students." *Change,* October 1976, pp. 7, 63-64.

Gellhorn, A. "Premedical Curriculum." *Journal of Medical Education,* 1980, *55,* 616-617.

Golden, J., and others. "A Summary Description of Fifty 'Normal' White Males." *The American Journal of Psychiatry,* 1962, *119,* 48-56.

Gonzalez, N. "In Defense of Elitism." *Science,* 1981, *213,* 1.

Heath, D. "Academic Predictors of Adult Maturity and Competence." *The Journal of Higher Education,* 1977, *48,* 613-632.

Heins, M. "Medicine and Motherhood." *Journal of the American Medical Association,* 1983, *249,* 209-210.

Heins, M., and others. "Comparison of the Productivity of Women and Men Physicians." *Journal of the American Medical Association,* 1977, *237,* 2514-2518.

Hough, D., and Marder, W. "State Retention of Medical School Graduates." *Journal of Medical Education,* 1982, *57,* 505-513.

Jones, R. *Association of American Medical Colleges.* "From MCAT to M.D.: Predicting Success in Medical School." Paper presented at the American Educational Research Association meeting, New York, March 15, 1982.

Lister, J. "By the London Post: Selection of Medical Students, Occupational Mortality, and William Harvey." *New England Journal of Medicine*, 1978, *298*, 1182-1184.

Mattson, D. "Use of a Formal Decision Theory Model in the Selection of Medical Students." *Journal of Medical Education*, 1969, *44*, 964-973.

Meredith, K., Dunlap, M., and Baker, H. "Subjective and Objective Admissions Factors as Prediction of Clinical Clerkship Performance." *Journal of Medical Education*, 1982, *57*, 743-751.

Moore-West, M., and Health, D. "The Physically Handicapped Student in the Medical School: A Preliminary Study." *Journal of Medical Education*, 1982, *57*, 918-921.

Niemi, R., and Phillips, J. "On Nonscience Premedical Education: Surprising Evidence and a Call for Clarification." *Journal of Medical Education*, 1980, *55*, 194-200.

Palmer, J. "Can Meritocracy in Academe be Saved?" *Science*, 1979, *203*, 1.

Pellegrino, E. "Pruning an Old Root: Premedical Science and Medical School." *Journal of the American Medical Association*, 1980, *243*, 2518-2519.

Petersdorf, R. "Beliefs and Biases." *The Pharos*, Spring 1980, pp. 11-15.

Prewitt, K. "Usefulness of the Social Sciences." *Science*, 1981, *211*, 1.

Quinton, A. "Elitism: A British View." *The American Scholar*, Winter 1975/1976, pp. 719-732.

Reid, J. "Little Latin and Less Greek." *The Pharos*, Fall 1979, pp. 20-22.

Rhoads, P. "Premedical Students, Admissions Committees, and 'the Physician as an Educated Person'." *Journal of the American Medical Association*. 1982, *247*, 2671-2673.

Rosenberg, M. "Increasing the Efficiency of Medical School Admissions." *Journal of Medical Education*, 1973, *48*, 707-717.

Sarnacki, R. "The Predictive Value of the Premedical Grade-Point Average." *Journal of Medical Education*, 1982, *57*, 163-169.

Saxon, D. "Liberal Education in a Technological Age." *Science*, 1982, *218*, 1.

Schofield, J. "The Stork and the Competition for Medical School." *The Advisor*, 1964, *1*, 1.

Schofield, J. "The Stork, Admission to Medical School, Going to a Foreign School, and Other Hazards." *Journal of Medical Education*, 1973, *48*, 693–695.

Schofield, J. "Competition for Medical School: The Stork Revisited." *The Advisor*, 1978, *14*, 1.

Sherman, S., Tonesk, X., and Erdmann, J. "1981–82 Enrollment in U.S. Medical Schools." *Journal of Medical Education*, 1982, *57*, 495–498.

Silver, H. "Admission to Medical School." *Journal of the American Medical Association*, 1982, *248*, 1717.

Stillman, P., and others. "Students Transferring into an American Medical School: Remediating Their Deficiencies." *Journal of the American Medical Association*, 1980, *243*, 129–133.

Vaillant, H., and others (Eds.). *Report to the Alumni Council on the Need to Consider Modifications in the Premedical Education and Selection of Applicants to the Harvard Medical School.* Cambridge, Mass.: Harvard Medical School Alumni Council, 1980.

Walsh, J. "Does High School Grade Inflation Mask a More Alarming Trend?" *Science*, 1979, *203*, 982.

Weingartner, R. "Premed Students Need Broader Education." *American Medical News*, April 23–30, 1983, p. 17.

Wirtz, W. (Ed.). *On Further Examination: Report of the Advisory Panel on the SAT Score Decline.* New York: College Entrance Examination Board, 1977.

Zuckerman, H. "The Sociology of the Nobel Prizes." *Scientific American*, 1967, *217*, 25–33.

III. The M.D. Curriculum

Abrahamson, S. "Diseases of the Curriculum." *Journal of Medical Education*, 1978, *53*, 951–957.

Ausburn, L. "Educational Methods and Structure: Driving a New Chariot on the Same Old Track?" *Educational Technology*, October 1978, pp. 12–15.

Becker, H., and others. *Boys in White: Student Culture in Medical School.* New York: Irvington, 1961.

Beering, S. "The Spark Within." Commencement address at Texas

A & M University College of Medicine, College Station, Texas, June 6, 1981.

Beeson, P. "Priorities in Medical Education." *Perspectives in Biology and Medicine*, 1982, *25*, 673-687.

Black, P. "Must Physicians Treat the 'Whole Man' for Proper Medical Care?" *The Pharos*, Spring 1976, pp. 8-11.

Bunce, D. "Medical Student Participation in Academic Affairs." *British Journal of Medical Education*, 1970, *4*, 4-8.

Burke, W., and others. "An Evaluation of the Undergraduate Medical Curriculum: The Kentucky Experiment in Community Medicine." *Journal of the American Medical Association*, 1979, *241*, 2726-2730.

Cluff, L. "The Integrative Function of Physicians in Making Medical Decisions." *The Pharos*, Fall 1978, pp. 2-4.

Connars, E. "Technological Forecasting: An Overview for Educators." *Educational Technology*, February 1978, pp. 32-35.

Cooper, J. "Medical Education: Past, Present, and Future." *New England Journal of Medicine*, 1977, *297*, 941-943.

Culbert, A., Blaustein, E., and Sandson, J. "The Modular Medical Integrated Curriculum: An Innovation in Medical Education." *New England Journal of Medicine*, 1982, *306*, 1502-1504.

Denny, F. "Old Skills and the Future of Medicine." *The Pharos*, Summer 1980, pp. 26-31.

De Solla Price, D. *Science Since Babylon*. New Haven, Conn.: Yale University Press, 1961.

Dixon, M. "What Are the Deficiencies in Undergraduate Medical Education?" *Association of Canadian Medical Colleges Forum*, 1982, *15*, 4.

Dock, W. "Curiosity, Culture, and Curricula." *Journal of the American Medical Association*, 1960, *99*, 643.

Donald, J. "Knowledge Structures: Methods for Exploring Course Content." *The Journal of Higher Education*, 1983, *54*, 31-41.

Ebert, R. "Can the Education of the Physician Be Made More Rational?" *New England Journal of Medicine*, 1981, *305*, 1343-1346.

Eichna, L. "Medical School Education, 1975-1979: A Student's Perspective." *New England Journal of Medicine*, 1980, *303*, 727-734.

Engel, G. "'The Best and the Brightest': The Missing Dimension in Medical Education." *The Pharos,* Fall 1973, pp. 129–133.

Fritts, H. "Mark Van Doren and the Search for a Rational Curriculum." *The Pharos,* Fall 1977, pp. 10–12.

Funkenstein, D. *Medical Students, Medical Schools, and Society During Five Eras: Factors Affecting the Career Choices of Physicians, 1958–1976.* Cambridge, Mass.: Ballinger, 1978.

Gessner, P., Katz, L., and Schimpfhauser, F. "Sociomedical Issues in the Curriculum: A Model for Institutional Change." *Journal of Medical Education,* 1981, *56,* 987–993.

Graves, G., and Ingersol, R. "Comparison of Learning Attitudes." *Journal of Medical Education,* 1964, *39,* 100–111.

Halasz, N., and others. "Gross Anatomy Taught by a Department of Surgery." *Surgery,* 1970, *68,* 231–237.

Hamilton, J. "The McMaster Curriculum: A Critique." *British Medical Journal,* 1976, *1,* 1191–1196.

Holden, W. "The Interface Between Undergraduate and Graduate Medical Education." *Journal of the American Medical Association,* 1979, *241,* 1148–1150.

Hubbard, W. "The Educational Environment in the Large Medical School." *Journal of Medical Education,* 1967, *42,* 633–641.

Hubbard, W., Gronvall, J., and DeMuth, G. (Eds.). *The Medical School Curriculum.* Washington, D.C.: Association of American Medical Colleges, 1970.

Irby, D., and others. "A Model for the Improvement of Medical Faculty Lecturing." *Journal of Medical Education,* 1976, *51,* 403–409.

Jason, H., and Westberg, J. *Teachers and Teaching in U.S. Medical Schools.* New York: Appleton-Century-Crofts, 1982.

Kapp, M. "A New Way of Teaching Medical Students About the Law." *American College of Physicians Observer,* May 1982, pp. 11, 25.

Kulik, J., Kulik, C., and Carmichael, K. "The Keller Plan in Science Teaching." *Science,* 1974, *183,* 379–383.

Leaf, A. "The Harvard Medical Curriculum." *Harvard Medical Alumni Bulletin,* May/June 1980, pp. 4–11.

Lepore, M. *Death of the Clinician: Requiem or Reveille?* Springfield, Ill.: Thomas, 1982.

Levenson, S. "The Search for a Philosophy of Medicine." *The Pharos,* Winter 1979, pp. 2–8.

Levin, S. "Some Comments on Learning Problems in the Medical Student." *The Pharos,* Spring 1967, pp. 21–25.

Linn, B., and Zeppa, R. "Going Against the Educational Grain: Can Learning Occur Backward?" *Journal of Medical Education,* 1982, *57,* 325–327.

Loiterman, D., and Pickoff, R. "Medical Schools Without Walls: Self-Instruction Abroad." *Journal of the American Medical Association,* 1981, *246,* 1801–1803.

McKendry, J. "The Medical Student and His Clinician." *Queen's Medical Review,* 1968/1969 Annual, pp. 17–22.

McWhinney, I. "The Reform of Medical Education: A Canadian Model." *Medical Education,* 1980, *14,* 189–195.

Marton, F. "Skill as an Aspect of Knowledge." *The Journal of Higher Education,* 1979, *50,* 602–614.

Mawby, R. *Health System Out of Sync: Reform Through Health Professions Education.* Battle Creek, Mich.: The W. K. Kellogg Foundation, 1982.

Maxmen, J. "Future Forecasting and Medical Education." *Journal of Medical Education,* 1975, *50,* 34–36.

May, D. and Clark, I. "Cuckoo in the Nest: Some Comments on the Role of Sociology in the Undergraduate Medical Curriculum." *Medical Education,* 1980, *14,* 105–112.

Merton, R., and others (Eds.). *The Student-Physician: Introductory Studies in the Sociology of Medical Education.* Cambridge, Mass.: Harvard University Press, 1957.

Miller, G. "The Contribution of Research in the Learning Process." *Medical Education,* 1978, *12,* 28–31.

Mosteller, F. "Innovation and Evaluation." *Science,* 1981, *211,* 881–886.

Moy, R. "Critical Values in Medical Education." *New England Journal of Medicine,* 1979, *301,* 694–697.

Neame, R., and Powis, D. "Toward Independent Learning: Curricular Design for Assisting Students To Learn How To Learn." *Journal of Medical Education,* 1981, *56,* 886–893.

Osmond, H. "God and the Doctor." *New England Journal of Medicine,* 1980, *302,* 555–558.

Peck, C. "Increasing Patient Compliance with Prescriptions." *Journal of the American Medical Association,* 1982, *248,* 2874-2877.

Peddiwell, J. *The Saber-Tooth Curriculum: A Satire on Education.* New York: McGraw-Hill, 1939.

Petersdorf, R. "Academic Medicine: No Longer Threadbare or Genteel." *New England Journal of Medicine,* 1981, *304,* 841-843.

Piel, G. "The Medical University." *Journal of Medical Education,* 1981, *56,* 16-22.

Praiss, I. "Cost Containment Through Medical Education." *Journal of the American Medical Association,* 1980, *244,* 53-55.

Prywes, M. "A Look to the Future." *British Journal of Medical Education,* 1972, *6,* 264-267.

Ratzan, R. "On Teachers." *New England Journal of Medicine,* 1982, *306,* 1420-1422.

Regelson, W. "The Weakening of the Oslerian Tradition: The Changing Emphasis in Departments of Medicine." *Journal of the American Medical Association,* 1978, *239,* 317-319

Reynolds, R. "Medical Education—1980s." *Journal of Medical Education,* 1980, *55,* 718-719.

Rippey, R. *The Evaluation of Teaching in Medical Schools.* New York: Springer, 1981.

Rogers, D. "Some Musings on Medical Education: Is It Going Astray?" *The Pharos,* Spring 1982, pp. 11-14.

Rosinski, E., and Blanton, W. "A System of Cataloguing and the Subject Matter Content of a Medical School Curriculum." *Journal of Medical Education,* 1962, *37,* 1092-1100.

Ross, S. *Learning and Discovery.* New York: Gordon and Breach, 1981.

Rushmer, R., and Huntsman, L. "Biomedical Engineering." *Science,* 1970, *167,* 840-844.

Sanders, C. "On Experiments in Medical Education." *New England Journal of Medicine,* 1977, *297,* 1347-1349.

Schwarz, M. "Medical Self Perception: The Mirror Image." Address to Colorado Medical Society, September 23, 1982.

Schwarz, M. R., and others. "Communication Satellites in Health Education and Health Care Provision." *Journal of the American Medical Association,* 1983, *250,* 636-639.

Shapiro, E., and Lowenstein, L. (Eds.). *Becoming a Physician: Development of Values and Attitudes in Medicine.* Cambridge, Mass.: Ballinger, 1979.

Shortt, S. "History in the Medical Curriculum: A Clinical Perspective." *Journal of the American Medical Association,* 1982, *248,* 79-81.

Sieker, H. "A New Curriculum for Medical Education." *Clinical Research,* 1965, *13,* 3-6.

Simon, H. "Applying Information Technology to Organizational Design." *Public Administration Review,* 1973, *33,* 268-278.

Simpson, M. *Medical Education: A Critical Approach.* Woburn, Mass.: Butterworth, 1972.

Smythe, C., and others. "Departmental Review in Medical Schools: Focus and Functions." *Journal of Medical Education,* 1979, *54,* 284-293.

Somers, A. "Moderating the Rise in Health-Care Costs: A Pragmatic Beginning." *New England Journal of Medicine,* 1982, *307,* 944-947.

Sorensen, A. "A Note on Medical Education at Cambridge and Rochester." *Medical Review of University of Rochester,* Fall 1980, pp. 14-16.

Stemmler, E. J. "Medical Education-Adaptation to Change." *Health Affairs,* Univ. of Pennsylvania, Fall/Winter, 1983; pp. 12-17.

Strassman, H., Taylor, D., and Scoles, J. "A New Concept for a Core Medical Curriculum." *Journal of Medical Education,* 1969, *44,* 170-177.

Swazey, J., and Fox, R. "Medical Sociology." *Journal of the American Medical Association,* 1982, *247,* 2959-2962.

Tosteson, D. "Learning in Medicine." *New England Journal of Medicine,* 1979, *301,* 690-694.

Walbroehl, G., and others. "Family Practice Undergraduate Education." *Journal of the American Medical Association,* 1981, *245,* 1552-1554.

Waltz, J., and Inbau, F. *Medical Jurisprudence.* New York: MacMillan, 1971.

Welch, C. "Cost Containment." *Archives of Surgery,* 1980, *115,* 571-572.

Wescoe, W. "Tomorrow's Medicine." *The New Physician,* November 1967, pp. 293-296.

Wright, R. "Nutritional Assessment." *Journal of the American Medical Association,* 1980, *244,* 559-560.

IV. Teaching Clinical Medicine

Blois, M. "Clinical Judgment and Computers." *New England Journal of Medicine,* 1980, *303,* 192-197.

Bressler, D. "Are Medical Schools Neglecting Clinical Skills?" *Journal of the American Medical Association,* 1981, *245,* 1637-1638.

Cassileth, B. "The Care of the Patient, Revisited." *Archives of Internal Medicine,* 1982, *142,* 1087-1088.

Cousins, N. "The Physician as Communicator." *Journal of the American Medical Association,* 1982, *248,* 587-589.

Eddy, D., and Clanton, C. "The Art of Diagnosis: Solving the Clinicopathological Exercise." *New England Journal of Medicine,* 1982, *306,* 1263-1268.

Engel, G. "The Education of the Physician for Clinical Observation." *The Journal of Nervous and Mental Disease,* 1972, *154,* 159-163.

Engel, G. " 'The Best and the Brightest': The Missing Dimension in Medical Education." *The Pharos,* Spring 1973, pp. 129-133.

Engel, G. "The Prerequisites for Graduate Medical Education." *Bulletin of the New York Academy of Science,* 1974, *50,* 1186-1193.

Engel, G. "The Information Explosion in the Education of the Medical Student: An Historical Analysis." *The Pharos,* Fall 1975, pp. 21-24.

Engel, G. "Are Medical Schools Neglecting Clinical Skills?" *Journal of the American Medical Association,* 1976, *236,* 861-863.

Engel, G. "The Care of the Patient: Art or Science?" *The Johns Hopkins Medical Journal,* 1977, *140,* 222-232.

Engel, G., and Morgan, W. *Interviewing the Patient.* Philadelphia: Saunders, n.d.

Gonnella, J., and Veloski, J. "The Impact of Early Specialization on the Clinical Competence of Residents." *New England Journal of Medicine,* 1982, *306,* 275-277.

Gordon, H. "Advice to Medical Students Preparing for Clinical Clerkships." *The Pharos,* Spring 1979, pp. 9–16.

Grosse, M., Cruft, G., and Blaisdell, R. "The American Board of Surgery In-Training Examination." *Archives of Surgery,* 1980, *115,* 654–657.

Heimbach, D. "Why the Clinical Clerkship? A Statement to Students." *The Pharos,* Summer 1976, pp. 103–105.

Irby, D., and Rakestraw, P. "Evaluating Clinical Teaching in Medicine." *Journal of Medical Education,* 1981, *56,* 181–186.

Jewett, L., Greenberg, L., and Goldberg, R. "Teaching Residents How to Teach: A One-Year Study." *Journal of Medical Education,* 1982, *57,* 361–366.

Lindenmuth, N., Stone, A., and Donaldson, M. "The Effect of Third-Year Clinical Clerks on Physician Productivity in a Primary Care Practice." *Journal of Medical Education,* 1978, *53,* 357–359.

McGuire, L. "Unintended Secrets of an Internship Interviewer." *The Pharos,* Fall 1975, pp. 169–171.

Meier, R., Perkowski, L., and Wynne, C. "A Method for Training Simulated Patients." *Journal of Medical Education,* 1982, *57,* 535–540.

Morgan, W., Engel, G., and Wria, M. "The General Clerkship: A Course Designed to Teach the Clinical Approach to the Patient." *Journal of Medical Education,* 1972, *47,* 556–563.

Mumford, E. *Interns: From Students to Physicians.* Cambridge, Mass.: Harvard University Press, 1970.

Pawlson, L., Schroeder, S., and Donaldson, M. "Medical Student Instructional Costs in a Primary Clerkship." *Journal of Medical Education,* 1979, *54,* 551–555.

Wolf, S. "Ward Rounds: Teaching the Art of Medicine." *The Pharos,* Winter 1982, p. 36.

V. Three-Year Curriculum

"Getting Off Fast Track Sounds Good to Most." *College of Medicine Journal,* Ohio State University, 1979, *30,* 8–9.

Hejna, W. "It Takes Four Years . . . Reversing the Acceleration Trend." *Journal of the American Medical Association,* 1975, *234,* 387–388.

Stetten, D. "Projected Changes in Medical School Curriculum." *Science*, 1971, *174*, 1303-1306.

"The Three-Year Medical School Curriculum: What's Happening." *Medical World News*, December 20, 1974, pp. 52-53.

VI. Programmed Instruction

Barrett, G. "The Computer and Clinical Judgment." *New England Journal of Medicine*, 1982, *307*, 493-494.

Fraley, L., and Vargas, E. "Academic Tradition and Instructional Technology." *Journal of Higher Education*, 1975, *46*, 1-16.

Gibbons, J., Kincheloe, W., and Down, K. "Tutored Videotape Instruction: A New Use of Electronics Media in Education." *Science*, 1977, *195*, 1139-1146.

Marion, R., and others. "Computer-Based Instruction in Basic Medical Science Education." *Journal of Medical Education*, 1982, *57*, 521-526.

Miller, R., Pople, H., and Myers, G. "Internist 1, An Experimental Computer Based Diagnostic Consultant for General Internal Medicine." *New England Journal of Medicine*, 1982, *307*, 468--476.

"Now That's a Different Way to Go Through Medical School." *College of Medicine Journal* (Ohio State University), 1971, *21*, 2-5.

Postlethwait, S. *The Audio-Tutorial Approach to Learning*. Minneapolis: Burgess, 1964.

Small, P. "Science Education: Simulation Methods for Teaching Process and Content." *Biomedical Education*, 1974, *33*, 2008-2013.

Weisman, R., and Shapiro, D. "Personalized System of Instruction (Keller Method) for Medical School Biochemistry." *Journal of Medical Education*, 1973, *48*, 934-938.

VII. Teaching Geriatrics

Dans, P., and Kerr, M. "Gerontology and Geriatrics in Medical Education." *New England Journal of Medicine*, 1979, *300*, 228-232.

Duthie, E., Priefer, B., and Gambert, S. "The Teaching Nursing Home: One Approach." *Journal of the American Medical Association*, 1982, *247*, 2787–2788.

Goodwin, J., and others. "Association Between Nutritional Status and Cognitive Functioning in a Healthy Elderly Population." *Journal of the American Medical Association*, 1983, *249*, 2917–2921.

Johnson, J., and others (Eds.). *Incorporating Geriatric Knowledge in Medical Education Programs*. Washington, D.C.: Association of American Medical Colleges, 1982.

Katz, S., and others. "Active Life Expectancy." *New England Journal of Medicine*, 1983, *309*, 1217–1223.

Portnoi, V. "What is a Geriatrician?" *Journal of the American Medical Association*, 1980, *243*, 123–125.

Schneider, E., and Brody, J. "Aging, Natural Death, and the Compression of Morbidity: Another View." *New England Journal of Medicine*, 1983, *309*, 854–855.

Somers, A. "Long-Term Care for the Elderly and Disabled: New Health Priority." *New England Journal of Medicine*, 1982, *307*, 221–226.

VIII. Evaluation of Student Performance

American Association of University Professors. "Statement on Teaching Evaluation." *American Association of University Professors Bulletin*, Summer 1974, 168–170.

Barrett-Conner, E. "Whither National Boards?" *New England Journal of Medicine*, 1980, *303*, 1356–1357.

Canaday, S., Mendelson, M., and Hardin, J. "The Effect of Timing on the Validity of Student Ratings." *Journal of Medical Education*, 1978, *53*, 958–964.

Eckenhoff, J. "Should the Pass-Fail System Be Abolished?" *The Pharos*, Fall 1980, pp. 20–25.

Gessner, P. "Evaluation of Instruction." *Science*, 1973, *180*, 566–570.

Holden, W., and Levit, E. "Medical Education, Licensure, and the National Board of Medical Examiners." *New England Journal of Medicine*, 1980, *303*, 1357–1360.

Hubbard, J. *Measuring Medical Education.* (2nd ed.) Philadelphia: Lea and Febiger, 1971.

Hubbard, J. (Ed.). "Examinations and Their Place in Medical Education and Educational Research." *Journal of Medical Education,* 1966, *41* (Part 2), 1–69.

Irby, D., and others. "Legal Guidelines for Evaluating and Discussing Medical Students." *New England Journal of Medicine,* 1981, *304,* 180–184.

Jason, H., and Westberg, J. "Toward a Rational Grading Policy." *New England Journal of Medicine,* 1979, *301,* 607–610.

Katz, A. "More on Pass/Fail." *New England Journal of Medicine,* 1980, *303,* 1182.

Kennedy, W., Kelley, P., and Saffran, M. "Use of NBME Examinations to Assess Retention of Basic Science Knowledge." *Journal of Medical Education,* 1981, *56,* 167–173.

Levine, H. "Competency Based Evaluation in Medical Education." *Journal of Medical Education,* 1978, *53,* 82.

Linn, B., and Zeppa, R. "Measuring Performance in the Surgical Clerkship." *Journal of Medical Education,* 1974, *49,* 601–604.

Linn, B., and others. "Where National Board Examinations Pass and Fail in Evaluating Knowledge of Surgical Clerks." *Journal of Surgical Research,* 1979, *26,* 97–100.

McGuire, C. "A Process Approach to the Construction and Analysis of Medical Examinations." *Journal of Medical Education,* 1973, *38,* 556–563.

Maeroff, G. "'Pass-Fail' Grades Called Drawback." *New York Times,* November 11, 1973, p. 10.

Millar, R. "Examania—North American Style." *British Medical Journal,* 1979, *1,* 1408–1410.

Moyer, E., and Cohen, M. "Prediction of Medical School Achievement Based on the Performance of Ten Classes." *The Boston Medical Quarterly,* September 1964.

O'Donnell, M. "NBME Part I Examination: Possible Explanations for Performance Based on Personality Type." *Journal of Medical Education,* 1982, *57,* 868–870.

Rippey, R. *The Evaluation of Teaching in Medical Schools.* New York: Springer, 1981.

Sandifer, M. "The Norm-Referenced Examination." *Journal of Medical Education*, 1978, *53*, 81.

Scott, L., and others. "The Effects of Commercial Coaching for the NBME Part I Examination." *Journal of Medical Education*, 1980, *55*, 733–742.

Wigton, R. "The Effects of Student Personal Characteristics on Evaluation of Clinical Performance." *Journal of Medical Education*, 1980, *55*, 423–427.

IX. Humanism in Medicine

Banks, S., and Vastyan, E. "Humanistic Studies in Medical Education." *Journal of Medical Education*, 1973, *48*, 560–564.

Burrows, A. "A Medical Student on Call." *Journal of the American Medical Association*, 1983, *249*, 1128.

Collins, F. (Ed.). "The Medical Dilemma: Professional Demands and Personal Needs." *The Pharos*, Spring 1978, pp. 29–34.

Falk, L., Page, B., and Vesper, W. "Human Values and Medical Education From the Perspectives of Health Care Delivery." *Journal of Medical Education*, 1973, *48*, 152–157.

Fine, V., and Therrien, M. "Empathy in the Doctor-Patient Relationship: Skill Training for Medical Students." *Journal of Medical Education*, 1977, *52*, 752–757.

Glick, S. "Humanistic Medicine in a Modern Age." *New England Journal of Medicine*, 1981, *304*, 1036–1038.

Rogers, W., and Barnard, D. (Eds.). *Nourishing the Humanistic in Medicine: Interactions with the Social Sciences.* Pittsburgh: University of Pittsburgh, 1979.

The Value of the Humanities in Public Life and Education: A Summary Report. Report of Forum on Colorado Humanities Program, Denver, May 27, 1982.

X. Medical Ethics

"Beyond Sensitivity Training: Education in Ethics Essential for Future Physicians." *Medlines*, September 1982, pp. 6–7.

Chapman, C. "On the Definition and Teaching of the Medical Ethic." *New England Journal of Medicine*, 1979, *301*, 630–634.

Clements, C., and Sider, R. "Medical Ethics' Assault Upon Medical Values." *Journal of the Association of the American Medical Association*, 1983, *250*, 2011–2015.

Clouser, K. "Medical Ethics: Some Uses and Limitations." *New England Journal of Medicine*, 1975, *293*, 384–387.

Inglefinger, F. "The Unethical in Medical Ethics." *Annals of Internal Medicine*, 1975, *83*, 264–269.

Kass, L. "Professing Ethically." *Journal of the American Medical Association*, 1983, *249*, 1305–1310.

Mitscherlich, A. *Doctors of Infamy: The Story of the Nazi Medical Crimes*. New York: Schuman, 1949.

Nyiszli, M. *Auschwitz: A Doctor's Eyewitness Account*. New York: Fell, 1960.

Pellegrino, E., and McElhinney, T. *Teaching Ethics, The Humanities, and Human Values in Medical Schools: A Ten-Year Overview*. Washington, D.C.: Institute on Human Values in Medicine Society for Health and Human Values, 1981.

Schafer, A. "The Ethics of the Randomized Clinical Trial." *New England Journal of Medicine*, 1982, *307*, 719–724.

Siegler, M. "Teaching Clinical Ethics at the Bedside." *Journal of the American Medical Association*, 1978, *239*, 951–956.

XI. Student Adjustment to Medical School

Coombs, R. *Mastering Medicine: Professional Socialization in Medical School*. New York: Free Press, 1978.

Coombs, R., and Vincent, C. (Eds.). *Psychosocial Aspects of Medical Training*. Springfield, Ill.: Thomas, 1971.

Knight, J. *Doctor-To-Be: Coping with the Trials and Triumphs of Medical School*. New York: Appleton-Century-Crofts, 1981.

XII. Stress: Student and Physician Impairment

Blackwell, B. "Medical Education: Old Stresses and New Directions." *The Pharos*, Spring 1977, pp. 26–30.

Carey, R. "Doctors Who Commit Suicide." *The Washington Post*, April 23, 1978, p. 12.

Earley, L., and Johnson, D. "Medical Student Health." *Journal of Medical Education,* 1969, *44,* 36–45.

Gerber, L. "The Search for Clinical Role Models As a Way of Coping With Clerkship Stress." *Journal of Medical Education,* 1979, *54,* 659–661.

Grover, P., and Smith, D. "Academic Anxiety, Locus of Control and Achievement in Medical School." *Journal of Medical Education,* 1981, *56,* 727–736.

Hales, R. "Physician Burnout." *American Medical News,* July 31, 1981, pp. 3–12.

Holmes, T., and Rahe, R. "The Social Readjustment Rating Scale." *Journal of Psychosomatic Research,* 1967, *11,* 213–217.

Huebner, L., Royer, J., and Moore, J. "The Assessment and Remediation of Dysfunctional Stress in Medical School." *Journal of Medical Education,* 1981, *56,* 547–558.

Kirkland, J. "The Medical Student as a Loner." *Journal of the American Medical Association,* 1970, *213,* 278–279.

McCue, J. "The Effects of Stress on Physicians and Their Medical Practice." *New England Journal of Medicine,* 1982, *306,* 458–463.

Maeroff, G. "Stresses Are the Common Denomination Among Medical School Students." *The New York Times,* November 17, 1976, p. B6.

Marshall, R. "Measuring the Medical School Learning Environment." *Journal of Medical Education,* 1978, *53,* 98–104.

Miller, G., Miller, E., and Peck, O. "Medical Student Needs Assessment and Student Affairs Programming." *Journal of Medical Education,* 1981, *56,* 518–520.

Okie, S. "The Shock of Learning to Become a Doctor." *Washington Post,* April 30, 1978, pp. B1–B5.

Palarea, E. "It's Time to Eliminate the 'Conspiracy of Silence' Pertaining to Impairment." *Federation of State Medical Boards Bulletin,* March 1982, pp. 74–76.

Rabkin, J., and Struening, E. "Life Events, Stress, and Illness." *Science,* 1976, *194,* 1013–1020.

Rosenberg, D., and Silver, H. "Medical Student Abuse." *Journal of the American Medical Association,* 1984, *251,* 739–742.

Scheiber, S., and Doyle, B. *The Impaired Physician.* New York: Plenum, 1983.

Shore, J. "The Impaired Physician: Four Years After Probation." *Journal of the American Medical Association,* 1982, *248,* 3127–3130.

Steppacher, R., and Mausner, J. "Suicide in Male and Female Physicians." *Journal of the American Medical Association,* 1974, *228,* 323–328.

Thomas, C. "What Becomes of Medical Students: The Dark Side." *The Johns Hopkins Medical Journal,* 1976, *138,* 185–195.

Thoreson, R. "The Professor at Risk." *Journal of Higher Education,* 1984, *55,* 56–72.

XIII. Graduate Medical Education

Campbell, J. "The Internship: Origins, Evolution, and Confusion." *Journal of the American Medical Association,* 1964, *189,* 273–278.

Curran, J. "Internships and Residencies: Historical Background and Current Trends." *Journal of Medical Education,* 1959, *34,* 873.

Federman, D. "Will Pass/Fail Pass?" *New England Journal of Medicine,* 1978, *299,* 43–44.

Girard, D., and others. "Survival of the Medical Internship." *Forum on Medicine,* July 1980, pp. 460–463.

Kane, R., and others. "The Future Need for Geriatric Manpower in the U.S." *New England Journal of Medicine,* 1980, *302,* 1327–1332.

Levit, E., and Holden, W. "Specialty Board Certification Rates." *Journal of the American Medical Association,* 1978, *239,* 407–412.

Mason, H. "Effectiveness of Student Aid Programs Tied to a Service Commitment." *Journal of Medical Education,* 1971, *46,* 575–583.

Mason, H. "Medical School, Residency, and Eventual Practice Location." *Journal of the American Medical Association,* 1975, *233,* 49–52.

Moss, T., Deland, E., and Maloney, J. "Selection of Medical Students for Graduate Training: Pass/Fail Versus Grades." *New England Journal of Medicine,* 1978, *299,* 25–27.

Petersdorf, R. "The Doctors' Dilemma." *New England Journal of Medicine*, 1978, *299*, 628–634.

Sackett, D. "The Increasing Dispersion of Specialists." *New England Journal of Medicine*, 1980, *303*, 1058–1060.

Schwartz, W., and others. "The Changing Geographic Distribution of Board Certified Physicians." *New England Journal of Medicine*, 1980, *303*, 1032–1038.

Stein, L. "Education of Residents." *Journal of the American Medical Association*, 1981, *246*, 1299.

Steinwachs, D., and others. "Changing Patterns of Graduate Medical Education." *New England Journal of Medicine*, 1982, *306*, 10–14.

Tardiff, K. "The Effect of Pass/Fail on the Selection and Performance of Residents." *Journal of Medical Education*, 1980a, *55*, 656–661.

Tardiff, K. "Views of Residency Directors on Pass/Fail." *New England Journal of Medicine*, 1980b, *302*, 972.

Task Force on Graduate Medical Education, Association of American Medical Colleges. *Graduate Medical Education: Proposals for the Eighties*. Washington, D.C.: Association of American Medical Colleges, 1980.

Thier, S., and Berliner, R. "Manpower Policy: Base It On Facts, Not Opinions." *New England Journal of Medicine*, 1978, *299*, 1305–1312.

Veloski, J., and others. "Relationships Between Performance in Medical School and First Postgraduate Year." *Journal of Medical Education*, 1979, *54*, 909–916.

Wilbur, R. "Progress in Graduate Medical Education." *New England Journal of Medicine*, 1940, *114*, 1141–1146, 1146–1147, 1147–1151.

XIV. Continuing Medical Education

Baue, A. "Why Recertification?" *Archives of Surgery*, 1980, *115*, 11–14.

Dryer, B. (Ed.). "Lifetime Learning for Physicians: Principles, Practices, and Proposals." *Journal of Medical Education*, 1972, *37* (Part 2), 1–134.

Ell, S. "Five Hundred Years of Specialty Certification and Compulsory Continuing Medical Education, Venice 1300–1801." *Journal of the American Medical Association*, 1984, *251*, 752–753.

Houle, C. *Continuing Learning in the Professions*. San Francisco: Jossey-Bass, 1980.

Oetting, G. "Continuing Medical Education: Pro and Con." *American Medical News*, December 25, 1981, p. 4.

Ohliger, J. "Continuing Education for Professionals: Voluntary or Mandatory?" *Journal of Higher Education*, 1982, *53*, 593–598.

Relman, A. "Recertification: Will We Retreat?" *New England Journal of Medicine*, 1979, *301*, 778–779.

Sanazaro, P. "Limitations in Physician Performance Evaluation." *Federation Bulletin*, 1978, *65*, 195–204.

Sibley, J., and others. "A Randomized Trial of Continuing Medical Education." *New England Journal of Medicine*, 1982, *306*, 511–515.

Suter, E., and others. "Continuing Education for Health Professionals: Proposals for a Definition of Quality." *Journal of Medical Education*, 1981, *56*, 687–707.

XV. Research and Scholarship

Braunwald, E. "Can the Medical School Remain the Optimal Site for the Conduct of Clinical Investigation?" *Journal of Clinical Investigation*, 1975, *56*, i–vi.

Carter, C. *Higher Education for the Future*. Oxford, England: Blackwell, 1980.

Friedrich, R., and Michalak, S. "Why Doesn't Research Improve Teaching?" *Journal of Higher Education*, 1983, *54*, 145–163.

Highet, G. "The Scholarly Life." *The American Scholar*, 1972, *41*, 522–529.

Linsky, A., and Straus, M. "Student Evaluations, Research Productivity, and Eminence of College Faculty." *Journal of Higher Education*, 1975, *46*, 89–102.

Sample, S. "Inherent Conflict Between Research and Education." *Educational Record*, 1972, *53*, 17–22.

Stetten, D. "High-Powered Research and the Microscopic Viewpoint." *Journal of Medical Education*, 1981, *56*, 3–7.

XVI. Learning

Bruner, J., Goodnow, J., and Austin, G. *A Study of Thinking.* New York: Wiley, 1956.

Chase, W., and Ericsson, K. *Cognitive Skills and Their Acquisition.* Hillsdale, N.J.: Erlbaum, 1981.

Cross, K. P. *Accent on Learning: Improving Instruction and Reshaping the Curriculum.* San Francisco: Jossey-Bass, 1976.

Daedalus. Special issue on intellect and imagination, Spring 1980.

Ericsson, K., and Chase, W. "Exceptional Memory." *American Scientist,* 1982, *70,* 607–615.

Hunt, E. "On the Nature of Intelligence." *Science,* 1983, *219,* 141–146.

Piaget, J. *The Psychology of Intelligence.* New York: Harcourt Brace Jovanovich, 1950.

Puff, C. (Ed.). *Memory Organization and Structures.* New York: Academic Press, 1979.

References

American Medical Association and Association of American Medical Colleges. "Joint Statement on Health Manpower." *Journal of Medical Education,* 1968, *43,* 1009–1010.

American Medical Association. *Directory of Residency Training Programs.* Chicago: American Medical Association, annual publication.

American Medical Association. *Profiles of Medical Practice, 1977.* Chicago: American Medical Association, 1977.

American Medical Association Council on Medical Education. "Fifty-Ninth Annual Report on Medical Education." *Journal of the American Medical Association,* 1959, *171,* 1507–1579.

American Medical Association Council on Medical Education and Hospitals. "Policy on Foreign Medical Graduates." *Journal of the American Medical Association,* 1960, *172,* 1045.

American Medical Association Newsletter, July 26, 1982, p. 4.

Anderson, J., and Graham, S. "A Problem in Medical Education: Is There an Information Overload?" *Medical Education,* 1980, *14,* 4–7.

419

Association of Academic Health Sciences Library Directors. *Annual Statistics Medical School Libraries in the United States and Canada.* (4th ed.) Houston: Houston Academy of Medicine, Texas Medical Center, 1980-81.

"Approved Examining Boards in Medical Specialties." *Journal of the American Medical Association,* 1949, *141,* 63-89.

Arey, L. *Northwestern University Medical School, 1859-1959.* Evanston, Ill.: Northwestern University Press, 1959.

Association of American Colleges. *A Search for Quality and Coherence in Baccalaureate Education.* Washington, D.C.: Association of American Colleges, 1983.

Association of American Medical Colleges. "Proceedings of the Association of American Medical Colleges for 1957." *Journal of Medical Education,* 1958, *33,* 63-66.

Association of American Medical Colleges. *Association of American Medical Colleges Directory of American Medical Education, 1960-1961.* Washington, D.C.: Association of American Medical Colleges, 1960.

Association of American Medical Colleges. *Association of American Medical Colleges Curriculum Directory, 1973-74.* Washington, D.C.: Association of American Medical Colleges, 1973.

Association of American Medical Colleges. *Association of American Medical Colleges Curriculum Directory, 1980-1981.* Washington, D.C.: Association of American Medical Colleges, 1980a.

Association of American Medical Colleges. *Association of American Medical Colleges Directory of American Medical Education, 1980-1981.* Washington, D.C.: Association of American Medical Colleges, 1980b.

Association of American Medical Colleges. *Graduate Medical Education: Proposals for the Eighties.* Washington, D.C.: Association of American Medical Colleges, 1980c.

Association of American Medical Colleges. *Association of American Medical Colleges Directory of American Medical Education, 1981-1982.* Washington, D.C.: Association of American Medical Colleges, 1981.

Association of American Medical Colleges. *Academic Information in the Academic Health Sciences Center: Roles for the Library in*

Information Management. Washington, D.C.: Association of American Medical Colleges, 1982a.

Association of American Medical Colleges. *Association of American Medical Colleges Curriculum Directory, 1982–1983.* Washington, D.C.: Association of American Medical Colleges, 1982b.

Association of American Medical Colleges. *Medical School Admissions Requirements.* Washington, D.C.: Association of American Medical Colleges, 1982c.

Association of American Medical Colleges. *Report on Medical School Faculty Salaries.* Washington, D.C.: Association of American Medical Colleges, 1982d.

Association of American Medical Colleges. *Medical School Admissions Requirements.* Washington, D.C.: Association of American Medical Colleges, 1983.

Association of American Medical Colleges Committee on the Expansion of Medical Education. "A Bicentennial Anniversary Program for the Expansion of Medical Education." *Journal of Medical Education,* 1971, *46*, 105–116.

Association of American Medical Colleges Committee on the Financing of Medical Education. "Undergraduate Medical Education: Elements, Objectives, and Costs." *Journal of Medical Education,* 1974, *49*, 101–128.

Association of American Medical Colleges Council of Teaching Hospitals. Annual Survey of resident stipends. Unpublished data, n.d.

Association of American Medical Colleges Division of Educational Measurement and Research. Unpublished data on U.S. medical school enrollments for 1980–1981, October 10, 1980.

Association of American Medical Colleges Division of Operational Studies. Unpublished data, 1961, 1970, 1980.

Association of American Medical Colleges Division of Student Services. Unpublished data on national applicant pool and entering class statistics for 1978–1982, November 1, 1982.

Awad, W., Harrington, W., and Pepper, E. "The Ph.D. to M.D. Program." *New England Journal of Medicine,* 1979, *301*, 863–867.

Bane, F. *Physicians for a Growing America.* DHEW Pub. No. (PHS) 709. Washington, D.C.: U.S. Department of Health, Education and Welfare, 1959.

Barrows, H. *Simulated Patients (Programmed Patients)*. Springfield, Ill.: Thomas, 1971.

Barrows, H. "Problem-Based, Self-Directed Learning." *Journal of the American Medical Association*, 1982, *250*, 3077–3080.

Bayne-Jones, S. *Final Report of the Secretary's Consultants on Medical Research and Education*. Washington, D.C.: U.S. Department of Health, Education and Welfare, 1958.

Beran, R., and Krimer, R. *Study of the Three-Year Curricula in the U.S. Medical Schools*. Washington, D.C.: Association of American Medical Colleges, 1978.

Berger, S., and Roth, C. "Prospective Payment and the University Hospital." *New England Journal of Medicine*, 1984, *310*, 316–318.

Bickel, J., and others. "The Role of M.D.-Ph.D. Training in Increasing The Supply of Physician-Scientists." *New England Journal of Medicine*, 1981, *304*, 1265–1268.

Billings, F., and Spickard, A. "Alcoholism in a Medical School Faculty." *New England Journal of Medicine*, 1981, *305*, 1646–1648.

Bloomquist, H. "The Status and Needs of Medical School Libraries in the United States." *Journal of Medical Education*, 1963, *38*, 145–148.

Bonner, T. *American Doctors and German Universities: A Chapter in International Intellectual Relations, 1870–1874*. Lincoln: University of Nebraska Press, 1963.

Booker, H. "University Education and Applied Science." *Science*, 1963, *141*, 486–557.

Bowers, J. "Admission to Medical Education in Ten Countries." *Danish Medical Bulletin*, 1980, *27* (Supplement to No. 1), 29–31.

Boyer, E. *High School: A Report on Secondary Education in America*. New York: Harper & Row, 1983.

Bradford, W., and Schofield, J. "Survey of Required Clerkship Experiences in Internal Medicine." Unpublished paper, 1983.

Braunwald, E. "Can the Medical School Remain the Optimal Site for the Conduct of Clinical Investigations?" *Journal of Clinical Investigation*, 1975, *56*, i–vi.

British Information Service. *Education in Britain*, 1979, *15*, (whole issue).

Broad, W. "Journals: Fearing the Electronic Future." *Science*, 1982, *216*, 964–968.

Broad, W., and Wade, N. *Betrayers of the Truth: Fraud and Deceit in the Halls of Science*. New York: Simon & Schuster, 1983.

Bronson, G. "New Medical Schools in Carribean Provoke Controversy in U.S." *The Wall Street Journal,* June 19, 1979, pp. 1, 20.

Bureau of Health Manpower. *Selected Tables on Basic Projections of the Supply of Physicians, 1977.* BHM Report No. 77-80. Washington, D.C.: U.S. Department of Health and Human Services, 1977.

Burn, B. *Admission to Medical Education in Ten Countries.* New York: International Council for Education Development, 1978.

Butler, P., Bentley, J., and Knapp, R. "Today's Teaching Hospitals: Old Stereotypes and New Realities." *Annals of Internal Medicine,* 1980, *93,* 614-618.

Califano, J. "The Government-Medical Education Partnership." *Journal of Medical Education,* 1979, *54,* 19-24.

"California Considering Action to Deal with a Physician Surplus." *American Medical News,* 1981, *24,* 11.

Carnegie Commission on Higher Education. *Higher Education and the Nation's Health: Policies for Medical and Dental Education.* New York: McGraw-Hill, 1970.

Carnegie Council on Policy Studies in Higher Education. *Progress and Problems in Medical and Dental Education: Federal Support Versus Federal Control.* San Francisco: Jossey-Bass, 1976a.

Carnegie Council on Policy Studies in Higher Education. *A Classification of Institutes of Higher Education.* (Rev. ed.) Berkeley, Calif.: Carnegie Foundation for the Advancement of Teaching, 1976b.

Carter, C. *Higher Education for the Future.* Oxford: Blackwell, 1980.

Case Western Reserve School of Medicine. "Call for Curriculum Changes." *Medline,* January 1983, p. 6.

Castleton, K. "Are We Building Too Many Medical Schools?" *Journal of the American Medical Association,* 1971, *216,* 1989-1992.

Chapman, C. "The Flexner Report." *Daedalus,* 1974, *103,* 105.

Charles, L. "Implications of Off-Shore Medical Schools in the Commonwealth Caribbean." *Education medica y salud,* 1979, *13,* 42-59.

Chesney, A. *The Johns Hopkins Hospital and The Johns Hopkins University School of Medicine: A Chronicle.* (2 vols.) Baltimore: Johns Hopkins University Press, 1943.

Cline, J. "Medical Education and the Medical Profession." *Journal of the American Medical Association,* 1952, *148,* 1273-1274.

Cluff, L. "Medical Schools, Clinical Faculty and Community Physicians." *Journal of the American Medical Association*, 1982, *247*, 200–202.

Coggeshall, L. *Planning for Medical Progress Through Education*. Washington, D.C.: Association of American Medical Colleges, 1965.

College Entrance Examination Board. *Admissions Testing Program of the College Entrance Examination Board*. Princeton, N.J.: College Entrance Examination Board, 1980.

Collins, J. "Congressional Staff Cuts." *Congressional Record*, 1981, *127*, H47–H50.

Congressional Record, untitled article, H7646–H7653, July 28, 1975.

Cooper, J. "Undergraduate Medical Education in the United States." In J. Bowers and E. Purcell (Eds.), *Advances in American Medicine: Essays at the Bicentennial*. Vol. 1. New York: Josiah Macy, Jr., Foundation, 1976.

Cooper, J., and Prior, M. "A New Program in Medical Education at Northwestern University." *The Superior Student*, 1960, *3*, 14–17.

Crawford, S. "Medical School Libraries in the United States: 1960 Through 1975." *Journal of the American Medical Association*, 1977, *237*, 464–468.

Creswell, H. *The Honeywood File*. London: Faber and Faber, 1972.

Curran, J. "Internships and Residencies: Historical Backgrounds." *Journal of Medical Education*, 1959a, *34*, 873.

Curran, J. "Internships and Residencies: Historical Background and Current Trends." *Journal of Medical Education*, 1959b, *34*, 883–884.

Darley, W. "The Financial Status of Medical Education." *Journal of Medical Education*, 1953, *29*, 11–20.

Daubney, J., Wagner, E., and Rogers, W. "Six-Year B.S./M.D. Program: A Literature Review." *Journal of Medical Education*, 1981, *56*, 497–503.

Davis, F. D. Personal communication, 1983.

De Solla-Price, D. *Science Since Babylon*. New Haven, Conn.: Yale University Press, 1961.

Deitrick, J., and Berson, R. *Medical Schools in the United States at Mid-Century*. New York: McGraw-Hill, 1953.

Drew, E. "The Health Syndicate: Washington's Noble Conspirators." *Atlantic Monthly*, December 1967, *220*, 75–82.

Drucker, P. "Professional Schools Ought to Reap Some of Their Graduates' Earnings." *Chronicle of Higher Education,* November 10, 1982, p. 64.

Durant, W. *The Story of Civilization: The Life of Greece.* New York: Simon & Schuster, 1939.

DuVal, M. K. "University of Arizona College of Medicine." In V. Lippard and E. Purcell (Eds.), *Case Histories of Ten New Medical Schools.* New York: Josiah Macy, Jr., Foundation, 1972.

DuVal, M. K. "Anticipating Community Relationships." *Journal of the American Medical Association,* 1975, *194,* 1303-1305.

Eichna, L. "Medical School Education, 1975-79: A Student's Perspective." *New England Journal of Medicine,* 1980, *303,* 727-734.

Evans, J. "Organizational Patterns for New Responsibilities." *Journal of Medical Education,* 1970, *45,* 988-999.

Ewing, O. *The Nation's Health: A Ten Year Report to the President.* Washington, D.C.: U.S. Government Printing Office, 1948.

Flexner, A. *Medical Education in the United States and Canada: A Report to the Carnegie Foundation for the Advancement of Teaching.* Bulletin No. 4, Boston: D. B. Updyke, The Merrymount Press, 1910.

Flexner, A. Statement made at testimonial dinner in celebration of Flexner's 90th birthday, New York City, 1956.

Fordham, C. "The Bane Report Revisited." *Journal of the American Medical Association,* 1980, *244,* 354-357.

Fredrickson, D. "Biomedical Research in the 1980s." *New England Journal of Medicine,* 1982, *304,* 509-517.

Fuhrman, F. *Multiple Discipline Laboratories for Teaching the Medical Sciences.* Palo Alto, Calif.: School of Medicine, Stanford University, 1968.

"Full Time Faculty in Seventy-Eight Medical Schools." *Journal of Medical Education,* 1967, *42,* 798-799.

Gardner, H. *Frames of Mind: The Theory of Multiple Intelligence.* New York: Basic Books, 1983.

Garrison, F. *An Introduction to the History of Medicine.* Philadelphia: Saunders, 1966.

Gay, R. "The Machine in the Library." *The American Scholar,* Winter 1979-80, 49, 66-77.

Gifford, J. *The Evolution of a Medical Center: A History of Medicine at Duke University to 1941*. Durham, N.C.: Duke University Press, 1972.

Ginsberg, E. *Men, Money, and Medicine*. New York: Columbia University Press, 1969.

Ginsberg, E. Presentation to Section on Medical Education, American Medical Association, San Francisco, December 3, 1980.

Glaser, R. "The Medical Deanship: Its Half-Life and Hard Times." *Journal of Medical Education*, 1969, *44*, 1115.

Gordon, T. "Medical School Applicants, 1977-78." *Journal of Medical Education*, 1979, *54*, 677-702.

Graduate Medical Education National Advisory Committee. *Report of the Graduate Medical Education Committee to the Secretary, U.S. Department of Health and Human Services*. Washington, D.C.: U.S. Department of Health and Human Services, 1980.

Grant, W., and Eiden, L. *Digest of Education Statistics*. Washington, D.C.: National Center for Education Statistics, 1982.

Gray, G. *Development of the Curriculum in American Medical Schools*. Unpublished thesis for M.D. degree, Baylor College of Medicine, 1961.

Joseph S. Green, Sarina J. Grosswald, Emanuel Suter, David B. Walthall III (Eds.). *Continuing Education for the Health Professions: Developing, Managing, and Evaluating Programs for Maximum Impact on Patient Care*. San Francisco: Jossey-Bass, 1984.

Greer, W. *Western Reserve's Experiment in Medical Education and Its Outcome*. New York: Oxford University Press, 1980.

Gregg, A. *Challenges to Contemporary Medicine*. New York: Columbia University Press, 1956.

Hampton, C. L., and others. *Journal of Medical Education*, 1979, *54*, 90-95.

Harlow, R. *The United States*. (3rd ed.) New York: Holt, Rinehart and Winston, 1959.

Harrell, G. *Planning Medical Center Facilities*. University Park: Pennsylvania State University Press, 1974.

Haynes, R. B., Davis, D. A., McKibbon, A., and Tugwell, P. "A Critical Appraisal of the Efficacy of Continuing Medical Education." *Journal of the American Medical Association*, 1984, *251*, 61-64.

Health Insurance Institute. *Source Book of Health Insurance Data*. Washington, D.C.: Health Insurance Institute, 1982.

Highet, G. "The Scholarly Life." *The American Scholar*, 1972, *41*, 522-529.

"Hill Seen Agreeable to Abort Military School Plan." *Washington Post*, February 26, 1977, p. A7.

Hilles, W., and Fagan, S. *Medical Practice Plans at U.S. Medical Schools*. Washington, D.C.: Association of American Medical Colleges, 1977.

Hinsey, J. "The Medical School and the Federal Government." *Yale Journal of Biology and Medicine*, 1967, *39*, 404-411.

Horowitz, G., and Bleich, H. "Paperchase: A Computer Program to Search the Medical Literature." *New England Journal of Medicine*, 1981, *305*, 924-930.

Houle, C. O. *Continuing Learning in the Professions*. San Francisco: Jossey-Bass, 1980.

Huang, C. "Physical Facilities of Medical School Libraries in the United States, 1966-1975: A Statistical Review." *Bulletin of the Medical Library Association*, 1976, *64*, 173-178.

Hudson, J. (Ed.) *Health Maintenance Organizations and Academic Medical Centers, 1981*. Menlo Park, Calif: Henry J. Kaiser Family Foundation, 1981.

Hyde, D., and others. "The American Medical Association: Power, Purpose, and Politics in Organized Medicine." *Yale Law Journal*, 1954, *63*, 937-1022.

Iglehart, J. "The New Era of Prospective Payments for Hospitals." *New England Journal of Medicine*, 1982, *307*, 1288-1292.

"In Portland, the Doctor Is In, and In, and In." *Washington Post*, March 31, 1981, p. 2.

Institute of Medicine, National Academy of Sciences. *Costs of Education in the Health Professions*. Washington, D.C.: National Academy of Sciences, 1974.

Isaacs, J. *Council of Teaching Hospitals Survey of University Owned Teaching Hospitals' Financial and General Operating Data*. Washington, D.C.: Association of American Medical Colleges, 1980.

Isaacs, J., and Madolf, M. "Undergraduate Medical Education in Prepaid Health Care Plan Settings." Unpublished paper, 1983.

Jacobson, R. "Curtailing the Cost of Search Committees." *Chronicle of Higher Education*, June 21, 1976, p. 8.

Jarco, S. "Medical Education in the U.S., 1910-1956." *Journal of Mt. Sinai Hospital*, 1959, *8*, 339-385.

Johnson, D. G. *Physicians in the Making: Personal, Academic, and Socioeconomic Characteristics of Medical Students from 1950 to 2000.* San Francisco: Jossey-Bass, 1983.

Johnson, V. "The Council on Medical Education and Hospitals." In M. Fishbein (Ed.), *A History of the American Medical Association.* Philadelphia: Saunders, 1947.

Joint Committee of the Association of American Medical Colleges and the Medical Library Association. "Guidelines for Medical School Libraries." *Journal of Medical Education,* 1965, *40,* 7-61.

Jolly, P., and Smith, W. *Medical Practice Plans at U.S. Medical Schools.* Washington, D.C.: Association of American Medical Colleges, 1981.

Jones, B. "Federal Support of Medical Research." Report of the Committee on Consultants on Medical Research to the U.S. Senate Committee on Appropriations. 86th Congress, 2nd Session, 1960.

Journal of the American Medical Association, 1922, *70,* 633.

Journal of the American Medical Association, 1940, *115,* 699.

Journal of the American Medical Association, 1951, *134,* 695.

Journal of the American Medical Association, 1961a, *178,* 632.

Journal of the American Medical Association, 1961b, *178,* 645-646.

Journal of the American Medical Association, 1961c, *178,* 647.

Journal of the American Medical Association, 1964, *190,* 613.

Journal of the American Medical Association, 1971, *218,* 1206-1207.

Journal of the American Medical Association, 1972, *222,* 974.

Journal of the American Medical Association, 1975, *231,* 49.

Journal of the American Medical Association, 1980, *244,* 2829.

Journal of the American Medical Association, 1981a, *246,* 2914.

Journal of the American Medical Association, 1981b, *246,* 2917.

Journal of the American Medical Association, 1981c, *246,* 2925.

Journal of the American Medical Association, 1981d, *246,* 2940.

Journal of the American Medical Association, 1981e, *246,* 2965-2967.

Journal of the American Medical Association, 1982, *248,* 3249.

Journal of the American Medical Association, 1983, *250,* 1542.

Journal of Medical Education, 1966, *42,* 798.

Keyes, J., and others. *Medical School-Clinical Affiliation Study.* Washington, D.C.: Association of American Medical Colleges, 1977.

Kilpatrick, J. "Mr. Collins' Complaint: Neighborhood Bloat." *Washington Post,* January 17, 1981, p. A11.

King, L. "Medical Education: Elitisms and Reform." *Journal of the American Medical Association,* 1983, *250,* 2457-2461, 3100-3104.

Knight, J. *Doctor-to-Be; Coping with the Trials and Triumphs of Medical School.* New York: Appleton-Century-Crofts, 1981.

Knowles, J. "The Hospital." *Scientific American,* 1973, *229,* 128-137.

Kunz, J. *"Index Medicus:* A Century of Medical Citation." *Journal of the American Medical Association,* 1979, *241,* 387-390.

Lang, C., and Harrell, G. "Guidelines for a Quality Program of Laboratory Animal Medicine in a Medical School." *Journal of Medical Education,* 1972, *47,* 267-271.

Lawrence, S. "New Medical Schools Chartered in the Caribbean Begin Classes—Sometimes Amid Legal Disputes." *Forum on Medicine,* October 1978, pp. 19-25.

Lawrence, S. "Caribbean Medical Schools—Business is Booming." *Forum on Medicine,* January 1980, pp. 63-64.

Leake, C. "The Students' Unit Medical Laboratory." *Journal of the American Medical Association,* 1924, *82,* 114-117.

Liaison Committee on Medical Education. Annual Questionnaire.

Liaison Committee on Medical Education. Confidential records.

Liaison Committee on Medical Education. *Functions and Structure of a Medical School.* (Rev. ed.) Washington, D.C.: Association of American Medical Colleges, 1973a. (Orginally published 1957.)

Liaison Committee on Medical Education. *Special Criteria for Programs in the Basic Medical Sciences.* Washington, D.C.: Association of American Medical Colleges, 1973b.

Liaison Committee on Medical Education. *Guidelines to Functions and Structure of a Medical School.* Washington, D.C.: Association of American Medical Colleges, 1976.

Library Study Committee of the Association of American Medical Colleges. "The Health Sciences Library: Its Role in Education for the Health Professions." *Journal of Medical Education,* 1967, *42* (Part 2), 1-63.

Liebelt, R. Personal communication, 1958.

Lippard, V. "The Medical School—Janus of the University." *Journal of Medical Education,* 1955, *30,* 698-706.

Lippard, V. *A Half-Century of American Medical Education, 1920-1970.* New York: Josiah Macy, Jr., Foundation, 1974.

McCarn, D., and Leiter, J. "On Line Services in Medicine and Beyond." *Science,* 1973, *181,* 318-324.

Manning, P. "Continuing Medical Education." *Journal of the American Medical Association*, 1983, *249*, 1031–1045.

Marchand, E., and Steward, J. "Trends in Basic Science Instruction Affecting Role of Multidiscipline Laboratories." *Journal of Medical Education*, 1974, *49*, 171–175.

Margarell, J. "Extra Work Found to Add Twenty-One Percent to Base Salaries of Most Professors." *Chronicle of Higher Education*, November 17, 1980, p. 13.

Mathews, J. "In-Doctor-Glutted West, Home Visits to Patients Are Resuming." *Washington Post*, April 21, 1982, p. A9.

"Medical Legislation." *Journal of the American Medical Association*, 1951, *145*, 737–738.

"Military Medical School." *Chronicle of Higher Education*, May 27, 1975, p. 12.

Miles, W. *A History of the National Library of Medicine: The Nation's Treasury of Medical Knowledge.* Washington, D.C.: U.S. Government Printing Office, 1982.

Miller, G. *Educating Medical Teachers.* Cambridge, Mass.: Harvard University Press, 1980.

Moy, R. Minutes of faculty retreat, Southern Illinois University School of Medicine, January 1972.

Moy, R. Minutes of Faculty Retreat, Southern Illinois University School of Medicine, May 1972.

Moy, R. Personal communication, September 28, 1982.

National Academy of Sciences (National Research Council). *Personnel Needs and Training for Biomedical and Behavioral Research: 1981 Report.* Washington, D.C.: National Academy of Sciences, 1981.

National Advisory Commission on Health Manpower. *Report to the President.* Washington, D.C.: U.S. Government Printing Office, 1967.

National Board of Medical Examiners. *Annual Report: 1982.* Philadelphia: National Board of Medical Examiners, 1983.

National Center for Education Statistics. *Digest of Education Statistics.* Washington, D.C.: National Center for Education Statistics, 1981.

National Commission on Excellence in Education. *A Nation at Risk: The Imperative for Education Reform.* Washington, D.C.: U.S. Government Printing Office, 1983.

National Fund for Medical Education. *Annual Report.* Hartford, Conn.: National Fund for Medical Education, 1979.

National Institutes of Health (Office of Program Planning and Evaluation, Division of Research Grants). *Basic Data Relating to National Institutes of Health.* Washington, D.C.: U.S. Government Printing Office, 1952, 1954, 1960, 1964, 1970, 1975, and 1980.

Norwood, W. *Medical Education in the United States Before the Civil War.* Philadelphia: University of Pennsylvania Press, 1944.

Norwood, W. "American Medical Education from the Revolutionary War to the Civil War." *Journal of Medical Education,* 1957, *32,* 433-440.

Norwood, W. "Critical Incidents in the Shaping of Medical Education in the U.S." *Journal of the American Medical Association,* 1965, *194,* 715-718.

Norwood, W. "Medical Education in the United States Before 1900." In C. O'Malley (Ed.), *The History of Medical Education.* Berkeley: University of California Press, 1970.

Opie, E. "Adoption of Standards of the Best Medical Schools of Western Europe by Those of the United States." *Perspectives on Biology and Medicine,* 1970, *13,* 309-342.

Page, R., and Littlemeyer, M. *Preparation for the Study of Medicine.* Chicago: University of Chicago Press, 1969.

Pannill, F. "The University of Texas Medical School at San Antonio." In V. Lippard and E. Purcell (Eds.), *Case Histories of Ten New Medical Schools.* New York: Josiah Macy, Jr., Foundation, 1972.

Patterson, J. "University of Connecticut School of Medicine." In V. Lippard and E. Purcell (Eds.), *Case Histories of Ten New Medical Schools.* New York: Josiah Macy, Jr., Foundation, 1972.

Peddiwell, J. *The Saber-Tooth Curriculum.* New York: McGraw-Hill, 1939.

Perry, D., Challoner, D., and Oberst, R. "Research Advances and Resource Constraints." *New England Journal of Medicine,* 1981, *305,* 320-324.

Perry, J. "Periodicals Prices." *Bulletin of the Medical Library Association,* 1980, *68,* 303.

Petersdorf, R. "The Role of the Department Chairman in Schools of Medicine." *Journal of Medical Education,* 1971, *46,* 1069-1073.

Petersdorf, R. "The Academic Mating Game." *New England Journal of Medicine,* 1978, *298,* 1290-1294.

Petersdorf, R. "Some Issues in Medical Education." *Forum on Medicine,* March 1980a, pp. 203-209.

Petersdorf, R. "Some Perturbations in Medicine." *Journal of the American Medical Association,* 1980b, *248,* 2098-2101.

Petersdorf, R., and Wilson, M. "The Four Horsemen of the Apocalypse: Study of Academic Medical Center Governance." *Journal of the American Medical Association,* 1982, *247,* 1153-1161.

Philbrick, I. "Medical Colleges and Professional Standards." *Journal of the American Medical Association,* 1901, *36,* 1700-1702.

Porterfield, J. "A State Plans for Its Future in Medical Education." *Journal of the American Medical Association,* 1965, *194,* 127-130.

Powers, L., Darley, W., and Littlemeyer, M. "Physician Giving to Medical Schools." *Journal of Medical Education,* 1965, *40,* 414-422.

President's Commission on the Health Needs of the Nation. *Building America's Health: Findings and Recommendations.* Washington, D.C.: U.S. Government Printing Office, 1952.

"Proceedings of the Washington Session of the Clinical House of Delegates of the American Medical Association, December 6-9, 1949." *Journal of the American Medical Association,* 1949, *141,* 1159-1174.

Rappleye, W., and others. *Medical Education: Final Report of the Commission on Medical Education.* New York: Commission on Medical Education, 1932.

Ravitch, D. *The Troubled Crusade.* New York: Basic Books, 1983.

Rayack, E. *Professional Power and American Medicine: The Economics of the American Medical Association.* New York: World, 1967.

Reinhardt, V. "Health Cost Culprit May Be Manpower Policy, Argues Economist." *Health Manpower Report,* July 20, 1977, pp. 1-2.

Reiter, B. *Saturday Night Knife and Gun Club.* New York: Bantam, 1977.

Relman, A. "Americans Studying Medicine Abroad: The Distressing Facts." *New England Journal of Medicine,* 1978, *299,* 887.

Robinson, G. *Adventures in Medical Education.* New York: Commonwealth Fund, 1957.

Rogers, D. "Reflections on the Medical School Deanship." *The Pharos,* Summer 1975, pp. 13-16.

Rogers, D. "On Humanism in Medicine." *The Pharos,* Fall 1981, pp. 8-11.

Romano, J. (Ed.). *To Each His Farthest Star: The University of Rochester Medical Center, 1925-1975*. Geneva, N.Y.: Humphrey Press, 1975.

Rosenthal, J. Unpublished analysis of data collected by the Association of American Medical Colleges and derived from Liaison Committee on Medical Education annual questionnaire for all medical schools, n.d.

Rosenthal, J. "State Funds in Support of Public and Private Medical Schools, 1979." *Journal of Medicine Education*, 1980, *55*, 885-887.

Ross, S. *Learning and Discovery*. New York: Gordon and Breach, 1981.

Ruhe, C. Personal communication, May 1982.

Sackett, D. "Compliance Practicum For the Busy Practitioner." In R. Haynes and others (Eds.), *Compliance in Health Care*. Baltimore: Johns Hopkins University Press, 1979.

Sackett, D., and others. "Randomized Clinical Strategies for Improving Medication Compliance." *Lancet*, 1975, *1*, 1205-1207.

Savoy, R. "State Government Payments to Out-of-State Medical Schools for Enrolling Their Residents." *Journal of Medical Education*, 1977a, *52*, 694-696.

Savoy, R. "State Roles in Financing Medical Education." *Journal of Medical Education*, 1977b, *52*, 607-610.

Saxon, D. "Is the Medical School a Proper Part of the University?" *Journal of Medical Education*, 1976, *51*, 991-995.

Schmidt, C., Zieve, P., and D'Lugoff, B. "A Practice Plan in a Municipal Teaching Hospital." *New England Journal of Medicine*, 1981, *304*, 259-263.

Schmidt, G. *The Liberal Arts College*. New Brunswick, N.J.: Rutgers University Press, 1957.

Schwartz, W., and others. "The Changing Geographic Distribution of Board Certified Physicians." *New England Journal of Medicine*, 1980, *303*, 1032-1038.

Severinghaus, D., Carman, H., and Cadbury, W. *Preparation for Medical Education in the Liberal Arts College*. New York: McGraw-Hill, 1953.

Shannon, J. "The Advancement of Medical Research: A Twenty-Year View of the Role of the National Institutes of Health." *Journal of Medical Education*, 1967, *42*, 97-108.

Shem, S. *The House of God*. New York: Dell, 1978.

Shepherd, G. "History of Continuation of Medical Education in the United States Since 1930." *Journal of Medical Education*, 1960, *35*, 740-758.

Sherman, J. Personal communication, 1981.

Shrylock, R. *Medicine and Society in America: 1660-1860.* New York: Cornell University Press, 1962.

Siegerist, H. "An Outline of the Development of the Hospital." *Bulletin of the Institute for the History of Medicine*, 1966, *4*, 573-581.

Silber, D. "Southern Illinois University Medical Curriculum: A Systemwide Application of Objectives-Based Instruction." *Journal of Medical Education*, 1978, *53*, 473-479.

Singer, C., and Underwood, E. *A Short History of Medicine.* New York: Oxford University Press, 1962.

Sirridge, M. "The Docent System: An Alternate Approach to Medical Education." *Pharos*, 1980, *43*, 25-28.

Smiley, D. "Our Need for Doctors." *Journal of Medical Education*, 1949, *24*, 248-250.

Smith, W. *Report on Medical School Faculty Salaries, 1981-1982.* Washington, D.C.: Association of American Medical Colleges, February 1982.

Smythe, C. "Developing Medical Schools: An Interim Report." *Journal of Medical Education*, 1967, *42*, 991-1004.

Smythe, C. "Toward a Definition of Department Size: A Study Based on Six Departments in Twenty-Five Medical Schools." *Journal of Medical Education*, 1970, *45*, 637-660.

Smythe, C. "New Resources for Medical Education: Start-Up Expenditures in Twenty-Two New U.S. Medical Schools." *Journal of Medical Education*, 1972, *47*, 690-701.

Smythe, C., Jones, A., and Wilson, M. "Tenure in Medical Schools in the 1980s." *Journal of Medical Education*, 1982, *57*, 349.

Smythe, C., and others. *Departmental Review in Schools of Medicine.* Washington, D.C.: Association of American Medical Colleges, 1978.

Snow, C. *The Masters.* New York: Scribners, 1960.

Sparks, R., and others. Personal communication, 1980.

Spaulding, W. "The Undergraduate Medical Curriculum (1969 Model). McMaster University." *Canadian Medical Association Journal*, 1969, *100*, 659-664.

Spilman, E. "The Multiple Discipline Laboratory." *Journal of Medical Education*, 1958, *33*, 168-174.

Spilman, E. "Some Advantages and Disadvantages of Multiple Discipline Laboratories." *Journal of Medical Education,* 1966, *41,* 143-149.

Stead, E., and others (Eds.). "Educational Technology for Medicine: Roles for the Lister Hill Center." *Journal of Medical Education,* 1971, *46* (Part 2), 1-97.

Steinfeld, J. Personal communication, November 9, 1982.

Stevens, R., and Vermeulen, J. *Foreign Trained Physicians and American Medicine.* DHEW Pub. No. (NIH) 73-324. Washington, D.C.: U.S. Department of Health, Education, and Welfare, 1972.

Stimmel, B., and Graettinger, J. "Medical Students Trained Abroad and Medical Manpower." *New England Journal of Medicine,* 1984, *310,* 230-235.

Stimmel, B., and Smith, H. "Career Choice and Performance on State Licensing Examinations of 'Fifth Pathway' Students." *New England Journal of Medicine,* 1978, *299,* 227-230.

Strauss, R. "Departments and Disciplines: Status and Change." *Science,* 1973, *182,* 895-898.

Strickland, S. *Politics, Science and Dread Disease.* Washington, D.C.: Howard University Press, 1972.

Suter, E., and Waddell, W. "AVLINE: A Data Base and Critical Review System of Audiovisual Materials for the Education of Health Professionals." *Journal of Medical Education,* 1982, *57,* 139-155.

Taksel, L. *Report on Medical School Faculty Fringe Benefits.* Washington, D.C.: Association of American Medical Colleges, 1982.

Taylor, L. "The Natural History of Windows: A Cautionary Tale." *British Medical Journal,* 1979, *1,* 870-875.

Tead, O. *The Climate of Learning.* New York: Harper & Row, 1958.

Thomas, L. "Notes of a Biology Watcher: How to Fix the Premedical Curriculum." *New England Journal of Medicine,* 1978, *298,* 1180-1181.

Tittle, C., and Rowe, D. "Fear and the Student Cheater." *Change,* 1974, *6,* 47-48.

Tonesk, X., and Nelson, J. "Indebtedness of Senior Medical Students." Washington, D.C.: Association of American Medical Colleges, 1981.

U.S. Bureau of the Census. *1980 Census of Population: Supplementary Reports.* Washington, D.C.: U.S. Government Printing Office, 1981a.

U.S. Bureau of the Census. *Statistical Abstract of the United States, 1981*. Washington, D.C.: U.S. Department of Commerce, 1981b.

U.S. Department of Education Office for Civil Rights. *1980 Elementary and Secondary Schools Civil Rights Survey: National Summaries*. Washington, D.C.: U.S. Department of Education, March 1982.

U.S. Department of Health, Education and Welfare. *The Supply of Health Manpower, 1970: Profiles and Projections to 1990*. DHEW Pub. No. (HRA) 75-38. Washington, D.C.: U.S. Department of Health, Education and Welfare, December 1974.

U.S. Department of Health, Education and Welfare. *Health in America: 1776-1976*. DHEW Pub. No. (HRA) 76-616. Washington, D.C.: U.S. Department of Health, Education and Welfare, 1976.

U.S. Department of Health and Human Services. *Chronology of Health Manpower Legislation, 1956-1979*. DHHS Pub. No. (HRA) 80-69. Washington, D.C.: U.S. Department of Health and Human Services, 1979.

U.S. Department of Health and Human Services. *Health in the United States*. DHHS Pub. No. (PHS) 81-1232. Washington, D.C.: U.S. Department of Health and Human Services, 1980.

U.S. Department of Justice, Immigration and Naturalization Service. Unpublished data, 1972-1979.

U.S. General Accounting Office. *Study of Health Facilities Construction Costs*. Washington, D.C.: U.S. Government Printing Office, 1972.

U.S. General Accounting Office. *Policies on U.S. Citizens Studying Abroad Need Review and Reappraisal*. Report to the Congress of the U.S. by the Comptroller General. Pub. No. (HRA) 81-32. Washington, D.C.: U.S. General Accounting Office, 1980.

U.S. House of Representatives, Committee on Armed Services. Hearings on H.R. 2, "To Establish a Uniformed Services University of the Health Sciences." 92nd Congress, 2nd Session, 1971.

U.S. House of Representatives, Committee on Interstate and Foreign Commerce. Hearings on H.R. 4999, H.R. 8774, and 2nd H.R. 8833, "Training of Physicians, Dentists, and Professional Public Health Personnel." 87th Congress, 2nd Session, 1962.

U.S. House of Representatives, Committee on Interstate and Foreign Commerce, Subcommittee on Health and the Environment. *Current Health Manpower Issues*. 96th Congress, 1st Session, 1979.

U.S. Public Health Service. *Medical School Facilities: Planning Considerations.* Pub. No. 874. Washington, D.C.: U.S. Government Printing Office, 1961.

U.S. Public Health Service. *Medical School Facilities: Planning Considerations and Architectural Guide.* Pub. No. 875. Washington, D.C.: U.S. Government Printing Office, 1961, 1964.

U.S. Senate Committee on Labor and Public Welfare, Subcommittee on Health. Hearings on S. 1323 and S. 434, "Aid to Medical Education." 84th Congress, 1st Session, 1955.

Veterans Administration. *1980 Annual Report.* Washington, D.C.: U.S. Government Printing Office, 1981.

Vogel, M. *The Invention of the Modern Hospital: Boston, 1870-1930.* Chicago: University of Chicago Press, 1980.

Volker, J. *The Arizona Medical School Study.* Tucson: University of Arizona Press, 1962a.

Volker, J. "Arizona Medical School Study in Retrospect." *Arizona Medicine,* 1962b, *19,* 41A-50A.

Wackym, P. Personal communication, 1983.

Wagner, C. Letter to Morton Levitt, University of California at Davis School of Medicine, January 2, 1974.

Waite, F. "Medical Degrees Conferred in the American Colonies and in the United States in the Eighteenth Century." *Annals of Medical History,* 1937, *9,* 314-320.

Walsh, J. "Universities Face New Accounting Rules." *Science,* 1980, *210,* 34-36.

Wasserman, M. "Historical Chronology and Selected Bibliography Relating to the National Library of Medicine." *Bulletin of the Medical Library Association,* 1972, *60,* 554.

Wearn, J. "Western Reserve: 1. Background of an Experiment." *Journal of Medical Education,* 1956, *31,* 516-518.

Weiskotten, H., and others. *Medical Education in the United States, 1934-1939.* Chicago: American Medical Association, 1940.

Weiss, R., and others. "Foreign Medical Graduates and the Medical Underground." *New England Journal of Medicine, 1974a, 290,* 1408-1413.

Weiss, R., and others. "The Effect of Importing Physicians—Return to a Pre-Flexnerian Standard." *New England Journal of Medicine,* 1974b, *290,* 1453-1458.

Weston, D. "How To Reduce the Budget." Paper presented at meeting of the Association of American Medical College's Council of Deans, Kiawah Island, S.C., May 1982.

Whipple, H. (Ed.). "Medical Schools and Teaching Hospitals: Curriculum, Programming, and Planning." *Annals of the New York Academy of Sciences,* 1965, *128,* 457–720.

Wiggins, W., and others. "Medical Education in the United States and Canada." *Journal of the American Medical Association,* 1959, *171,* 1507–1509.

"Will Surplus of M.D.s Be Good for Patients? Look at San Francisco." *The Wall Street Journal,* March 13, 1980, p. 2.

Willard, W., and others. "New Medical Schools: Some Preliminary Considerations" *Journal of Medical Education,* 1960, *35,* 93–107.

Williams, G. *Western Reserve's Experiment in Medical Education and Its Outcome.* Oxford, England: Oxford University Press, 1980.

Wilson, L. "Intensive Care Delirium: The Effect of Outside Deprivation in a Windowless Unit." *Archive of Internal Medicine,* 1972, *130,* 225–226.

Wilson, M. P. "Medical Schools in the Planning State: Are More Schools Needed?" *Journal of Medical Education,* 1972, *47,* 677–689.

Wilson, M. P. "Developing Management Leaders." University of Pennsylvania, National Health Care Management Center, Issue Paper No. 6. Philadelphia: University of Pennsylvania Press, 1980.

Wilson, M. P., and McLaughlin, C. P. *Leadership and Management in Academic Medicine.* San Francisco: Jossey-Bass, 1984.

Wilson, M. P., and Smythe, C. M. "Medicine." In C. H. McGuire, R. P. Foley, A. Gorr, R. W. Richards, and Associates. *Handbook of Health Professions Education: Responding to New Realities in Medicine, Dentistry, Pharmacy, Nursing, Allied Health, and Public Health.* San Francisco: Jossey-Bass, 1983.

Winslow, R. "A Nation of Doctors in Debt?" *New York Times Magazine,* November 9, 1981.

Wolfe, G. "The Site of a Medical School." *Journal of Medical Education,* 1965, *40,* 506–509.

Wolfe, T. *From Bauhaus to Our House.* New York: Farrar, Straus & Giroux, 1981.

World Health Organization. *World Directory of Medical Schools.* Geneva: World Health Organization, 1979.

Worthen, D. Personal communication, 1981.

Wray, N., and Friedland, J. "Detection and Correction of House Staff Error in Physical Diagnosis." *Journal of the American Medical Association,* 1983, *249,* 1035–1041.

Wright, J. *On a Clear Day You Can See General Motors.* New York: Avon, 1979.

Youmans, J. "Experience with a Postgraduate Course for Practitioners: Evaluation of Results." *Journal of the Association of American Medical Colleges,* 1935, *20,* 154–173.

Zaleznik, A. "Managers and Leaders: Are They Different?" *Harvard Business Review,* May/June 1979, pp. 67–78.

Index

Note: Page numbers followed by *n* refer to notations within parentheses (that is, the in-text reference citations).